THE JOLLY PILGRIM

PETER BAKER

The Jolly Pilgrim
©Peter Baker

ISBN: 978-1-906316-85-3

Published in 2011 by HotHive Books, Evesham, UK.
www.thehothive.com

A CIP record of this book is available from the British Library.

Printed in the UK by CPI Cox & Wyman, Reading.
Front cover image courtesy of NASA.
Author photo courtesy of Michael Roberts.
All other photos © Peter Baker.

The author takes full responsibility for all the observations recorded and views expressed
within these pages.

This book is dedicated to the memory of

Elizabeth Jyl Marsh

May her breathtakingly beautiful soul rest in peace

THE JOLLY PILGRIM

Jolly, adjective:

1) ... in good spirits, merry: *In a moment he was as jolly as ever.*

2) ... cheerfully festive or convivial: *A jolly party.*

3) ... joyous; happy.

4) ... (chiefly British informal) delightful, charming.

Pilgrim, noun:

1) ... a person who journeys, esp. a long distance, to some sacred place as an act of religious devotion: *Pilgrims to the Holy Land.*

2) ... a traveller or wanderer, esp. in a foreign place.

Contents

Maps

A Primer

We're not thinking big enough. When we consider what's happening on this planet – the problems we've got and the direction the world is heading in – we get too wrapped up in the immediate and short term. The scope of human knowledge has exploded in recent centuries, but we're still thinking about our affairs within parameters that were set out before we really knew anything.

At the dawn of this twenty-first century the human race is in a position to start being more realistic about which of its world's features are transient and which are enduring, and about what is actually real and what's only real in our heads. It's time we took a step back and synthesised a more complete narrative of ourselves.

For me the vehicle for that synthesis was a journey. The journey lasted two years and, when I went on it, I kept a diary. Whenever I got the chance I would email that diary's latest entry to anyone who'd registered an interest in what I was doing.

Here is how the book works: each diary entry is numbered and dated, any entry prefixed 'Musings' is a commentary on the unfolding story and any prefixed 'Global Musings' is part of the book's core thesis regarding this whole seven-billion-humans-on-a-planet gig.

Due to my subject matter, I've had to use the term 'civilisation' a lot. I believe the fact there are no synonyms for this word in English is indicative that we, as a species, don't spend enough time thinking about the big picture. This book, as much as anything, is an attempt to start addressing that.

I've been asked about the title. It was, first of all, the email address used to post back the diary. The 'pilgrim' part will become clear. As for the 'jolly', let's just say I'm a happy guy.

Finally, for the record, I'm not really trying to start a new religion. That would be silly.

Part 1

The Bicycle Ride

1: Canterbury and Other Tales
31 May 2005

At 45 Hewitt Road in north London, we've had a lot of parties. I once calculated that, in the seven years I've lived there, we've had more than 500 gatherings, dinners and shindigs. A thousand people must have – at some time or other – stayed over, sleeping on the sofa, the futon and the carpet or, occasionally, in the back garden. Sometimes they just never went to sleep.

When shutting the front door for the last time I made a promise to myself: I vowed never to forget how much fun we'd had in that house, how many shared experiences we'd all enjoyed and what an amazing part of my life it had been. As I got on my bicycle and set off, a chapter in that life came to its close.

Heading south, I took a route I know like the back of my hand: freewheeling down Hewitt Road; hanging a right onto Green Lanes; down through Clissold Park, filled with a springtime glory of picnics and ballgames; and then on into central London.

This time instead of turning right towards the West End or left into the City – where my now ex-colleagues still work – I went straight down, across London Bridge and into the suburbs beyond. An hour after crossing the Thames the urban landscape gave way to the rolling hills of Kent. Istanbul, here I come.

That first afternoon I had three important learning experiences at the same time: becoming massively dehydrated; having no idea where I'd camp; and being reminded that shops outside the city close at six (so I didn't have any food).

With the light failing and hunger's pangs beginning to gnaw, I stopped beside a likely-looking meadow to eye it up as a camping spot. A nearby householder, cutting bushes in his back garden, told me to go ahead. It was seven o'clock. I was just outside Rochester.

Said householder turned out to be the local doctor. After I'd set up my tent he invited me in for dinner. He and his family were very impressed by my cycling-to-Turkey scheme. I might be dining out on that one a lot. His wife had cooked a rack of chicken wings on a whim, but her two sons had shown no interest. As I gratefully tucked in she looked me in the eye and declared my arrival to be destiny. The idea rather appealed.

On my second day Mum came to say goodbye and join me for some cycling. I met her off the train at Rochester in the morning and we set off east together. The sun shone into late afternoon as we peddled our way through the countryside, stopping to watch a village cricket match, browse farm shops and eat a picnic.

In the evening we reached Canterbury. There we ate Italian food and talked about what a great day we'd had. Then, with a lump in my throat, I saw her off at the train station. I'll see you in two years.

The next morning, a light drizzle falling, I made my way across Kent and late that afternoon reached the south coast at Dover. Zipping around town in search of a campsite, I became lost.

Finding myself on a path above the cliffs, I stumbled upon an older gentleman wearing a trench coat and an enormous beard. He was living in a Roald Dahl-style fantasy camp. Pots, pans and iron kettles hung from a tightly knit canopy of trees. Bits of carpet and corrugated iron lay scattered about. It was rather cosy.

The old fellow was charming, if a little eccentric. With the English Channel spread below, we shared a moment. His accent was eastern European and, while he initially claimed to be called Wally, following a cigarette he confided that his real name was Vladimir. Between ramblings and a confused lecture on calculus, snatches of Vladimir's life story emerged.

He'd been born in western Russia in 1925 and, as German divisions advanced across the motherland, had become caught up in the sharp end of World War II. Life never really went back to normal after that and, decade following decade, the tides of the twentieth century bounced Vladimir around Europe, finally washing him up on those Dover cliffs; the scattered flotsam of a passing era.

He wasn't one of life's complainers.

Dover is my last pit stop before crossing the Channel to the Continent. I'm staying on a campsite above the cliffs and have spent the last two days exploring the castle and looking out over the sea. I'm beside a retired couple called Brian and Yvonne. It turns out they're from Colchester – my home town – and Brian used to work with my late uncle Bill, of whom we were both very fond.

Brian's a renaissance man. He learned French when he was 40 to feed a passion for nineteenth-century literature, and plays guitar in what used to be a four-piece band. Unfortunately, they had to start using a drum machine after their vocalist eloped with the drummer. It's all terribly rock 'n' roll.

Days since leaving London: 5

2: Asterix, St Joan and the Normans
6 June 2005

After writing that last email I made my way to the port and boarded a ferry to France. I spent that afternoon and the following morning in Calais, then began cycling south into Normandy.

I took the opportunity to stop at Agincourt, site of the battle where Henry V and 6,000 Welsh and English lads snotted the French in 1415. When the locals asked where I was heading, I felt mildly embarrassed to admit I was going out of my way to visit the place where the cream of their nobility had been massacred. Not to worry. They were very intellectual about it. 'A culturally iconic moment similar to our storming of the Bastille,' I was told.

That evening I watched the sunset while eating a picnic of Camembert and salami, and listening to Beethoven's Ninth with the last of the power in my iPod. As darkness fell tendrils of mist crept from a nearby river and filled the valley below. Mesmerised, I picked my way down to a fence at the bottom of the field to get a closer look. A grizzled old French dude appeared at my elbow. 'La nature,' he said, gesturing with his huge weathered hand, 'c'est si magnifique.'

Cycling across Normandy the sun beat down and the countryside was an idyll of green perfection. In the pristine village restaurants the set menus are to die for and a bottle of wine with lunch is de rigueur. They're also into extravagant facial hair, generally sporting vast and elaborate moustaches. I keep thinking I've spotted Asterix or one of his chums.

I've had my first bad patch. It started with a thunderstorm, a flat tyre, changing said tyre in the rain, having the new tyre burst (*psheet* it went), then running across town – drenched and frantic – to reach the bicycle shop before it closed, all with wet feet and an empty belly.

The next day a gale blew in my face from dawn till dusk while I crawled along at a miserable nine kilometres per hour. That was really unpleasant. I cheered myself up by camping in a dark forest with deer running around. That was really satisfying.

I've reached Rouen, ancient capital of the Normans. It was an English base during most of the Hundred Years War and is where Joan of Arc was burned at the stake.

The old city seethes with history. Narrow alleys lead to cobbled squares where faded cupids piss into clear pools. Walls carved after the Black Death are filled with manacles and skulls, and decades-spun cobwebs are an arm's length away. It's chock full of amazing churches. The cathedral is astounding.

Legs getting stronger. Rapidly developing a tan.

Days since leaving London: 11
Distance travelled: 559 kilometres

3: Gothic Transcendental
13 June 2005

I first learned of Chartres Cathedral from Kenneth Clark's *Civilisation* series about the history of European art. That, along with David Attenborough's *Life on Earth* and Carl Sagan's *Cosmos*, probably taught me more than my five years at high school put together. The cathedral was completed in the year 1220 and is 90 kilometres south-west of Paris. Lord Clark characterises its construction as the symbolic unleashing of post-Dark Ages Europe and one of the crowning architectural achievements of Western civilisation.

I've been to a few of Europe's grandest churches in my time; although, as you can tell, I was expecting Chartres to be pretty special. Nonetheless, the sight of it rising from the French agricultural plains (you can see it from *miles* away) and totally dominating the town itself didn't prepare me for what I would find inside.

My eyes were attuned to the bright sunny morning and it took them a few moments to readjust. This church is dark – very dark – with hundreds of fantastically complex stained-glass windows alongside three great roses of colour. A symphony in stone. A cry of affirmation by now-forgotten artists. Gloomy. Foreboding. Gothic.

Jaw-dropping.

My mind set ablaze, I spent two hours sitting in the aisles, scribbling in my notebook. To think that during the Revolution they came within a hair's breadth of tearing it down. How frail is the thread by which our human heritage is preserved. When I finally see the Aya Sophia – Justinian's great cathedral in Istanbul – I may have to fall to my knees for dramatic effect.

Chartres vignette: a portly, hamster-like lady is yelling to her friend across the nave using only her nasal passages. The acoustics are ricocheting her words around the building. A robed man approaches and asks her (in French) to be quiet. '*Neeeow,*' she whines, '*Ing*-lish?' He puts a finger to his lips. She gets the message. The man was a priest and the hamster, bless her heart, was an American.

After leaving the cathedral I ambled around Chartres for a while, bought bread, cheese and a bottle of Bordeaux and spent the rest of the day sprawled beside my tent in the city's camping ground. As the shadows lengthened through the afternoon I delved into the library in my saddle bags and mused.

The geniuses who built that sublime architecture had a sense of how they related to the universe: a sense defined by things such as God and faith. A spiritual architecture.

And yet eight hundred years ago, in that pre-scientific era, we humans had a relatively limited understanding of what we were and where we'd come from. We didn't conduct our affairs based on any sort of informed assessment of ourselves, but through a set of complex behavioural strategies that had been hard-wired into us by evolution. We lived in a world of half-formed and inconsistent myth that was a dim reflection of the truth we'd begun to grasp while lifting ourselves from the mud and pandemonium of Earth's ecosystems.

But it led to that church. And that was the end of the beginning. Something deep inside us, which had been germinated on the African savannah, was beginning to flower.

Following my epiphany at the great temple, I cycled south for two days until I reached the city of Orléans in the valley of the River Loire. There I turned west and, today, I'm in the delightful town of Blois (pronounced: blwah).

I keep meeting people called Peter in different languages. One was a German fellow on the cliffs above Boulogne last week. His wife had died in her thirties, leaving Peter to face the world alone. He ran an organisation called 'Motor Homes for Singles' (which came out as something labyrinthine in German) and was researching routes. The guy running my Blois-based campsite is also called Peter (in French, obviously). Pierre is cross-eyed, humoursome and runs a slick operation.

I have decided to discard the word bicycle in favour of the sexier term 'cyclatron'. I've also awarded my cyclatron a name. Henceforth, she shall be known as 'Nelly'.

Yesterday, while pedalling along with Nelly and smothered in factor 15, my arms and legs became coated in the small black insects which hang out beside the river. Some of them started to have sex on me. Cheeky little blighters.

Days since leaving London: 18
Distance travelled: 904 kilometres
Average daily banana consumption: 3.67 bananas

4: Captain Haddock, French Poetry and the Loire
18 June 2005

Being a Tintin fan, I always understood that the comic book hero reporter was Belgian. However, I liked to imagine that his best friend, Captain Haddock, was English. I've now visited the real Marlinspike Hall (also known as Château de Cheverny) where Captain Haddock lived. Tintin was from Brussels and Captain Haddock, it turns out, resided in the valley of the River Loire.

Château de Cheverny is set among exquisite gardens of manicured lawns and venerable trees. In addition to its physical magnificence and substantial Tintin exhibition, one of the château's notable features is the pack of 100 hunting dogs its owners keep. During my visit, I witnessed them being fed.

Feeding a hundred lean, mean and hungry hunting dogs requires 90 kilograms of animal parts and a prodigious quantity of biscuits. That equates to a metal tray eight metres long and one metre wide, piled with food.

When the kennel doors are opened, the tray vanishes to be replaced by a heaving mound of white and brown fur. When it reappears, two minutes later, it's been licked clean. I feel pretty sorry for the stag.

The morning I cycled to the château I'd been struck by the lush and sunlight-filled forest paths I was passing. So, the next day, I postponed my journey west, left my bags at the campsite, grabbed a compass and headed into the forest with Nelly. I'm told they call it 'off-roading'.

Unfortunately, it rained all day. This meant there was no one to witness my – frankly inspired – renditions of 'Falling in Love Again' (as sung by Marlene Dietrich), 'The Man in the Moon Stayed Up Too Late' (*The Lord of the Rings*, book one, volume one) and 'Raindrops Keep Fallin' on My Head' (like in *Butch Cassidy and the Sundance Kid*), which I delivered – repeatedly and with great gusto – to the trees and forest animals.

That afternoon, in a village called Bracieux, I came across a restored medieval barn housing an exhibition by local artists. The only other person there was an elderly lady called Janine Desmars. We struck up a conversation during which she informed me that her hobby was to write poetry (in French) and send it to various world leaders. I was initially sceptical, until she produced replies from Tony Blair and Jean-Pierre Raffarin (Prime Minister of the Fifth Republic). It's a crazy world.

Continuing west the next day I came to Montrichard, a market town on the banks of the River Cher. I decided to stay a night and camped beside an English couple called Basil and Lis. As soon as I'd pulled out my tent, Basil was over to advise on shade options and the on-site facilities. This was swiftly followed by an offer of tea.

Basil and Lis had recently retired and were tearing around Europe in a camper van with two sea kayaks and a couple of mountain bikes. We drank their beer and talked into the night about the wonders of France and the wild blue yonder.

Amusingly, as I cycled down an overgrown path on my way to the city of Tours yesterday, I came across a couple 'getting biblical' on the river bank. 'Pardon! Pardon! Bonjournay!' I yelled as Nelly and I whizzed past. I reckon they were having a very bonne journée.

Days since leaving London: 23
Distance travelled: 1,174 kilometres

French word of the day: 'trembler' meaning 'quiver'

Musings
One Man and His Bicycle

The precise chain of events which led to me cycling to Istanbul is rather convoluted, but basically it all came down to girls. Specifically, three girls.

The first girl was called Josephine Shepherd. Seven years earlier, when I'd just moved to London, Jo had been my girlfriend. She was a student at the Slade – a posh London art school – and was blonde, bohemian and drop-dead gorgeous.

Jo shared a house with her brother Kit, who was lovely but not very sociable. Because he lived with my girlfriend, I looked for ways to make friends with him. It turned out Kit was an editor for the Folio Society – a highbrow London publisher – and worked on history books. Kit and I got talking about that, and he started lending me books.

The first book he lent me was a thick biography of Julius Caesar. I devoured it. Next, a three-book series on the Crusades set in the storybook world of the medieval Near East. Lots of the action takes place in a city called Constantinople, which would later be known as Istanbul. I devoured that too.

Two months later, Jo dumped me. I wasn't man enough for a girl like her back then. But I never stopped reading history books.

The second girl was called Rachel Barlow. Five years before the bicycle ride, when I'd just established myself in London, Rachel had also been my girlfriend. Rachel was a nuclear physicist at the Royal Free – a big London hospital – and was willowy, athletic and extremely clever.

Rachel used to cycle to work and would come home every evening full of excitement and stories of mist-shrouded London canals at daybreak. Following her lead, I bought a bicycle and began cycling to work.

Six months later, Rachel dumped me. I was too flighty for a girl like her back then. But I never stopped cycling.

The third girl who led me to cycle to Istanbul had never been my girlfriend, but is of much more immediate relevance to this story. I'll tell you all about her later.

* * * * *

My plan was to go around the world for two years, starting with a bicycle ride across Europe.

I'd cooked up my scheme a year earlier, given my bosses four months' warning that I was leaving and then finished at my job six weeks before setting off.

I used those six weeks to go through every possession I owned, throwing (or giving) things away and leaving the rest with trusted companions. I then visited the important people in my life, spent a week with my parents, tied up all my loose ends and threw an enormous going-away party.

As for the practicalities, my assessment was as follows:

1) There's the ground.

2) There's a bicycle.

3) You've got a general idea what Europe looks like.

4) Head south-east and keep an eye on road signs.

5) Do not, under any circumstances, panic.

How hard could it be?

In the eyes of some, I didn't have my adventure well planned. Two weeks before leaving, a friend, checking on progress, asked about some of the equipment she felt I'd need, such as a compass, cycling shorts and bicycle panniers.

I didn't own any cycling shorts and had never even heard of 'panniers', but proudly showed her the star chart I'd acquired and my copies of the Bible and the Qur'an: all essential equipment for the sort of adventure I had in mind.

Then, on the glorious spring afternoon of the 27th of May 2005 it was just me, a bicycle and the long road to Turkey.

During the first few days it's basically all in the mind. Anyone can climb onto a bicycle and say they're going to Istanbul. Then – after one week – the culture shock hit me.

I was alone in the middle of a French corn field, I'd left my entire life behind and there was no one to talk to. The idea of five months in the wilderness was suddenly a little frightening. The day before reaching Rouen – with the wind blowing in my face from dawn till dusk – the distance across Europe was starting to look ominous and it crossed my mind that I might not be able to do it.

It was heading west along the Loire Valley – body hardening and mind adjusting to its new realities – that I hit my groove and my confidence soared. From then on, it was just a matter of time.

* * * * *

I'd made the strategic decision to follow the Romance, rather than the Germanic, route across Europe. In essence, that meant going anti-clockwise, rather than clockwise, around the Alps.

I'd also decided to avoid the big cities (because, on a bicycle, they're a drag) and there were two items on my 'must-see' list: Chartres Cathedral and the Viaduc de Millau. In addition, I had visits to pay in southern France, northern Italy and Slovenia.

Apart from that, I had no idea which route I'd follow. So I looked in my guidebook, picked spots which seemed interesting and headed in their direction.

I dealt with navigation one step at a time. I found Dover by reading road signs. Then, after crossing the Channel, I looked in the big road map book of France (I'd had the foresight to buy), found the page with Calais on it and worked out which road would take me to Boulogne.

After that it was a step-by-step process. Travelling one town at a time, I made my way across that first page, then turned to the next one and repeated the procedure. As the weeks went by, page following page, I made my way across France, and then Europe. It was enormously satisfying.

Map 1

Europe, from London to Istanbul

Boxes denote from where each email was sent.

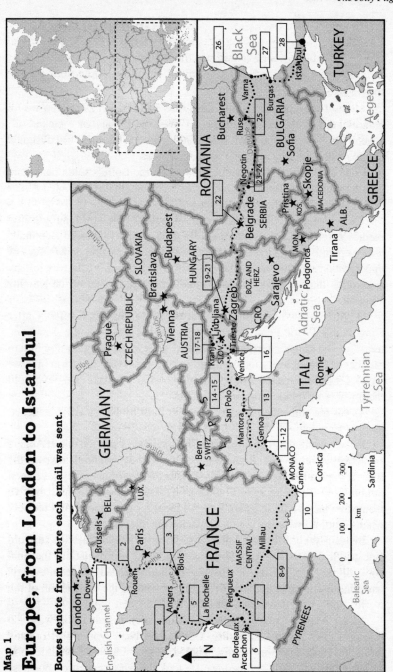

.... **Route of the bicycle ride**

5: Golden Brown,
Texture Like Sun
25 June 2005

I've been looking at castles.

Most of the châteaux along the Loire Valley are basically pleasure palaces built by the French aristocracy after the Renaissance kicked off. Visually they're stunning but, fortification-wise, a bit girly: not designed to cope with battering rams or rapacious armies.

Eight days ago at the town of Chinon, on the Loire's south bank, and 40 kilometres after Tours, I came across a château that represented a very different brand of military architecture.

The château at Chinon is a full-blooded 400-metre-long gigantic medieval fortress. It sits dramatically atop a rocky spur and contains three separate compounds, an underground tunnel system and masses of underground chambers. Graffiti cut onto its dungeon walls was left by none other than Jacques de Molay: the last Grand Master of the Knights Templar.

De Molay was imprisoned at Chinon in the fourteenth century after King Philip IV of France resolved to get his paws on the Templars' treasure. The king's interrogators went to work, eventually forcing him to say that he denied Jesus and trampled on the cross (very bad form in those days). Later he recanted, so they burned him at the stake. He never told them where he'd hidden the cash though.

As for the stupendous castle: that was built by Henry II Plantagenet, King of England.

If I was excited by the fortress at Chinon, when I saw the one at Angers I practically wet myself. Right in the centre of the city and rising over the river, it's spread across 20,000 square metres and surrounded by seventeen jumbo-sized, 30-metre towers linked by a 600-metre wall so thick they've planted a vineyard on it. There's even a moat for good measure. Precisely what's required when facing that rapacious medieval army.

Beneath the castle is a vault containing a 103-metre, 700-year-old tapestry. It depicts the Apocalypse as described in Revelation, the final book of the Bible. Bizarre imagery of multi-headed dragons. Angels wrestling bat-winged demons. Prophetic visions of the destruction of the world. God's final defeat of Satan.

At the Angers campsite I met a bloke called Gerald, who was also having a solo cycling adventure. Gerald had been working at organic farms in France and was heading back to England to serve organic food at music festivals. You get the idea. He took the whole cyclatron business much more seriously than Nelly and me, and had bits of equipment we didn't even know existed. Did you know you can now get 'micro pumps' only slightly bigger than mascara brushes?

Angers was the last city on the Loire I visited. After that I turned south-west and, yesterday, hit the Atlantic coast at La Rochelle, which looks over the Bay of Biscay and is filled with fishing boats, seafood and tourists. I'm resting up for a couple of days before heading south to find a beach.

I don't tan well, or easily, but four weeks of being outside all day seems to be doing the trick. I'm slowly turning a rather fetching golden colour and developing freckles.

Days since leaving London: 30
Distance travelled: 1,624 kilometres
Most distance covered in a single day: 113 kilometres (yesterday)

French word of the day: 'patauger' meaning 'splash about'

6: Out of the West
5 July 2005

Heading down the Atlantic coast it got *really* hot. By midday on the second day south of La Rochelle, I had to retreat into a village café to escape the mind-bending temperatures. It wasn't until six in the afternoon that a cool breeze blew in from the Atlantic and it became possible to operate once more. By then I was exploding with energy.

Zooming up and down the line of hills that overlook the coastal plain provided a dramatic view of the darkening skies and thousand-foot wall of black cloud heading our way from over the ocean. As the wind picked up and lightning began leaping across the heavens, my excitement levels went nuclear.

Soon, Nelly and I were sweeping along the empty roads like a cackling pair of avenging angels: whooping and yelling as we topped each rise, sucking power from the electrified air and bounding across the hills as though they were mere hummocks.

Only when the violent wall of rain crashed past did I call a halt to the adrenaline-fuelled madness to camp on a village green as the storm's heart descended. The next morning, when I awoke, the tent was smothered in fallen leaves and surrounded by broken branches. Heart-pounding stuff.

Things you would never see in Britain:

1) At a street carnival south of La Rochelle, one float consists of four

guys with blacked-up faces, fake afros and bones in their hair, dancing with two guys dressed in monkey suits. Tasteful.

2) A sign outside a restaurant near Arcachon reads: 'Menu 10 euros, vin à volonté' (unlimited wine). Ah ha, ah ha, ah ha ha ha. I'll have the fish, and two carafes of rosé, please.

I've just spent a week staying beside the ocean near a town called Arcachon, towards the southern end of France's western coast. The campsite is large and well resourced (a pool, a shop and English newspapers) and it's only an afternoon's bicycle ride from Bordeaux, so red wine is cheap and plentiful.

I've been reading, writing, swimming, exploring, and chilling out in bars playing Caribbean music.

We're beside 'Europe's Largest Sand Dune'. At more than a hundred metres high it takes 15 minutes to climb the thing and its summit is a splendid place to watch the sun turn red over the Atlantic. I decided the only way to properly appreciate such a titanic dune was to slide down it using a sand board while listening to the Beastie Boys on my iPod.

Thus far, my numerous attempts to construct an effective sand board have been in vain. The Beastie Boys, however, are rocking it.

Tomorrow it will be time to call an end to this lazy beach life, turn away from the wide expanse of the ocean and begin my long journey into the east.

Days since leaving London: 40
Distance travelled: 2,041 kilometres
Proportion of
    EU budget spent on agricultural subsidies: 40%
    EU output attributable to agriculture: 1.8%

French word of the day: 'réjoui' meaning 'joyful'

7: London's Mourning
9 July 2005

I'm in Périgueux, in the Dordogne Valley, 150 kilometres from the Atlantic coast.

I logged on to the internet at seven o'clock last night completely ignorant of events in London over the last two days. The fact I had an unusually large number of emails didn't initially faze me. However, the first one I checked was from somebody who didn't know I was abroad, asking was I OK 'given the bombings in London'. Those words sent a shiver down my spine.

I went straight to the BBC News website to find out what had happened. When I saw the basics my first feeling was actually relief; it wasn't a nightmare scenario like a 747 crashing into the Canary Wharf tower.

Then I read a long list of messages from the UK filled with surreal accounts of a day of chaos, wild rumours and London buses abandoned in the street. It appeared that everyone I knew was safe until I reached the last message on the list: the first to have been sent.

My friend Susan Harrison is a good and feisty woman. She works as a nurse at Great Ormond Street Hospital in central London and was heading there on the Piccadilly line when the bomb went off outside King's Cross station. If she'd caught an earlier train she'd have been looking after the victims.

It took her boyfriend, Mike, all night to find her. She'll live, but they've amputated her left leg. I feel a strange sort of powerlessness. Not now so jolly a pilgrim.

Back at the campsite I hooked up with Christophe, William and Mel, who were sharing my field beside the river. They're a warm-hearted, hard-drinking crowd. Just what I needed.

William has a massive canoe tied to the roof of his car and is wandering around France, looking for watercourses to provide adventure. He was a full-blown lunatic in his day and told a life story rich with fighting and scrapes with penury. At two o'clock this morning, as we drank warm Pernod together, he recited me Lewis Carroll's *Jabberwocky*. 'Twas brillig, and the slithy toves did gyre and gimble in the wabe ...'

Christophe is lean, swarthy and blue-eyed. He's also on a pilgrimage: to Spain to visit the Cathedral of Santiago de Compostela in Galicia on behalf of his ailing mother, now too weak to make the trip. He's travelling by moped, pulling a trailer for his dog, Fonzo.

Christophe is stopping in Périgueux to pay his respects at old haunts from 20 years ago. Back then he was a successful businessman and claims to have lived in the biggest house in town. Then the cops caught him with 40 boxes of dodgy foie gras and locked him away.

When he was released six months later, he resolved to try a new country and had his then wife blindfolded before dropping a pen onto a map of the world. The pen chose Madagascar, so Christophe moved there and ended up running a company fitting out business jets.

Christophe's girlfriend arrives this afternoon. However, two days ago he got picked up by the woman behind the butcher's counter at the local supermarket. He assures me she put the moves on him over the pâté section. These French, you know.

Mel is a bearded, nervous type with woman complications of his own. He's in Périgueux to visit his girlfriend, but it appears she's more interested in other girls than Mel. They also have serious communication problems, which culminated in her pulling a gun and threatening to shoot him, hence his presence at the campsite. We all had a laugh about that one.

Days since leaving London: 44
Distance travelled: 2,298 kilometres

> *If you can get people to believe in absurdities you can get them to commit atrocities.* – Voltaire

8: Shadows of Forgotten Ancestors
16 July 2005

I've just come from the Vézère Valley in the Dordogne, where the famous prehistoric cave paintings at Lascaux are located. I spent three days there.

The area is dotted with subterranean grottos that have walls covered in images of the bison, rhinos and aurochs which roamed the area in prehistory. There are 147 prehistoric sites, 25 decorated caves and a stunning museum chronicling the cultures which have ebbed and flowed across the region for a score of millennia.

The paintings are the most sophisticated art produced by hunter-gatherers that has ever been documented and the oldest man-made thing I've seen by 12,000 years. Even after all that time, they're still exceptionally evocative. Our guide summarised the diligent analysis of the paintings carried out by scholars in recent decades. The more one learns, the more interesting they become.

Animal images appear in undeciphered patterns; geometric signs symbolic of who-knows-what are repeated at caves throughout the region; and there's the suggestion of an antler-headed 'sorcerer' figure. High art made by long-passed ancestors. A tantalising window into the physical and emotional world they inhabited.

That world seems so distant. When you look at those paintings, or some ancient artefact behind glass at the museum, the lives of the people that created them – lives of hunting and gathering in the prehistoric valleys – can seem irrelevant to our immediate world of technology and modernity. But they're not irrelevant.

The people who created that art had kids. They taught those kids to walk, talk and wipe their bums. Those kids then had kids of their own, and so on, in an unbroken chain of humanity right down to all of us. In the meantime, some of those descendants figured out agriculture, wheels, writing and cities.

The reason we relate so effortlessly to their art is because it constitutes an intellectual and emotional response to the world by minds almost identical to our own. Everything about us – our language, our culture and our genes – is defined by the way those artists struggled through their lives. Because they made it, here we are.

We're part of the same story. The human endeavour. A spirit has been passed down across the generations through people about whom we know nothing, but to whom we owe everything, and if all the world's a stage, this is one hell of a play.

France is full of amazing cycle paths. However, off a road called the D704, just south of Sarlat-la-Canéda, I found the best one ever: a perfectly straight track through a tunnel of deep green, flanked by steep gullies, sheer cliffs and looming vine-covered rock formations.

I freewheeled down it for an unfeasibly long time, at a tidy 20 kilometres per hour, shouting 'Oh what a beautiful world' to various nameless tunes. I fully expected some mad old druid character to appear from the bushes and begin leaping about.

Awed by the beauty of Mother Nature, I've taken to collecting sprigs of wild flowers and inserting them into the strap of my handlebar bag. This may make me look silly, but I don't care about that and at least people will know I come in peace.

Days since leaving London: 51
Distance travelled: 2,741 kilometres
Population density of

France:	107 persons per square kilometre
The UK:	240 persons per square kilometre

French word of the day: 'franc-parler' meaning 'outspokenness'

Musings
How to Cross a Continent on a Bicycle

Life was throwing up a series of unanticipated challenges. One day in a remote village on the Atlantic coast I'd been subjected to the full

American Werewolf in London treatment from a bar full of locals who fell silent and blank-faced when I popped in looking for water.

In the Dordogne one evening, Nelly ran over a patch of ground thorns that punctured her tyres in 12 places. By the time I'd fixed them all it was two hours later and pitch-black, and there was nowhere to camp. Trust me, at the time it was stressful.

France experienced a major heat wave that June. The day I left Angers it was so hot that I'd taken the precaution of leaving at four in the afternoon after first drinking two litres of water. Nonetheless, after a wimpish 25 klicks, I retreated to a ditch, skull splitting open, head in hands and trying not to throw up.

I didn't have a strong grasp of French geography. I knew the basic shape of the country and where the major cities were located, but that was about it. Crucially, I didn't understand the topography and, when you're travelling by bicycle, hills are a really big deal.

Northern France is quite flat so, after the first month, I had an inflated sense of the distances I could cover. Then I hit the Massif Central.

The Massif Central is an elevated region of mountains and plateaux in south-central France covering one-sixth of the country. The volcanism that created It wound down about 10,000 years ago (and there hasn't been an eruption since 5760 BCE) so now it's all grassy cones, rich volcanic soils and very steep hills.

Before reaching it I was more concerned with exploring than actually getting to Istanbul. But by the time I was through the mountains and onto the French Riviera, it was the end of July and making it across Europe before winter was beginning to look like an issue. After that, I travelled pretty much in a straight line.

That left one major navigational decision: should I cycle through the Balkans?

The series of bloody episodes that constitute the Yugoslav Wars of 1992–2001 were extensively covered in the British media. In the summer of 2005 they were still fresh in the imagination.

Yet, from the UK, it was difficult to know if cycling and camping there was a reasonable risk or absurdly reckless. Initial enquiries from London proved inconclusive. The British Foreign Office's website mentioned unexploded land mines in out-of-the-way places. This was not a promising sign.

* * * * *

Here are the five cardinal rules for pan-continental bicycle adventures:

1) Drink water all the time. You don't really understand this until you've spent four hours cycling up an extinct volcano with a dehydration-related headache. During the hottest periods I was drinking four and a half litres of water a day.

2) Eat lots of food. Bananas are a winner. It's not like you're going to get fat.

3) Never cycle in the dark.

4) Don't be shy about where you camp. People who've never cycled across a continent love to fling around fourth-hand warnings about angry farmers. Ignore them. Farmers tend to be nice. Anyway, if you find a forest and camp 20 metres from the nearest footpath, you're in more danger of being taken out by a stray meteorite than harassed by an uncivil landowner.

5) Stay clean. This is very important and makes the difference between feeling stupendous and feeling rough as hell. I talked to other long-distance cyclists who, when away from campsites (and their showers), didn't wash. Big mistake.

Five months living in the wilderness is absolutely no reason to practise poor personal hygiene. The side effects of not washing involve irritation and redness around one's 'bits' which rapidly stops one enjoying life. I learned that lesson the hard way early on, then washed my whole body – showers or no showers – every evening, for the rest of the trip.

No shower? No problem. Simply apply the Wilderness Bottlewash System. Equipment: one litre bottle of water. This is what you do:

1) Strip naked.

2) Pour ¼ litre of water (slowly) over head.

3) Lather up (be methodical).

4) Pour remaining water (slowly) over head, ensuring all relevant areas are thoroughly rinsed.

5) Dry off.

6) Job done.

As the weather grew colder at the end of the bicycle ride this became an increasingly demanding feat of physical endurance. The most bracing occasion was when the only water available was from the fridge of a dwarf-like Bulgarian lady. Standing naked in a cold dark Bulgarian forest while slowly pouring icy water over one's head is a genuine test of one's mettle; but infinitely preferable to being dirty.

* * * * *

I've come across a lot of people who, when undertaking long-distance bicycle rides, treat the experience as some sort of race: getting up at six o'clock, getting on the road as early as possible, cycling as fast as possible etc. That's not really my style.

By the end of the first month, I'd settled into a routine. I'd sleep about nine hours a night, get up mid-morning, have a bit of breakfast, hang out at my campsite for a couple of hours, begin cycling around midday, break for coffee if I saw a nice spot, cycle for as long as I fancied and stop daily to buy food and water.

Each evening I'd camp in the most beautiful place I could find, apply the Wilderness Bottlewash System, then settle down to eat, read and daydream. Once I'd made my daily shop, I could stop wherever I wanted, and if the day ended in a forest, on a mountain or (one time in Serbia) in a swamp, so be it. Every now and again I'd roll into towns, send out my weekly email and stock up on reading materials.

That was the manner in which I cycled across Europe during the summer of 2005. I was supremely fit, getting loads of sleep and spending my days filled with incredible highs like freewheeling down mountains in the sunshine. Not only was that an extremely healthy lifestyle, but it was punctuated by powerful and affecting experiences such as my visits to Chartres Cathedral, the Vézère Valley and the Viaduc de Millau.

All these things feed into your state of mind, and the way that you feel about the world.

And, as I made my way across Europe, the story of that world marched along. Power was shifting east to India and China. The misadventure in Iraq – sliding deeper into catastrophe – was on everyone's lips. Globalisation and environmental degradation were setting parameters on the new century.

In southern France, engineers were beginning the construction of an experimental fusion reactor and, in America, other engineers were getting ready to send a spaceship to Pluto. The world was evolving:

travelling – generation by generation – into an unknown future. Meanwhile, I was living the solitary existence of a solo traveller, beholden to nobody, able to wander, weigh up the world and reading, reading, reading ...

The library I carried was ever changing. Here were its contents (stuffed into my overcrowded saddle bags) when I first left London: French road map, French guidebook, French dictionary, French phrasebook, *Perfume* by Patrick Suskind, *Cosmos* by Carl Sagan, a star chart, the Qur'an and the Bible.

My rationale for reading these last two was that, as the founding texts of Judaism, Christianity and Islam have been instrumental in shaping this world, I should find out what they say. I reasoned five months under the stars would provide the required head space.

9: The Two-Legged, Two-Wheeled Groove Machine
18 July 2005

I've finally started reading the Bible I brought with me and have now completed the first two books – Genesis and Exodus. The beginning is gripping: all the famous stories such as God creating the universe, Adam and Eve, and Noah and the Flood. Following that, however, I was dismayed to learn that the well-known Old Testament patriarchs (Abraham, Isaac, Jacob etc.) were ghastly (keeping slaves and lying for material gain).

I assumed that Joseph (the one with the technicolor dreamcoat) was going to be nice, but he used the seven years of famine as a pretext to take from the people of Egypt (in the following order): all their money, all their livestock and all their land. Then, when they had nothing left, 'Joseph reduced the people to servitude, from one end of Egypt to the other'. Then he gloated about it. What a bastard. It's a shame; he seemed so nice in the musical.

Apart from Chartres Cathedral, my must-see list for France contained one other item – the Viaduc de Millau, the new bridge over the Tarn Gorge above the town of Millau. The bridge is the final link in the A75 autoroute providing a continuous motorway from Paris to the western Mediterranean. I spent half of yesterday staring at the viaduct. Like the great temple, it didn't disappoint.

At 2.6 kilometres long, 342 metres high and supporting a four-lane motorway, the bridge is straight out of some far-out science-fiction book.

It breaks all sorts of records for height and general impressiveness and was opened in January 2005, just six months ago. It is surely set to become acknowledged as a wonder of the modern world.

At the time of Napoleon just two centuries ago, the main roads in Europe were still the ones put there by the Romans. Now you can drive by motorway from Paris to Madrid, while leaping 380-metre gorges along the way. Here we have an engineering masterpiece of the highest order, a triumph of industrial art and a solid example of how the hardware of civilisation can complement nature.

Welcome, ladies and gentlemen, to the third millennium.

Plan update: Millau is about halfway across the country, in the Massif Central. The scenery is spectacular, but the cycling is really hard. I'm heading east towards Avignon.

Singing update: Heading down a wonderfully scenic road beside the winding River Lot, I cycled through a series of tunnels cut into the rock. One was just long enough to handle a tune, so I belted out verse two of 'Jerusalem' at maximum volume. The acoustics were supernaturally perfect and it came out *really* loud. Very satisfying.

In addition, after reading about Chinese efforts to reconstruct Kublai Khan's summer capital I've added 'Xanadu' (as sung by Olivia Newton-John) to my cycling-singing repertoire. Finally, I've reconstructed the words of 'The Animals Went in Two by Two', discarding verses I deemed inadequate. Apart from that, it's almost all Led Zeppelin.

Millau is conveniently close to the village of Roquefort, where they make the world's finest blue cheese. I was thrilled to make a visit there a part of my pilgrimage. After being taken on a tour of the natural caves where the smelly blue stuff is matured, I expressed my adoration by purchasing a full half round.

Back at the Millau campsite last night, I wrestled with the cheese for hours, bringing to bear the additional firepower of two baguettes and some very acceptable Côtes du Rhône. But, in the end, the Roquefort got the better of me. Still, that's why they call it the King of Cheeses.

On the 27-kilometre climb through the valleys to Roquefort I stopped beside a VW van, and its owners – Daniel and Simone – fed me fruit and cold drinks. They were cruising around with their dog, Pauline, and their three tortoises: Coco, Cocette and Jean-Philippe. Daniel and Simone were friendly and unpretentious with a natural, understated style. Jean-Philippe, however, was rather grumpy and extremely fussy about his lettuce.

Days since leaving London: 53
Distance travelled: 2,797 kilometres

Maximum speed so far achieved by Nelly the cyclatron: 64.8 kilometres per hour (on descent into Millau)

French word of the day: 'taquin' meaning 'playful'

10: Mediterranean Blue
27 July 2005

Tuesday, 19 July, the day I left Millau, was in all respects a perfect day. It began with an hour-long climb out of the valley, getting me fully in the mood to expend energy. After that I flew like a phoenix through 130 kilometres of tree-thronged valleys in the Massif Central: my muscles burning with fire and my head burning with poetry. That evening I camped beside a clear river, which I threw myself into twice. Then I ate a picnic of bread, cheese and olives, lit a fire on the bank and considered the stars.

Twenty-four hours later I rolled into Avignon following a gruelling day in furnace-like temperatures. My finely tuned party antennae immediately told me something was up. Sure enough, I'd inadvertently arrived during the city's annual month-long arts festival. The streets were filled with clowns, South American pipe bands and fat men dressed as nuns. The city's campsite was chock-a-block with beautiful olive-skinned art-house types armed with hammocks, guitars and dreadlocks.

Bulls-eye.

I was camped with a couple of Algerian guys and a vivacious gaggle of Swedish and French chicks with a mean line in sarcasm. I immediately adopted them as my gang and spent the next two days hippying out, watching street theatre and attending rowdy nocturnal music venues where they danced flamenco until 5 a.m. to the harmonies of Spanish guitar.

I left Avignon on the 23rd and had been travelling through the heart-stoppingly beautiful hills of Provence for four days when, yesterday afternoon, my entire body beaded with sweat, I topped a rise and felt cool, salty air wash over me. Below – stretching to the horizons like a huge turquoise adventure playground – lay the Mediterranean.

Through some nifty planning I'm here at the same time as my Colchester-based neighbours, Jane and Richard. They've been friends of my family since I was 13. Richard is a successful businessman and entrepreneur (massive house, drives a Porsche etc.). His wife, Jane, is elegant and gregarious, with something to say about everything and holding court wherever she goes.

They're staying at a villa on the edge of Cannes with their mate Kate and a cluster of amusing children. I'm being so well looked after it's almost embarrassing. The French Riviera is in its summer swing with full beaches and a buzzing nightlife.

The villa has a pool and, last night, for the first time in two months, I slept in a real bed and used a real pillow instead of a rolled-up pair of jeans. I've been talking about the views over the Côte d'Azur, drinking Richard's wine and generally freeloading.

Richard, showing his true bohemian colours, has brought his guitar, harmonica and assorted songbooks. It didn't take much to persuade me to play Mick Jagger to his Keith Richards. We tackled some Bob Dylan and Beach Boys numbers. Our audience was very appreciative.

I'm hanging out to rest up, sort out my administration and buy some new maps. Then, in two days, Nelly and I head east towards Italy.

It's been a great couple of months. *Vive la France*.

Days since leaving London: 62
Distance travelled: 3,212 kilometres
Life expectancy at birth in France: 79 years (third highest in the world)
Proportion of French population below the poverty line: 6.1%

French word of the day: 'pétillant' meaning 'sparkling'

11: Ice Cream and Supercars
1 August 2005

Bible update: some people react to reading the Bible – and learning about Jesus – by overhauling their spiritual architecture. I have trumped their card and upped the ante by growing a beard. My beard is officially light blond with distinguished ginger bits. I've taken to stroking it when I'm about to say something particularly insightful.

After three days of love and recharging from Jane, Richard and their crew, I said my farewells and continued east. Cannes, Nice and Monte Carlo all lived up to expectations: exotic-looking women, designer shades and Ferraris.

In Nice, I slept on concrete next to another long-range cyclist: Frederick, from Sweden. Frederick has been following the Tour de France and going hard through the Alps and Pyrenees. He was a serious cycling dude covering as much distance in a day as I cover in two. Unfortunately, he'd found it necessary to get rid of his cyclatron computer (the electronic wizard box that tells you your speed and distance) because it stressed him out when he wasn't covering enough ground. For me, stress isn't proving to be a problem.

On crossing the Italian border, the locals wasted no time in living up to the stereotypes about their chaotic driving. The traffic laws are clearly regarded as little more than vague guidelines and, when you're on a bicycle, it's up close and personal.

Going over my first roundabout was a particularly involving experience of furiously beeping horns and aggressive gridlocked insanity, although everyone – myself included – seemed to be enjoying themselves. I would periodically throw up my hands and shout 'mamma mia' so they knew I was in the gang.

Heading along the gorgeous and sun-baked Italian Riviera, I caught sight of British newspapers outside a shop. I stopped long enough to ascertain the key development: that the 21/7 bombers, who attempted to set off a second round of explosions on the London Underground, have all been caught alive. I have to admit that news caused my heart to swell with nationalistic pride.

This afternoon I stopped at the charmingly named town of Cogoleto to have a swim in the sea. There I was immediately set upon by a super-friendly bunch of older Italians, who, within minutes, had got my entire plan and itinerary out of me, proving that with enough enthusiasm and hand-waving a shared language really isn't necessary.

One elderly gentleman, brow appropriately furrowed, decided to give Nelly an inspection. He paid particular attention to her front forks and computer before sagely tapping the latter and pronouncing 'bene' (good). I was most relieved.

Days since leaving London: 67
Distance travelled: 3,474 kilometres
Population of Italy: 58,103,033

> *When man invented the bicycle he reached the peak of his attainments. Here was a machine of precision and balance [and]… the more he used it, the fitter his body became … a product of man's brain that was entirely beneficial to those who used it, and of no harm or irritation to others.* – Elizabeth West

Musings
Writing Home

As a younger man, in the summer between school and university, I'd spent two months with family in the USA. After I had bummed around for a week, my Uncle Jack, seeing I was in need of some direction, suggested I buy a go-anywhere bus ticket and do some exploring.

Good idea, Uncle Jack.

Two days later I was riding the Greyhound into New York City, watching Manhattan's skyscrapers emerge from the morning's haze while Simon and Garfunkel's 'America' played through my headphones. It was a powerful experience for a young man. Six weeks later I'd been coast to coast through 26 states, gone bungee jumping, visited the Grand Canyon and caught the travel bug for life.

Thirteen years later, when I set off across Europe on that bicycle, I was richer, stronger and a great deal better informed about the world than I'd been at 18. My objectives, on this occasion, were rather more imaginative. Let me explain.

I believe that there are certain duties which we, as human beings, must discharge if we're to live fulfilled and self-actualised lives. One set of duties is to the wider community of which one is a part. Discharging them involves looking after your family, working productively for the benefit of society and being there for the people who rely on you for moral, social and other kinds of support. Much of life's wider significance, and the satisfaction that can be gained from it, results from the way in which one discharges those duties. Personally, I take them very seriously.

But there is also another duty.

Underneath the multifaceted construct that is a person's character and psyche, and behind the layers of social and cultural conditioning which carve each individual's value system, goals and identity, there is a core inner self. The psychoanalytic terms describing this central architecture of the human personality are the id (our underlying animal drives) and the ego (our executive, conscious, awareness). That inner dynamo – a cauldron of seething excitations thrown up, in a beautiful and mysterious way, by the carbon atoms in our brains – gets just the one chance to experience this cosmos.

For all practical purposes, the world is infinitely complex and interesting. There are more fascinating things to know and extraordinary experiences to have than can possibly be taken advantage of in a single human lifetime.

Yet, at the age of 31, I'd become aware that it was possible to go through life without ever understanding the fulfilment to be gained from conducting a proper intellectual and emotional exploration of one's home universe. It is possible to live and die without ever understanding how much fun you can have if you really put your mind to it; and it is possible to spend a lifetime obsessed by the smokescreen of trivia that fills human culture, and never seriously dive into the infinitely more fascinating and bottomless ocean which lies beyond.

In failing to do those things (for reasons of small-mindedness or handed-down notions of respectability, or because nobody around one does them) one is neglecting a basic duty to that core inner self.

When I left on my grand tour there were certain experiences I felt I should put myself through if I was to have the full life to which I aspired. A time was approaching when responsibilities to my wider community might make some of those experiences inappropriate, or at least undignified.

I did not, therefore, just want to see the world. I wanted to immerse myself in it. I wanted to take tea with Peruvian matriarchs high in the Andes, to discuss philosophy with Turkish motorcycle mechanics and calculus with wild-eyed Russian tramps. I wanted to circle the globe, read the ancient holy texts and ponder the mysteries of reality.

But first, I wanted to cycle topless across Europe, with a rainbow-coloured peace flag tied around my head while singing Led Zeppelin songs.

It only seemed appropriate to record the experience.

*****

In this age where email addresses and international travel are commonplace, so are electronic communiqués from distant lands. I felt the medium had untapped potential.

My first consideration was my audience. The initially small group of individuals who received my emails were busy people. They did not have time to read rambling accounts of the minor crises and mountain of logistics implicit in a two-year around-the-world adventure. They just wanted some escapism with their morning coffee. My ambition, therefore, was to convey the spirit of the trip.

There were two principal problems in achieving that. First, I was not of a mind, at the time, to articulate the most difficult, heartbreaking or depressing episodes. As a result, those reading the original diary were only getting half the story. But don't worry, I'm going to tell *you* everything.

The second problem was that, for the most important things, there are no words. One cannot adequately explain, using prose, what it feels like to stand alone, on a summer's day, atop the forest-shrouded folds of the Massif Central; to float in the warm waters of the equatorial Pacific as the sun sets in the west; or to be alone in a forest at night, and look up to see the faint red mote of Mars hanging in the blackness of space.

The way I dealt with that problem, as the journey continued, was to write about what those experiences did to my head. As you will see, following five months in the wilderness with Nelly, some curious things began happening in there.

12: A City with Orange Trees
2 August 2005

I'm loving Italy: the coffee is cheaper, the road signs more confused and the tunnel acoustics about the same. Because it's so hot I've started cycling topless and because I can no longer bear to use the helmet (it gives me a headache) I've started tying stuff around my head. All this, along with the flowers in my handlebar bag and signature red sunglasses (Greenwich Village, darling), comprises my new cycling image.

Due to this über-hippie look, and the excitability of the locals, I get quite a lot of people shouting at me. I reckon some of it's rude, but I have the advantage of not having a clue what they're saying, so I just wink knowingly, point Fonz-style and sweep on with Zen-like calm.

Nelly and I cruised into Genoa yesterday afternoon and knew at once we were going to like the place. The scooterists were in vocal mood, the buildings grand and august, and the avenues were lined with orange trees.

This city is a particularly appropriate stop as its history is intimately bound up with that of my destination. In the Middle Ages there was big money in the pan-Mediterranean sea routes, and the era's great trading cities (Venice, Genoa, Pisa etc.) fought for control of them in an ever-shifting web of alliances. Traditionally, the Genoese fought on the side of Byzantium.

In the year 1453, as the tides of history prepared to bring to an end a millennium of Graeco-Roman rule over Constantinople, its defenders stood hopelessly beleaguered by a vast Ottoman army. It was a Genoese galleon that broke out to beg help from Christian Europe. When no help was forthcoming, the crew took a vote and decided to return to Byzantium as it faced its nemesis. Now *that's* heroic.

Bible update: I'm on page 300. I had no idea how bad the Old Testament was going to get. There's an account in the Book of Numbers of how the Israelites go through the Midianite women and murder all the ones who aren't virgins. I was so sickened by this that I had to put the book down and stare at the roof of my tent awhile.

Then, during the civil war at the end of the Book of Judges, the fighting is topped off by the breathtakingly misogynistic finale of the mass abduction of girls from Shilah, which follows shortly after their killing all the women who aren't virgins (again). Monsters.

Last night at the Genoa campsite – high in the ancient and earthly atmosphere of its old city – I got drunk with a thoughtful and good-looking Belgian couple called Donovan and Linsey. They were driving to Rome with a car full of cheap Italian rum, so the three of us got stuck in. I awoke this morning to find that I'd only made it halfway into the tent last night. I think I may also have been snoring. Most undignified.

Days since leaving London: 68
Distance travelled: 3,483 kilometres
French GDP: US$2.22 trillion
Italian GDP: US$1.83 trillion

Either this man is dead or my watch has stopped. – Groucho Marx

13: The Freakazoid
5 August 2005

After getting through the stupendously beautiful Apennine Mountains north of Genoa, Nelly and I have been tearing along the valley of the River Po, trying out a new Italian cheese every day.

The city of Mantova looked so big on my map that I reasoned it was bound to have a campsite. On arriving yesterday evening I asked around but lucked out. No campsite.

I'd cycled 114 kilometres in very hot weather. I was tired, hungry and sweaty. It was nearly dusk and setting up camp in the dark is a bad idea, so I needed a fast solution. Mantova is by the shores of a boomerang-shaped lake crossed by several causeways. I could see a line of trees stretching away from the far shore: camping territory.

After cycling over one of the causeways we turned down a path into the forest and, on finding a lakeside meadow, I pulled out the tent and prepared to set up. That's when the mosquitoes mobbed us. It was a ferocious surprise attack. There must have been 50. One little devil even got inside my ear. Camping in Mosquito Central was not an option.

The light was failing fast, so we picked the first path leading away from the lake and set off. After 20 minutes, the trees and thick undergrowth became open field. As we made our way across I immediately felt something go wrong with Nelly's wheels. I looked down and both tyres were dead flat. Ground thorns: nasty. Camping on a field of ground thorns was not an option. Off we set again, this time with me pushing.

By the time we found some actual grass we were lost and miles from anywhere, the light had gone, I was drenched in sweat, Nelly had two flat tyres and there were still a couple of mozzies in pursuit. I pitched up and went in search of firewood.

Ten minutes later I had a pile of branches and was preparing to strip off, clean myself, light a fire and eat. That's when I noticed someone had appeared at the far end of the field and was pacing back and forth. I'd seen him by the light of his cigarette.

I needed to eat and wash at once and I wasn't taking my clothes off with a random stranger hanging about. The only person who might have business in an obscure mosquito-infested Italian field at night would be a farmer. Nothing was being grown there.

I went over. He was my height, thick-set, with black hair to his waist and wearing a black sarong. This dude clearly wasn't a farmer. I acted commanding and tried some pidgin English: 'You OK? Me sleep here. You here why?' It did the trick. He got on his moped and drove off. Problem solved.

Half an hour later the Jolly Pilgrim was cleaned, changed and sitting beside a vigorous camp fire, preparing to tuck into a meal of tomatoes, avocado and duck pâté. Then, at the far end of the field, a moped headlight appeared. Weird gothic sarong dude was back.

The guy was seriously encroaching my comfort zone. There was no reason for anyone else to be in that field and I couldn't relax with a freakazoid hanging about. If there's a murderer loose in Italy, it's not like I'm reading the papers and if we were going to have a confrontation then I wanted to be full of adrenaline first. It had been a difficult day, I was really hungry and I really needed that guy to piss off. Working myself into a temper wasn't difficult.

Wearing dark jeans and a dark waterproof, I knew he couldn't see me crossing the field. My long-bladed penknife was in the jacket pocket and

I was physically pumped after a day on the cyclatron. I went right into his face and didn't need to speak Italian to get my point across. I think he was trying to say 'no problem' by raising his palms and shaking his head. I shouted some more. He hurried over to his moped and got lost. This time he didn't come back.

Final assessment: once eyeball to eyeball I was pretty sure freak man wasn't dangerous, just really peculiar. Applying appropriate paranoia, I returned to where he'd loitered after 10 minutes had passed to be absolutely sure he wasn't hiding. Behind his lurking spot there was a hedge with a gap. It was full of used condoms.

Of all the obscure fields near Mantova, I camp in the one where the gay men go to have sex with strangers, overreact, then nearly threaten someone with a knife. Oops.

Days since leaving London: 71
Distance travelled: 3,743 kilometres

14: Peace Flags and Sun-Dried Tomatoes
6 August 2005

Bible update: sitting in my tent every evening I dutifully get out my Bible and keep reading. After announcing the Ten Commandments in Exodus (Book 2 of 66), the only commandment which gets any attention is 'Thou shalt have no God but me'. Apart from that it's basically the grubby politics of those nasty biblical Israelites, with whom I've completely lost sympathy.

I was hoping the appearance of King David would calm everyone down. It didn't. The bits dealing with him read like a list of excuses for the things he did and he comes across as a bit of a bandit. If this is what the people who venerated him thought, I wouldn't want to read what his enemies had to say.

It's clear in advance when someone is going to end up on the winning side. Joab – David's main military dude – keeps getting bad press despite always supporting David and continually winning battles for him. I correctly predicted this bad press was a sign he would come to a sticky end. Sure enough, the moment Solomon took the throne, Joab was executed on the flimsiest of excuses.

Last night, on a river bank a few kilometres north of the town of Legnano, Nelly and I found our best camping spot so far. It was an isolated clearing in a dense copse of trees discovered only after much scouting. Getting Nelly there meant slinging her over my back and wading through a deep layer of undergrowth. Then I set up the tent and collected a huge pile of wood.

I sat by the fire, 15 metres above the running river, beneath a great canopy of trees and a greater one of stars and galaxies beyond, eating an elaborate picnic of olives, anchovies and sun-dried tomatoes. A chorus of frogs sang to me while I looked into the flames and burned stuff. Then I fell into a long and restful sleep. This morning I was so content that I relit the fire and hung out until noon.

This afternoon we've been exploring Legnano's market and I found a man selling rainbow-patterned peace flags ('pace' in Italian). I bought two.

One flag I have just posted to Sue – currently recovering from the London bombs – in a parcel with some dinosaurs (plastic, not actual dinosaurs) and a few other knick-knacks I found at the market. The other flag will henceforth be worn around my head as an act of solidarity with her. As for the dinosaurs, they're bound to come in handy.

Plan update: my next pit stop will be with Italian friends near Venice. I'm particularly looking forward to seeing their daughter. Her name is Linda.

Days since leaving London: 72
Distance travelled: 3,830 kilometres

> *Then David sent messengers to Ish-Bosheth son of Saul demanding 'Give me my wife Michal, whom I betrothed to myself for the price of a hundred Philistine foreskins.'* – The Book of Samuel

Musings
Linda Maria Pevere

In London there are lots of jobs and lots of people, but never enough space. Housing is expensive and house shares are common. If you get them right, they can be uniquely rewarding social environments.

At 45 Hewitt Road, the north London home where I lived before the bicycle ride, there were three bedrooms. Moving in didn't just mean changing living arrangements, it meant joining a family. The most important quality in a prospective housemate was a well-developed sense of community. Linda Maria Pevere comes from a sprawling and cheerful Italian clan. Community is something she has a very clear understanding of.

When she moved in on 7 October 2001 – the day American and Northern Alliance forces began their offensive in Afghanistan – she was 23, sweet and a bit lanky; one of the tens of thousands of young Europeans living in Britain's capital. From that autumn, I began following the story of Linda's life.

In the next four years I saw her recover from a car accident, nurse a friend back to health, be made redundant, take a sabbatical in Berlin to organise a festival, launch a new career and be betrayed for the sake of money. These are intense experiences to live through with someone; the sorts of experience that bind people together.

She got to know my family. My friends became her friends. Her mother, brother, sisters and endless cousins came to stay. In this way, our lives became joined.

As she grew in worldliness and confidence, Linda became ever more complex and glamorous. You could take her anywhere and she'd always know what to say, what to wear and how to act. Within a year of moving in she'd become my best friend, closest confidante and most trusted adviser.

But there had never been anything sexual about it.

The thought had, of course, crossed my mind. But Linda and I were already deep inside each other's heads and the relationship as it stood had become a key plank in both our lives. I was old enough to know that some lines, once crossed, cannot so easily be passed back over. There was much to lose, so the thought had been deliberately set aside and a block put on it.

I remember exactly where I was standing when that block was removed.

In the summer of 2004, ten months before I left, we were in the garden discussing my plan for a global adventure. That plan was to cycle to Istanbul, then make my way to Australia and meet up with my old travelling buddy Sol. Out of the blue, Linda said she'd come to Australia too. I hadn't seen it coming.

The moment she said it I knew, if she joined me in Australia, we'd get together. I knew it in my heart.

So I began reassessing our relationship.

Getting together in London would have created a tangled web. But meeting your best friend – who is conveniently also the best-looking person you know – on the far side of the world? The more months that went by, the more I thought about it. The more I thought about it, the clearer things became. I therefore faced a dilemma: what to do?

Being a few months away from leaving to cross a continent on a bicycle seemed an inappropriate time to propose a relationship. However, I soon came to realise that, if I said nothing, and she didn't come, I'd never forgive myself.

So, I could tell her how I felt, but that I thought we should wait. Or, ask to have her for a few months and then again in Australia. That would feel weird. Anyway, I didn't want her for a few months. I wanted everything.

I made the judgement call. Rather than introducing a wide ball into our relationship in the final months before leaving, I'd wait. But, before setting off, I'd tell her my mind.

So I waited. In those final months living together, things between us changed. We both knew it.

Ten days before I set off we were making dinner in the kitchen. 'Lindy, are you really going to come to Australia? It's a big move. Are you sure you're up for it?' She smiled. Linda has big dark eyes and a very beautiful smile. 'Don't worry, baby, I'm coming.'

Two days later I went to spend a week with my parents to say goodbye. She came for a couple of days too. We both slept in the summer house in the orchard. Late that night, I told her.

'I can't imagine getting together with anyone but you. We've lived together four years and we're already like a family. I think we'd make an amazing couple.

'When you come to Australia, we'll have the best time in the world and if you want me, I'm all yours. I'll give you half my money, do whatever you want and dedicate the rest of my life to you.'

They were carefully chosen words.

She was shocked. She said she'd think about it. That was cool. I wasn't expecting an immediate response. The following day, she told me I'd chosen the right time to tell her. That meant a lot to me.

One week later, on the 27th May 2005, the two of us spent the morning alone together at 45 Hewitt Road. She made me breakfast and we sat and talked in the back garden.

Then we kissed goodbye and I cycled off to Canterbury.

*****

I didn't announce any of this in my diary. It wasn't anybody else's business what was driving me across Europe.

*****

The Pevere family have a tradition. Every summer they spend two weeks on Isola di Sant'Andrea, an island in the Laguna di Marano Lagunare, near Venice. I'd been invited to join them that year. It was an honour, but more importantly it was a chance to see Linda before Australia.

However, plans had been left vague. I didn't have an exact date to meet her. I didn't even know precisely where she lived, or the name of her village, only that it was somewhere in the vicinity of Venice.

I wasn't carrying a phone, most of the public telephone boxes in the Po valley were broken and, when I found ones that worked, I could never get through. The further east I travelled, the more aimless my wanderings became.

When I finally got through, on Sunday, 7 August, the sound of her voice was electrifying. Linda was waiting for me. Her village was called San Polo di Piave. I immediately ate all the food I was carrying, got on Nelly and hit the road. It was 3 p.m.

The journey from Montagnana to San Polo would normally have taken two days. I covered the 140 kilometres in six hours with no breaks. At one point, on the outskirts of Padua, I mistakenly ended up on a motorway (a no-no) going in the wrong direction (a big no-no) and had to U-turn across the traffic in order to get off (an oh-no-no). It was reckless, but I was really looking forward to seeing Linda.

I arrived at San Polo just before 10 p.m. and found myself next to a grand white church in the village's main square. Suddenly all these Italians appeared and then there she was, radiant and perfect, emerging from the night.

15: Italian Summer
16 August 2005

I'm at the home of the family of Linda Pevere, my Italian soul sister and ex-London housemate. Within half an hour of arriving, I was showered and sat at a long table in the garden eating supremely delicious home-cooked food, as my surrogate Mediterranean family swirled around and Laura (Linda's mum) massaged my tired legs while feeding me melted chocolate with a spoon.

The Pevere family live in a large house with a rambling garden that abounds with fruit trees, grape vines and a sizeable menagerie of animals. Their village is the kind of place where everyone knows everyone. Uncles, aunts and cousins are scattered in the immediate vicinity and often pop by.

This part of Italy is one of the richest regions in Europe. It's straight out of a glossy magazine: everyone dresses to impress, the cars are precision-made German instruments, and sunglasses are everywhere.

At one point, while sitting in the gorgeous piazza of the nearby town of Oderzo, Linda's super-cool brother Paolo arrived looking excited. He proceeded to have an intense exchange with all assembled (lots of hand-waving and passion). I was terribly impressed and imagined some exotic scheme was afoot. It was only afterwards that someone explained to me that they'd been talking about aftershave. God, I love the Italians.

We took a day trip to Venice. The last time I visited was in 1993 as a penniless 19-year-old backpacker. This time I was given a personal tour by three elegant Italian women: Linda, her cousin Giulia (fiery and occasionally throws things) and their friend Chiara (an expert in space law). My encounter with the city was considerably richer on this occasion.

That evening, Paolo drove us south to watch superstar DJ Tiesto deliver a set at one of the big coastal nightclubs. In this glammed-up part of the world, clubs come with their own in-house waterfalls and car parks filled with Mercedes and BMWs. That was only Tuesday night.

The next day brought the main event, the *pièce de résistance* if you will. They call it 'The Island'.

Here's the deal:

1) Take 10 Italians aged 21–59.

2) Plonk on an island encircled by beaches, in a lagoon by the Adriatic.

3) Provide with the following amenities: one tap.

4) Stir in enough red wine to freak out a large rhinoceros.

5) Leave for two weeks.

The whole family, and numerous hangers-on, descend annually for this hard-drinking lagoon-based fiesta. Operations are led by Ido, Linda's dad, and he's the kind of guy that likes to lead from the front. We're talking about a man with more than a hundred ducks and chickens, and who makes his own salami from scratch, starting with the pig.

Our three days on the island consisted of sunbathing, getting drunk in the rain, large quantities of extremely fresh seafood and lots and lots of messing about in boats.

Absolutely fantastic.

Days since leaving London: 82

Distance travelled: 4,009 kilometres
Number of sand particles on all the beaches on planet Earth:
7,500,000,000,000,000,000
Number of stars in the Milky Way Galaxy: 200,000,000,000

Italian word of the day: 'cazzo' (vulgar) meaning 'cock'

Musings
August and Everything After

I knew at once that Linda wasn't going to come to Australia. I could tell from the look in her eyes. Worse, there was a barrier: our intimate relationship had become formal, the warmth had turned to cold and we made nothing but small talk. It was a shock.

In the 10 weeks it took me to cycle from London to Linda's house, something had been lost. During the seven days in San Polo, the three on the island and the afternoon in Venice that followed, I kept my cool, but in reality I was in disarray; anxious, confused and struggling with increasing desperation for a way to get it back.

In 10 days, I couldn't find one. Then I was alone again, with Nelly, heading east.

There are many ways one might deconstruct what happened. At the time, I saw it simply. I'm hardly the first person to fall for their best friend, and hardly the first to do so under awkward circumstances. Transforming a relationship while changing continents is a tough call, but making dreams come true isn't supposed to be easy. There was a test. I'd failed.

It wasn't like there would be a second chance. If Linda didn't come to Australia, I wouldn't see her again for nearly two years. By then, so much would have changed.

In the 21 months that followed my visit to San Polo there were some very unpleasant episodes. Getting hospitalised in Zagreb was painful; my first months in Australia were crushing; and I was really pissed off about getting abandoned in the Bolivian desert. But the lowest point in the entire adventure was the two days cycling east towards Trieste. My mind was saturated with thoughts of her. Grinding through my head. The blackest sort of pain.

It was a huge watershed. Linda was my best friend. A major bond had been broken. I felt much more alone than before. What was really so glorious about staying with Serena and Matteo in Trieste was that they broke that spell and drew me from my bleak downward spiral.

It was the only time I considered cutting the adventure short. Should I return to London to win her? But I'd chosen to throw myself against the wild blue yonder in a once-in-a-lifetime adventure. If I'd backed out at that point, I wouldn't have had much to offer as a partner in London. Anyway, I still had a plan: get to Istanbul, get to Australia, then meet Sol. Then we'd see.

*****

The plan had a hole in it. It took me to Australia and no further. Once I met Sol I was confident we'd find something with which to fill it, and there was a reason for leaving things open-ended: to leave fate space to develop in interesting ways.

At this point in the journey, I had no idea what those interesting developments might be and a very specific constellation of circumstances would have to align before I'd find out. I'd thought the trip would be about high-octane adventure and that my visit to San Polo would be the prelude to an Australian romance. But, like this story you're reading, those things were just the facilitator.

You don't really understand people until you've met their families. I'd lived in close proximity to Linda for four years. I'd seen her ride life's roller coaster and cope when the chips were down. In my time at San Polo I saw for myself the environment in which her mind had been shaped and, after that, a lot of things about Linda made sense.

The Pevere family grow things, make things, keep animals, ride in boats, go dancing and spend weeks camping together on beaches. Watching them frolic, chatter and squabble for 10 days was a chance to witness, first hand, the complex social conditioning that goes on around a lively dinner table and how there is a magic passed down the generations which is learned, but not taught ...

All those families, at different points in their cycles. All those people, at different chapters of their lives. All those societies, at different moments in their histories. And the Viaduc de Millau and Chartres Cathedral and the Lascaux Caves.

You see, during that stupendous bicycle ride, and the adventures which followed, I had a palpable feeling of witnessing a snapshot of a larger dynamic and of travelling through a moment in time. It was in Australia – with my body broken and plans smashed – that I began to try to capture that feeling systematically. That was an experience which would, in turn, prompt me to go to Ecuador, get an apartment high in the Andes and write it all down.

16: Four Glorious Days in Trieste
21 August 2005

One of the great things about knowing Linda is that you get to meet some really groovy Italians. I left her clan on the 17th and headed towards the Balkans. The following afternoon I was picked up in Trieste by Serena, an old friend of Linda's who used to visit us in London.

To understand what Serena is like, imagine something out of *A Midsummer Night's Dream* mixed with a healthy twist of gypsy chic. She's a very entertaining young lady.

The two of us first took Nelly to a bicycle repair shop for some much-needed love and mechanics. Then we went back to Serena's flat in the hills rising behind the city. The flat has views over the Gulf of Trieste, is filled with eastern throws and inhabited by a mischievous cat. The weather was to die for, so we sat on the sun-filled balcony with her boyfriend Matteo (bearded-hippie-rock-god), played cards and listened to the blues.

Trieste is where the Latin, Germanic and Slavic worlds meet. Its Austro-Hungarian heritage is close to the surface in the opulent facades of its period buildings. There is also a well-preserved Roman amphitheatre and I managed to catch a ritual at the Serbian Orthodox Cathedral. The priest was black-robed and square-bearded and swung a golden smoking censer to the sound of Gregorian chant. As he proceeded down the nave I could feel Constantinople draw closer.

This is my fourth day in Trieste. Serena and Matteo's friends are a sprightly bohemian crowd of musicians and trade union activists: terribly friendly and full of beans. Since I arrived we've drunk cocktails on a grand plaza built by the Archdukes before World War I; spent an evening laughing beside the Adriatic under a full moon; and, on a poignant night, considered the ways of the world at Matteo's spacious house, before being lulled to sleep by the mournful, melancholy and magnificent music of Edvard Grieg.

Things I've learned in Italy:

1) The greatest team in Italy's Serie A football division is, without doubt, the all-conquering Inter Milan. I've been inducted into a fan club and everything. As for those pigs at AC Milan, henceforth, they

shall be referred to as 'The Enemy'.

2) Contrary to what I previously naively thought, pineapple is not – repeat not – a suitable topping for pizza. Any attempt to even raise the subject for debate will be met with shaking heads, steely looks and dark mutterings about the foolishness of the English.

3) Napoleon was Italian. He was brought up in Corsica, but his dad was Italian, so he's basically Italian. Don't tell the French.

My stay here has left me feeling profoundly regenerated and, since arriving, I've learned the words to three whole Bob Marley songs. Tomorrow, I break for the border with Slovenia. Matteo is hiring a bicycle to join me for the uphill ride.

Serena really came into her own last night. Surrounded by empty wine bottles and sat between two guitar enthusiasts, she lowered her eyes, leaned across the card table and whispered, in her heavily accented English: 'Vood ju laak to play … poka?'

Laugh? I nearly died.

Days since leaving London: 87
Distance travelled: 4,153 kilometres

Eyak (Alaskan) word of the day: 'xuqu'liilx'aax'ch'kk'sh' meaning 'are you going to keep tickling me on the face in the same spot repeatedly?'

17: Critics
23 August 2005

The first thing I saw on crossing the Slovenian border was a naked man standing beside a parked lorry, furiously masturbating himself. Evidently, the guy had issues.

Ninety minutes later I was 30 klicks from the border, night was about to fall and I'd left it late to camp, when I spotted a path leading into a damp forest of enormous pine trees. I made my way in.

Camping at times like that is much more fun if you have a fire. However, it had been raining hard for three days and last weekend Slovenia suffered extensive flooding. The forest was utterly waterlogged. There was no dry wood. Undeterred, I rose to the challenge.

The trick is to find several sizes of different twigs (to use as kindling) that are long dead (so they're dry) and suspended above the forest floor (so they haven't become soaked by the rain). If you arrange the right combination of twigs, get lucky with your wood type and blow on it really hard it *can* be done, but it isn't easy.

Using the last light of dusk to collect wood, and a bit of tissue and the card from a battery box to light it, I created a roaring blaze on my first, carefully constructed, attempt. Feeling pleased with myself I then settled down to eat a dinner of ham, mustard and pickle under the trees. That's when I noticed the ants.

Over the last three months, I've become rather familiar with Europe's ant populations. Since leaving London several species have taken it upon themselves to eat my food, explore my tent and (during the hottest weather) climb into my water bottles for a slurp. They are a minor nuisance but, fundamentally, ants are nice.

The ones pouring into my camp from the blackness of Mirkwood last night weren't nice at all. They were big, aggressive and travelling in alarming numbers. Once they started sinking their mandibles into me, hostilities were open and it was game on.

For the next 40 minutes I half-heartedly ate dinner while periodically throwing batches of the little varmints into the avenging flames of my expertly constructed campfire. Many hundreds of ants were reduced to ashes that night.

It took a while for me to comprehend the scale of my ant problem. By the time I'd eaten, the antish offensive showed no sign of abating. It had become clear that this was no ordinary ant incursion. These ants meant business. I gave up the struggle, brought everything inside the tent, sealed it as best I could, then went to sleep.

The next morning, the clouds had cleared and daylight illuminated the forest. On opening my eyes I saw a teeming multitude of ants covering the tent. There were thousands of them. A swarm of black army ants was marauding its way across the forest's floor and I'd camped right in the middle of them. Unlucky.

My quickly formed plan was to find a clear area on which to dump my equipment, then get ready for the day free of ant harassment. I ran to and fro, but the moment I put down an open-sandalled foot anywhere five or six of the little critters would crawl between my toes and chomp on me. I have no idea how big that ant swarm was, but after minutes of searching I couldn't find a single square foot of forest not covered with horrid black biting things.

I eventually threw down a blanket and spent quarter of an hour hopping from foot to foot while frantically breaking camp. I decided to skip breakfast.

Ants 1: Pilgrim 0

Days since leaving London: 89
Distance travelled: 4,295 kilometres
Time for an army ant to walk 20 metres: 1 hour
Global ant population (estimate): 10,000,000,000,000,000 (ten thousand trillion)

18: Gandalf on Guitar
29 August 2005

The evening after being assailed by the black ants, I arrived at the last of my scheduled European stops: the house of my old friends Maja and Cani in the Slovenian town of Kranj.

I first met Maja and Cani on a felucca meandering along the Nile in 1999, where we hit it off over a bucket of freshly caught perch. Maja is the orchestrator, always in the centre of the action and with an ever-sunny disposition. Cani has a million crazy projects and a habit of pulling them off. The man can build – and grow – anything. Their family has grown by one since I last saw them: Vid is ginger-haired, awash with energy and 22 months old.

On arrival, I was given my own room with a soft double bed and a balcony. The view outside is of mountains running horizon to horizon. There are two kitchens and – joy of joys – English Breakfast Tea. I'd originally planned on staying just two or three nights. Maja insisted on at least ten. OK.

The house is an enormous alpine-style arrangement split into three big flats. Floating around is Maja's brother Uros, an intellectual computer-literate type drafting a dissertation on Jewish fundamentalism during his summer break from university. Uros has a much-appreciated propensity for cooking brunch on behalf of Englishmen who rise late in the day.

Maja's mum and dad – Tanja and Bogdan – live on the ground floor. I spent an evening drinking wine with Bogdan, the details of his life being fascinating to me. His uncles and aunts fought as partisans during World War II and were imprisoned by the Italians. Bogdan himself was conscripted into the Yugoslav People's Army in the early 1970s and he spent two years at General Headquarters in Belgrade. He reports that it was a hardening, stoic experience which he did not enjoy and on returning home, his beloved baby daughter was terrified of him.

As for Tanja, she studied English and when Maja showed her one of these emails, she described it as 'perfect', so I like her.

Bible update: stop press for the Book of Job. Incredible. The best bit of the Old Testament so far by a wide margin. Hard contemplation about very difficult things. It deals with how to make sense of life when it's insufferably cruel. I particularly love the bit at the end where God says to Job: 'Well, I created the universe, what did you contribute?' You have to admit, He has a point.

Slovenia is right at the forefront of the rapid blurring of Europe's old Iron Curtain division. It's well organised, visibly prosperous and busy making the most of the summer. On my second night we attended a free open-air concert in a vampire-style ruined castle. The headline act was a feisty local folk band with a comedy accordion player and, inexplicably, Gandalf on guitar. They delivered much of their excellent stage banter in English and rocked the house.

The next evening we saw an Italian blues band play a local jazz festival with Maja and Cani's crew: a free-spirited, open-minded bunch who danced barefoot on the grass until midnight. I've also been exploring the countryside by bicycle and spent an afternoon by the river in Ljubljana – Slovenia's funky capital – drinking beer under the sun with Maja's extraordinarily attractive colleague Dunya. Then we walked uphill to the city's castle and took in the surroundings.

We've just got back from a weekend on the coast. Cani, Maja, Vid and I swung down there to stay at their cottage by the sea, where we slept, read and lazed around. Excellent for the soul.

Since leaving the UK I've been trying to decide which route to take from here. Option one is back into Italy, south, then by boat to Greece. Option two is straight through the Balkans. Of late I've received several warnings that option two could be problematic. Ido, Linda's dad, said I'd be foolish to go that way and urged me to strike south. Bogdan is practically forbidding me to continue east, talking of ambush by Serbian bandits.

Nevertheless, I've decided to take the land route. At this point I'm confident I can deal with any confrontation and the idea of ambush appeals to my sense of fun. The plan therefore is to travel south-east through Croatia, Serbia, Romania and then Bulgaria. I'll tell you how I get on.

Days since leaving London: 95
Distance travelled: 4,314 kilometres
Slovenian population: 2,011,070

Where were you when I laid the earth's foundation? Tell me, if you understand. Who marked off its dimensions? Surely you know! Who stretched a measuring line across it? On what were its footings set, or who laid its cornerstone – while the morning stars sang together and all the angels shouted for joy? – The Book of Job

19: Dazed, Confused and Mildly Infected
17 September 2005

After 10 days of luxury at Maja and Cani's house, I finally dragged myself away and headed for the Croatian border. The storm gods of Slovenia decreed that my last days in the country would be much as my first: intermittent rain, thunder rolling through thickly forested valleys and hilltops lost in overhanging cloud.

I first began talking to myself early in this pilgrimage as a way of focusing the mind. From there it was an obvious step to start talking to Nelly ('Well, Nelly, today we're heading for XYZ town. We'll find a bike shop, get that spoke sorted …' etc.). It was somewhere in Provence that I caught myself answering back on behalf of the cyclatron: essentially carrying out both sides of a conversation with an inanimate object.

Following the best part of a month with real human contact between the French Riviera and Kranj, Nelly and I stopped talking to each other. But three days of sleeping in the Slovenian and Croatian countryside and the bicycle began piping up once more.

Those conversations were halted in Zagreb. My maps showed three campsites in the city. None of them turned out to exist, so I was forced to use a youth hostel, which brought sudden and unanticipated immersion into the global backpacking community.

My first evening in the city was therefore spent with Phil – an entrepreneurial type from Chicago squeezing every drop of fun from a month in Europe – and a bunch of mad-for-it Australian and American girls who'd descended from the Greek coast, where bar owners had been paying them to dance in clubs. We had a great night, but since then I've been feeling rather ill.

Just before the Croatian border I got stung on the leg by an aggressive flying thing. By yesterday, this insect wound had developed into a multicoloured bruise accompanied by full swelling of the left shin. That, in turn, led to a tour of three of Zagreb's medical facilities, which were quite modern, apart from the odd typewriter.

All this culminated in a consultation with a very nice doctor called Marcus, who spoke perfect English (albeit, sadly, with an American accent).

Dr Marcus informed me of the following:

1) My heart rate is now extremely low ('Sports heart,' he said). I was very pleased by this news.

2) I have a mild bacterial infection of the skin called Streptococcus, courtesy of said flying thing.

I was then handed over to a nurse called Joanne (four kids, aged 8–14, likes collecting foreign coins) who had the inestimable pleasure of giving me my first ever bottom jab. It was very painful and I was forced to lie down for some moments afterwards.

I've been ordered to stay put a few days, before hitting the road for Belgrade. I shall, of course, follow this advice, but I'm gagging to get on. I do, after all, have a continent to cycle across.

Days since leaving London: 104
Distance travelled: 4,567 kilometres
Croatian population: 4,495,904

> *I hate to advocate drugs, alcohol, violence, or insanity to anyone, but they've always worked for me.* – Hunter S. Thompson

20: The English Patient
20 September 2005

My claim to be suffering a mild infection turned out to be an understatement. After two days of waiting for my multicoloured shin bruise to clear, I returned to the infection hospital for what I thought was a paranoia check.

The doctor examined my leg, asked a few questions, declared the infection out of control and then hospitalised me. This was a most unexpected turn of events.

The last time I was an inpatient was when I was five and they were carving up the bones of my lower legs so I could walk properly. It was therefore very strange to find myself suddenly dressed in baggy blue pyjamas and immersed in a world of bossy matrons, haughty doctors and eccentric bald men with sideburns, wandering around in dressing gowns.

The morning after my internment, our ward was invaded by six high-energy nurses. As I stumbled out of bed bleary-eyed they thrust towels at me and ordered that I take a shower. The fact I was half asleep and everyone was shouting in Serbo-Croat gave the experience a strange phantasmal quality.

For the first four days, I was given hard-core antibiotics, delivered intravenously four times a day, which had me writhing on the bed in pain. On day five I was downgraded to once-a-day penicillin bum injections which, while rather undignified, were considerably less painful and a subject of great hilarity for everyone else.

In the next bed is Minja (stomach infection), who has become my top hospital buddy. Minja can't understand why I don't want to spend the rest of my life in Croatia and I've been forced to insist, repeatedly, that I'm going to Turkey. On day two Minja's cousin – blessings upon his soul – brought a television into the ward, giving us access to cheap American drama, football and *The Simpsons*.

When planning this trip, a stint in an infection hospital wasn't high on my must-do list, but it's been a great chance to bond with the Croatians (I love 'em) and I've rather enjoyed the attention from all the lovely nurses.

My favourite nurse is called Adrien. She regularly sneaks me into the rose garden, where we drink Turkish-style coffee together. Adrien is half-Serbian, quite fancies Mel Gibson and has vivid stories of working at the hospital during the Yugoslav Wars.

Those wars have been a favourite topic of conversation on the ward. These guys are still pretty pissed off about the whole thing. Adrien tells first-hand accounts of casualties from the Croatian-Serbian phase of the fighting and asks why more help wasn't forthcoming from western Europe (and I quote: 'Where were you?').

Minja points out that the Soviet Union fractured into republics without having a war, as did Czechoslovakia. He also likes to tell me the numbers: the tens of thousands killed and billions of dollars it all cost (and I quote: 'For what?'). We all agreed better uses could probably have been found for that cash.

It's comforting to know that I can show my face at a foreign medical institution, with a condition I don't understand and have a team of strangers swing into action with proficiency, humour, and compassion for my rather lonely situation. My respect for medical professionals has been greatly enhanced, as has my hatred of needles.

To keep me occupied, one of the doctors was kind enough to collect an English-language magazine from downtown, so I've been learning all about how Hurricane Katrina has swamped New Orleans. I've also been reading the Bible.

Days since leaving London: 117
Distance travelled: 4,571 kilometres
Proportion of New Orleans currently under water: 60%

Don't try. I'm sleeping inside with a big dog, an ugly woman, two shotguns and a claw hammer. – Sign on Oriental Rugs, St Charles Ave, New Orleans

21: Received Scripture
21 September 2005

So, there I was, lying in a Croatian infection hospital, reading my Bible.

I'd resolved to use my internment to finish the holy book and was ploughing through Acts when I noticed that Miljan – in the next bed – had acquired an A4 picture-book version of the New Testament. That day Jadranko moved into the bed on the other side. He was only 16, and training to be a priest. You can guess what he was reading. We were all dressed in identical sets of blue pyjamas. What a sight. I was the only one making notes.

If that bee hadn't savaged me on the Slovenian border and forced me to lie in bed for 12 days, I might not have got through all 1,380 pages. But with nothing else to do, I max out at around 80 Bible pages a day, before reaching scriptural overload. The first 600 pages took me two and a half months, the final 780 just 10 days.

The Old Testament is a hard read. Its first 300 pages are mainly rambling accounts of archaic rituals and animal sacrifice, interspersed with horrifying acts of premeditated murder and genocide, although there are a few good bits.

The Book of Job is amazing. Job is blameless and upright, but when the things he most fears are delivered upon him he is overwhelmed by hopelessness and wishes to be swallowed into oblivion. Then God comes along and puts it all in perspective. He describes – in express and melodious language – what the experience of being the creator of the universe is like and points out that He is not subject to judgement or questions from any of His creatures, no matter how blameless. It was humbling.

The end of the Old Testament goes downhill again. By the Book of Isaiah the Israelites are proclaiming God's curses on all their enemies, which is basically everyone else. Then, for good measure, the divinely inspired devastation of the world is predicted.

The prize for the best Old Testament character goes to Nebuchadnezzar, ruler of Babylon. In between ruling a mighty empire and overseeing the construction of the Hanging Gardens, Nebuchadnezzar finds time to have wacky dreams, throw tantrums and chuck people into furnaces when in a huff.

After all that, the New Testament was a relief. I love the way the Gospels tell the same story from different angles. It's a clever literary trick. Maybe I'll borrow it. By the Gospel of Luke, I was genuinely gripped by a good read. Then, 26 pages from the end, in the first Book of John, it finally proclaims: God is love.

Hallelujah.

Days since leaving London: 118
Distance travelled: 4,577 kilometres

Have you seen the gates of the shadow of death? Have you comprehended the vast expanses of the earth? Tell me, if you know all this. – The Book of Job

Musings
A Jealous and Avenging God

To assert that a book was directly, deliberately and uniquely inspired by God, that God is perfect and can do *anything* and that the book in question contains His complete and eternal message for humanity is a very big set of claims. One would expect such a book to be – at the very least – comprehensively spectacular and overflowing with transcendent wisdom.

After reading the Bible in its entirety my view is that, whichever holy spirits inspired its authors, the words they wrote have the signs of humanity stamped all over them. Reading what those words actually say (as opposed to what other people say they say) was most enlightening. The whole thing is considerably more confused and ambiguous than I'd previously been led to believe.

For example, the reputation of the city of Sodom comes down to a single incident. Lot's house is surrounded by locals who want him to send out his guests so they can have sex with them (Lot instead offers his virgin daughters). Whether or not Sodom was actually full of raging homosexuals is difficult to judge (though for millennia it's been interpreted that way). However, God is evidently pissed off as he destroys the city with burning sulphur.

I was under the impression that King Solomon was a paragon of goodness and wisdom. The only story I knew was the one with the two women, where they both claim a child; Solomon threatens to cut it in two, then awards the baby to the woman who objects. What I hadn't understood is that that's the *only* wise thing Solomon does. Apart from that it just goes on (for pages and pages) about how wise he is, along with gushing about how many chariots he's got, his 700 wives, 300 concubines and the slave labour he uses to construct prestige buildings. He doesn't actually *do* anything else wise.

The Book of Psalms contains 150 intensely beautiful religious poems. However, with a handful of exceptions they deal exclusively with a few closely related themes: God is great, the righteous man will seek God, the unrighteous will be punished, God will protect the righteous, and the righteous will triumph over the unrighteous.

Here's an excerpt from Psalm 9:

> *The Lord reigns for ever;*
> *he has established his throne for judgement.*
> *He will judge the world in righteousness;*
> *he will govern the peoples with justice.*

It's gorgeous stuff, but it doesn't seem very *substantial* to me. It doesn't provide concrete instructions on how to conduct oneself, and the overwhelmingly most important difference between righteousness and unrighteousness is belief in God. But if being righteous means saying you believe in God and believing in God involves being righteous then the arrangement is circular. Unless, of course, one is prepared to be a little more specific about what one means by the word 'God'.

Jesus is marvellous. He is against elitism and materialism and in favour of humility, compassion and love. Fabulous. I also note that he makes it pretty clear that if you're rich, you're going to go to hell. Unless, of course, you can get a camel through the eye of a needle. Jesus is very specific about it and it's mentioned three times.

St Paul seemed to write most of the New Testament. I didn't like him. He goes around proclaiming willy-nilly who will, and will not, go to heaven. This is downright cheeky as such things are clearly a matter for God. Whereas Jesus says things like 'Love thy neighbour', Paul says things like 'I don't like the following people ...'. The list of people Paul doesn't like is long and includes homosexuals (who commit 'shameful lusts'), women (who must be silent and submissive) and people with long hair (which I personally felt was just creepy).

I had not anticipated that studying the Bible would trigger my conversion, but I had expected more in the way of world-illuminating insights. As regards that expectation, I must admit to a pang of disappointment. Glimpsing into the minds of those Middle Eastern holy men was fascinating, but if the voice of the divine is hidden in their ancient words then I could not make it out.

*****

The evening of the day after I drew these conclusions, I had dinner with one Dr Santini. Among the matters we discussed was her Catholic faith. She told me about how that faith had given her great strength and how she had witnessed it guide so many people through, and make sense of, the trials, tribulations and struggles of birth, life, marriage and death.

There's a position on religion which holds that it is mere ancient superstition, programmed into each generation by the next. I don't regard that as a very thorough narrative. It is true that many evil and preposterous things have been said, and done, in religion's name. Yet, as a phenomenon, it has been central to the human adventure and key to many of the most awesome things we've accomplished.

Isn't the *underlying* point that this universe we all live in is profoundly mysterious and wonderful, and that something extraordinary and magnificent is clearly going on – right here, right now – on this planet?

22: Belgrade Calling
28 September 2005

On finally leaving hospital in Zagreb I found that the skies had turned grey, the winds cool and the leaves brown. Autumn had arrived.

As one moves deeper into the Balkans, recent history becomes more traumatic. This is reflected in the life stories of those you meet. My final evening in Zagreb was spent in the company of Dr Maria Santini, who first declared my infection out of control and hospitalised me two weeks earlier. We drove into the hills and checked out some sights, then she bought me a horse steak dinner.

Dr Santini went to medical school (in Zagreb) during the Croatian-Serbian phase of the Yugoslav Wars, even though she was living in what was technically Serbia when the fighting started. To enrol, she therefore had to undertake a secret and indirect four-day journey to the city, moving from town to town to avoid battlegrounds and awkward questions from military types.

She then studied as an undergraduate while the city was under artillery bombardment from the army of the land she'd just left. While this was happening her family (who were still in Serbia) had lost all contact with her. Following six months with no word from their daughter, Dr Santini's mother and father, along with her 16-year-old brother, decided to make their own way north through the war zone, to Croatia, where they were reunited and still live today.

Dr Santini's paternal grandfather, a navy man, was imprisoned by the Germans during World War II, but escaped when the Allies bombed the jail where he was being held. He then made his way into the mountains, tracked down a partisan band and spent the rest of the war fighting as a guerrilla. My life seems so dull by comparison.

The morning after my dinner with Dr Santini, following two and a half weeks in the Croatian capital (and buying enough maps to get us to Turkey), Nelly and I finally left Zagreb on the 22nd, made our way south through the city and headed for Serbia.

For two days, raindrops kept falling on my head. In the evenings I slept in wet hillside meadows, where I was forced to make friends with distressingly tactile slugs and spiders. Then, as I approached the border, the sun showed his face and life became less damp and more wonderful.

On our final evening in Croatia we camped deep in an ancient forest of gnarled trees, where I lit a fire, drank a bottle of Zinfandel and was kept company by the wails of nocturnal wildlife. The next morning a thick mist had descended and visibility was down to yards.

By the time Nelly was loaded and I was pushing her back to the path, two figures had appeared out of the gloom. They were gruff old men bearing huge wicker baskets full of the woodland fungi they were gathering. They were very friendly, so I took photos of them proudly showing off their mushrooms.

That afternoon, two rainstorms crashed past and the sun – hanging low in a bank of bleak cloud – made a mirror of the arrow-straight road into Serbia. The first town we came to was called Sid, and there I treated myself to a slap-up Balkan-style mixed grill with lashings of cold pink wine.

Dragomir, the waiter, was anxious I might think all Serbians were crazy (Slobodan Milošević and all that). I didn't. I was worried he might be offended that six years ago British warplanes were dropping bombs here. He wasn't.

Striking deeper into the Balkans, I feel like the ultimate cycling hippie: topless, wearing big red sunglasses and with a multicoloured peace flag around my head. As I rode into the suburbs of Belgrade yesterday my joy was such that I began spontaneously belting out Pink Floyd numbers. Then, on reaching the city proper, we came to the wide expanse of the great river cutting through it. At that point I flipped to – what else – Johann Strauss' *The Blue Danube*, as I meandered along its venerable banks. 'La-daa-daa-daa-daaaaa da-da da-da …'

Days since leaving London: 125
Distance travelled: 5,054 kilometres
GDP growth, planet Earth, 2004: 3.8%

Inuit word of the day: 'areodjarekput' meaning 'to exchange wives for a few days only'

23: Pianists, Moonshine and Coconuts
5 October 2005

In Belgrade I stayed with a cousin of my Slovenian friends Maja and Cani. Her name is Maca (pronounced: 'matza' meaning 'cat') and she lives with her son Filip. They're both accomplished pianists (she teaches, he's just graduated) and dwell in a tower block in the city centre which, on the outside, is concrete and Soviet-style.

On the inside, however, their apartment is a pristine haven with bookshelves lined with Proust and Dostoevsky, a forest of pot plants and, of course, a piano.

Maca welcomed me to the city with a bottle of home-brewed schnapps, which smelled like fresh apricots and went down like ouzo. With waist-length red hair, she is enthusiastic about everything and generally a bit of a beatnik. The two of us got on like a house on fire.

That evening we headed downtown to join another cousin, Josif, in a turn-of-the-century house share filled with his UK-educated, English-speaking friends. Six hours after arriving in Belgrade I was in the back of a saloon, flanked by drunk Serbians, being driven to an all-night taverna by a man called Igor. On arriving everyone seemed to know the words to all the songs and the folk band had oomph, so we sang along and danced on tables until morning.

NATO's air offensive of 1999 threw up some mad stories. When

American F16s were taking out the country's military compounds and bridges there was no school and no work, so the Serbians spent most of their time partying. Everyone reports that it was a happy time which brought them together.

Belgrade totally rocks. It's one of the most amazing cities I've ever been to. There's a military museum with exhibits back to the Romans, a huge white temple to St Sava, Byzantine-style mosaics and masses of hip hop. I spent three days there, during which I did all the touristy things, hung out in cavernous neon-lit internet cafés deep under the city and spent many happy hours at Maca and Filip's flat while they practised their Chopin and Bach.

From Belgrade, I followed the Danube east through mountainous undulations of white rock. Immense sheets of the stuff, crowded with forests and meadows, soared up on either side. Just after the town of Veliko Gradiste I stumbled upon a titanic Dungeons & Dragons-style castle sprawled along the cliffs. A sign revealed its name to be Golubac Grad. I had it all to myself and clambered on its walls until evening. In England it would cost 20 quid to get into a place like that.

The next day we came to a section where the road went through 16 tunnels in a row, cut through the rock. I tested the acoustics of each and every one. After my (now traditional) rendition of 'Jerusalem', I embarked upon a selection of cockney medleys and soft rock numbers. I can report that 'I've Got a Lovely Bunch of Coconuts' reverberates beautifully behind 60 feet of solid rock. U2 doesn't work so well.

I'm now at the town of Negotin, right on the border. From here I follow the Danube east for another few hundred kilometres into Romania. Then I drop south into Bulgaria. Beyond that is Turkey.

Days since leaving London: 132
Distance travelled: 5,356 kilometres
Galaxy to human ratio in the observable universe: 33:1

The weirder you are going to behave, the more normal you should look. – P. J. O'Rourke

24: The Old Serbian Bicycle Shop
7 October 2005

At Negotin, Nelly needed some spokes replacing and I found a ramshackle bicycle repair shop where it looked like they could fix anything. The guy running it was round-faced, solidly built and called Nenad. We got talking and, sure enough, it turned out the shop had been in continuous use since Nenad's grandfather set it up 70 years ago.

As we talked about bicycles the grandfather appeared. He had huge workman's hands, was still drinking and smoking, and remained in contact with Jewish families in Israel he'd helped escape the Nazi death camps. He even still repaired the odd bicycle. He was 92.

Nenad invited me for tea at his house and, that afternoon, I was plunged into yet another lesson in the outstanding hospitality of the Serbians. I've just spent two days with Nenad, his mate Miljan and their two beautiful wives.

They hadn't come across many English cyclists and wanted to know my opinions on everything. I was asked question after question beginning with: 'What do you think about ...?' (George W. Bush, Tony Blair, Slobodan Milošević, Margaret Thatcher ...) Boy, were they asking the right person if they wanted opinions.

That first night together we ended up at Miljan's house and drank until 5 a.m. while they regaled me with stories of Serbian history, ancient and modern.

On 28 June 1389 – St Vitus' Day – the Serbian army of Prince Stefan Lazar was broken by the advancing Ottoman Empire at the history-turning Battle of Kosovo. Following their defeat, one of the Serbian knights, Milos Obilic, went to the Turkish camp on the pretext that he wanted to surrender. Obilic was brought before Sultan Murad I. But just prior to kneeling, he drew out a concealed knife and drove it into Murad's stomach, slaying him moments before being slashed to pieces himself by the Sultan's bodyguards. Nenad's enthusiastic stabbing action was particularly convincing.

They talked of the 1990s, of economic meltdown, riots and protesting before the building of the government-controlled television station. They told surreal stories of government thugs bursting into homes at night to conscript men for war. As we chatted, a BBC documentary on the rise and fall of Slobodan Milošević came on the TV; right on cue.

In the person of Mr Milošević, Serbia and Yugoslavia elected a president with the instincts of a Cold War warrior carved during an era that had already passed. When Yugoslavia's regions began breaking away, he reacted by trying to grab all he could for its Serbian heartland.

Acting like the Stalinist throwback he was, Mr Milošević hijacked the Serbian media and fashioned it into an instrument for sowing a 1984-style hate campaign to cajole his countrymen into initiating a grotesque series of ethnically charged conflicts that went on for nearly a decade, first in

Croatia, then Bosnia, then Kosovo.

By 1999 Milošević's cronies were filling buses with the corpses of murdered Kosovans and dumping them in the Danube. Finally, the Americans intervened.

Mr Milošević was told that if he didn't cease, air strikes would begin taking out Serbia's military and civilian infrastructure. Mr Milošević called their bluff. The Americans weren't bluffing. A year later, he was gone.

Here are some numbers. The first major conflict of the Yugoslav Wars was that between Serbia and Croatia in 1992. At the time, Serbia had seven and a half million people and Croatia four and a half million. They both had a GDP per head (broadly: the size of the economy per person) of around US$7,500.

Italy, the closest of Europe's (four) trillion-dollar economies, had 57 million people and a GDP per head of around US$18,500.

To put it another way, the Italian economy was around 11 times larger than those of Serbia and Croatia combined – a crude, but not unreasonable illustration of relative resources. The economies of Germany, France and the UK were even bigger. Yet as genocide exploded across the Balkans, the nations of western Europe dithered.

The catastrophe unfolding in Iraq clearly demonstrates what a bad idea it can be to charge into other people's countries with lots of guns, but no game plan. But European complaints about American arrogance would ring more true if – when the flames of war burned for a decade in a part of the world that is European by every geographic, historical and cultural definition – we'd done something about it.

On my second night with the Negotin gang, we hit the town. It turned into another late night and, as one drinking venue after another closed its doors, we were forced into ever less glamorous establishments. At two o'clock this morning, we entered the seediest dive I've ever seen.

The decor was beer-stained and filthy. A chubby middle-aged lady wearing spangly underwear would gyrate in front of punters for a small fee. In dark corners, drinkers were asleep, face down on tables, after long evenings of self-abuse.

The company, however, was top notch.

We discussed communism. I was conscious that my Western background could bias me against the political arrangements that dominated eastern Europe last century. As it happened, though, Miljan and Nenad had very clear views as to the merits of those political arrangements: Serbia had wasted 50 years while western Europe lived through its post-war golden age.

They told story after story of waste, inefficiency and corruption. Like the time the secret service burst into Nenad's grandfather's shop to commandeer two bicycles. When they'd finished with them, they dumped the bicycles in a forest to rust away. When his grandfather protested he was threatened: 'Are you a capitalist?'

The twentieth-century political systems of eastern Europe were supposed to be about creating better societies, rather than allowing lazy secret service people to waste bicycles. But giving one set of humans power over another without making them accountable, and then expecting them not to act in a dysfunctional way, is always naive. It ignores the underlying realities of what we – as humans – are, and how and why we behave in the way that we do.

As for those communist command economies: their success was predicated on the assumption that the relevant political and bureaucratic decision-makers were in a position to make strategic and economic judgements that were orders of magnitude beyond their abilities. By believing that they had the mental wherewithal to administer a country (when they couldn't even administer a bicycle), they'd persuaded themselves that they had answers they weren't predisposed to have. They were seeing the world through a very narrow lens.

Serbia has been through a dark period. It has many difficult struggles ahead. But the underlying fabric of its society is strong and it is well positioned to make the most of the dawning century. As for its people: they're clever, remarkably cosmopolitan and tremendous fun, and they won't let me pay for anything.

Days since leaving London: 134
Distance travelled: 5,356 kilometres
Amount by which the Serbian economy shrank during the Yugoslav Wars: 50%

The doors of heaven and hell are adjacent and identical – Nikos Kazantzakis, The Last Temptation of Christ

Musings
Wide-Angle Lens

In the 1980s, when I grew up, one was acutely aware of living in the shadow of the Cold War. The geopolitical reality of the day was that the most industrially and technologically developed parts of the world were divided into two camps. Each camp sat on an enormous pile of nightmarish weapons and they periodically flirted with a military confrontation, the consequences of which would have been horrifying beyond imagination.

Mercifully, it appears we're now past that bottleneck. Attention has become focused on new problems: terrorism, climate change, economic instability and the disruptive aspects of globalisation. Two things surprise me about how we treat these problems: first, how quickly they went from being second-order to all-consuming concerns; second, how they're treated with equal seriousness to the problems which ceased with the fall of the Iron Curtain. It's difficult to think of much that compares with having tens of thousands of thermonuclear warheads ready to annihilate civilisation at a few hours' notice.

In the Balkans, recent history was both more traumatic and much closer to the surface. Yugoslavia's break-up was well within living memory. Everyone had first-hand experience of war. Yet it was extraordinary how quickly that legacy was being buried by the energy and dynamic modernity of the Balkan states. Even there, conversation would often turn to those confoundedly cheap goods from China.

I think this is because the human mind – the window out of which we comprehend reality – is inclined to think within certain time frames and find significance in certain sorts of things. For example, humans have a tendency to overemphasise the scale of their biggest problems and think short term even when kidding themselves that they're thinking long term. This creates a bias in the way we reflect upon our world and our civilisation, and what's happening to them.

The most apparent such bias is our fascination with the alpha male, or female, and their doings. In day-to-day culture, this translates into an overestimation of the significance of individuals who are, for whatever reason, famous. In current affairs it translates into an obsession with the top politician (in this era generally the President of the United States of America). But the place where it has traditionally caused most distortion has been when we thought about history.

Until quite recently, when we thought about history, what we were really thinking about was political history: who was king, when the big battles took place, who won them, which empires controlled what territory, and the biographies of great men. This is the history of Serbian knights and Ottoman sultans and it is dominated by the long list of alpha males who've directed politics down the ages, from Julius Caesar to Charlemagne to Napoleon.

And yet it is not princes or presidents that shape the destiny of this world. Understanding their machinations is interesting, but it is a very narrow lens through which to consider the story of which we're a part.

As human scholarship has become more insightful, this has been recognised. In recent decades, history has been deconstructed to the underlying forces that truly shape our global society and upon which politics is just the surface froth: demographics, economics and the technological advances upon which all other political and social developments since the dawn of agriculture have been built.

As this investigation gathers pace, an increasingly rich narrative of our past is being brought to light. It is a narrative characterised by the rise and fall of civilisations, the mutation and evolution of culture, the diffusion of ideas and technologies, greater contact between peoples and increasingly elaborate systems of political organisation. It's a very interesting story.

But it's not the whole story.

Looking at a small part of a big picture in isolation is not the most productive way to understand it. Even the sophistication of present-day historical wisdom captures only some of the more easily visible aspects of the very large iceberg of which we're a part. There are deeper fires driving this human venture.

There's a fable – about you – sometimes told. It takes place on a beach. It goes like this ...

You're standing on a beach looking out to sea. To your left, also looking out to sea, stands your mother. The two of you hold hands. Standing to your mother's left, also looking out to sea, stands her mother. They too hold hands. To your grandmother's left, stands her mother, with whom she holds hands, and so on; and so on; all the way into the far distance and beyond.

Once you've travelled down that beach for around 60 metres you come to a woman who was alive during the construction of Chartres Cathedral. After 120 metres you come to a woman who lived during the fall of the Western Roman Empire.

After one and a quarter kilometres you come to a woman who lived when the Vézère Valley's cave paintings were painted. It is well within the realms of possibility that she herself was one of the artists. Now we're scratching the surface.

After 11 kilometres you come to a woman of great interest to anyone who might read this book. We don't know her real name, so we call her Eve. Eve was the ancient grandmother of every human alive on planet Earth today: the most recent female ancestor of the entire human race. She was fully anatomically modern and, 150,000 years ago, she brought up her children in Africa.

But Eve also had a mother.

After 400 kilometres you come to a being for whom we have no name. This being was your ancestor, my ancestor, Eve's ancestor and the ancestor of every human that has ever lived. But she was not human, and she was also the ancestor of a chimpanzee.

It gets stranger still.

After approximately 300,000 kilometres you come to a being that was your ancestor, my ancestor, Eve's ancestor, the ancestor of every human that has ever lived, the ancestor of every chimpanzee that has ever lived and also the ancestor of a Tyrannosaurus rex.

Eventually, if you go a long way down that beach you come to something that was the ancestor of all those things and which was also the ancestor of the oak tree.

*****

Let me tell you about my epiphany beneath the Gothic masterpiece of Chartres Cathedral, which was to define the intellectual and spiritual journey that followed.

One hundred and three years before I set off from London on my bicycle, a man called Herbert Walker Wells delivered a speech called 'The Discovery of the Future' to the Royal Society in London. It was a remarkable piece of prose. Seventy-seven years later, another man, called Carl Sagan, copied some of the words from that speech into a book he was writing and, 26 years after that, I lay outside my tent at Chartres, a plastic cup of Bordeaux in hand, and read them. They affected me deeply.

Here they are:

We look back through countless millions of years
and see the great will to live struggling out of the inter-tidal slime,
struggling from shape to shape and from power to power,
crawling and then walking confidently upon the land,
struggling generation after generation to master the air,
creeping down into the darkness of the deep.

We see it turn upon itself in rage and hunger
and reshape itself anew,
we watch as it draws nearer and more akin to us,
expanding, elaborating itself,
pursuing its reckless inconceivable purpose,
until at last it reaches us
and its being beats within our brains and arteries,
throbs and thunders in our battleships, roars through our cities,
sings in our music and flowers in our art.

It is possible to believe that all the past
is but the beginning of the beginning,
and that all that is and has been is but the twilight of the dawn.
It is possible to believe all that the human mind has accomplished
is but the dream before the awakening.

Out of our lineage minds will spring
that will reach back to us in our littleness
to know us better than we know ourselves,
and reach fearlessly forward
to comprehend a future that defeats our eyes.

This world is heavy with the promise of greater things.
A day will come,
one day in the unending succession of days, when beings,
beings who are now latent in our thoughts and hidden in our loins,
shall stand upon this earth as one stands upon a footstool,
and shall laugh and reach out their hands amidst the stars.

Each one of us, all of our problems, human civilisation and the whole phenomenon of humanity are the ephemeral expression of a deeper arc of events. Owing to the events of the last few centuries we now have access to a great deal of information about that arc, yet we've been slow to reinterpret many basic features of our society and civilisation with reference to it. We therefore not only misapprehend but underestimate our current circumstances.

The time has come to embark upon a reinterpretation. Once we do, everything will make much more sense, be far less scary and leave us feeling a great deal more optimistic about ourselves, our species, our planet and our future.

But we have to think big. Really big.

25: Six Hundred Kilometres Along the Danube

11 October 2005

I've now travelled 648 kilometres along the River Danube. Here are some incidents and observations from along the way:

1) One night I hauled Nelly 200 feet up a hill beside the river to watch the sky in a meadow where no one would find us. I spent the evening on my back, star chart in hand, studying the heavens. The next morning the mist receded to reveal two bovines, one ancient Serbian shepherdess and a billy goat gruff. By nine o'clock not only had they found us, but we were already surrounded.

2) Bulgaria employs only top-quality comics as border guards. The joke 'You carrying hashish, ecstasy, ammunition, slaves?' never goes out of fashion.

3) At one point we crossed the river on a small ferry shared with some tobacco smugglers. I chortled while watching them Sellotape packets of Marlboro to themselves. One chubby fellow managed to get 50 packets under his clothes before I lost count.

4) Stopping at a roadside shack in Romania to drink a small coffee, I observed a gypsy girl arrive wearing a bright-red headscarf, chequered skirt and massive hoop earrings. She went straight to the bar and ordered an enormous flagon of beer. The gypsy girl was a couple of inches south of five feet, while the flagon must have held a litre. She did the lot in two gulps. It was ten in the morning.

The best camping spots in Europe can only be found by a country boy and a cyclatron with a sense of adventure. After nearly five months on the road, Nelly has become super-adept at traversing forest floors to interesting, out-of-the-way places …

The swamp we slept in the day after leaving Belgrade was a mistake (we were desperate). But the magic orchard on our last night in Romania was a triumph of rural exploration: wet and uninviting from the outside but – for those who dared within – dry, flower-filled and inhabited by fairies.

Bonkers update: whizzing down dusty Balkan roads, I am entirely tickled by the pleasure of life and periodically stop to express myself through the furious scribbling of poetry. When camped at night I now rave almost constantly to myself, singing snatches from songs and shouting things at Nelly. I've named both my bicycle bags. The left one is called Doris and the right one Mildred. My tent has been christened Larry. We're quite a team.

I'm in the Bulgarian city of Ruse, still in the Danube Valley. It's starting to get really cold. I'm heading south.

Days since leaving London: 138
Distance travelled: 5,727 kilometres

> *Be happy young man, while you are young, and let your heart give you joy in the days of your youth. Follow the ways of your heart and whatever your eyes see.* – The Book of Ecclesiastes

26: Bulgarian Rhapsody
14 October 2005

Wild animals keep approaching us. They're mainly deer, snuffling things investigating us at night and, on one occasion, a wild boar. Two nights ago, camped off the E70 after the town of Razgrad, a pack of feral dogs – angry and barking – appeared out of the night.

We had a very big campfire burning, so I armed myself with a firebrand and a club then shouted really rude words at them, very loudly, until they scampered off. Nelly and I are unafraid of pesky woodland mongrels and the dogs knew it. I imagine dogs can smell that sort of thing.

Bonkers update: I've started bonding with trees. When I see a particularly impressive one I stash Nelly, approach the target tree and then lay a hand on its trunk while closing my eyes. I then contemplate the size and impressiveness of said tree and the transitory nature of my own existence. I don't care if it's silly, I'm really enjoying myself.

The Bulgarian hinterland has produced some of the best cycling of this trip. I've been pedalling merrily away, free as a bird, lost in my own world.

The best day so far was near the town of Madara. Nelly and I had ridden up onto a plateau to consider an ancient carving of a horseman beside medieval Greek inscriptions that had been hewn in a cliff face in the eighth century. The horseman holds a pike in one hand and a wine cup in the other. His steed tramples upon a lion, beside him runs a dog, before him flies an eagle and behind him stands a god. Descending from the plateau, we were confronted with a vista of green plains as far as the eye could see and several kilometres of freewheeling as we descended onto them.

With the sun on my face and spirits ascending to the stratosphere, I decided it was time to pay my respects to Ms Gloria Gaynor. 'At first I was afraid, I was petrified ...'

I'd stayed the previous night in a remote hostel and I awoke that morning after 10 hours sleep to be served a breakfast of cheese and tomatoes on toast (for free) by a Bulgarian lady with pigtails and a penchant for naff soap operas. I was in very good voice indeed.

The local agricultural workers looked on in bemusement, sickles in hand, and completely failed to applaud my performance. It was as though they'd never seen a topless hippie on a bicycle, with a rainbow-coloured peace flag tied around his head, singing 'I Will Survive' before. I bowed and waved anyway. It was a good moment to be alive.

Yesterday afternoon we reached the city of Varna. It's on the Black Sea.

Days since leaving London: 141
Distance travelled: 5,931 kilometres

I figured that if I said it enough, I would convince the world that I really was the greatest. – Muhammad Ali

27: Istanbul or Bust
18 October 2005

My joint-favourite Byzantine emperor is Basil II. Absolute monarchy is a terrible system of government, but as absolute monarchs go, Basil was as good as they get. He was clever, hard-working, unmaterialistic and attentive to the best interests of his people. He was also a very successful general and ruthless on the battlefield, a characteristic which led to his nickname: The Bulgar Slayer.

On 29 July 1014, at the end of a dozen years of bitter and grinding warfare, Basil finally pinned down and destroyed the Bulgarian army at Kleindion. The Byzantines took 14,000 prisoners that day and Basil had 99 out of every 100 blinded (think: red-hot pokers and eyeballs). The remaining 1 in 100 were left with a single eye to guide the others home. When Samuel, the Bulgarian emperor, saw what had happened, he had a heart attack and died of sorrow the next day. It's not a story I'll be repeating around here.

Back in Slovenia, when I was getting ready to leave for Zagreb, they warned me to be careful of the Croatians. They're a wily people, I was told, and not to be trusted. Two weeks later, after the Croatians had selflessly spent 12 days curing me, they, in turn, cautioned that the Serbians were dangerous and unpredictable. That wasn't my experience of the Serbians.

In Serbia they said that the *really* dangerous people in this corner of the world are, in fact, the Bulgarians. Last night, I told this story to a Bulgarian man called Rado, assuming that he'd find it amusing. 'Ah!' he exclaimed. 'Well, there are *some* parts of the country …'

Of all the countries I've visited, Bulgaria was the one I knew least about before arriving (apart from that it's got a major problem with corruption). After nine days, here is my personal verdict: friendly and polite people, good roads, well-stocked shops and stunning value for money. I think it's a fantastic place.

After hitting the Black Sea at Varna, we've travelled south down the coast to Burgas in Bulgaria's south-eastern corner. Turkey is now very close. We're resting at a proper hotel for a couple of days to prepare for the final stage.

The time has come to wrap this sucker up. All we lack is an attendant rock band to play a theme tune as we head out on the last leg. The plan is simple: strip to the waist, strap the team to Nelly, don my lucky peace bandanna, then break for the border.

I'll tell you how I get on.

Days since leaving London: 145
Distance travelled: 6,081 kilometres
Typical price of a cup of coffee in

France:	2 euros
Italy:	1 euro
Croatia:	0.6 euros
Romania:	0.3 euros
Bulgaria:	0.2 euros

The prize for the best coffee goes to: Italy. No question.

I'm a churning urn of burning funk. – James Taylor

Musings
Long Road East

Exercise is the closest thing we have to an elixir of youth. It's the ultimate feel-good drug and brilliant for your skin, body, looks and sense of wellbeing. Having nine hours of sleep, followed by six hours of exercise and then being clean and alone in the wilderness, with good food and the stars for company; and doing that day in, day out, for five months puts you in a very beautiful place physically, mentally and emotionally.

Along the border that separates Bulgaria from Turkey there is a ridge of mountains. Those mountains are characterised by deep valleys, thick forests and spectacular views. On my final night in Bulgaria I camped high in them, on a deer trail, about a hundred metres from the road.

It was freezing, so I spent the evening inside the tent with the door zipped up and my head torch on, eating a meal of bread, cheese and apples, washed down with red wine.

Sitting there, cross-legged, alone in the mountains, cutting up apples with my penknife and singing away to myself, I stopped what I was doing in a moment of introspection. I suddenly realised how intensely happy and content I was feeling …

A lot of people asked me why I ever stopped cycling, suggesting I could have pushed through Turkey into western Asia. I've met quite a few long-distance cyclists in my time. There was a Swiss fellow in Pakistan who'd started in Alaska two years previously. He was extremely physically robust, but he didn't make eye contact when he spoke and had almost nothing to say for himself.

Then there was an American couple who'd been cycling around the world for years. They were really friendly, but a bit obsessive and, considering the number of places they'd been, remarkably ignorant. Although, to be fair, they knew a great deal about bicycles.

I wanted an adventure that was rich and diverse, not one that was just about cycling. I wanted to get inside my home world – inside its nooks, its crannies and the heads of its different peoples – and the bottom line is that there's a limited amount that one can learn from the back of a bicycle.

Those 150 days in the wilderness were some of the best in my life. But, by the time I reached Istanbul, I was done with cycling.

28: The City of the World's Desire
24 October 2005

Ladies and Gentlemen:

At 1.39 p.m. on Sunday, 23 October 2005, 150 days after setting out from London and with 6,424 kilometres under our belts, Nelly and I arrived in Istanbul: formerly known as Constantinople, formerly as New Rome, and formerly as the city of Byzantium.

Three days earlier, on reaching the Turkish border, my excitement had become infectious. I had all the border guards laughing before I'd even got my passport out. Then, freewheeling down the mountainside into Turkey proper, I lost it: singing and yelling in joy for an hour, before stopping to admire my first mosque, eat my first kebab and calm down.

Yesterday – the day I entered the city – will now always remain seared into my memory. Our last map only covered the land up to 50 klicks before the suburbs and the road signs all directed me to the motorways (which I can't use). Rather than seek out a new map I decided I'd wing it and follow my nose.

My strategy was to drop south until I reached the coast, then east until I saw the Aya Sophia. What I didn't realise was that several large estuaries stretch north from the Sea of Marmara, so you have to take a very indirect route. I cycled really fast, followed my guts and got all my guesses right. After crossing two causeways, we finally reached the coast and found a road running east–west. From there, there was only one way to Istanbul.

The final run-in involved 30 kilometres of undulating, roller-coaster, six-lane freeway with very bad tarmac. Turkish drivers are aggressive and they don't use their indicators. It was a hair-raising ride and I lost all feeling below my wrists as I gripped tightly onto Nelly while chanting 'Don't get killed, don't get killed' through gritted teeth.

As the road flattened and the traffic slowed, I came to a flyover where someone had strung a blue and white sign. The sign read: 'Welcome to Istanbul'. Welcome indeed.

In the fifth century, when Attila the Hun set eyes on the great fortifications of Theodosius, it is said that he shook his head and turned away, knowing that they would be too strong for him. In the twenty-first century, when the Jolly Pilgrim saw those same walls, he stood, momentarily delirious, and laughed in delight beneath the ancient sun-baked stone.

Then the forest of minarets of Sultanahmet – the old city – appeared. It was the third Sunday of Ramadan and the place was jam-packed. A hippie on a bicycle with a rainbow flag tied around his head was like a red rag to a bull. I was briefly mobbed, but too happy to care. Then I was beside the Aya Sophia. I had arrived.

Leaving London that fateful spring afternoon seems a long time ago. As regards this whole 'I'm going to cycle to Istanbul' malarkey, I think I've made my point.

Here's the trip by the numbers:

Days on the road:	150					
Days spent in:	UK	5	Slovenia	13	Romania	3
	France	60	Croatia	21	Bulgaria	10
	Italy	23	Serbia	12	Turkey	3
Distance travelled:	6,429 kilometres					
That equates to:	2.14 x the Tour de France					
	16% of the way around the world					
	0.00000006796% of a light year					
Nights spent in a tent:	100					
Different camping spots:	69					
Nights in a hospital bed:	11					
Highest speed:	69.9 kilometres per hour (downhill in Monte Carlo)					
Most distance in a day:	146.1 kilometres (along the Po valley to Linda's house)					
Punctures fixed:	21					
Maps used:	8					
Poems written:	29					

The day before yesterday – my last in the wilderness – I had wanted to camp somewhere memorable. Late that afternoon, while cycling across a moor-covered ridge, I saw a rocky spur in the distance, high above the surrounding land. That was the spot.

The outcrop was hundreds of metres from the road. It took over an hour to haul Nelly and the gang there one by one, carrying each aloft in turn over the heather. I pitched up as the sun set, ate my picnic and then clambered up one of the rock columns.

Sitting Buddha-like on its summit I sang several songs. The penultimate verse of the last song went like this:

> *To think I did all that*
> *And may I say, not in a shy way*
> *Oh no. Oh no, not me*
> *I did it my way.*

Wolves started howling in the distance. Miles from anywhere, the wind on my face and a blanket wrapped around me, I looked up at the clear field of stars above, down at the twinkling lights of the towns in the distant valleys below and thought about the previous five months.

There are some moments – moments such as those – that one has a vain urge to try to capture. They cannot be captured, except as a fading memory which will never adequately recall what it was really like. Moments like that are fleeting, destined to sparkle and then pass away, just like men. But, of course, that's what makes it all so beautiful.

Part 2

Metropolis

29: New Rome
26 October 2005

Here I am, like a dream: Istanbul – not just any city, but for 2,000 years a key theatre for the drama of the human race and a central nexus around which the story of our species has flowed.

It was originally Greek. The legend goes that, two and a half millennia ago, the Oracle of Delphi told King Byzas of Megara to found a city on the Bosporus where Europe touches Asia. Byzas, being a king, named it Byzantium after himself.

The Romans conquered the city in 196 CE back when they ruled this half of the world, but the foundations for its pivotal role in history were laid 100 years later when the emperor Diocletian declared the empire too big to be ruled as a single state and split it into east and west.

After single-handedly redirecting the development of a continent Diocletian retired to grow cabbages (I'm serious – apparently he really liked cabbages) but, 40 years later, his successor, Constantine, established the future capital of the eastern of those two empires at Byzantium. He named the re-founded city New Rome, but to posterity it would always be known as Constantinople.

Within two centuries the Western Roman Empire had descended into anarchy and the Dark Ages. The Eastern Empire (also known as the Byzantine Empire) was to rule the Mediterranean and Middle East until the emergence of the Arab Caliphate in 636 CE. Constantinople, the empire's beating heart, was the most coveted city in the world.

As Islam rose, the fortunes of Byzantium were eclipsed by those of the Caliphate, which devoured its Middle Eastern possessions. However, it remained the richest and most civilised part of Europe for a further eight centuries. That era was brought to a close in 1204 when Constantinople was sacked by the soldiers of the Fourth Crusade, leaving it an impoverished shadow of itself and the crippled Byzantine Empire a weakened target for the rising power of the Turks.

They came from the steppe: that vast expanse of grass and scrub, stretching between China and the Black Sea, from which – since man tamed horse – nomadic warriors have periodically poured forth. The Turks emerged in the eighth century, arriving first in Persia then, generation by generation, picking their way across the Islamic civilisations of the Middle East. By 800 years ago they'd reached the Mediterranean.

That was just as another wave of plainsmen – the Mongols – were turning Asia on its head. Osman, a Turkish king, took advantage of that chaos and the refugees fleeing west, to found a new empire: an Ottoman

Empire. It was well placed to envelop the crumbled ruins of Byzantium and, in 1453, Constantinople fell to the Turks.

For the great metropolis this brought repopulation and another wave of fabulous buildings. With the city as their base, the Ottomans conquered vast swathes of Europe, Asia and North Africa, becoming lords of the Middle East and building an empire that stretched from Gibraltar to the Persian Gulf. Constantinople became the centre of the richest and most cosmopolitan empire on Earth. As pogroms and inquisitions gripped Europe it was the 'haven of the universe' and dubbed 'the city of the world's desire'. Of course, the Turks had always had their own name for it: Istanbul.

Suns always set on empires and heroic periods are universally followed by lulls and stagnation. The Ottomans were not immune to this historic pattern and, as the second millennium reached its closing centuries and Europe rose up to rule the world, they went from Lords of the Horizon to the sick men of Europe. Their empire was finally brought to its close in 1922, and a Turkish Republic declared by the legendary war hero Mustafa Kemal Atatürk.

In the twentieth century Turkey had its ups and downs, but in this opening decade of the third millennium, the government of Recep Tayyip Erdoğan (which is mildly Islamic and very effective) presides over low inflation, robust growth, stable macroeconomics and an ever more dynamic society. One of his policies is to make Turkey a part of the European Union. The future is bright.

Atatürk moved the capital to Ankara, in Turkey's Asian hinterland, but Istanbul remains its most important metropolitan centre, the country's cultural, economic and intellectual hub and the largest city in Europe. After arriving three days ago, Nelly and I have taken a room in the shadow of the Blue Mosque.

Days since leaving London: 153

> *If the Earth were a single state, Istanbul would be its capital.* – Napoleon

Musings
The Transition

It was a shock. During those final months of the bicycle ride I'd been on top of the world, wrapped in a multi-month surge of inspiration. I'd imagined my first evening in Istanbul several times: seen myself bursting into a hotel, announcing what I'd done, then leading a party into the city for an adventure replete with colourful escapades and eccentric characters. Following my euphoric arrival, the reality was less romantic.

The first hotel wouldn't have me when I said I wanted to stay some weeks. The second was more open-minded, but minutes after checking in I found myself alone and perched at the end of a bed with the reality of the aftermath washing over me. I wouldn't change a thing about the following weeks, but that first night was tough. I went to the bar and began talking to strangers.

I ended up with a personable trio of Germans named Heinrich, Wolfgang and Giselle. They wore clothes based on Indian styles and their blond hair in dreadlocks. I didn't mention the bicycle ride. Instead, they told me how angry they were. They were angry about the politicians who failed to serve the general good, the corporations that thrived on the globalisation they loathed and the modernity which would – they predicted – bring ruin upon planet Earth.

I was to hear a lot of this sort of thing as I made my way around the globe: people seeing the problems the world has, comparing it to a hypothetical world in their heads, then judging the state of humanity based on that comparison.

Yet it is the image of Heinrich, doomsaying the future on that first night in Istanbul, that stayed with me. The youth of the rich world, on visa-free travel to Turkey, complaining about globalisation. The most well-nourished, educated and culturally free generation that has ever lived bemoaning a world in decline.

Here's the thing: I think that view is mistaken. I think it's born of assessing our world in terms of short time frames and through a narrow set of bourgeois, early twenty-first-century parameters. I think it's about time humanity set out a more ambitious interpretation of its collective condition. It took me a while to find the resolve, but in the end I decided to do it myself.

*****

The next morning I adopted an internet café and sent the email announcing my arrival. When I went back two days later, a friend had replied telling me that Linda had a new boyfriend. The friend wasn't to know what effect that news would have on me.

After two more days Linda herself wrote saying she'd gone back to an old flame and, while she didn't want this to be the end between us, she wouldn't be coming to join me. I went back to my room, but I couldn't sleep that night. The following morning, in a dark frame of mind, I went to pay my respects to the church of Justinian.

30: Outdoing Solomon
29 October 2005

Istanbul's heart is packed with sparkling mosques, timeworn basilicas and a massive Ottoman palace. Where the Roman hippodrome once stood, three pillars mark time back to prehistory: the walled obelisk was erected by the Byzantines a thousand years ago; the swirl of green metal that is the Serpent Column was cast a thousand years before that; and the Obelisk of Thutmose III, shipped from Egypt by Theodosius the Great, is 3,500 years old.

Beside all these, and eclipsing them in my eyes, is the squat red pile of the Aya Sophia: the Church of the Holy Wisdom of God, symbolic centre of Istanbul, supreme architectural masterpiece of late antiquity and the spiritual culmination of my journey across Europe.

When it was built, in 537 CE, contemporary western Europe was a dark-age backwater where life consisted of eating gruel and living in huts, barbarian warlords consumed a meagre food surplus, no one took baths and hardly anyone could read. Contemporary Constantinople was the axis of west Eurasian civilisation, a haven of human high culture, capital of a vast empire and the greatest city in the world. The Aya Sophia was where its people set out their relationship with infinity.

It pre-dates all the major churches in western Europe by a solid 600 years and was the largest ever built until the one at Seville a millennium later. It was converted to a mosque by Mehmet the Conqueror and to a museum by Mustafa Kemal Atatürk. It's borne witness to 73 emperors and 31 sultans; when Justinian, the emperor who built it, entered the finished cathedral he is said to have exclaimed: 'Solomon, I have surpassed thee.' He had.

I went to see it alone, with reverence, this afternoon. It's been emotional.

For hours, wandering beneath its giant dome, I daydreamed about the millennium and a half of drama that has played out there. It was here that Heraclius – the greatest Roman since Caesar – completed his homecoming after bringing to an end the five-century-long Roman-Persian wars. He had charged the Persian flank at Adana, broken their armies at Nineveh, shattered their empire and wrested the True Cross from their grip. On 14 September 628 CE, in a solemn mass of thanksgiving, the holiest relic of Christendom was raised within these walls.

It was here, on 16 July 1054, that Christianity broke into schism. An Italian legation burst into the great church and, in the presence of a congregation assembled for the Eucharist, laid the papal Bull of Excommunication on the high altar, throwing the city into chaos and opening a wound between Catholic West and Orthodox East that still bleeds today.

Picked out in mosaic are the ancients. There's Constantine and Justinian themselves, offering the city and church to Jesus; John 'the Beautiful' Comnenus (a heroic warrior king, but not a looker – his soul was beautiful, his nickname ironic); and arch-femme fatale and imperial ball-breaker, the outrageously beautiful Empress Zoe.

Zoe's first husband, Emperor Romanos III, curtailed her expenditure (i.e. shopping) only to be found dead in his bath. Zoe married her second husband, Emperor Michael IV, later that day but upon the death of Michael IV the new emperor, Michael V, banished Zoe to a nunnery. That was a mistake. Zoe was ruthless and popular, and being a nun wasn't really her style.

She soon returned, usurped Michael, gouged out his eyes and packed him off to be a monk. Her final husband, Emperor Constantine IX, outlived her. Lucky fellow.

As I made ready to leave, I stumbled upon the tomb (bones removed) of one Enrico Dandolo, the Doge of Venice who orchestrated the sacking of Constantinople by the armies of the Fourth Crusade in 1204: one of the darkest episodes of murder, rape and cultural vandalism there has ever been.

Standing beside his burial place, musing on how the treasures of antiquity were lost and the greatest seat of Christianity brought low, I realised that the crowds had cleared. Gripped by the moment, I checked no one was looking, leapt the rope barrier and danced on the man's grave.

I left feeling satisfied and in a rather good mood.

Days since leaving London: 156

Major world cities (and present-day location) by population, 600 CE:

Constantinople (Turkey)	500,000	Alexandria (Egypt)	200,000
Ch'ang-an (China)	500,000	Teotihuacán (Mexico)	100,000
Loyang (China)	400,000	Tikal (Mexico)	50,000
Ctesiphon (Iran)	300,000	Rome (Italy)	50,000

Somali word of the day: 'guree' meaning 'to make room for someone to sit on a loaded camel'

31: Urban Geography
1 November 2005

To reach the Black Sea from the Mediterranean you must first travel across the island-dotted Aegean (nestled between Greece and Turkey), to the Dardanelles strait in its north-eastern corner. Travelling through that strait (of which the Gallipoli Peninsula forms the western flank) leads to the small, inland, Sea of Marmara. On that sea's far side, 280 kilometres away, lies the entrance to another strait: the Bosporus. That 30-kilometre channel (between one and three kilometres across) leads to the Black Sea, and built onto either side of its southern end lies Istanbul.

The Bosporus is a major shipping lane. Massive tankers and container ships plough north and south along it, dodged by passenger ferries travelling east and west between the shores. Istanbul is the world's only metropolitan area straddling two continents. The eastern side (Anatolia) is in Asia while the western (Thrace) is in Europe. That European side includes the city's historic centre, Sultanahmet, where Nelly and I have based ourselves.

Sultanahmet is a travellers' crossroads. Its main drag ('The Street') is crowded with bars, laundries and kebab stalls. Halfway along is the Orient Hotel. In the hotel's basement is a belly dancing club. In a courtyard behind it, Nelly stands chained to a railing. Next to that railing is the window to my room, the biggest in the place: Room 32.

The Orient is a major operation. In addition to the belly dancing club, there's a bar, a rooftop restaurant and a travel agency. The travel agency is managed by Dilara, who used to run nightclubs in London and is now one of The Street's bigwigs. She's very glamorous. We've made friends.

Yesterday, Dilara took me to a party. Getting there involved a 40-minute taxi ride into the eastern, Asian, flank of the city. During that drive we passed hills covered in rank after rank of tower blocks and I came to grasp just how stonkingly vast this place is. The apartment where the party was held was lined with deep pile carpets and filled with hardwood furniture. They were playing progressive trance music downloaded from servers in Israel and Japan. Everyone spoke English.

The host was swarthy, solidly built and named Okhan. With a degree in automotive engineering, Okhan is a successful businessman and a registered Harley Davidson mechanic; in the garage below, he showed me his gobsmackingly beautiful chrome and yellow V-twin air-cooled beast. He has a reputation as a fixer: someone it's good to know in a crisis. His friend Zeheb showed me Okhan's entry in his mobile phone. It reads 'call in case of emergency'.

Zeheb is a producer and has just made a documentary about Turkey's accession to the EU. I asked for his thoughts on the subject. He told me that the specifics of Turkey's political status were less important than the process its journey to EU membership was helping to facilitate (adopting certain elements of modernity). If anyone has any preconceptions that the Turkish people lack political or cultural sophistication, then they should set them aside.

I awoke this morning to find myself on Okhan's sofa with soothing trance still quietly pumping from his state-of-the-art sound system. As I crossed the Bosporus back into Europe by taxi, the weather was both sunny and rainy at the same time. Across the hills of the Golden Horn, dozens of bulbous Ottoman-style mosques sparkled through the haze. Magic.

My family are big on adventures. Forty-two years ago Mum went to Australia when getting there still involved spending six weeks on a boat. A year earlier, in 1962, my aunt Lyn had walked to Moscow to protest against the insanity of the nuclear arms race. A decade and a half before that, Dad spent 1946 and 1947 in Palestine. Most famously of all, my great-uncle John sailed around the world in a tall ship (for two years) back in the 1930s.

I've been doing my best of late to contribute to this illustrious tradition. Nonetheless, my family's matriarchs and patriarchs observe my exploits with a critical eye and are sending a delegation to check on me. Mum (no surprises) volunteered for the task. She arrives this afternoon. I'm off to the airport to collect her now.

Days since leaving London: 159
Budget for ITER, the experimental fusion reactor: US$12.8 billion

Turkish word of the day: 'sevinç' meaning 'delight'

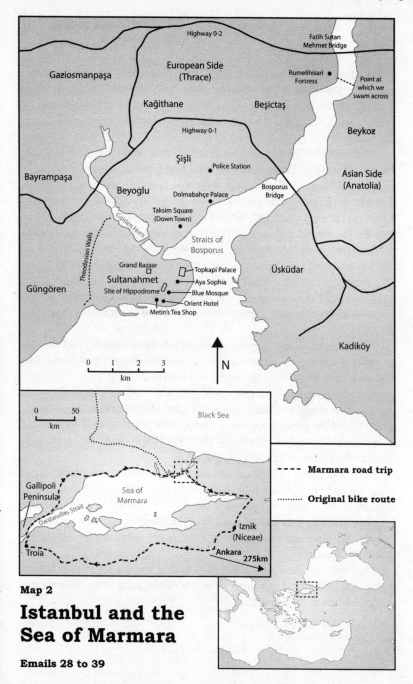

Map 2

Istanbul and the
Sea of Marmara

Emails 28 to 39

32: Marmara Road Trip
9 November 2005

After Mum arrived we spent three days wandering around the Grand Bazaar, trying out hubbly-bubbly pipes and playing backgammon in Turkish coffee shops (she cackles when she wins). Then we stored her stuff, hired a car and set off on a three-day road trip around the Sea of Marmara.

At the end of the first day we reached Iznik, which used to be called Nicaea. It's one of Anatolia's most important historic towns and has acted as capital of both the Byzantine and Ottoman empires. Nicaea is where, in 325 CE, the emperor Constantine called the first worldwide conference of Christian bishops where they argued about the nature of the Trinity, set the date for Easter and outlawed self-castration. Remarkable that they had to.

The town is on the shores of a great lake, set beside mountains, and full of palm trees and petite green mosques. It's sleepy, tranquil and delightful. We wandered over its intact walls and amphitheatres and stayed at a pension where the owner, Ali, did John Wayne impressions and pointed Elvis-style while saying 'hokey dokey'. I found it difficult to take him seriously.

The next day we drove east around the lake and through grass-covered foothills to the shores of the Aegean and an even more august set of ruins that are now called Troia, but were once known as Troy.

Nine cities have stood there. The first was built five thousand years ago, the last abandoned three thousand after that. Homer's Troy was the seventh city. Its great stone ramps and slanted walls remain formidable: grand enough to allow visions of Hector's broken body being dragged behind the chariot of the vengeful Achilles.

After a morning of meandering through excavations and dreaming of mythological Greeks, we followed picture-postcard coastal roads north, crossed to the Gallipoli Peninsula and sang songs all the way back to Istanbul. Thelma and Louise may have had better anarchist credentials than us, but Mum and I have a better voice range to harmonise 'When The Saints Go Marching In'.

That was two days ago. Since then, we've spent a lot of time talking and bought an expensive carpet for my sister Ruth. This afternoon, I dropped Mum at the airport.

Days since leaving London: 167

Turkey's

Population:	69,660,559
Life expectancy at birth:	72.36 years
National GDP:	US$508.7 billion
GDP per person:	US$7,400
Population below the poverty line:	20%

World peace is inevitable. – Sign on the front of the Sinbad Hostel, Sultanahmet, Istanbul

33: Nelly No More
11 November 2005

Nelly and I have parted company.

Her new companion is Metin, who runs the book exchange/gift shop/ internet café from which I'm sending these emails. It felt more appropriate to gift her to a friend than enter negotiations with a Turkish bicycle merchant, so I swapped her for 30 lira, unlimited computer access and free tea for the rest of my stay in Istanbul. In celebration of the exchange, Metin and I wrote our names on Nelly in permanent marker, along with 'Jolly Pilgrim' and Metin's new cyclatron name: 'Happy Hajj'.

My love affair with Nelly was always limited by the fact that I'm a carbon-based life form, while she's a bicycle. Nevertheless, we went through a lot together and I will probably never again feel such affection for an inanimate object. Doris and Mildred are staying with Nelly. Larry the Tent went back to England with Mum.

I've fallen in with a fellow named Tarik. Tarik is gangly, wears a beard and is a teacher somewhere in the city's outer sprawl. He arrived in Istanbul four weeks ago from Korea, a country he skipped following complications that arose with the police after crashing a motorcycle into a parked vehicle. We've been japing around, discussing philosophy and drinking tea.

Tarik believes there's a dichotomy in the human world between our animal selves – hard-wired to obsess over power and status – and spiritual beings with the capacity to reshape their environment sufficiently to construct a world-spanning civilisation. He's a thoughtful bloke.

One of Tarik's pastimes is to get drunk, then climb UNESCO World Heritage Sites. He made it halfway up the Great Pyramid of Cheops on Christmas Eve 1999 before falling asleep and, several weeks ago, got to stage one of the Aya Sophia before being chased off. The other night he persuaded me to make an attempt on the Blue Mosque (I was drunk). We were foiled by attentive security personnel and angry guard dogs, which is probably for the best.

Another new person in my life is Eden. Eden is impish, athletic, from Sydney and touring Europe having adventures. He ran with the bulls in Pamplona after partying through the night, fell asleep covered in bull's blood, awoke to find that his bags had all been stolen, and then spent his last 12 euros on cheap beer and hitchhiked to Paris. Cracking stuff. Eden is technically helping out at the Orient, though I've not actually seen him do any work. We've been drinking vodka and staying up late.

Days since leaving London: 169
Days the Spirit rover has been active on the Martian surface: 680

Are you going to come quietly, or do I have to use earplugs? – Spike Milligan

34: Istanbul Character Diaries
13 November 2005

A backpack of clothes and other flotsam has arrived for Major Tom from ground control in London. This has allowed me to deck out my Istanbul pad with homely touches, including a mini bookshelf containing a fat tome on world history, a book of English ballads, the Qur'an, the Bible and a star chart; the ever-present peace flag (on the wall); and a picture of Muhammad Ali (for inspiration).

This is my base for investigating Sultanahmet's subculture, which is made up of the business people running the tourist infrastructure; a semi-permanent crew of bar keepers and tour guides; and an ever-shifting assortment of adventurers, party animals, freaks, misfits and pilgrims. It's a rich pageant of colourful characters and a great place to meet people.

Stephan (also known as the 'Step Man') is from Bonn. Stephan's gig is to go around the world climbing steps in unusual ways. The list of monuments he's scaled is impressive. Notable achievements include carrying a bicycle to the top of the Empire State Building and spending 24 hours going up and down the stairs in a tower in a vineyard in France (some sort of world record). Stephan comes with a comedy German accent and his own website. He is scornful of the forms he's often made to fill in by bureaucrats and wears bright orange trousers so that he's easy to spot in photographs.

I was introduced to Stephan by Halil. Halil is Kurdish, from Mardin, and is the Orient's cook, handyman and DJ. He's learned English (from scratch) on the job and has developed a hybrid Australian-Turkish lingo full of phrases like 'How's it gown, mate?' and 'What's up, mate?' Halil periodically appears at my door to update me on the latest gossip from The Street while hopping from foot to foot and saying 'mate' a lot. Sometimes, when working at the belly dancing club, he gets up on the bar and has a go himself. It really gets the party started.

That was how I met Leila. Leila is from Toronto and gave up her job as an underwear designer for Wal-Mart in order to visit her sister in Scotland. Somehow she ended up in Istanbul. Her appearance always carries a few sassy touches which betray the life she left behind, but a few searching questions revealed her as a society girl, aspiring female drag queen and lynchpin of Toronto's gay community.

Don't say 'fag hag', say 'diva'.

Days since leaving London: 171
Countries in the world that grow bananas: 132

> *It's hard to be humble when you're as great as I am.* – Muhammad Ali

35: The Vodka Collection
17 November 2005

I should have known it was a bad sign when Eden and I started a collection of empty vodka bottles. The game has become to quietly chat up the people staying at the Orient, then at night round up the interesting ones and take them clubbing. Everyone always seems to end up in my room by sunrise, which is how we're getting through so much vodka. Tarik occasionally shows up and goads people into climbing something old.

On Sunday evening things spun out of control. Danica, a Californian girl, dragged me to the local dive bar to meet her crew: Juna and Jess. There we were joined by a travelling band of Cambridge punters (Craig, Kent and Naomi) and a wandering Australian surf dude (Cameron). It was one of those moments when the chemistry between a group of strangers just goes …

click.

After that, one thing kept leading to another. I only slept for 3 of the following 66 hours. On Monday morning we all arrived for breakfast as

Halil, catching our mood, loaded perfectly uplifting disco onto the stereo, then pumped up the volume as winter's sun blazed across the ship-dotted Sea of Marmara spread below us. We then returned to Room 32 to sit in the light beams falling through the window, smoke rolled-up cigarettes and talk of our homelands. As the sun sank once more, we piled down to a murky and alcohol-soaked club on The Street where the singer implored us to go west wearing flowers in our hair.

Sleep deprivation has left memories hazy after that, but my chums at the internet café inform me that I was spotted with a woman on each arm, heading towards my favourite kebab stall early on Tuesday afternoon. Hours later I found myself in bed in a room full of people I hadn't known 48 hours earlier, drinking neat vodka, straight from the bottle.

Cheap, dirty and Turkish – just the way I like it.

Days since leaving London: 175
Empty vodka bottles standing on my wardrobe: 12

> *Tragedy is when I cut my finger. Comedy is when you walk into an open sewer and die.* – Mel Brooks

Musings
The Crush

It was all about a woman.

Danica Kumara had stayed at the Orient several times in the previous weeks. She was using it as her base for trips around Turkey. We'd talked, swapped email addresses and eaten breakfast together. That Sunday evening, when she told me to come and meet her friends, there was a fire in her eyes. Those eyes were big and brown. She also had shoulder-length red-brunette hair, a languid west-coast drawl and the body of a gymnast. She was from San Francisco.

The following morning, when we all sat above the Sea of Marmara with the sun on our faces, and I gazed across the table at her, that was it. I couldn't stop thinking about her. The entire three-day party was for her entertainment. Unfortunately, I somehow lost control of it. These things do have a habit of snowballing.

Holding court in Room 32 was all very well, but because it was always full of people, we never got a moment alone. Before I knew it, the moment had passed and I'd never kissed the girl.

Danica now lives in Kosovo working with Romany refugees. She writes occasionally. However, it took me a couple of days to get over that particular episode of her company. To be brutally honest, I spent them holed up alone in Room 32 writing forlorn poetry.

Late in the evening of the second day, I received an unexpected phone call.

36: Byzantine Twilight
23 November 2005

Simon Peace is one of my best friends. We met at Durham University in England's north, where his digs were conveniently close to the city centre, so I used them as a doss house, sleeping mat and floordrobe. Simon is a top-end capitalist with the brain of a scholar and follows me on even my most tangential and abstract musings. We argue a lot, but only about highbrow stuff.

Simon and his beautiful, petite, doctor wife, Savita, are supposed to be on holiday in Jordan. Those plans were complicated when Savita went down a mountain on a mountain bike shouting 'Yeehah', fell off and broke her arm. When the bombs went off in Amman on 9 November the two of them resolved 'not to be beaten by global terrorism', but Savita's orthopaedic surgeon forbade their Jordanian scheme, so they redirected to Istanbul at the last minute.

The first order of business was a night out. Eden gathered a posse and we hit the town by taxi convoy.

Club Babylon lives in a century-old ex-carpenters' workshop down neon-lit backstreets and was being rocked by a live New York dance outfit. The acoustic design was cutting-edge, the crowd oozed confidence and the dancing continued through to the morning.

Then, on Monday, we got down to business.

The Rumelihisari was constructed by Mehmet the Conqueror when he decided to finish off the already crippled Byzantine Empire. Constantinople (at that point already surrounded by land for nearly a century) was receiving food aid from Genoese colonies on the Black Sea. Mehmet resolved to cut off that lifeline. The fortress, built right on the banks of the Bosporus, was completed in five months. The Turks nicknamed it Boazkesen: throat-cutter.

One brave Venetian captain, Antonio Rizzo, tried to break through to the stricken and starving city, but Mehmet's cannons found their target. He had the surviving crew executed and Rizzo impaled on a stake by the water's edge. Byzantium's end was nigh.

Five hundred and fifty-two years later Simon, Savita and I arrived in high spirits after a morning at the sumptuous palace of Mehmet's nineteenth-century descendants. The Rumelihisari is built into the land's topography with no safety railings, towers screaming to be clambered upon and abundant vertigo-inducing drops. From its uppermost ramparts, one is presented with a vista of the Bosporus' evergreen-lined banks and the vast suspension bridge which leaps between them. Enormous ships, humming with industrial power, cruise past beyond a foreground of perfectly preserved medieval fortifications.

The following afternoon – yesterday – we visited Istanbul's awesome archaeological museum. There we bore witness to the cultures and peoples that have washed across this Earth, morphed into one another down the ages and brought us to this point. We stood mesmerised before dark stone statues of Babylonian governors and Assyrian kings, who gazed back at us across the millennia, above ancient inscriptions which proclaimed their mastery over the world.

Days since leaving London: 181
Duration of the

Japanese Monarchy, Jimmu to Akihito:	2,665 years
English Monarchy, Egbert to Elizabeth:	1,176 years
Byzantine Empire, Constantine to Constantine:	1,123 years
Ottoman Empire, Osman to Ataturk:	623 years
American Empire, Washington to Bush:	222 years (and counting)

> *And on the pedestal these words appear:*
> *'My name is Ozymandias, king of kings:*
> *Look on my works, ye Mighty, and despair!'*
> – Percy Bysshe Shelley

37: The Planetary Adolescence
24 November 2005

It's raining in Istanbul.

Simon and Savita left at midday. As their airport-bound bus pulled out into the rain-drenched street, I waved them off from under an umbrella. See you in two years. I've spent the afternoon at the internet café with Metin and our friend Emrah, a calm-spirited, handsome fellow who works locally as an English teacher. I've been writing, musing and drinking tea.

I've just learned some depressing news: the details of the man who blew up my friend Sue (and himself) in a tunnel next to King's Cross underground station in July. Germaine Lindsay was an immigrant from Jamaica who converted to Islam at the age of 15. He was 19 when he killed himself. His wife was seven months' pregnant. As far as anyone can tell, he did it for an idea called 'ummah', which defines some people as being members of a community of brothers, and other people as being outside that community.

On the subject of ideas, community and brotherhood, a current hot topic around here is the European Union (EU). The week I left Britain, it was going through a crisis because the people of Holland and France had rejected its new constitution. In my tent above the Dover cliffs I read about that and the bout of soul-searching it had led to regarding whether the EU could work. I find such soul-searching strange, seeing that it's already given structure to a phase of European history characterised by six decades of unprecedented peace and prosperity, in contrast to the two vast wars which preceded it.

Turkey has a unique role in this grand story. A half-Asian giant sitting on the sidelines, will it join or won't it? The arguments against Turkey becoming a member of the EU include that it's too big, too poor and has too many expensive farmers. Some people also have a problem with its Muslim heritage.

The arguments in favour include that a young, fast-growing country is exactly what Europe needs and that its integration will encourage the sort of moderate and democratic Islam championed by the Turkish people. This position also holds that Europe needs this country at least as much as this country needs Europe and that, if the Europeans aren't willing, Turkey might look elsewhere for strategic alliances. Russia maybe? That would be interesting, or a geopolitical catastrophe, depending on one's point of view.

However, there's a deeper and more interesting angle on what's happening that isn't about the politics of this decade or the next one.

The globalisation that obsesses this twenty-first century is part of a narrative that's already gone from tribes, through city states, silk roads and trans-oceanic voyages. That story isn't driven by treaties and constitutions. It's driven by the people of the world changing the way they think. Here, on the streets of central Istanbul, one can see it taking place.

Sultanahmet is as international as anywhere on Earth. Strangers are constantly striking up ice-breaking conversations in which the second bit of information exchanged is one's nationality. The idea of nationality as an aspect of identity is so entrenched in contemporary thought that it's easy to forget how arbitrary it is.

Seventeen thousand years ago, when those prehistoric artists painted aurochs on cave walls in the Vézère Valley, such ideas would have been meaningless. In 15,000 BCE there were no such things as nations. Back then, people would have described themselves into other ideas, maybe tribal ones. In the intervening millennia our mental landscape has grown relentlessly larger.

This epoch, where we define ourselves as British or Turkish, is a phase in the story of a planet of people slowly learning how to act like a planet of people. A tribe, a city state, a country, an empire or a European Union, they're all abstractions: conceptual tools that we've crafted in our heads. A line dividing countries exists in two places: on maps and in the minds of men.

During this current phase of history it's impossible to know what will follow the nation state as the basic political unit, or how the threads of macrohistory and geopolitics will one day intertwine. Will the EU be the kernel of something that defines politics for a millennium, or a prototype for the ideas which follow? Time will tell.

But whether Turkey joins the EU in the next decade or the next five decades, or joins something that comes after the EU isn't the point. This planet is coming together whether we like it or not and that process isn't driven by politics, it's driven by the business people and travellers who treat the world as one and it's bound together by cheap airfares, international sports and the internet.

The human race can spend another thousand years agonising over who is a brother and who is not, but such torments represent a confusion between things which are truly infinite and things that are only of today. Beneath such transient matters there is a more interesting narrative one can ponder: the narrative of a species of impetuous, hormonal and fantastically clever primates, which have evolved on this planet and are making up civilisation on the fly. Once we start assessing our affairs in *that* context we'll find that our deliberations become more productive and our conclusions less provincial.

Germaine Lindsay will never have the privilege of engaging in such deliberations because he's killed himself, apparently confused by socially constructed barriers and anaemic fairy tales, spreading death as he snuffed himself out. Meanwhile, the occasional passer-by hurries along the drenched streets outside my adopted internet café, Metin is making the tea again, Emrah is in the back, prayer mat laid out, bowing in submission, and it's still raining in Istanbul.

Days since leaving London: 182

Current American casualties in Iraq: 2,029
People killed during the Mongol conquests: 30,000,000

> *When we go to war, whether as part of a nation state or as part of a*
> *disaffected minority, we commit ourselves to the atrocity of murder*
> *... Moralising against those who return the favour is as much human*
> *nature as it is hypocrisy.* – Bill Coffin

38: Lord Byron's Footsteps
27 November 2005

I awoke at two this afternoon to be informed that Tarik and Eden have been arrested for climbing the dome of the Aya Sophia. Here's what's been happening in the past 48 hours …

At 11 p.m. on Friday night Eden came to my room to recruit me for the ridiculous plan of swimming the Bosporus. Lord Byron did it, apparently. My initial reaction was 'no way'. An hour later I was sold. We set off to the harbour following two hours' sleep and, at the harbour-side fish market, persuaded a Turkish boatman to ferry us north. It took 90 minutes for his chug-chug vessel to reach the thinnest part of the strait, where we disembarked.

There were Tarik, Eden, five other Australians, two Germans (to watch the bags) and me. We had one wetsuit. It snowed during the week, but we didn't bother testing the water. We just stripped down, fired up with an Antipodean war dance and leapt in. That may, in hindsight, have been a little rash.

As Her Majesty's only representative I expected to easily out-swim the colonials. However, like them, I'd underestimated how punishing a kilometre swim in ice-cold water from Europe to Asia would be. A hundred metres out, my extremities were numb and I was struggling to breathe so, despairing at the amount of filthy salt water I was swallowing, I turned to face the sky, thought of England, and hit the backstroke.

The following 30 minutes were at the edge of what I could physically cope with, and a struggle to avoid thick shoals of jellyfish or being obliterated by a passing freighter. Approaching the opposite shore we swam through a patch of gooey black 'scum' (don't ask), which had us screaming in defiance before finally stumbling onto the Asian shore.

There followed ten surreal minutes while our escort boat looked for a place to pick us up and several companions threatened hypothermic collapse, then a fumbling attempt to dress on the boat with hands torpid from cold. Half an hour later we were drinking hot coffee in the morning sun. We'd just swum from Europe to Asia. A real moment of satisfaction. Job done.

Back at the Orient everyone else went to bed, while I showered and then went to the airport to pick up two actresses. Katherine Manners was my housemate in London and first arrived in my world in 2003: vibrant, enthusiastic and fresh out of drama school. She taught me about acting, I taught her about washing up. She brought her delightful, statuesque buddy Anna. They're both taking breaks from shows at the National, one of London's premier theatres. I got them back to Sultanahmet and we ate as the swimmers woke up. Halil organised the club.

Shiva was five floors of invitation-only, stupendous, banging techno and had a music system to die for. The gang of actresses and swimmers mooched, smooched, shook it up and wove through the madding throngs of trendy Turks. With everyone high on life it was a very special night: gorgeous, blissful, a moment of unity. The last thing I remember is being back at Room 32 with Tarik and Eden. They were talking about girls and trying to keep me awake, but I was just so very tired …

When I awoke there was a random Australian asleep on my sofa. Things like that are always happening. Someone came to the door and told me the news. Apparently, Tarik tried to do a runner after they'd been arrested. The cops are really pissed off about it. I've been called to the police station.

Days since leaving London: 185
November water temperature of the Bosporus: 9°C

Do not be too timid and squeamish about your actions. All life is an experiment. The more experiments you make the better. – Ralph Waldo Emerson

39: Istanbul Endgame
2 December 2005

Anyone who hasn't been to Istanbul may not appreciate how outrageous it is to climb the dome of the Aya Sophia in broad daylight. On the evening of the 27th of November the police sent a car to take me to the station. I arrived at 11 p.m. with Tarik's and Eden's stuff, two bananas and a friendly face. I pieced together what happened.

11.00	Tarik and Eden leave Room 32 (and my unconscious form) after drinking a bottle of raki.
12.00	They begin their ascent of Justinian's Church of the Holy Wisdom of God.
12.10	As the call to prayer reverberates around the city, Tarik (a good Muslim) faces Mecca, drops to his knees and prays.
12.31	Reaching the dome's summit they sit and smoke cigarettes.
12.35	A crowd starts gathering in the square below.
12.50	Fearing terrorism, the police call in a team of snipers.
13.00	Their legend secure, Tarik and Eden begin to descend.
13.02	They are arrested.
15.00	After two hours of standing around, Tarik bolts for freedom. He doesn't get far.
15.05	Their shoe laces are removed and they are handcuffed together.
16.00	They go to jail.

I chatted to the police for a while, then left the boys in their cell and returned to the hotel. Katherine, Anna and I spent the following days exploring bazaars, mosques and palaces, and being cleansed in a 300-year-old bath house. In the evenings we sat in my room, finished the last of the vodka and discussed what we'd learned in Istanbul.

The day following their exploit, Eden and Tarik were presented to a judge who shook his head and sent them on their way. Tarik then returned to the distant reaches of Istanbul's sprawl, while Eden split town to meet a Polish girl. The Bosporus swimming team have dispersed and Katherine and Anna went back to London two days ago. There's only me left, but not for long.

I've spent the morning throwing away all the empty bottles, gathering up my home away from home and thinking about everything that's happened here: the dozens of people who have washed through this room, the building vibe, the gathering crowd, the passing storm. Now it's time to go. I'm feeling rather melancholy. Another moment has come and gone.

I have one or two more goodbyes to say, then tonight I fly to Thailand.

Days since leaving London: 190
Empty vodka bottles standing on my wardrobe this morning: 24
Today's weather in

London:	10°C and raining
Istanbul:	19°C and bright
Bangkok:	33°C and sunny

Musings
Forty Days

A query I received several times during those 40 days was: 'Is it really necessary to drink all that vodka?' Some regarded my partying as frivolous and silly, and felt the time could have been more constructively spent.

I would dispute that. If you want to share your moment in time with those who walk beside you – to really *connect* with them – stonking great parties provide a context for collective experiences for which there is no substitute. Sitting around drinking tea and discussing philosophy is all very well, but there are times in life when you simply have to look deep into someone's eyes and pass them the vodka bottle.

While travelling to Istanbul, I imagined my experience there would involve the contemplation of its venerable history; paying my respects at the site from which, for two millennia, the politics of half a world were dictated; and musing about Byzantine emperors and the Ottoman sultans who replaced them. But in the end it wasn't about those things.

Here was my experience of Istanbul: after the 150 most cosmically stimulating days of my life, as I cycled across Europe, I arrived at a destination where the echoes of history are as palpable as anywhere on Earth. I arrived at a point in that city's story when it was no longer a base for the imperial domination of one people by another, but for a coming together of peoples. With that as my stage, I enjoyed an experience that was defined by community.

The lesson I drew from that experience was that the way our civilisation evolves – the *mechanics* of how it is achieved – is not high politics. That's the surface froth upon a deeper, communal experience. If you want to understand what's happening on this planet, you won't get very far by thinking about the differences between a Byzantine emperor and an Ottoman sultan, because they're nearly identical expressions of the same underlying phenomenon.

I wasn't mentally in a place, during that Turkish winter of 2005, to do something as left field as using a travel story to set out a reinterpretation of human civilisation. It would take a few more twists of my own story before that would happen. Anyway, there was something else on my mind: someone I'd met in Istanbul, but hadn't mentioned in my emails – a girl.

When Simon and Savita left, I spent that day hanging out with

Metin at the internet café. Then I went to the bar to eat, following which I had every intention of an early night. That isn't what happened. Her name was Melanie Michaelson.

Melanie was tall, pale-skinned and outspoken. Her dad had been in the army, so she'd grown up on German military bases. She lived in the same part of north London as me, where she ran a nursery. She was on the last day of a week-long holiday.

The next morning, when she came to say goodbye, she mentioned that she'd be in Thailand in December. That afternoon I went to see Dilara at the travel agency and changed my ticket to Australia so that it went via Bangkok. Then I wrote Melanie an email asking if I could meet her off the plane. The next day she wrote back from London saying I could.

So when I finally flew east out of Istanbul, it was to meet a woman. It was pretty exciting. As for that great metropolis: captivating, exhilarating, bombastic, fantastic, ancient, wicked and wild. Leaving was a sorrow, but of the sweetest kind.

Part 3

Asian Fluctuations

40: Back in Bangkok
4 December 2005

I've been here before.

In 1996, shortly after graduation, I had gone to India as a volunteer physics teacher. The school was in the village of Kulathapuza, high in the forest-covered Western Ghat Mountains of Kerala, India's most south-westerly state. I worked there for five formative months, alongside a brilliant team and a headmistress with an instinct for how children learn.

During the fifth month her husband, the school's owner, returned from the north. Then I witnessed the dark side of how a man may publicly treat his wife in India: of inequality of rights, sexual jealousy and violence; and how these things are allowed to trump human dignity.

In disgust, I resigned.

That left me at something of a global loose end. A month earlier, on the lakes of Kottayam, I'd been told by a traveller who'd been there once that there was work for English speakers in Thailand. That's what they call a lead. A week later I was in Calcutta with a flight booked to Bangkok.

Bangkok was then, and remains now, a world city in the truest sense: huge, diverse and genuinely multicultural. It's also the social, political and economic focus of South-East Asia, and its transport hub. Khao San Road, in Banglamphu district, is planet Earth travellers central. Arriving at the age of 22 on the far side of the world, with US$250 to one's name and no ticket home, focuses the mind wonderfully. I soon got a job, becoming in-house English teacher at the Stock Exchange of Thailand.

I met a man called Sol. He was one of the best guitarists in the city of York, held a degree in physics and had an unerring knack for getting into hare-brained adventures. He became one of my best friends and we started a band (I sang), spending the evenings on stage at a seedy Bangkok nightclub. They were happy-go-lucky days of youth.

That was nine years ago. It's good to be back.

My old stomping grounds have not so much changed, as been obliterated under an ocean of new development. The Buddhist temple where one could reliably expect to be mobbed by mangy dogs has been sparklingly made over. The club where I sang is now a brothel.

Mama, who still runs the Apple Guest House where I lived, was right where I left her nine years ago. She looks frailer and is a grandmother now, but still makes the best iced coffee in the world.

My plane flew in yesterday morning, and last night it was the birthday of His Majesty King Bhumibol Adulyadej. The Thais held a mini-Glastonbury in the centre of town – any excuse for a party.

Entertainments included:

• Rock stage: an unnecessary number of guitars (everybody seemed to have one) and widespread headbanging.

• Teeny-pop stage: lots of attractive young women and a couple of token gay blokes performing a dance routine.

• Kickboxing ring: I caught the kiddies' competition – pubescent boys beating the shit out of each other for the pleasure of a screaming crowd. Lots of blood. I did chuckle.

On 11 December I'm meeting a friend here. That gives me six days to kill. I've decided to go to Cambodia.

Days since leaving London: 192
Proportion of Thailand's GDP generated in Bangkok: 44%
Bangkok's population in

1880:	255,000
1947:	1,178,881
1970:	3,077,371
2005:	6,642,566

41: The Temples of Angkor
7 December 2005

I've wanted to see the temples of Angkor since reading, many years ago, an account of their uncovering from the cloak of the jungle by a team of French archaeologists.

My base of explorations has been the town of Siem Reap, 150 kilometres from the Thai border. Reaching that border from Bangkok involved an ultra-modern, air-conditioned double-decker coach. Then, on the Cambodian side, we transferred to a jalopy bus which navigated, very slowly, down comically bad, potholed roads for eight sweaty hours.

I decided to explore by bicycle (the term 'cyclatron' having yet to catch on here). As all cyclatrons need a name, I christened my new steed 'Rhubarb'. The bicycle-hire person at the guest house assured me that three days of Cambodian sun and a daily 20-kilometre round trip would be too strenuous for an Englishman such as me. 'Don't worry,' I said, 'I know what I'm doing,' and off I set.

Angkor (once a sprawl of residential districts, farms and ceremonial centres) was the world's largest pre-industrial city and seat of the Khmer

Empire, which flourished between the ninth and thirteenth centuries: the classical period of Cambodian history. The temples, representing half a millennium of building, are dotted across the 3,000 square kilometres the city once covered, all now swathed in tropical forest.

Technology drives civilisation. Generals and presidents may get into the history books, but if people didn't invent stuff, we'd all still be living in caves. At Angkor it was their agricultural infrastructure which was the key. Towards the end of the first millennium, the Khmer began using a highly effective irrigation system which allowed the production of two rice crops per year. A large food surplus ensued.

Just as in Egypt four millennia earlier, that meant some members of Khmer society could start being more imaginative about what they did with their time. By the ninth century they were erecting some of the most spectacular monumental architecture the world has ever seen.

Rhubarb and I have just finished our second day of exploration. It's world-class stuff – acre upon acre of Dr Seuss-style jungle filled with fairy-tale old things: bat-infested towers; stone-carved images of gods, men and monsters; ancient trees, plump with Druidic power, their roots enveloping tumbledown ruins; and tiny, white-robed Buddhist nuns mooching about with joss sticks.

Angkor Wat, the most famous structure, and the only part of the city that was never lost to the forest, has been an Asian site of pilgrimage since the city was abandoned. It's still the largest religious building in the world, filled with angelic devas and demonic asuras. The temple was erected by King Suryavarman II in the twelfth century to celebrate his symbolic union with Vishnu.

Kinky.

Days since leaving London: 195
Years since the completion of:

Chartres Cathedral	1,785
Colosseum in Rome	1,924
Angkor Wat	853 (circa)
Stonehenge	3,500 (circa)
Aya Sophia	1,468
Great Pyramid of Cheops	4,585 (circa)
Pyramid of the Sun (Mexico)	1,805 (circa)

42: Cambodian Damage Control
9 December 2005

I've always taken pride in my consciously cultivated antennae for danger and fierce paranoia about valuables while on the road. Cambodia was a really unfortunate place to get complacent.

It was my third day exploring the temples. For the first time in months I'd not worn jeans, so my passport and wallet were not, as usual, snug against my bum and thigh. They were in my day bag, which was in Rhubarb's basket. I'd also taken out one of my reserve cash stores and my plane ticket to Australia. They were in the day bag too.

The lock I'd been using to secure the bag had, just an hour before, broken. By that evening I was feeling so la-di-da I'd even stopped taking the elementary precaution of looping the bag's strap around Rhubarb's handle bars to guard against exactly what was to happen.

Amateur.

I was cycling back into Siem Reap after sunset, marvelling at the ancient groovy things looming out of the twilight and singing 'Sally MacLennane', my favourite Pogues number. Happy as Larry. High on life. That was when they got me.

Two guys on a motorcycle crashed into me from the left, knocked me to the ground, grabbed the bag and accelerated into the swarms of identical scooters inhabiting these roads. In addition to my passport and wallet, the bag contained my glasses, sunglasses, camera and – most heart-wrenching of all – the big black book in which I write these diary entries and so much more. Following the most creatively productive period of my life it was full of notes, quotes, essays, tables and poetry: the irreplaceable artefact of the last seven months.

A simple moment and everything changes. It took a few seconds for the enormity to sink in. I was in big trouble. My stomach clenched up.

At the tourist police station it took five minutes to find anyone. They were zero help. At the main station I sat, drenched in sweat and trying not to throw up, as the fat man behind the desk took an hour to fill out two A4 forms while watching a soap opera over my shoulder.

Preliminary investigations revealed that the conventional course would be to go to Phnom Penh (I have no money, remember), spend ten days titting about with bureaucrats and miss my onward flight to Australia. That wasn't a course I was prepared to countenance, so I hatched a plan.

Because I used to live in Thailand, I know it quite well. Once there, I'm safe. I therefore resolved to break myself over the border illegally, get to a cash machine (I have a secret spare cash card) and then throw money at the problem. Once in Bangkok I would cast myself upon the mercy of the British Embassy. What were they going to do? Refuse me a new passport?

I didn't sleep well last night. By 8.15 this morning I was in contact with the Thai underworld. By 9 a.m. I'd initiated negotiations with the cops. It wasn't going to be cheap.

Said cops insisted on completing a 'situation' report (let's just say they hadn't helicoptered in a forensics team), which meant going to the scene of the crime and drawing diagrams. As far as I was concerned it was a way of wasting time before we got down to the time-honoured custom of bribery. We were faffing around on the tarmac when one of the policemen took a call on his radio. He turned to me and asked: 'Are you Peter *Thomas* Baker?'

A moment of clarity. I hadn't given them my middle name.

Days since leaving London: 197

Musings
Unspoken

I wrote the above on 9 December. Not all my communiqués were as measured. Here's the text of the email I sent to a few close friends and family the night before, on 8 December.

Hello

It's 10 p.m. local time.

To cut a long story short, this evening I had everything of value stolen, including my passport, cash card and plane ticket to Australia. There is no infrastructure to get cash wired and Cambodia doesn't have any ATMs, so I can't use the spare card taped (thank God) to the inside of my star chart.

There are two possibilities. The first is that I go to Phnom Penh. Unfortunately, the British Embassy there doesn't issue passports but orders them from Bangkok, which takes at least 10 days, meaning I miss my flight to Australia. The second possibility is that I find a way to break myself over the border to Thailand, and civilisation. That basically involves bribing a load of people.

I'm safe and trying hard to find a way out of this shit. It's been a really tough day. I'll call as soon as I'm able, which might be a while.

I have 45 dollars and 10 pounds to my name. Wish me luck.

P.x

But the unspoken story of that Cambodia misfortune was that there was no way I was letting a couple of random motorcycle-riding bag snatchers stop me from meeting up with Melanie. She was arriving in Bangkok two days later, so I was going to Thailand no matter what. If that meant paying off South-East Asia's criminal underworld, so be it.

43: Cambodian Damage Assessment

10 December 2005

Against all the odds, they found my bag dumped by the roadside. In the end I lost my camera, glasses, ATM card, 3,000 Thai baht and some bits. The important thing was that I got back my passport, plane ticket and big black book. Everyone kept telling me: 'lucky man'. Too right.

With the hell the Cambodians have been through in the past three decades, I've nothing to complain about. It was an educational experience. The debrief this end is that while the cops and snatchers weren't in cahoots, they probably knew each other. I don't resent that. My fault for getting sloppy.

On that difficult night of sweat and pidgin English, while the shit was hitting the fan, I met three blonde and friendly Aussie chicks called Caroline, Ceridwen and Justine. Straight into my darkest hour, some angels to guide the way. I was adopted and christened 'Passport Pete'.

Following my deliverance, they took me to dinner then a French-run bar to get drunk on mojitos. We all shared the long, hot bus journey back to Thailand this morning. Song of the moment: 'Bring Me Sunshine' as sung by Morecambe and Wise. Every cloud has a silver lining.

Learning points:

1) Paranoia is your friend.

2) The time-wasting bureaucratic lethargy of the police was in marked contrast to the industry, energy and 'can-do' attitude of the guys

running my guest house, who let me live on credit for two days.

Following the robbery, when everything was sorted, a callow young policeman turned up to make a thinly veiled attempt to extort money from the guest-house boys (and I quote: '... it was a faulty bicycle'). If the 'authorities' would let them get on with business (instead of hassling them for bribes and getting in the way) they could make that country rich real quick.

In the 1980s, when I grew up, there was a received wisdom about the economic geography of planet Earth: a billion rich people (in Europe, North America, Australia and Japan) and four billion poor people (everywhere else). That model no longer describes our situation.

Material wealth creation across the developing world has ballooned since the 1980s to levels unprecedented in history. China, the great dragon, is the star of that show. A new model to describe the economic shape of human civilisation is: over a billion rich people, four billion people getting rich very quickly and another billion who are not.

That sixth of the world's population not moving towards a long-term future of material prosperity live mainly in sub-Saharan Africa, but some of them live in other economically disastrous nations such as Cambodia. Perhaps their biggest obstacles are the webs of entrenched power systems designed to serve the few over the many: humans instinctively manipulating their fellows using tools carved into shapes we call habit and culture.

Cambodia's current difficulties were not caused by one of those despots who squander hundreds of billions of dollars and yet cannot build roads, but rather three decades of catastrophic war and genocide. Nonetheless, the contrast between cosmopolitan Thailand and semi-medieval Cambodia is stark and writ on the faces of corrupt young men in uniform, the unwitting tools of a dysfunctional system.

My experiences with the country's crooked police and pointlessly hindered business people could therefore turn me into a small-government free-market fundamentalist or an anti-establishment revolutionary. I've yet to decide which.

It's Sunday. I'm back safe and sound in Bangkok. Khao San Road is a riot of colour and life. God, I love this town. Tomorrow I'm meeting my friend Melanie at the airport.

Days since leaving London: 198

To be born a gentleman is luck, to die a gentleman is an achievement.
– Abraham Lincoln

44: It's a Jungle Out There

14 December 2005

Following the kerfuffle in Cambodia things started to look up when my dazzling chum Melanie showed up. We had met during the closing days of my stay in Istanbul, clicked at once and decided to hook up in Thailand. Melanie is grade A party material and will drop everything to shake ass at the first sign of some funky house. The evening she arrived, we hit the town.

Our first breakthrough was a Thai innovation known as a bucket. It's like a sandcastle bucket except, instead of filling it with sand, one fills it with loads of ice, a can of coke, a can of Red Bull, half a bottle of rum and as many straws as you fancy. It's communal, potent and really gets the job done.

Melanie is an ambitious drinker and disregarded my warnings that bucket number two might be enough. The next morning our journey to the airport was consequently an experience of profound rock and roll. As the taxi cruised down sun-baked highways, I distracted the driver while Mel was sick into a bag behind him. Live the dream. She slept on the hour-long flight south to Surat Thani, then we hired a driver to take us west, into the jungle.

The Khao Sok National Park is located just south of the Isthmus of Kra, on the mountainous ridge separating the Thai peninsula's east and west coasts. It's the oldest evergreen forest in the world: the remnant of a 160-million-year-old ecosystem. Melanie snoozed on my lap as we travelled inland, passing titanic limestone columns hundreds of metres high. After two hours we reached the lodge at which we're now staying.

The lodge is made of wood with the Thais' typical flair for design. An amusing troop of monkeys live nearby. They prance around, squabble and take food from your hand. There's also a clear, swimmable river and a rope swing allowing one to go in Tarzan-style. The lodge is inhabited by a small eccentric assemblage. There's Brian, a 40-something Aussie bloke with a goatee and a smile, and his two lady travelling companions: Gemma (his 17-year-old daughter) and Dutimas (one of his old Thai pals).

Brian did the Asian hippie trail back in the 1970s during the now legendary pre-guidebook era. I quizzed him on it. He informs me it was cheaper then, everyone smoked marijuana and Afghanistan was an Asian highlight. I haven't grasped the details of his relationship with Dutimas, but she's exceptionally good-looking and I think she might be trying to steal Melanie off me.

Most interesting of all is Jimmy, the Thai guy running this joint for his brother. Until six months ago Jimmy was living life in Bangkok's fast lane (which is a very fast lane indeed). His mates were successful, rich, young and up for it: working hard, playing dangerously hard.

Things started to get out of hand. Jimmy realised that, with all the sex, drugs and madness, something had to give. He bailed, left his job, packed up his life and came south. He didn't tell his former associates where he'd gone, but called them from a public phone (so they couldn't trace the call) to tell them he was safe. He'd seen stuff.

Melanie and I are staying in a two-room tree house. It's a romantic and serene space, 15 feet above the ground. Outside are tremble-winged beetles, rainbow orchids and the jungle, crouched, humped in silence.

Days since leaving London: 202

I spent a lot of money on booze, birds and fast cars. The rest I just squandered. – George Best

45: Full Moon
19 December 2005

The final stop Melanie and I made together was Koh Pa-Ngan, the iconic island venue for the notorious full moon parties (think: a moon, a beach and some really powerful speakers). We arrived the day before kick-off. It was teeming. There were pot-bellied Europeans with young Asian girlfriends, hippies trying to score drugs and masses of ravers (who are typically dreadlocked, Swedish and off their heads).

Regrettably, two such ravers drowned earlier in the week so the police cancelled the gig. By then, there were already thousands of people on the island. It was too late to stop all hell breaking loose, which it promptly did.

Melanie and I joined a crew of Turkish men, and armed ourselves with 2,000 bahts' worth of magic shake. We hit the beach at sunset and, for the following 18 hours, danced and sang through a hundred moonlit adventures which blurred into one.

One of our Turkish friends (a two-week holidaymaker) had a Thai girlfriend. Tasanee was a major asset to the party but she wasn't in the habit of opening up to men. She opened up to Melanie though. Turns out she was from the west coast. The 2004 tsunami killed her father, uncle and three cousins, impoverishing the family. That's why she was working as a prostitute. So many shades of grey in this world.

The morning after the moon party found Mel and me lounging on a cliff top, with reggae music playing in the background while the sun yawned above white sand, green palms and a tranquil turquoise sea. Words cannot describe.

Melanie is an amazing woman: kind, cheerful and passionate. Our week-long love affair has been one of the most fulfilling and joyful experiences of my entire life: coming down to breakfast, still drunk from the night before, into the hippie wonderland of Khao San Road; making out in the soothing calm of our jungle tree house; and the otherworldly merriment of the island of the moon.

But I left the island alone yesterday morning. Melanie has a month in Thailand. I have a Melbourne-bound plane to catch. Our last embrace was a quiet, unemotional affair. Cheeks pressed. Vaguely concerned to avoid a long goodbye, the moment came and then suddenly went in the flow of the day. It was only when I was alone on the boat to the mainland that it hit me.

All the things I should have said. How I should have properly thanked her. How I should have told her how perfect it's been to be with her hour by hour during these last long, adventurous days. Dancing around – just the two of us – in our beach hut. Her dozing beside me. Reading while I showered. Doing her nails.

As the white surf churned I put on dark glasses to hide the welling.

Travelling back across Thailand wasn't the same without her. The return to the north was arduous and frustrating, while together we'd flown along. Now I'm back in Bangkok for the third time in 16 days. Walking past the places we'd been, and the bars where we'd got drunk or stared across the table at each other. But this time I'm alone, and tonight I fly to Australia.

Days since leaving London: 207
Cruising speed of

Nelly the cyclatron (London to Istanbul):	22 kilometres per hour
Flight BA7312 (Bangkok to Melbourne):	922 kilometres per hour
New Horizons probe (Earth to Pluto):	58,536 kilometres per hour

Musings
The Australian Rationale

Here was my rationale for going to Australia. Life in London had been full of known quantities: people who knew me, who liked me, who I could trust. I was looking for character-building experiences and the thing I felt would be good for me was to go to a foreign city where nobody knew who I was, set up from scratch and see what kind of a life I could build. Australia looms large in the British consciousness. It also has key advantages, such as a liberal visa regime and a common language.

Melbourne would be my first port of call. Then the plan was to go to Sydney, find a beach, become a barman and see what happened. Sol would be joining me. Then the adventure was to become a two-person excursion.

Or maybe three-person?

Despite everything, there was someone I couldn't get out of my head. Someone I genuinely could not, deep in my heart, imagine my future without. The thought wouldn't go away and it stayed my hand from any other course.

Things between us in Italy had not been what they'd been in London. However, at this point in the adventure, I'd successfully cycled across Europe, fostered an international community of fun in Istanbul and navigated my way out of a very tight spot in Cambodia. I still had over £12,000 in my bank accounts and I was strong, lean, fit and hard. I had a lot to offer a woman. Boyfriend or no boyfriend, once I'd set up a base in Australia, maybe, just maybe, Linda could still be persuaded.

You see together, Sol and I are quite a team. Team enough to persuade an Italian lady that her immediate destiny lay in the southern hemisphere. A brand new stage was about to begin.

It seemed like such a good plan.

Part 4

Down Under

46: Phase Four
30 December 2005

I arrived in Melbourne 10 days ago to 33 degrees Celsius and a clear cobalt-blue sky. It's summertime in the southern hemisphere.

My old friend Carla picked me up from the airport. She's a dancer by trade, of Egyptian-Irish descent and possessed of extensive fairy-like qualities. Her holidays began the day I flew in and she talked through her plans for us as we drove back to the apartment she shares with her buddy Amelia.

Amelia is a florist, and their apartment is behind her flower shop. She's also a leggy blonde with a laid-back attitude and a deep Australian drawl. On my first afternoon she regaled me with stories of life in the outback: hard-bitten men in hard-bitten towns with Filipino wives. Then the next day, she rambled on about Nietzsche. Down-to-earth and full of surprises.

It's blisteringly hot. I hide from the sun while a blonde Australian florist lectures me on German philosophy and her friend, the dancer, picks fresh lemons off a tree in the garden to go in our drinks. This is a very agreeable way of adjusting to a new continent.

Christmas Day was spent with Carla's mum, eating salmon and horseradish with champagne, followed by platters of fresh crayfish. Apart from that, we've been having barbecues, touring the city and going to the beach. There's a plague of flies – they're unbelievably annoying.

My Australian visa lasts a year. The plan is to acclimatise here, move to Sydney, meet up with Sol and then set up a base.

Yesterday I was hospitalised by a bee again. The little blighter surprise-attacked me on the beach when I was buying ice cream. The sting itself was a minor annoyance: the symptoms which followed, anything but. They were, in order: itchy crotch, itchy scalp, swelling of the head and neck, light-headedness, a rising feeling of nausea, extreme shortness of breath and a red blotchy rash spreading uncontrollably across my body.

I was rushed to a state-of-the-art hospital, where the consultant was distinguished and supremely comforting. He injected my arm with adrenaline, arranged a sandwich and then sedated me.

Apparently, my immune system was so upset by its experience in Croatia that it now freaks out at the first sign of bee poison. The doc informed me that next time my throat could swell up and asphyxiate me.

Bees are now my enemy. How did it come to this?

Days since leaving London: 218

English word of the day: 'apiphobia' meaning 'fear of bees'

Musings
Communication Breakdown

I'd been in Australia eight days and things were not as hunky-dory as I was making out. Carla was in an unhappy place. She'd left the UK earlier that year because they wouldn't extend her visa. She was angry about that and the breakdown of her relationship with a boyfriend in London.

She was also desperate for me to stay in Melbourne. I wouldn't be persuaded. Before leaving I'd asked Linda where she wanted to live in Australia. She'd been very definite: Sydney. So I was going to Sydney, but there's a rivalry between the two cities; Carla thought I'd be better in Melbourne and she wouldn't let it lie.

None of this overly worried me. I was grateful for the hospitality and Carla had always been pretty highly strung. Then it started to get really intense.

I was expecting to hang out with her, but whenever we made plans to spend time doing separate things she'd always have reason to change them at the last minute. After my first week in the country we'd been together nearly every waking hour and the tension was rising. We spent the afternoon of 29 December at the beach having a heart-to-heart and starting to clear the air. Then I got hospitalised by that bee.

The following afternoon we left Melbourne to drive to the house of her friends in the mountains. As we reached the city limits she exploded. 'I'm fed up with driving you everywhere,' she fumed. 'I don't like having you here and it's ruining my holiday.' After going on like this for 15 minutes she stopped talking to me. We were heading to a place with no public transport to stay with people I hardly knew.

When we arrived, our hosts immediately took control and by working a magic of common-sense counselling, mixed with liberal doses of red wine, they quickly depressurised the situation. By bedtime, Carla and I had made up.

47: Shangri-La
5 January 2006

For New Year's Eve, Carla and I drove to the house of her friends Anna and Will in the mountains 90 minutes north of Melbourne. Their village is called Kinglake.

The two of them live in an eco-heaven set among bush forest. The house uses collected rainwater for all its liquid needs and the garden is filled with dreamcatchers, Tibetan prayer flags and a Neolithic-style log circle. Flocks of cockatoos periodically invade its trees.

Anna is enormously welcoming, talking expansively about how great everything is and how they live in 'the best house in the world'. She has shelves crammed with books detailing magic spells and providing explanations as to the meanings of zodiacal signs.

Will is trained in law and psychology. He has degrees coming out of his ears and his conversation ranges from how Western systems of justice might be redesigned from first principles, to describing how humans react to other people not as they really are, but in accordance with the context in which they find each other. Deep shit, man.

Amelia and lots of other nice people turned up for New Year's Eve. We drank cold beer in the sun then took a walk in the evening so the girls could collect flowers. Midnight found us standing in ceremony around the garden's log circle, dancing under the black sky and sharing a moment of exultation at the magnificence of Mother Nature.

Carla and Amelia went back to Melbourne on Monday, while I stayed at Anna and Will's until this morning. They put me to work raking their lawn, clearing their drains and painting their chicken coop. The three of us talked late into every night, drinking buckets of tea, and Anna and I went for a long walk in a forest where real live wallabies roamed.

I hitchhiked back to Melbourne this afternoon. It took 90 minutes for the first car to go past, but that one picked me up. Sean, the driver, was the first person I've met to actually use the word 'sheila' instead of 'woman'. He also managed to get the phrases 'I'm not a racist' and 'dog-eater' (slang for a person of Korean origin) into the same sentence. I engaged him vigorously as to whether that was playful or offensive and, by the time we reached the city, we were top mates.

Days since leaving London: 224

Nicest places to live (ranked according to UN Human Development Index; selected countries):

Norway	1	Britain	15	Turkey	94
Australia	3	France	16	India	127
USA	10	Slovenia	26	Niger	177

Australian phrase of the day: 'budgie smuggler' meaning 'tight male swimwear'

Musings
The Tram Stop

Here were the items on my page-long to-do list that first fortnight on the continent: send out next diary email; write to Dilara and Metin in Istanbul; call Mum and Dad; call Sol; get a tax file number; get a haircut; set up a bank account; get a Medicare card; get Australian visa stamped; buy new jeans, work trousers, shoes, bag, notebook, socks, boxer shorts, contact lenses, an Australia guidebook and a mobile phone; and buy thank-you presents for Carla (the new Apple Wireless Mouse she'd been talking about, but couldn't afford) and Amelia (*Consider Phlebas*, one of my favourite books, which had come up during one of our discussions).

By the time I returned to Amelia and Carla's apartment that Thursday evening I'd barely dented this task list, so I pressed on at once with the administrative side of setting up in Australia. On the evening of Saturday, 7 January, I met with Carla and her friends at Federation Square in downtown Melbourne. Carla was angling for me to accompany her to a barbecue the next day, but I had stuff to get on with and said I'd give it a miss.

She went silent for two minutes then began shouting across the table. 'You're the worst house guest I've ever met. You're completely selfish, you only think of yourself and I've had all I can take of you.' Momentarily dumbfounded, I made my excuses then went back to the apartment. When Carla returned at 2 a.m. she wasn't sober and wouldn't talk.

The next morning I went downtown, booked into a hostel, returned to the house and gave the girls their thank-you presents; then I told Carla: no hard feelings, but I was leaving. Then I left.

I'm pretty sure Amelia persuaded her to follow me. Twenty minutes later, at the bottom of the hill, the tram to Federation Square was late.

Just as it pulled up, Carla came around the corner and asked to talk. So we sat on a wall while she talked.

She talked about how hard it was coming back to Australia, about how badly her ex-boyfriend had acted towards her and about how unfairly so many of the people in her life were treating her. At the time it felt as though she needed me to reassure her that none of it was her fault. But I wasn't going to do that, so she went around in circles for two hours until it all became so tawdry that I couldn't listen any more. Seeing a tram approaching, I stood to get it.

'Before you go, can we just agree that all this trouble between us has been half your fault and half my fault?'

'I'll have to think about that, Carla.'

'Yeah, but can you promise not to mention this to anyone in London?'

'I'm not in the zone to make promises right now, Carla. I think I should go.'

'But first can you just agree that all of this was half your fault?'

Those were the words ringing in my ears as the tram's doors closed. That was the moment I lost my cool. By the time the tram reached Federation Square, I was seething with rage.

*****

Carla was a good person in a dark place and old friends sometimes fall out. And yet that jovial and open frame of mind I'd been in on reaching Australia cannot simply be switched on and off. Something in my spirits broke that evening and I began sliding downhill, just as my difficulties were beginning.

I didn't want to be in Melbourne an hour longer, but had to wait three days for my appointment with the bee doctor. The news wasn't good. Following my experience in the Balkans, I suffer anaphylactic shock from bee poison. Anaphylaxis is a severe allergic reaction which occurs when a person's immune system becomes sensitised to a particular allergen. It can be catastrophic and fatal.

The doctor issued me, there and then, with a six-inch-long plastic tube containing 300 milligrams of adrenaline and told me to carry it everywhere for the rest of my life.

48: Australian Intercity
13 January 2006

Bee update: after a long meeting with an allergy specialist I've been issued with an anti-bee adrenaline auto-injector, which I must carry at all times. If I am once again savaged by a black and yellow mini-monster, I must self-inject, then get to a hospital. If through bad luck or bad planning I'm unable to do either, then I'm in big trouble. Henceforth, I shall be no fun at picnics.

For my last few days in Melbourne I stayed in the city centre. Then I caught a 12-hour overnight train to Sydney on which I sat beside a six-foot-six half-Fijian called Kye.

Kye was in the army but had just been discharged following eight months of knee and shoulder reconstruction after being blown up by a rocket-propelled grenade in Iraq. He'd been there two years and stationed in Falluja, which last year saw some of the nastiest urban warfare since the invasion. After learning that detail I just kept firing questions at him.

Kye was in awe at Iraq's beauty and expressed deep admiration for its people, particularly the members of the new defence forces he'd been training. However, he took a dim view of his American colleagues, telling one story of receiving a letter from 'the insurgents', apologising for accidentally hitting an Australian armoured vehicle. Apparently, they'd been aiming for you-know-who.

On discharge, Kye received a six-figure sum due to his injuries. He said he thought it was ridiculous to give a 19-year-old that kind of money. All he wanted was to go back into the army.

As for the cash, he'd burned through an eye-watering AU$60,000 (25 grand UK) funding a two-week 'bender' for the colleagues who'd dragged him from the wreckage last year, then used a good chunk of the rest to pay off his parents' mortgage. Good lad. And I quote: 'There's nothing quite like being really pissed in a foreign country, with a gun.'

I emerged bleary-eyed from Sydney train station this morning. The weather was overcast and humid as I ambled, overloaded with bags and blinking stupidly, down George Street and into the city.

Days since leaving London: 232
Current American casualties in Iraq: 2,383
American casualties in Somalia, which caused the USA to pull out of the country: 29

Work, consume, be silent, die. – Graffiti stencilled onto pavement outside Central Station, Sydney

Musings
No More Pilgrims

Sol wasn't coming. The day I arrived in Sydney I called to check in with him. His plan was to fly over at the end of January, spend two weeks with me, fly back to the UK, then back to Australia again after a month. The plan had an ominous ring, and sure enough, a week later his arrival had been indefinitely delayed.

This was not good news. My rationale for being in Australia was unravelling just as I was alone, paying $50 a night at a hotel and in a bad state of mind. But there I was. When you're in an unfamiliar country with no support network there are two overwhelming priorities: get a house and get a job.

On my first night in Sydney I hit the pavement with a stack of CVs, wearing my newly purchased, second-hand, $8 work trousers. I went bar to bar asking for work, but was told I'd need a certificate to serve drinks. The course took a day.

I got straight on the course, got the certificate, then hit the pavement again. This time I was told I'd need another certificate to cover gambling (in New South Wales, fruit machines are everywhere). It would take a week to get on a course, so I booked onto one and began looking for a house.

49: The Sydney Reconnaissance
21 January 2006

As I plan to be in Sydney a while, finding the right place to live is important. I've been scouting the city.

My first survey mission was to Coogee Beach. It has a small intense centre dominated by pubs crammed with English people. The crowd were fat, badly dressed and couldn't hold their alcohol. Not my scene.

Next I checked out Bondi. The beach was nice but it rained all day and the vibe didn't thrill. I then spent a day walking around the leafy inner-city quarters of Surry Hills and Darlinghurst. Nice, but no banana. Randwick? Nope. Kingsford? Naa.

I was looking for something special and felt sure I'd know it when I saw it, but nothing was electrifying me. I put in a call to Eden, my old Istanbul wingman. He suggested a neighbourhood called Newtown, so I went to check it out.

As I stepped off the bus a man with a bright pink beard went past on a bicycle. The main drag, King Street, was full of hip-looking coffee shops, recycled funky clothes stores and same-sex couples holding hands. There was a 30-foot-tall fresco of Africa on the side of one building and a huge painting of Martin Luther King on another. Aborigine-style lizards adorned the walls, along with koala bears, swivel-eyed sharks and multicoloured kangaroos. The whole place oozed cool bohemia. This, I was digging.

The next day I moved into a house five minutes from the King Street action with two natives: Adam and Chantel. The house has high ceilings, white walls, wooden floorboards and a yard. The beach is 35 minutes away.

I have my own kitchen for the first time in eight months and have been revelling in simple pleasures such as frying eggs in the morning. This week I visited a couple of second-hand furniture stores and have decked out my room with a clean, minimalist look. My new address is 119 Australia Street.

Days since leaving London: 240

Don't just do something, stand there. – Peter Rosier

Musings
One Thing, and Then Another

The day I moved into Australia Street an inch-wide lump appeared on my abdomen. I called a doctor and two days later at the surgery he diagnosed a hernia.

An inguinal hernia is a protrusion of the bowel through the sheets of muscle running up the inside of your torso. The doctor reasoned that five months with Nelly stressed the muscles, which then tore when I carried all my bags across Melbourne. Should have taken a taxi.

He informed me that there was a danger my internal organs could become stuck in the gap then malfunction, so he booked me in to see a surgeon. It would take three weeks to get an appointment.

Logistically, this was awkward. Life in Sydney was becoming expensive and finding a job was already taking longer than I'd anticipated. Now I had a sinking feeling that I was going to end up in hospital.

50: 119 Australia Street

4 February 2006

Newtown, where my new house is located, is in Sydney's Inner West. The university is just to the north. Downtown is half an hour away in moderate traffic.

Adam and Chantel, my new housemates, have known each other since they were 12, but we all moved into Australia Street at the same time. We've been assembling furniture, swapping bits of life story and watching the Australian Open together.

Chantel has six younger brothers and sisters, five of whom are exactly the same age. Their names are Ethan, Tahlia, Olivia, Mikaela and Madaleine. There are only three other sets of quintuplets among Australia's 20 million people. When this fact of her pregnancy emerged, Chantel's mum was advised by doctors that continuing with all the foetuses would be a bad idea.

She refused to relent, made it through the pregnancy, gave birth to five healthy babies and has now got them all to the age of 15. Whenever I feel my life is getting complicated I will remember the example of Chantel's mum.

This strength of character has been passed to her daughter, who is a black belt in Tai Kwon Do. Chantel is pathologically terrified of frogs, but has a no-nonsense approach to cockroaches, which she dispatches with efficiency and growling (while yours truly is squealing and flapping his arms).

Adam spent four years teaching and has thrown it in to go to drama school. He's at the elite National Institute for Dramatic Art. Mel Gibson and Cate Blanchett went there. He's a thoughtful, well-read sort with an extensive library, a decent stereo and a large music collection – these are all matters of great joy to me.

Australia Day fell during my first week here. There was much agitation among the natives about an annual ritual run by everybody's favourite radio station – JJJ – called 'Hottest 100'. Everyone votes for their favourite tunes, then cheers when they come up. I'm learning things about bands called Powderfinger and Wolfmother.

Things that happen in Newtown: in the main square at the end of King Street there's a plinth. A honky-tonk-style piano sits on it and a 'Public Piano Playing and Polishing' is being performed. Just as it sounds – two men are pottering with beeswax while another tinkles away. They let me have a go with a rag. Zen, dude.

Days since leaving London: 254
Population of Newtown: 15,027
Date Newtown established as a Sydney suburb: 1862

> *I have left orders to be awakened at any time in case of national emergency, even if I'm in a cabinet meeting.* – Ronald Reagan

Musings
Anything That Can Go Wrong

I suffer from a birth defect called talipes. It's commonly known as clubfoot.

When I was born my feet were twisted inwards and my Achilles tendons were too short. While I was still a baby they cut open my lower legs and lengthened those tendons. Then, when I was five, they opened me up again, sawed through my bones below the knees and swivelled my lower legs outwards.

I spent a lot of my early years in wheelchairs or on crutches and wore metal callipers until I was nine. I'm scarred and disfigured below the knees (whereas above the knees I'm all yummy). My feet are an unusual shape and they've never wholly done their job properly. I'm a slow, awkward runner and if I bend my knees even a fraction I'm effectively balancing on the balls of my feet. This limits the number of dance moves I can pull off, not that I've ever let that hold me back.

When I was young, getting shoes that fitted was an issue. As I became older it gradually became less of one. Until, that was, I got to Australia.

Normally I wear boots, even when it's hot, because they support my feet. But if you're cycling across a continent, you only get to take one pair of shoes and boots don't cut it; so I'd bought a pair of trainers.

Those trainers got me all the way through Europe, Istanbul, Thailand, Cambodia and Melbourne. By the time I arrived in Sydney they were wrecked, so I did what I always did: I went to an army surplus store and bought a pair of boots. Then I threw the trainers in a bin. That was a mistake.

By the end of that day I was in agony. I went back to the shop and bought a new pair of boots. They seemed fine when I tried them on, but by the time I got back to the house I couldn't feel my feet. I went back again and spent two hours trying on different pairs of boots. I found some that seemed OK at the time, but by the day's end it was the same result. Eight months in trainers had changed the shape of my feet.

Two weeks after I moved into Australia Street I was heading to the suburb of Leichhardt to hand out CVs when the stinging in my abdomen became so acute that I had to duck into an alley. I sat on the pavement's edge, put my head in my hands, gritted my teeth and waited for the pain to subside.

I had no job. My money was disappearing in rent, shoes and medical expenses. Sol wasn't coming. Linda wasn't coming. My feet were in agony. My abdomen was so painful I couldn't walk and I was probably going into hospital.

And this all begged the question: what am I doing in Australia?

I didn't need to be there. I could have gone backpacking, or stayed with Nelly. But I'd had this romantic notion of being a barman in a seedy Sydney dive bar. The reality was looking entirely less romantic.

After 20 minutes I could walk again, so I picked up my CVs and carried on to Leichhardt.

51: Kill All Bees
20 February 2006

I've got a job. I'm working for a hospitality agency called Nosh and my first shift was at the Sydney Opera House serving coffee at the memorial service for Kerry Packer: formerly Australia's richest man. He died on Boxing Day.

Mr Packer was a larger-than-life, lovable-rogue type of fellow. Exploits included overseeing a six-billion-dollar business while having trouble reading; spending six minutes clinically dead in 1990; and having the taxpayer pay for his funeral even though he was famous for not paying taxes (it's a bit of a sore point).

In the 1970s Mr Packer single-handedly overhauled world cricket and, when buying off the Australian Cricket Board, came out with the line: 'There is a little bit of the whore in all of us, gentlemen. So then, what's your price?' What a cool guy.

His memorial service was well attended. I star-spotted John Howard (Oz PM), Bob Hawke (ex-Oz PM) and Russell Crowe (movie star).

Things that happen in Newtown: in the main square I pass a man dressed in a puffy white cat suit. He's playing a two-foot-long electric guitar hooked up to a six-inch-tall speaker and breaking out crazy riffs. In front of him is a donation box. The sign reads: 'money to buy drugs'.

This suburb is also a hotbed for a certain sort of political radicalism. I'm keen to expose myself to new thinking so, on a whim, I attended a meeting of the Socialist Alternative Party. The discussion point was: 'Where does racism come from?'

The gentleman in charge gave a long speech. His thesis was as follows: racism is a modern invention manufactured by the capitalist ruling classes and it will only be eradicated through a workers' revolution and the creation of a socialist new world order. I can report that it was some of the most intellectually vacuous, woolly-headed ignorance I've heard in some time.

Lovely people, but I wouldn't vote for them.

As part of my ongoing war with bees everywhere, I've attended an allergy clinic to see what else freaks out my immune system. I was put in the care of a nurse called Luke wearing a death metal pendant (he lived in, you guessed it, Newtown), who tested me for 42 different allergies. The resident professor then called the hospital in Melbourne where I recovered after the bees' last assault against me and checked the results of the blood test they'd given me.

The tests confirmed that there's nothing else with which my system has a problem. Not even wasps. Just bees. Curses upon them all.

I was angling for them to use their power over twenty-first-century medicine to bionic me up with some cyborg-like, anti-bee abilities. Unfortunately, such treatments take years and I won't be here long enough. For the time being I am condemned to remain in a constant state of fear, haunted by the ever-present threat of the dreaded black and yellow ones.

Days since leaving London: 270
Average number of deaths per year in the USA as a result of

| Bears: | 0.5 | Spiders: | 6.5 |
| Sharks: | 1.0 | Bees: | 53 |

Musings
The Vigil

After three weeks of handing out CVs, I was offered three permanent jobs and some agency work within a 48-hour period. The next day I had my appointment with the surgeon. He confirmed that part of my small intestine was poking through the hernia and that it would be necessary to operate. He booked me into hospital for the following week.

So I had to turn down all the jobs, do shift work for the Nosh agency and cram in as many hours as I could to stem the rapid disintegration of my finances.

The hospital called the day before my operation and told me to be there at six in the morning. I was already on a 12-hour shift that ended at midnight. I got back to Australia Street at 1 a.m.

Adam and Chantel were living opposite hours to me and I hadn't seen them in days. Heading off to be sliced open when it's late and dark and cold and you're alone in a foreign land is not a pleasant feeling. But it is an intense one. I booked a taxi for 5 a.m. and savoured it.

I arrived at the hospital – tingling with adrenaline and trepidation – 30 minutes before they opened the front door; so I sat on the pavement outside under a street light, got out my notebook and worked out how I was going to tell everyone about the whole hernia palaver.

52: Australian Medical Infrastructure
26 February 2006

Having developed a hernia (also known as a flipping, ruddy, bastard hernia) on the day after arriving in Newtown, I've found that life has become considerably more expensive and complicated than it might otherwise have been. My chief hernia adviser, Dr Story, wears a beard without a moustache, looks like a Methodist dairy farmer and decided to slice me open.

Within an hour of being let in to the hospital I'd been weighed, prodded and had my blood pressure taken (and I quote: 'It's perfect, Mr Baker'). All the attention from the nurses, along with sleep deprivation and the first of many injections, threw me into an excitable state of mind and, by the time I was gowned and being wheeled towards the operating theatre, I'd transformed into a comedian of world-class stature.

I had the porter and the anaesthetist chuckling as I fired off a series of quality hospital gags. Then Dr Story appeared above me dressed in blue. I said something incredibly funny about George Clooney as he pulled out his scalpel. I don't remember anything else.

I awoke that afternoon gas-masked, blood-spattered and distinctly less amusing. I was sharing a ward with two solid, old Aussie blokes and the three of us spent the next 24 hours being stoic while swapping bits of newspaper and illness stories.

I got back to Newtown three days ago and have been convalescing on the 119 Australia Street sofa. Today I'm finally walking around (albeit with a slight limp) and made it as far as the internet café from where I now write.

Days since leaving London: 276
Number of doctors I've dealt with professionally since arriving in Australia: 8
Per capita annual health expenditure:

Australia   US$3,158   Croatia   US$357   Cambodia   US$29

A wise man should consider that health is the greatest of human blessings, and learn how by his own thought to derive benefit from his illnesses. – Hippocrates

Down Time

Two people I knew had suffered hernias in the previous years: my dad and my mate Tony. They'd both told sanguine tales of standing up from the operating table and walking away afterwards. That wasn't my experience.

On my day in hospital after the operation, dog-tired and drifting in and out of sleep, even turning over in bed was agonising; forget standing up. Days two and three saw me back at Australia Street, but tied to the couch, dosed up with painkillers and emotionally washed out.

I was crashing and burning in Australia. When I'd boarded that plane to Melbourne, I'd been a fireball of enthusiasm. Two months later, on leaving hospital, my zeal had been stifled and my gusto squashed.

I didn't articulate that in my emails. Writing home saying I was ill, I couldn't work, my finances were shot to pieces, I never went out, I never saw my new flatmates and that I was being haunted by a physical deformity I thought long-conquered didn't seem appropriate. And it definitely wasn't my style.

Relentlessly looking on the bright side has always been one of my coping strategies, and other people have real problems, so I made light of mine.

In the end, that unhappy period between January and March 2006 changed the direction of my life. The forced inactivity meant I had time on my hands. Time to think. One of the first things I'd done was adopt a Chinese-run internet café on King Street. While I couldn't spend money or work, I could read and write. I could go through the notes I'd scribbled down between Chartres Cathedral and Angkor Wat, and I could pull out the Qur'an which had been lying in my bags since London.

53: Kill All Hippies
3 March 2006

Later in this pilgrimage than anticipated, I've tentatively begun reading the Qur'an, Islam's holy book. It's divided into 'Suras' (literally: chapters) and I'm on Sura 2 of 114.

The main themes are love, mercy and forgiveness. The text makes repeated calls for orphans, travellers and the needy to be cared for. It also stresses that God is forgiving and that people should be also. Fighting is only allowed under very specific circumstances. It is absolutely not endorsed. Then, catching me completely off guard, it announces its approval of anal sex. God is full of surprises.

The prose is marvellous. I'm extremely impressed. It stands in stark contrast to the medley of carnage and bizarre animal sacrifice which constitutes the beginning of the Bible. I'm making notes.

Things that happen in Newtown: on purchasing a bottle of wine at the bottle shop the cash register pings up $11.11. The eyes of a guy next in line (long hair, bad teeth) open wide: 'Yeah, man, like, you know they say there's, like, a gate opening, man and eleven eleven is the key. If you read government reports then, like, everything finishes in 2012, man.'

He didn't seem the type to read government reports to me. I tried to be nice, but couldn't help laughing in his face.

While waiting for my body tissue to heal, and inspired by the marvels of Islamic scripture, I've decided to found my own religion. Here are some details:

1) I'm now intellectually committed to the idea that capitalism is the most rational system for running economies. The moment of clarity came in a field in Serbia. It's all about the proper allocation of capital. Things just fell into place.

2) My ethical thinking is moving towards classic liberalism. Too many

people get off on telling other people what to do, then making up reasons (which are really excuses) for why they're doing it.

3) I've come across a spiritual belief system that summarises much of my recent thinking on the subject: naturalistic pantheism. It is not to be mistaken with classical pantheism: a heretic faith whose adherents are basically witches.

On announcing these conclusions from my recovery bed/sofa, Adam pointed out that I could not possibly be a hippie while also subscribing to capitalism. Something about mutual exclusivity. This threw me into days of emotional turmoil before I stumbled across the term 'neo-hippie' and found it most to my liking.

I am therefore in a position to officially announce the name of my new religion. Henceforth, I shall be a Naturalistic Pantheistic Neo-Hippie. Rolls off the tongue, don't you think? I herewith declare myself chief high priest. Nobody can join without my permission.

Days since leaving London: 281

A balanced Australia Day diet should consist of a few nice, juicy lamb chops and beer … Yet your long-haired, dole-bludging types are indulging their pierced taste buds in all manner of exotic, foreign, often vegetarian cuisine … It's an absolute disgrace … The soap-avoiding, pot-smoking, hippie vegetarians may disagree with me, but they can get stuffed. They know the way to the airport, and if they don't I'll show them. – Sam Kekovich

Musings
Tipping Point

One more thing went wrong: my insurance company screwed me. They were the first call I made when the doctor confirmed a hernia. From that moment I was plunged into a world of endless paperwork and feckless insurance administrators, where nothing was straightforward and no question I put to them trivial enough that they could simply tell me the answer.

For months I chased one employee after another while they sent me on wild goose chases for double receipts from every doctor in Sydney, then left the company or went on sick leave. This dragged on until August when a guy three rungs up the chain called and told me that my policy was invalid. The clause was deeply ambiguous and three-quarters of the way into page four of the small print. It was the only time in my life I'd made an insurance claim. I ended up paying for everything.

But things were about to start getting interesting again. Mardi Gras would begin the re-injection of fun into the adventure, my feet were getting used to boots again and that problem was solved decisively when I discovered the Blundstone: the classic Australian workman's boot. It was practically designed for me.

54: Degrees of Separation
10 March 2006

One sure-fire way of creating an interesting social situation is to get 20,000 gay boys and girls, stick them in costume and declare a street party. Last week's Sydney Mardi Gras involved 120 floats, 6,000 participants and half a million spectators. Game on.

Chantel and I rocked down to Oxford Street. It was humming with a carnival atmosphere. We inserted ourselves in the crowd, then made friends with everyone in a five-metre radius. Adam was staffing the event for his drama school. We screamed boisterously when his float went past. The dykes on bikes were a highlight. The Newtown Gym had its own dance troupe.

The action then moved to Chantel's friends' flat where a spontaneous party kicked off. After some time I was dispatched into the throngs outside to find recruits and returned an hour later with three European girls and a sailor. It was that kind of evening.

All this was just after Adam introduced me to Georgia.

Georgia is a nurse, but wants to be a dietician. She comes from Brisbane, but works in Sydney and she's turning out to be a rock. The other day, she took me to a warehouse party.

We arrived via a nondescript backstreet which led to a dingy corridor vibrating to a muffled bass line. Then the happy hardcore washed over us as we entered a drop-down arena where giant pink beach balls hung from the ceiling and a line of decks was manned by a shifting crew of shaggy-haired DJs. Absolutely going off.

Three days later, Georgia took me to a picnic and introduced me to Karim.

Karim joined the British Army as a teenager. One day on the UNcontrolled zone in Cyprus he tested how far a ball bearing would go from a catapult with a tail wind. Further than he thought possible, as it happened. The smashed window of the Turkish watchtower set off the first gun battle on the buffer zone since the 1970s and earned Karim 60 days in a military prison and a punishment posting to Iraq (shortly after the 1991 Gulf War), cleaning up the road to Basra.

By the time he'd spent 14 days breaking charred bodies from the armoured vehicles to which they were welded, his enthusiasm for the military was at an end. Chance then led to a job on a survey ship and Karim's story permanently relocating to Australia. At first he got homesick. Now he's settled and loves the weather.

Qur'an update: I've reached the bit where it says it's OK to hit one's wife. Here is what it says specifically: if you fear that your wife will 'assume superiority over you' and behaves accordingly, then you should – first – remind her of God's teaching, then ignore her in bed, and finally – if none of that makes her see the error of her ways – hit her (a single blow).

Of all the European girls that joined us for Mardi Gras, the most interesting was Renata. Back in Prague, Renata runs studio space where artists from different disciplines create together. She's in Sydney to break open 'a new cultural sphere'.

I took her for a drink in a blue and yellow bar, where she told me of how she digs cyberpunk and holds William Gibson, its noir prophet, on a pedestal. I listened while she ruminated on cybernetics, consensual hallucinations and the new global matrix: lines of light, ranged in the non-space of the mind, clusters and constellations of data.

Days since leaving London: 288
Speed of New Horizons probe after Jupiter flyby: 82,000 kilometres per hour

The future is already here – it's just not evenly distributed. – William Gibson

55: Goth Shift
18 March 2006

I'm doing shifts at an alternative rock night in a bar called The Agincourt. Six hours of working to a soundtrack of the Cure and the Sisters of Mercy really floats my boat. Sometimes I sing along.

The goth crew wear black. Leather and PVC are a must, and the groove is to cover oneself in make-up while looking unhappy and mournful. They've also developed a fashion for cosmetic contact lenses which turn the whole eye white. It's a hell of a look under UV.

I've made it my project to wait until I'm passing them their drinks before cracking a smile and delivering a precision-guided compliment. For a brief moment they all look happy to be alive, no matter how much face paint they're wearing.

Qur'an update: the text has now explicitly spelled out its own place within the grand scheme of the cosmos. Here's the deal: Jesus came with the scripture (basically the New Testament) which confirmed the Torah (basically the first five books of the Old Testament); then Muhammad came with the final confirmation and authority over both of those previous messages. In this way, God has informed humankind of his will, for all time. Job done.

Eden of Istanbul has returned to my life. He requested my attendance at a bush-based music event on the Central Coast, north of Sydney. The details were left vague, but I decided to trust him. Renata – Czech cybergoddess – came along.

An hour north and we were in the countryside, where Eden met us off the train. We swam in the ocean, ate prawns, then went to meet the party squadron he'd assembled: Ali, Wozza and the magnificent Michelle.

Four hours later I was in a car full of foxalicious, high-attitude chicks heading into the night, a journey which ended via a 17-kilometre track of red sand and potholes: off the beaten track, Australian style.

The technical name, I'm told, is a 'bush doof'. Ten acres of wilderness, five sound stages, not many shoes and a couple of cops making a futile attempt to shut the thing down. For the next eight hours we meandered between the stages, wandered through the trees, lost each other and found each other again as the swirling crowds became more and more psychedelic.

As the evening progressed, many people went missing to sleep in the surrounding bush. Then, as twilight turned into morning, they began to reappear, shuffling back through the trees. They were confused and wide-eyed. They'd become lost in the dark, but now they were returning to us. They didn't know where they were, or in some cases who they were, but that was OK – we were all together at the end.

I've heard a lot of different DJs hit their stride in a lot of different ways over the years. When the moment of sublime musical perfection came in that dawn-lit Australian wilderness, it was in the shape of 1970s punk-pop. 'Gordon is a Moron' blared across the hills, we danced like maniacs around the remote forest clearing and the sun burned its way towards noon.

Back at Eden's house we cooled off in his pool, then Renata and I took the train back to Sydney. In retrospect, without at least one wacky outback bush rave the cultural side of my experience in Australia would always have seemed incomplete. Sleep is for wimps. Wicked.

Days since leaving London: 296
Sailors beaten at arm-wrestling by Oliver Reed before his fatal heart attack: 5

If you obey all the rules, you miss all the fun. – Katherine Hepburn

56: Going Hard
5 April 2006

Susannah May Colbert is a petite, talkative type, a research psychologist by profession and an old friend from my London years. To celebrate the completion of her PhD she's travelling around the world, but in the opposite direction to me.

Here's how our relationship works: as we're both a bit pushy and loud-mouthed we're always trying to get one over on each other. Naturally I dominate these contests, while allowing her to win just enough that she feels in the game. Susie likes to point out that while her basis for mild arrogance is a perfect academic record and several years with a globally renowned research team, mine is, well, the fact that I'm me.

Susie flew in from South America, where she was injured in a freak white-water rafting accident. This left her with a shattered humerus, a disabled radial nerve, an arm that will be in a sling for at least another five months and internal metalwork put in place by a team of good-looking Argentinian doctors. She's carrying a set of X-rays that detail all this and is showing them to everyone she meets.

Having just backpacked Peru with one arm, Susie made it clear that she was in Sydney to have fun and the morning I picked her up from the airport my shift was cancelled. Who should choose that moment to raise his impish little head? Eden. He and Susie immediately hit it off and I sensed at once that things were about to spiral out of control.

It was St Patrick's Day. A lot of Irish people live in Sydney. We purchased some picnic food and headed to Hyde Park, where an Irish festival was in full swing. On arriving we were met by a chorus of Gaelic laughter, so we threw down a blanket, cracked open some wine and stripped off. The weather was fantastic. We were all in the mood to boogie.

The highlight was when the penultimate band embarked on a series of perfectly executed Pogues numbers. It turns out that I'm an extremely talented Irish dancer. My technique is naive, but my enthusiasm is stellar and, crucially, I know all the words. The Irish themselves were more energised by the visually accurate but cheesy U2 tribute band that headlined.

By the time they'd finished their encore, Eden had hatched a plan to head out east with Brian, a lanky fashion designer from Cork who'd emerged from the crowd that day. They'd already talked Susie round. I insisted on popping back to Newtown and left them to it.

It was past midnight when I found them again on Bondi Beach. They were all very drunk and dragged me to the house of two expat girls, who were extremely polite, terrible housekeepers and almost certainly drug dealers. Brian appeared to be sleeping with both of them.

The next morning Susie's friend Abi arrived from New Zealand and for the last few days she's been staying at Australia Street. Susie has commandeered my bed for the two of them. I'm on the sofa.

Qur'an update: a lot of time is spent reviewing stories from the Old Testament. I've just got to some new material about Joseph (of technicolor dreamcoat fame). At one point, Joseph's master's wife gets all her mates together to check Joseph out and seduce him. Joseph, noble fellow that he is, says: 'I would prefer prison to what these women are calling me to do.'

Loser.

I've spent the last week working hard while Susie and Abi enjoy day trips to the Blue Mountains and Botanical Gardens. I come home every night to find them watching the Commonwealth Games and discussing their adventures. It's rather comforting.

Setting up a life in Sydney is not proving simple. Something urgent and unexpected has come up. The day after tomorrow I have to leave Sydney for a few weeks to attend the wedding of my friend Abhishek. It's in India.

Days since leaving London: 314
Foreign athletes missing, 24 hours after end of Melbourne Commonwealth Games: 19

Welcome to President Bush, Mrs Bush, and my fellow astronauts. – Dan Quayle

Musings
Sydney
Introspective

When you arrive in a new town you have to move fast to get your base in order: find a house, get a job, build a life. Things had not gone according to plan in Sydney. I'd spent most of the summer in enforced down time, my reasons for being in the city had evaporated and those collapsing finances were starting to limit my options.

That put me in an interesting corner.

I was alone on the far side of the world, with a head full of inspiration, a notebook full of ideas and free to do *anything* I wanted. In a life filled with preoccupations, moments like those don't come along very often.

So, if I could do anything I wanted, what did I really want to do?

I wanted to capture a way of thinking about the world that was singing out to me. I wanted to say some stuff which it was about time someone said – to set out a narrative of humanity that was big, optimistic and stripped of the assumptions implicit in human discourse since prehistory. In hindsight it's difficult to see how else I might have found the head space and chutzpah for such an undertaking. Once I'd made the decision, one thing just kept leading to another.

But I wasn't quite there.

The wedding seemed like bad timing when it came up, but it cleared my head. You see, there were two good reasons for going to India. Abhishek is a dear friend and I wouldn't have missed his marriage for the world. But there was another reason. Linda was going to be there.

Part 5

Hindustan

57: A Passage to India
7 April 2006

I met Abhishek in 2003 after he answered our advert for a housemate. We were particular about who lived at 45 Hewitt Road and his profile wasn't promising. An expat Indian computer programmer isn't top of one's list when running north London's premier party mansion. We couldn't have been more wrong.

Some people are so positive, so warm and so genuinely engaged by those around them that they couldn't hide it if they tried. It's an attitude which cannot be faked. Within minutes of coming through the door, the room was his.

Abhishek is a very clever man. He's worked as a consultant software engineer in Hong Kong, for prestigious banks in London and will soon be starting his MBA at a top US business school. The Sunday in 2003 when he moved into 45 Hewitt Road, we spent the afternoon discussing futurology and imagining the world views of tomorrow. By the time he moved out three months later, I'd learned of the virtuoso alliance between curry and whisky, and how to make the perfect mango smoothie.

Since then we've rarely been on the same continent, but I've been following his halting progress towards marriage for some time and that time, as it happens, is now. My attendance is non-negotiable, so this pilgrimage is now taking a detour to India. The last time I visited was in 1996, back during my physics-teaching days in the Keralan jungle. That was exactly a decade ago.

Due to flight-booking complications, I found myself taking an indirect route starting with a 10-hour stopover (plus four-star accommodation) in Kuala Lumpur. I used it to catch up on sleep and was fully recharged by the time I returned to the city's spanking new Thunderbirds-style airport, where I stood before its panoramic five-metre-high windows and watched the reds and oranges of sunset spread across the surrounding rubber plantations. India, here I come.

Then I was back in Bangkok for the fourth time in six months. I had two hours, and was served coconut milkshake by the most ludicrous ladyboy ever, before finally boarding my flight to Bengal. I arrived in Calcutta last night, the Qur'an in one hand, *The Economist* in the other. Abhishek was waiting.

As I hold him in such regard, I felt that the lady he'd decided to spend his life with had better be pretty special. She was with him.

Swetambali is tall, with high cheekbones and an easy smile. She asked me a series of searching questions, but hardly mentioned herself – the sort of understated attitude I find utterly disarming. Only after some coaxing did she reveal that she's just finished her master's degree and admitted that yes, she did do some modelling, but only when it was a designer she respected and she could spare the time.

The boy got his back slapped when that detail emerged.

Days since leaving London: 316

	India	Australia
Land area (square kilometres)	2,973,190	7,741,220
Population	1,095,351,995	20,264,082
Life expectancy at birth	64.71 years	80.5 years
Total GDP	US$3.61 trillion	US$640.1 billion
GDP per capita	US$3,300	US$31,900

A man who stands on a hillside with his mouth open will have to wait a very long time for a roast duck to fly into it. – Chinese proverb

58: Full Immersion
10 April 2006

Abhi and Swetambali come from the Maithil Brahmin community and speak Maithili as their first language. They were first put in touch by their parents in April 2005. At the time, he was living in Denver, she in Calcutta.

They hit it off, visited each other in June and October 2005, and soon slipped into a routine taking advantage of the Colorado–Calcutta time difference: each would call the other when returning from work to wake them as morning broke on the other side of the world. Abhi told me the size of his phone bill. It was well into the thousands of dollars.

On my first day in town the driver picked us up at 10 a.m. We dropped Abhi at L'Oréal for a pre-marriage tart-up, then Swetambali and I went off to bond through the medium of shopping.

First: jewellery. A trove of gold and bling had been ordered for the big day and we toured through shop after shop filled with baubles, finery and half-cut diamonds collecting it.

Second: wedding threads for the Jolly Pilgrim. This involved standing before an enormous mirror and trying on a series of spectacular suits and robes while three tailors fawned over me and an Indian model commented on how handsome I looked. You can probably imagine how strenuous I found that.

Following a day in the loved-up world of Swetambali and Abhishek the three of us went our separate ways: Swetambali to Siliguri at the foot of the Himalayas, where the wedding will be held; Abhi to his family in Bihar in the north-east to prepare for the main event; and I to Sudder Street in Chowringee on the eastern bank of the River Hooghly, where I found a cheap hotel and went to bed.

Qur'an update: on the plane to Bengal I reached a point where it sets out the argument for God's existence. The argument runs as follows: 'Our God created the world, what did your God create?' That's it. That's the argument.

Disappointed doesn't even begin to describe how that makes me feel.

Now it's claiming that it is 'God and his Messenger [who decide] on a matter that concerns them ...' His messenger decides? I was under the impression that God decided and Muhammad was his prophet. With growing perplexity, I read on ...

The day after Abhi and Swetambali left, life became even more agreeable when Linda – my perfect Italian soul sister, who is also attending the wedding – arrived in town. Meetal, a local lad, took me to the airport to collect her and I waited, in excited suspense, at the arrivals gate. After 20 minutes there she was, a little sadder than the last time I saw her, but as beautiful as ever.

She looked on wide-eyed as we drove back to the city and the awesome pandemonium of Calcutta's street life rolled by: human-powered rickshaws, ramshackle trams, herds of goats and the odd cow just mellowing out in the middle of the road.

Meetal is a grand master in the art of driving incredibly fast through unbelievably traffic-clogged streets. At one particularly hair-raising junction he announced, in a classic piece of Indian deadpan: 'See that policeman? If he stop me he cannot stop me.'

'Why is that, Meetal?' I enquired. Cue: wiggle of head from side to side.

'Because we are going *very* fast now.'

Linda and I are loving Calcutta's zany energy and she insisted we visit Mother Teresa's grave. A guy called Omitabho took 40 minutes to haul us, through clogged and frenetic backstreets, to her final resting place in the grounds of the Missionaries of Charity. Apart from that we've been hanging out on Sudder Street and have acquired a team of attendant chaps who shoot the breeze, drink tea and periodically try to get cash off us.

Days since leaving London: 319
Daily fatalities on India's roads: 270

Hurry burry spoils the curry. – Indian road safety sign

59: One Teardrop upon the Cheek of Time
13 April 2006

Shortly after arriving, Linda announced that as she'd never been to India before she wanted to see the Taj Mahal. We had four days before the wedding and Agra was 1,000 kilometres in the wrong direction. But what Lola wants …

The Mughal Empire was the last great imperium to dominate India before the British. Its rise was driven by the new gunpowder weapons spreading across Eurasia during the sixteenth century and it went on to control the subcontinent for 200 years, until the early 1700s.

The empire was founded when Babur (the warlord, not the elephant) led a series of invasions south from Kabul, culminating in his overthrow of the last Delhi Sultanate in 1526. However, the empire's true creator was his grandson, Akbar the Great, who reigned from 1556 to 1605 and extended its frontiers to incorporate the trading and agricultural wealth of the Ganges plain and the port cities along the Bay of Bengal and Arabian Sea.

Akbar was also the world's first great leader to promote reason as the highest value of the state, during a period in which Islam had much to teach Christianity about tolerance and enlightenment. The empire he ruled was one of the richest parts of the world. His revenues were 25 times that of his English contemporary, James I.

It was under Akbar's grandson, Shah Jahan, that the empire reached its zenith and developed the distinctive synthesis of Islamic, Persian, Indian and Mongol traditions which is reflected in, among other things, its architecture.

The Taj Mahal was built for love. In 1631 Shah Jahan's favourite wife, Mumtaz Mahal, died giving birth to her fourteenth child. The heartbroken emperor began construction of the mausoleum (in which they would both eventually be entombed) later that year. It took 20,000 workers and 1,000 elephants 22 years to complete it.

It's a romantic story. But as Linda pointed out, buildings like the Taj aren't really about love, they're about prestige, designed to make a point about the people that build them. Many of the workers who did the actual construction got a raw deal: Shah Jahan removed their thumbs lest they repeat the feat.

We spent a thoughtful afternoon admiring the tomb from every angle, then lay on the grass as the sun went down and the moon came up. As night fell, a black Taj appeared in the pools of its starlit gardens. Finally, as they prepared to close the site, we were shooed away by a good-natured policeman sporting a massive moustache.

Qur'an update: I've reached a brilliant bit describing a scene in heaven that takes place after the Final Judgement. A group of men (it's always men) are sitting around chatting in 'gardens of delight' while passing around a drink from 'a flowing spring' that is 'white, delicious to those who taste it, causing no headiness or intoxication'. One of them then mentions a friend he knew back on Earth pre-paradise and they all peer down to see the fellow in question, burning in the fires of hell. How way-out is that?

Yesterday Linda and I explored Agra Fort, a crescent-shaped complex with a forbidding military exterior hiding a paradise of pearl mosques, palaces and the marble tower where Shah Jahan – imprisoned by his son Aurangzeb – saw out his final years.

There we met Jocelyn, a French lady who last night joined us for dinner, along with Milo, a German history professor. We dined on bread and stew above the city's winding lanes. The main topic of discussion was the economic awakening of India and China. Milo and Jocelyn believed that awakening would cause the inevitable decline of Europe as wealth moved to Asia. I argued that in the future new industries would rise and sources of wealth would be different from those of today.

Not only would Milo and Jocelyn not accept that, they couldn't even imagine how such an eventuality might come to pass. They saw economics as a zero-sum game in which an industry leaving a country leads to an irreplaceable loss of wealth. A future in which all humanity was materially rich they found genuinely inconceivable. 'We've had our turn, now it's theirs,' Milo sighed.

This conversation was particularly remarkable given that it took place against the backdrop of 50 years during which western Europe's economies and living standards have reached heights unthinkable during any previous period of history – and that this wealth creation has been almost entirely driven by industries non-existent 200 years ago.

Clearly, living in one of the most stable, safe and fabulously wealthy societies that has ever existed is no proof against pessimism. Fifteen years of economically underperforming Asia has been enough to blind them not only to the age of unprecedented prosperity during which they've lived their lives, but also to the transforming two centuries before that, and the eight-thousand-year metamorphosis through which the human story has just passed.

It's a striking example of how narrowly we think when considering the context of our lives and the time frames in which we contemplate the events unfolding around us. One imagines those Mughal emperors weren't such pessimists. Despite their grubby foibles, I for one am grateful to them for their vision, their glory and their enduring monuments to love and death.

Days since leaving London: 322

Humans everywhere share the same goals when the context is large enough. – Carl Sagan

60: Monsoon Wedding
17 April 2006

Qur'an update: I'm having increasing difficulty entertaining the idea that if God was intending to instruct humanity on how to manage its affairs for eternity, He would have sent us this. For example, the text contains detailed instructions as to whether (and under what circumstances) one can marry one's adopted son's ex-wife, but nothing at all about economic policy.

At one point the text (purportedly God) berates worshippers for rushing out during prayers to listen to music, leaving Muhammad alone on the pulpit. I appreciate that sort of thing isn't on, but if one is the infallible creator of reality and one has 450 pages to deliver one's final and eternal revelation to humankind, surely attention could be paid to weightier matters? I read on …

The journey east from Agra to join the groom's party in Bihar involved a 27-hour train ride and the full kaleidoscopic bustle of India. We rolled into Ranchi with six hours to freshen up. Then Abhi arrived with his entourage.

Nothing had prepared Linda and me for the hullabaloo and carnival atmosphere as the full weight of his clan emerged from a convoy of 20-plus vehicles. After a quick get-to-know-you session, we piled onto yet another train for yet another overnight ride, this time to Siliguri: 75 Indians, four generations and one carriage. Just when we had thought it couldn't get any crazier, we found ourselves in a world filled with the hubbub of three score people talking over one another, in which food (from mangoes to Bombay mix) was being passed hither and yon.

My abiding memories of that journey are the boisterous singalongs, listening to the old guys lecture the young guys about cricket, and retreating to third class, where the drinking was getting done. There I had Urdu poetry recited to me and received a lecture concerning what India was *really* about: peace, love and prosperity, apparently. Yeah, dude, for real.

We were met at Siliguri train station with garlands of flowers, then loaded into yet another convoy of vehicles and driven to our hotels. The two days in and around Siliguri that have followed have been one long social event involving dancing, costumes, several religious ceremonies, almost continual eating, a visit to a tea plantation and an afternoon at a hilltop temple, where Linda and I sat close, but apart, beneath a bush on which purple flowers grew.

Swetambali's father is master of ceremonies. He's doing a brilliant job looking after his horde of high-spirited guests including: Abhi's cousins, his cousins' parents, his cousins' parents' friends, his cousins' parents' friends' children ...

Uncle Neeraj works for the Oil and Natural Gas Commission and spends a lot of time in Burma. I questioned the morality of doing business with a self-selecting elite whose members violently repress their own people, but are too feckless to run a country. Neeraj argues that Burma's junta draws disproportionate criticism from the West because Western influence is weak there.

Abhishek's brother-in-law's best friend, Surjeet, works for Indian military intelligence. He lives a James Bond lifestyle and has been ambushed, blown up and shot. He expresses confidence in India's glorious future and talks of when, not if, it becomes a superpower.

I was delighted to be reacquainted with Abhi's cousin Mayur. Mayur is a professor of computer science in Missouri, where he tackles insanely complex maths problems, thinks about quantum computers and designs the software of the future. It's always fun to pose Mayur an esoteric computer-related question. This leads to him going wide-eyed, waving his hands around and talking very quickly. He claims that when you discover something completely new, it's better than sex.

Mr Thakur – Abhishek's dad – is the main man. Abhi described him as 'a happy camper' and wherever he goes Mr Thakur can be found holding court and leading his gaggle of brothers and in-laws in a quest to make maximum mischief. These guys need little excuse to drop some bhangra tunes and rock out under the midday sun.

He works for Tata Group, India's biggest multinational with fingers in pies from energy to automobiles. One of Mr Thakur's roles is to arrange operations in the depths of rural Bihar, where bandits still rule. I asked him how one deals with an armed brigand operating outside the law. 'They're human beings. We talk to them.' Good point.

India's various cultural traditions arrange their marriage ceremonies in different ways. None are simple. On the evening of the main event the groom's party paraded through town, band in tow, dancing and throwing wads of cash into the air. At the main gate there was a stand-off orchestrated by Abhi's feisty brother-in-law Robin. We refused to hand over the groom until the bride's party produced a red handkerchief, a transistor radio and a buffalo. It's traditional I'm told.

Then the party unfolded: hundreds of guests and waves of food and chatter and hustle and fun. I strutted around in my white embroidered Nehru suit while Linda looked thoroughly ravishing in her sari. Meanwhile, on a brightly decorated stage, Abhishek and Swetambali were married in a six-hour ceremony, aloof and resplendent, as the celebrations swirled around them.

Days since leaving London: 326
Indian female literacy: 50%

> *By all means marry; if you get a good wife, you'll be happy. If you get a bad one, you'll become a philosopher.* – Socrates

61: Cloud Cities
26 April 2006

Following the wedding we had five days to get Linda back to Calcutta for her Europe-bound flight.

We began with a visit to a ramshackle viewing station in the Jaldapara Wildlife Sanctuary in the foothills of the eastern Himalayas. There we met an elephant called Matambula ('Honey Garland'), who carried us into a forest and past a rhinoceros going for a paddle. I thought Honey Garland seemed sad and questioned whether carrying humans was sufficiently dignified for such a magnificent elephant. Linda, who's something of a Doctor Dolittle, assures me that it's obvious when a 9,000-pound mammal is angry.

Next we drove to the mountain kingdom of Bhutan, where we stood beside an ancient Buddhist pagoda stretched with brightly coloured streamers and looked down through a cloud-filled valley upon the town of Phuentsholing. Then we made a seven-hour bus climb to Darjeeling, where we bought jars of tea and pashminas before rising at dawn to stand, blanket-wrapped on a mountain, watching light break through a veil of pale yellow mist and the sun rising over the roof of the world.

That afternoon we returned to the valleys and caught an overnight bus back to Calcutta, where our journey had begun.

When the goddess Sati, first consort of Lord Shiva, was humiliated by the rudeness of her father, Daksha, to her husband, she threw herself upon the sacrificial fire, praying to be reborn to a father she could respect. Shiva, enraged by the self-immolation of his beloved, decapitated Daksha and began dancing around the world with mad abandon.

Lord Vishnu, to pacify him, cut Sati's body into 52 pieces and, according to local tradition, where one piece fell a place of pilgrimage grew up: the great temple complex to Kali in Kalighat. On our final evening together, Linda and I went to pay our respects.

The priest had the green eyes and light skin of an Afghan. I asked him how many gods were recognised in Hinduism. He smirked and replied: 'It's all God.'

Then he took us to the inner sanctum and sat us before a stone image of Kali in a dark and violent mood. There we received our blessings and slipped into a meditative trance as they beat out their drums in long praise to Shiva's moody consort, the black goddess of annihilation.

The next day Linda flew back to London. I watched her walk away from me through the departure gate then lingered at the airport for a while, melancholic and doleful.

I made one more trip into the hinterland: to Abhi's village, where he and Swetambali, serene and confident, were being shown off and preparing for their new life together. I was off-duty most of the time, alone in a hotel with a good view and cable TV. I used the time to think about: what I'll do next, the world spinning around me and the nation outside.

For half a century, following the country's unification and independence in 1947, the Indian economy grew at a trend rate of four per cent: 'the Hindu rate of growth'. That was about the same as its population growth, a demographic and economic state of affairs which locked it into the stifling poverty for which it became synonymous.

In 1991 a man called Manmohan Singh (then finance minister) masterminded a series of reforms, including opening the economy, reducing government control and floating the currency. Economic growth jumped to a new trend rate of seven per cent, while population growth continues to inexorably decline. A transformation has thus begun.

And it's not just in the numbers. These changes are writ into the fabric of Indian society. If you talk to Indians born in the 1960s they typically have five or six siblings, as did Britons a couple of generations before them (my paternal grandfather – born 7 August 1892 – was one of 15 children). Yet Abhi's generation are almost all one of two (as was typical in the UK in the 1960s).

Compared to 10 years ago there are more ambitious infrastructure projects, much better roads and an intensified buzz. The country's self-confidence is in a completely different place. My old Irish mate Terry used to say that Calcutta in the 1990s was like Dublin in the 1950s.

In a place like India, with its huge reservoirs of penury, it will be a long time before the situation of the poorest improves. But if we want to make poverty history then we have to create wealth, and if we want to make civilisation sustainable then we have to stabilise its population. There is a global demographic transition taking place and it's spelled out in the family histories all around us. The same forces, driving the same patterns, are reconstructing humanity the world over.

I returned to a rain-lashed Calcutta this evening and caught a cab across town back to Sudder Street. Tomorrow, I return to Oz.

Days since leaving London: 335
India's share of world income:

1700	24%	(under the Mughal Empire)
1820	16%	(under the British)
1913	7.6%	(still under the British)
1952	3.8%	(post-Independence)
1973	3.1%	
2005	6.3%	

India's fertility rate (children born per woman):

1960	5.9
1980	4.7
2006	2.9

Rate at which Indian wealth per person set to double: every 20 years

The march of society, of social change, has not been fast enough, nor fundamental enough, so far. – K. R. Narayanan, the first dalit (untouchable) President of India, 1997–2002

Fate Amenable to Change

To a new arrival India can seem chaotic. However, anyone who's spent much time on the subcontinent will recognise the rhythms underlying its surface commotion.

Indian society is like a great social engine, humming down the ages, bound together by an ever-changing web of family ties. Its tempo is regulated by deeply entrenched cultural practices linked to the cycle of birth, marriage and death. The engine has retained its underlying integrity even as waves of invaders – from Muslim to Mughal to Briton – have washed over it, and its continuum can be traced through religious and artistic traditions to those most ancient civilisations on the banks of the River Indus.

Westerners sometimes look down upon the Indian custom of 'arranged' marriage, simplifying it to its most primitive stereotype. It's true that families as worldly as Abhishek and Swetambali's (and couples as desperately in love) are exceptional. Yet the custom has evolved to fulfil a role crucial to any society if it is to be stable in the long term: the need for a robust social institution to provide people with brides and grooms. In that it stands in contrast to the unreliable modern system of the West, an unreliability which leads to one of the great unspoken malaises of our time – that so many people are unable to find long-term partners.

On the other hand, for a region with probably the richest spiritual tradition humanity has yet produced, the Indians can be desperately bourgeois. The idea of cycling across a continent on the basis that it might provide experiences to deepen one's character isn't something many of them relate to. As for living the life of a Sydney barman in order to enrich one's understanding of humanity – it isn't just that the idea does not compute: it draws blank stares of incomprehension.

However, the observation from that 25-day Indian immersion of most relevance to the ideas for which this story is an agent is one regarding the economic (and related demographic) changes taking place in India (and other parts of the formerly 'third' world) at the beginning of the twenty-first century.

Because we're all part of these global patterns, we fail to step back and think about the wider implications of what's happening. Milo and Jocelyn couldn't get past seeing India's economic vibrancy as threatening because they couldn't separate it from their insecurities about Europe. Considering how insightful we are as a species, I think we could start being more realistic about our own historical context.

If one were to consider the economic and demographic changes reshaping twenty-first-century human society from the perspective of a dispassionate observer (maybe from that of a historian in some distant future), what might one make of them?

To my mind, what's really going on is that as a result of millennia of trial and error, and a growing awareness of our interconnectedness, we humans have made progress in one of the key logistical problems facing us as a consequence of this civilisation business we've stumbled into: how to orchestrate economies.

India's economic transformation is really an expression of the fact that, across a vast and ancient land, a billion people have got a little better at managing their affairs in this mysterious and bewildering universe we live in, and another hurdle has been crossed between ourselves and infinity.

*****

But at this point in the journey, that wasn't the main thing on my mind.

The most moving thing I've ever read is a letter J. R. R. Tolkien wrote to his son about his late wife. In the letter Tolkien says that the person with whom you share the most profound bond in this world is not the one to whom, in some theoretical way, your personality is best suited. It's the one with whom you actually share the experiences of your life.

From the moment Linda walked through the arrivals gate at Calcutta airport, I had her to myself for two weeks. You'd think that would be enough time to discuss our future. You'd think that, with two weeks thrown together, you'd be able to find, or create, a moment to initiate that conversation. Wouldn't you?

It never happened. Linda and I have always been comfortable in each other's company, but it wasn't the same. Our relationship lacked its former intimacy. The fire in my mind no longer saw a companion in the mirror of her face. Even with all that time, I was unable to rekindle it; or to express how much I wanted it back and wanted her.

Then she was disappearing through the departure gate and we'd grown even further apart.

I'd never envisaged that my adventure would be a solo affair. The thought it might end up being so preyed on my mind during those final days in India without her, along with another thought: this is ridiculous. This is *it*. These are our *lives*.

So I resolved to force the issue.

On returning to Sydney I decided to call, forego any niceties, tell her what I thought and insist we discuss it. You see, I genuinely believed that I could offer Linda a partnership no one else could, and that she knew me – and us – well enough to know that was true. She might be on the other side of the world, but you only live once and anything is possible.

I worked myself up to make that call. It's the people with whom you spend your days to whom you're bound. These are our days. Don't grow apart from me any more. I want you. I won't let you down. Please.

I made the call.

She was in.

'Pronto!'

'Ciao bello! Come siete?'

'Si bellissima. How was your journey to London?'

'It was fine. I'm back at work now. How're you, baby?'

'I'm cool; back in my lovely house in Sydney. Adam and Chantel are here. How're things with you?'

'They're good. I'm feeling a bit down after our holiday. My God, wasn't it *amazing*?'

'It was pretty cool, Lindy.'

'So, are you excited to be back in Australia?'

I was only mildly excited to be back in Australia. But I was very excited to have her on the other end of the phone. I started to tell her what I thought.

The line went dead.

It happens. International lines get cut off. It's no big deal. I called back. The phone rang but no one picked up. I put the phone down and called again. The phone rang and rang. Still no one picked up. I put the phone down and redialled the number very carefully. Still no one picked up.

The phone I was calling is in the hall at 45 Hewitt Road, at the bottom of the stairs on a shelf beneath a mirror. I lived in that house for seven years. I know that phone extremely well. I could think of no reason why she wouldn't pick it up, even if just to tell me to call another time. She must know I'd call straight back. She must know I'd be trying to get through. I tried her mobile. No one picked up.

It didn't make sense. I began casting around for reasons she might not take my call. I couldn't understand. I *needed* to talk to her.

Then I began to deflate. That feeling at the bottom of my stomach. The final throes of a rejection which began nine months earlier. No one picked up.

That was it. That was the moment. My path was chosen. My life forked.

The ultimate conclusion of this pilgrimage you're reading about is one of elation and joy. But the experience did not draw me closer to Linda or anyone else. For I would not get the girl and, in spite of my dreams, plans and expectations, I would undertake it alone.

Part 6

The Boiling Pot

Paying for All This

You might be interested to know how I paid for this escapade and how much it cost.

In 2000 I won US$5,000 in an essay competition in which one had to predict the future. At the time that was almost exactly £3,500. I used the money to take my then girlfriend to Mexico and to buy a stereo. With the £1,500 that remained I opened two savings accounts.

From then on I saved every month, come rain or shine, for five years. Even though I ended up in favour of capitalism, I never personally made much money out of it. However, I've always lived frugally, don't own a car and have no dependants.

When I cycled away from London I had £15,000 in those two savings accounts and during the first three months of the bicycle ride I received an additional £2,000 in deferred pay. By the time I returned to Britain, two years later, I was £3,000 in debt. Here is where the money went ...

During the 150 days it took me to cycle from London to Istanbul I spent £3,214. Or, to put it another way, £150 a week. In the five and a half weeks I partied my way around Istanbul I spent £1,930 (£338 a week). I wasn't exactly watching every dime at that point and quite a bit of it went on vodka. The one-way ticket from Istanbul to Melbourne, with a stopover in Bangkok, cost £528.

The 16-day roller coaster of Cambodia and Thailand, including one internal flight, cost £416 (£186 a week). Getting robbed at Angkor Wat cost £450. The main expenses were a new camera, £70 baksheesh for the boys who helped me out in a tight spot and £50 in bribes for the cops.

Those first three months in Melbourne and Sydney when everything went wrong cost £4,505, only £997 of which was actual medical expenses. Most of it was spent on living and paying rent in Sydney while not working.

My return ticket from Sydney to Calcutta cost £556. Twenty days in India, including one internal flight, cost £478 (£134 per week).

My income in Sydney was AUS$15,545 (£6,275), which paid for most of my Newtown lifestyle and the magical mystery tour which followed. However, I withdrew additional funds from my UK accounts during that time for big one-off expenses such as diving. The net effect was that the period between the end of April 2006 (when I returned to Sydney) and November 2006 (when I flew to the Americas) cost me

£1,018. A one-way ticket from Sydney to Quito, with stopovers in Los Angeles and San José, cost £873.

On the Pacific's western shore, life got cheaper again. My week rambling around Costa Rica cost £222, the two months and seven days drawing patterns in the stars in Quito cost £1,726 (£175 a week) and the four and a half months conducting a global deconstruction through South America cost £2,828 (£170 a week). The 10-day chill-out sessions in the Guyanese haven cost £223 and the flight out of Georgetown £362.

Total cost of the entire two-year pilgrimage: £20,326 and 33 pence. Bargain.

By the time I returned from India, any lingering hopes that my adventure might be anything but a solo affair had evaporated. That, and the fact I was halfway around the world without a ticket home or a plan, both freed and focused the mind wonderfully.

62: Return to Oz
14 May 2006

I've returned to Oz and my beautiful house in Sydney. The weather is cooler and the food less spicy. There are seven months left on my Australian visa.

At this point I can – if I wish – do something more financially rewarding than working in the hospitality industry. So this week, I had a meeting with an agency in the Central Business District interested in employing me in a role where I'd have to wear a suit and work in an office. They were positive meetings and good people, but I'm not interested.

For a start, working in a professional office job would require getting sponsored and staying in Australia for more than a year. That's not an option I'm even slightly moved to consider. I'm entirely happy with my life in England, I don't want to swap it for anything else and, if I want to work in an office, I can do that in London. As for the financial rewards, this is a pilgrimage, not a shopping excursion.

I will therefore make use of my Newtown base to get under the skin of Australian society, plan my next move and finish the Qur'an.

Qur'an update: there are some quarters where Islam is perceived as being warlike or misogynistic. I've always been wary of such perspectives. I believe the evolution of religion is intertwined with that of culture and impossible to disentangle from it. Reading the Qur'an is reinforcing, rather than challenging, that conviction.

However, I would say it's clear that the text was written within a culture which was misogynistic by twenty-first-century standards and *at* war. It's easy to see how, isolated from their context, individual passages could (through ignorance or deceit) be misinterpreted to mean something that they do not.

Things that happen in Newtown: on King Street there's a gentleman driving an electric wheelchair and holding a long-neck beer bottle. Not being able to walk is absolutely no reason not to dress in leather and cover oneself in tattoos. Attached to the wheelchair is a stereo and speaker system, which blasts out thrash metal while he manoeuvres his vehicle on and off the pavement like a lunatic. On a nearby wall is some black and white street art.

It reads: 'fashion kills individuality'.

Days since leaving London: 353
Proportion of
 Earth's population that lives in Australia: 0.31%
 Gold medals won by Australia at the 2004 Athens Olympiad: 5.65%

We are here on Earth to fart around and don't let anyone tell you different. – Kurt Vonnegut

63: Snake House
23 May 2006

Changes are afoot at 119 Australia Street.

Chantel has made a long-planned move back to Queensland to live with her boyfriend Kris. Adam and she are soul mates, so this is a big watershed in both their lives. We had a series of goodbye events during her last week in town, then on the final evening I left them to it. When I returned that night I noted that the furniture in the living room had been moved and guessed at once that they'd been dancing to 1980s music again. They do that pretty regularly.

To make the transition easier for Adam, I remind him that even though Chantel has a chiselled and devoted boyfriend to look after her in Brisbane, Adam has me. He doesn't seem to find that particularly comforting.

Eden will be our new housemate. His plans for the house include a revitalisation of the feng shui and a beer factory in the garden shed. He's also brought his pet, 'Chuck', a three-foot diamond python. At first I was alarmed by the prospect of sharing a house with a carnivorous reptile;

however, while I'm normally a people person rather than a pet person, I at once developed an uncharacteristic fascination for Chuck. I've been spending long periods staring into his glass tank and attempting to mind-meld with him. I believe he may be waiting until he's larger before trying to eat me.

I've commandeered Chantel's room (the biggest) and renamed it 'The Master Bedroom'. It has a large window with multicoloured glass panes, beneath which I've placed my bookshelf and desk. From here I shall look out onto Australia Street, muse upon the world and write it all down in my big black book.

Qur'an update: my copy comes with an extensive commentary by the translator, M. A. S. Haleem. In that commentary he often describes the text as offering 'proofs' or 'refutations' to claims made by unbelievers or others with whom it is taking issue. I don't agree that the text offers either proofs or refutations. What it does is make counter-statements, which is not the same thing at all. Saying 'God created the heavens and the Earth, therefore God exists' is not a proof.

Days since leaving London: 362

> *The known is finite, the unknown infinite; intellectually we stand on an islet in the midst of an illimitable ocean of inexplicability. Our business in every generation is to reclaim a little more land.* – T. H. Huxley

64: 365 Days on the Road
27 May 2006

It's one year since the spring afternoon when I got on Nelly the cyclatron outside my old London home and began heading east. I'm now halfway through this pilgrimage and halfway around the world. On the whole I'm feeling moderately pleased with the progress of my scheme to undertake a multifaceted adventure across planet Earth at the start of the third millennium and during the dawning of the Age of Aquarius.

Honk honk.

Sydney's bohemian quarter is proving an increasingly interesting waypoint. Newtown's current human geography involves a critical mass of artists, hippies and students grooving the place up; and the young urban professionals that have followed them in to soak up the atmosphere. Right now it's got the creativity of the former, the economic vibrancy of the latter and plenty of eccentrics (feeling comfortable just being themselves) who add spice.

The trend is towards gentrification. I'm told that 10 years ago it was much grungier. I suspect that 10 years hence, the artists will have moved on.

King Street, Newtown's heart, is the most interesting road in Sydney, with top-notch people-watching opportunities, ubiquitous coffee shops and rambling second-hand bookstalls. Surrounding it is an arc of solid, old housing stock in which garage sales are a social feature and VW vans have the names of Cat Stevens songs painted on them.

From there I walk downhill to Victoria Park's open-air pool and swim myself into physical highs beyond a vista of the downtown skyscrapers, sparkling beneath the clear blue air above.

I've finished the Holy Qur'an. To begin with I was extremely impressed. Its opening suras magnificently implore forgiveness, moderation and compassion between humans. However, after this glorious start it goes back repeatedly – almost obsessively – to the same things: 'disbelievers' will suffer eternal torment, 'believers' will go to heaven, 'God' is the only god, Muhammad is his prophet and, one day, there will be a Judgement Day. If this is God's supreme message for humankind, intended for all times and places, then the range of subjects upon which it makes pronouncements is startlingly narrow.

My new reading material is a field guide to whales, dolphins and porpoises (cetaceans). I'm starting to brim with knowledge regarding our splendid water-based cousins. When I'm at the pool, and think no one will notice, I sometimes pretend that I am one …

Splish splash.

Days since leaving London: 365
Number of verses in the Qur'an: 6,200
Verses dealing with

Ritual practice:	100	Penal laws:	30
Personal laws:	70	Judiciary matters and testimony:	20
Civil laws:	70		

Bear in mind that the present life is just a game, a diversion, a distraction, a cause of boasting among you, of rivalry in wealth and children. – The Qur'an

Cosmological Interlude

Before I say anything more about the Abrahamic faiths, here is some background as to how those faiths (Judaism, Christianity and Islam) and their respective scriptures (sacred texts) fit together.

The Jewish faith holds that God sent His message to humankind through a series of prophets, and that this message is recorded in the Jewish Bible (which Christians call the Old Testament).

The Christians agree with this, but also believe that God subsequently incarnated Himself on Earth in the form of Jesus Christ and that this, and associated events, are documented in the New Testament. Together the Old and New Testaments constitute the Christian Bible.

The Muslims agree with all of the above except that they believe that Jesus was a prophet, not God. The Muslims further hold that Muhammad (who lived about 600 years after Jesus) was God's last and greatest prophet and received His final message (technically via the Angel Gabriel), which he then delivered to humankind. That final message both complemented and completed the earlier ones and is recorded in the Qur'an.

Abraham was one of the first Old Testament patriarchs and is thought to have come from the Mesopotamian city of Ur. He is the traditional founder of the Jewish religion (and by extension the other two) and is revered by all three faiths.

All of this took place between around 2100 BCE (when the earliest Old Testament patriarchs lived) and 632 CE (when Muhammad died). The question of why God chose to reveal His final, eternal message to humankind over that period is not addressed, though I note that it was shortly after writing had been invented and towards the beginning of what would later be known as recorded history.

*****

The Abrahamic faiths all claim the same essential spiritual architecture for the universe. The essentials of that architecture are as follows.

A 'being' (God) exists. God is infallible, all-powerful and all-knowing, created reality and controls everything in the universe. God is possessed of at least some characteristics broadly comprehensible to humans (for example, He communicates with us). He also has plans for creation which are at some level comprehensible to humans.

God has chosen to impart certain ethical and cosmological information to humankind. For example: we shalt have no God but Him and, one day, there will be a Judgement Day. He has chosen to accomplish this by putting that information into the heads of certain individuals throughout history (the prophets and witnesses who wrote or inspired Abrahamic scripture) and, in the Christian view, at one point directly incarnating Himself as a human being.

He has done this in the knowledge that it would cause the relevant information to be written down (in the form of the various holy scriptures) and that those writings would subsequently act as a guide for humanity as to how to correctly manage its affairs until this current phase of reality draws to a close.

That drawing to a close will be marked by some sort of 'Armageddon' or 'Judgement Day'. Personally, I thought the Old and New Testaments were rather unspecific as to the wider purpose of that all-encompassing cosmic watershed.

The Qur'an, however, is unambiguous about it. Life is a diversion. This phase of reality is finite. Its purpose is to judge human beings in preparation for the next phase of reality, which will be infinite.

When the Day of Judgement comes all the humans who have ever existed will be divided up. Some will go to hell. Others, depending on how they lived, to heaven. Heaven is explicitly described. It consists of sitting on couches, drinking flagons of pure drink, eating fruit and meat and conversing on clean and wholesome matters, for eternity.

And that, in extreme summary, is what the Abrahamic religious systems claim is going on with this reality-universe-existence gig in which we find ourselves.

*****

When my Indian friends learned that I was reading the Qur'an, they became anxious that I should also read the Bhagavadgita (a key Hindu text), preferably at least two interpretations. Abhishek's sister's father-in-law delivered a compelling lecture on the multifaceted religious map of India and urged me to immerse myself in it.

But studying holy books is a time-consuming business and there were other things I wanted to muse upon during my journey. As a result of the holy books I did read, my ultimate thesis inevitably shows the influence of Middle Eastern, rather than Far Eastern or Indian,

religious traditions. Nonetheless, the way of thinking about the world I ultimately tried to capture is intended to be relevant across all traditions. Reading the Bible and the Qur'an gave structure to the journey which got me there.

65: Days Go By
27 June 2006

It's winter. Australia is a whirlwind of football, champagne and kangaroos – those cheeky little blighters get bloody everywhere. Here's what I've been up to.

Saturday 10ᵗʰ June

02.30 Australian Eastern Standard Time: Finish running a bar at the opening of the Sydney Film Festival on The Rocks above Sydney Cove. The crowd is chic and beautiful. I'm the free champagne guy. Everybody loves me.

03.30: Get back to Newtown in time to catch the end of Costa Rica vs Germany. The World Cup, in all of its gloriously epic pantomime, is under way on the far side of the world. Australia's team ('The Socceroos') are in the competition for the first time in 24 years. Anything could happen. It doesn't get any more exciting than this.

23.00: England win their first game. Phew.

Sunday 11ᵗʰ June

12.00: Summoned by Eden, Magnificent Michelle of bush doof fame rocks up with her sidekick Brittany, who is 18 and likes to shake it.

16.00: Arrive at We Love Sounds winter music festival at the Fox movie studios in Randwick. Eight thousand ravers are 'having it'.

20.00: The DJ mixes the Pet Shop Boys' 'It's a Sin' with the Beach Boys' 'Wouldn't It Be Nice'. It's one of those wondrous moments of musical clarity.

Monday 12ᵗʰ June

02.00: The festival closes so we take a taxi to Kings Cross, Sydney's infamous sleazy district, and hit the clubs.

06.00: Arrive back at 119 Australia Street to demand fine wine and cakes.

12.00: Drinking blue-and-green cocktails from Martini glasses in the living room. Adam has joined us. The music is unusually glorious.

15.00: In the yard. The chicks have left. The beer is cold. The sun is hot.

Tuesday 13ᵗʰ June

00.00: Still awake. The Socceroos annihilate Japan in their opening game, with three goals in the last 10 minutes. It's a fully fledged orgasmic Aussie sports moment.

07.00: Go to bed.

Friday 16ᵗʰ June

04.00: Football and time differences are playing havoc with my sleeping patterns. Wake up and go to work. Work eight hours, sleep three hours, work another eight hours, sleep another three hours, watch England game, sleep 90 minutes, work six hours, sit in a park with Japanese friend Shunji drinking beer, go for a swim, then back to work again.

18.00: One of my co-workers declares that Australia will win the World Cup before England. I roll my eyes in despair at the boy's ignorance. The shift lasts six hours, then I go home and go to bed properly.

Saturday 17ᵗʰ June

22.00: After sleeping all day I meet Glen, last seen at Club Babylon in Istanbul six months ago. He's just got back from the Nepalese civil war. The stories are harrowing. We talk through the night.

Sunday 18ᵗʰ June

23.00: The Socceroos are about to go up against Brazil. It's their biggest game ever. We're at Australia Street. The gang are arriving one by one. The mood is hopeful.

Monday 19ᵗʰ June

02.00: We arrive downtown at Circular Quay. There are 5,000 people and a very large screen. The atmosphere is boisterous.

03.30: Brazil smashes The Socceroos.

04.00: A fat man in the crowd is rude to me. I go after him, but am restrained by Georgia.

09.00: In the back yard at Australia Street with Glen. The sun is coming up and we can't stop drinking tea. The world is set to rights. Reconsidering my decision to go after that fat dude. Now feeling rather embarrassed about it.

17.00: Wake up, go straight to desk and start writing things down. Bursting with inspiration.

Wednesday 21ˢᵗ June

16.00: Work a shift at the Australian Museum at the opening of a new Egypt exhibition. The Coptic bishop arrives with a bulbous black hat and an authentic, bona fide gem-encrusted staff. I wait for him to cast some sort of magic spell. Straight from there to a cocktail party for an Antarctic exploration group. The room is filled with giraffe and elephant skeletons. I'm the free champagne guy. Everybody loves me.

23.00: Life in Sydney isn't sufficiently madcap. I go round the Pitt Street strip clubs, asking for a job as a barman. Get knocked back.

Thursday 22nd June

21.00: Work a charity fundraiser for the zoo at The Establishment on George Street, Sydney's swankiest club. Podgy businessmen in finely tailored suits and their fawning red-hot wives. Windows on worlds.

Friday 23rd June

05.00: Dragged out of bed by Eden to watch Australia vs Croatia. The Croatians go a bit mental. The referee loses control. There are five yellow cards and three players are sent off. Australia come from behind to secure a 2-2 draw and go through to the second round. They deserve it.

Saturday 24th June

17.00: Staff a wedding at a posh downtown convention centre. The groom is approaching 300 pounds and arrives with food poisoning. The DJ has no chin and keeps playing Bryan Adams. It's all a bit tense.

Monday 26th June

01.00: Straight from work to a pub full of Englishmen for England vs Ecuador. David Beckham's free kick is technically perfect. England go through to the quarter finals. Yeehah.

21.30: Watch Coldplay live at the Sydney Entertainment Centre. They are confident, up for it and at the height of their powers. Mesmerising.

Tuesday 27th June

00.00: Straight from the gig to Sydney's Leichhardt, the Italian quarter, to watch Australia vs Italy on a big screen with a bipartisan crowd of 10,000. It's rowdy.

00.30: The premier of New South Wales, when asked which team he supports, uses the fact that he has an Italian grandparent to make a tragic grasp for ethnic identity. And I quote: 'Aussie, Aussie, Aussie, si, si, si.' Tosser.

03.00: Italy win with a dodgy penalty in the ninety-third minute. Shocking.

After the game Italian supporters started letting off flares. As we made our way home towards Newtown, trails of thick red smoke swirled around forlorn bodies draped in Australian flags. I attempted to lighten the mood with the following gag: 'Well, at least England are through. That's the important thing.' Apparently, that wasn't in the slightest bit amusing. Funny old game.

Days since leaving London: 397

Note to reader: England were beaten 3-1 on penalties by Portugal in their next match. That will teach me not to brag.

66: The Enemy Within
30 June 2006

New South Wales has a colossal gambling problem. There are fruit machines ('pokies') in every joint in town. Put aside thoughts of Las Vegas-style razzle and bling. Think instead of morbid rooms full of chain-smokers feeding high-denomination bills into machines that flash lights while playing ghastly plinky-plonk music.

People have weird priorities. Don't they know that $50 could buy them a lovely meal and a bottle of wine at the restaurant I'm running upstairs? They could read a nice book or something?

I regard this as a serious challenge to my liberal principles. As a general rule I believe people should do as they please, including run or use fruit machines. Yet when I see them in action I feel a hankering to ban them as a senseless waste of money and time.

On one occasion I was put in charge of the fruit machine area. Naturally I interpreted this as fate inviting me to sabotage my brothers' and sisters' unhappy relationship with gambling and encourage them towards more rewarding pastimes. While cleaning ashtrays and singing to myself, a rather sad lady asked why I was happy.

I pointed out that money is a useful conceptual tool for ordering civilisation which has become linked to human status and, by extension, self-worth. I then pointed out that life is actually lived inside the box of one's own mind and that it doesn't matter how you fare in our human games of prestige, what other people think about you or, for that matter, how much money you've got. She left, there and then, with a smile on her face and holding the remains of her pay cheque. I'm convinced that this will lead to positive karma.

On the subject of karma, further to my recent readings of the Bible and the Qur'an, it's time to start talking spiritual architecture.

Whenever Abrahamic scripture turns its attention to women, their interests are automatically assumed to be subservient to those of men. The Bible is full of portrayals of women as evil sexual predators. Warnings against adultery concern themselves exclusively with the evils of women seducing men. The evils of men seducing women are never addressed, which seems inappropriate given the dynamics of sex in the real world. The Old Testament spends far more time condemning prostitutes than it ever does liars or murderers.

This is a shame. Dealing with the problems raised by sex – particularly the problem of how to protect the interests of women – is just the sort of area where humanity could do with a little divine guidance.

The Qur'an calls repeatedly for the protection of women's interests (with one hiccup where it says you can slap your wife). In fact I got the feeling that in the context of seventh-century Arabia, it was probably a progressively feminist creed. However, it's entirely written from a male point of view.

The instructions around divorce are addressed specifically to men, not people in general. When heaven is described (and it is described several times), the descriptions uniformly gush about the beautiful and good-natured maidens that will 'attend' to anyone who ends up there. Unless Islamic scripture contains a hidden lesbian dogma which I've missed, my assumption is that this information is provided for the benefit of men. It is never mentioned whether women who go to heaven will receive male attendants.

Of course, it's possible that this is a punishment for being deceived by the serpent in the Garden of Eden, which will teach those women for going apple scrumping.

Days since leaving London: 400
Rate of gambling-attributed suicides in New South Wales: 1 per week

67: Mozart and Other Miracles
5 July 2006

One of the fun things about working in the hospitality industry is the tips. My best tip so far was from some musicians: tickets worth $70 to see a rendition of Mozart's Requiem. The music was spellbinding: fervent, passionate and evoking a vision of humanity redeemed through its art and reconciled with nature and the infinite. It made my spine tingle.

The worst tippers are the politicians. Working at the New South Wales parliament I was appalled to learn that it's common for tables of eight to gorge themselves on (taxpayer-subsidised) food only to leave the most trifling of tips, if one at all.

On the important subject of whether spending decisions should be made by politicians, what is Australia (20 million people) doing with three levels of government (federal, state and local) anyway? The USA (300 million people) and India (1.1 billion) have the same number. After observing first hand the expensive infrastructure maintained by the taxpayer on behalf of the second tier, I can report that no expense is spared on it (except when it comes to tips). There's even a special bell which rings when not enough of them are in the chamber because they're too busy living it up (and not leaving tips). I listened to one (unimaginative) speech by the leader of the state opposition criticising the incumbent's taxation policy. Simply abolishing himself apparently hadn't crossed his mind.

I've been continuing my post-Qur'anic musings. Miracles are a recurring theme in both the Bible and the Qur'an. There is an unspoken assumption running through both books, and much of human culture, that miracles are a relevant way for God to prove His existence.

In the Old Testament there are many instances where the prophets use miracles to prove that they speak for God. This differentiates them from the false prophets, who do not speak for God and cannot therefore perform miracles. In the New Testament there are numerous miracles performed by, and associated with the life of, Jesus. The Qur'an records no new miracles, but states repeatedly that those described in the Old Testament (particularly those of Moses) prove that God is real. However, it then rejects the idea of producing additional miracles on the basis that God does not need to prove Himself.

In short, claims that God does not need to prove Himself with miracles lie alongside claims that past miracles prove the existence of God.

I reject the whole principle of supernatural miracles. I see miracles around me all the time. In fact, I live in one. The universe does not need to be reduced to a pantomime sound-and-light show in order to prove something about God as a short cut to enlightenment.

The conjecture that there is an entity ('God') who creates a universe that operates on rules but then needs to step outside those rules to get things done indicates a striking lack of imagination. God (who can do anything, remember) could simply be more cunning about His initial rules without recourse to this crude and silly miracle nonsense.

I believe supernatural miracles are an example of an archaic, abstract concept, stuck in our collective psyche, that is a relic of a time when things were explained in terms of magic. If the human race is to construct a functional long-term spiritual framework for thinking about how it relates to the infinite, surely such concepts should now be set aside.

Chuck the Python update: I've developed an almost paternal interest in Chuck the Python's welfare. I often find myself nipping over to his tank to see what he's up to. Having looked up diamond pythons on Wikipedia, I've now declared myself the house expert on constrictor snakes. I level criticisms at Eden that he is insufficiently responsible to look after a python. He taunts me that I am middle-aged and loopy. Whippersnapper.

Days since leaving London: 405
Length of fully grown diamond python: 3 metres (9 feet)
World's biggest snake: the green anaconda, 8.8 metres (29 feet), 227 kilograms (500 pounds)

A donkey with a bunch of holy books is still a donkey. – Sufi proverb

68: Bishops and Bohemians
11 July 2006

I first met Glen in Istanbul last year. The fact he's from Newtown is a coincidence. He returned from his own around-the-world odyssey last month, following a road trip across Alaska, a month in Kashmir and ending up in Kathmandu just as the Nepalese civil war was spilling onto its streets.

Glen holds a different view from me on the state of humanity. He takes a broadly pessimistic position: it's not looking good; the global establishment is made up of irredeemable bastards; civilisation will send the ecosphere into meltdown. Meanwhile, my position is largely optimistic: the human condition has never been better; we're fundamentally on the right track; planetary climate management was always going to be tricky.

Joint meditation on these matters has become a rewarding feature of Newtown life. Our other main discussion point has been the long-anticipated arrival of his girlfriend/lover/muse, Gemma-Lee.

Here's the deal: Glen and Gemma-Lee went out when Glen lived in the UK in 2005. They kept in touch. Gemma-Lee (21, from Leeds) has never left Britain before. A week ago she flew to Australia and straight into the house, room and bed of our lad. Culture shock. It's hare-brained and wilfully romantic and I wholeheartedly approve. Gemma-Lee turns out to be a bit of a character. Noteworthy attributes include great physical beauty, lots of piercings and a thick northern-English accent. Proper Yorkshire lass. Love it.

I've just run a lunch for Australia's number two Catholic bishop at his residence above Sydney Harbour. Bishop Anthony got to the top via the academic route. He holds a doctorate in medical ethics and has bookshelves filled with religious philosophy; on his cabinet there is a reliquary containing a bone fragment from the remains of Thomas Aquinas.

The lunch was for trainee priests. They were pleasant, but I found them an unworldly, wet-behind-the-ears bunch. No iron-willed Jesuits on missions from God, these. I had a long discussion with the bishop's assistant about the morality of contraception, abortion and masturbation. We also discussed the Bible ...

I'm of the view that religious systems are, and have always been, intrinsically more dynamic than is commonly assumed. I think it's in the nature of such systems to continually evolve in reflection of the communities for which they serve as a focus, but that evolution was disrupted by the invention of writing.

Before writing, religious systems were transmitted orally. New developments in the wider world could therefore be easily incorporated into them. However, once writing was invented, ideas became set in stone and, the more time that passed, the less relevant the form of the original written message became.

I imagine the Old Testament set out a perfectly relevant spiritual architecture for the ancient Middle Eastern agrarian societies in which it was written. But thousands of years later, when I was cycling across Europe and Leviticus solemnly declared that I should stone to death women who have sex with animals and not sacrifice my children to Moloch, it became a challenge to take Abraham's legacy seriously.

Reading the Bible and the Qur'an has convinced me that, despite the wisdom they contain, both are products of their own time, not all time; for time has, and continues to, move on.

Days since leaving London: 411
Approximate date of earliest

Proto-writing:	8000 BCE	(Sumer, southern Iraq)
Writing:	3200 BCE	(Eanna Temple Complex, Uruk, Sumer)
Literature:	2600 BCE	(Texts from Abu Salabikh, Sumer)
Stories in the Bible written down:		1200 BCE

Say nothing of my religion. It is known to God and myself alone. Its evidence before the world is to be sought in my life: if it has been honest and dutiful to society the religion which has regulated it cannot be a bad one. – Thomas Jefferson

69: Abraham's Legacy
19 July 2006

I do not hold the view that God made His will known to humankind between 2100 BCE and 632 CE, and that this will is recorded in the Jewish and Christian Bibles and the Muslim Qur'an. Nor do I believe that these texts represent God's attempt to outline for humanity its correct moral (and other) conduct for all time. I believe that if those texts were the work of an all-powerful being doing something so momentous, they would be … well … more comprehensive.

One could argue that their flaws are a consequence of them coming to us through the prism of the human prophets and witnesses who revealed them, and the translations that those unable to read the original tongues (like me) must study them in. However, bringing into being texts which, even given such factors, were still eternally and entirely meaningful is just the sort of thing an omnipotent God could, and even might, do.

I take the strong view that these texts, at least in a literal sense, are the product of human rather than divine hands and that this is clear from the themes they concern themselves with. For example, in the New Testament, the omnipotent creator of the universe supposedly condemns people for having long hair; and, in sura 16 of the Qur'an (named, chillingly, The Bee), those who call angels 'daughters of God' are denounced because daughters are apparently inferior to sons and this might therefore be offensive to angels.

However, the key example is the single ubiquitous theme running through all of these religious scriptures: the insistence that one must accept God as the only God and that not to do so is to utterly antagonise Him; that an infinite and infallible being has such an uneasy vanity that He is offended by those who doubt His existence.

Not only do I not buy that, I think it's silly. I believe that such condemnations are not the product of divine will, but of a different and less noble will.

But I am no spiritual nihilist. I do not take a negative view of these religious traditions nor of their role in the human world. I believe spiritual belief systems are a fundamental component of how we, as humans, relate to the universe. My wish therefore is to engage with, rather than reject, the established faiths.

I hope the human race is now reaching a point where unhelpful discussions about the literal truth of parts of those texts which are clearly metaphorical (e.g. God created the stars on a Thursday) can be set aside. We're now in a position to articulate a more complete understanding of these religious faiths, what they are and why they are a feature of our world: one in which they are a fundamental component of humanity's spiritual experience thus far and an intrinsic part of the journey that brought us to where we are.

That journey can now be used as the foundation for a more comprehensive appreciation of how humanity relates to the rest of the universe: one in which our lives are not just purposeful, but an element in a grander, bolder and wildly more exciting narrative.

Days since leaving London: 419

Among the repulsions of atheism for me has been its drastic uninterestingness as an intellectual position. – John Updike

Musings
Straight to Camera

The zany corner of Australia I'd found to live in was an excellent place to extrapolate the infinite from the everyday. Life was simple but colourful, with lots of inspiration and plenty of time to think. My feet were firmly in the gutter, but my head was in the clouds and my eyes were fixed, unwaveringly, upon the stars.

Here's how I read it: you, me, everyone alive, everyone who's ever lived and everyone who ever will live are on an adventure together. Until recently, the wisest understood this in principle, but no one had a handle on the parameters. Myths, legends and religious parables were our main tools for making sense of infinity and humanity's relationship to it. That's now changing.

Collectively, the human race has begun to piece together its own story and comprehend what it's part of. The past is turning out to be remarkable, the future enigmatic and the cosmos mind-blowing. As for this epoch, its most striking features – it transpires – were shaped by two transitions through which the human world has recently passed. Together they have sent that world into flux.

The first of these transitions was the shift to agriculture as our main method of food production, a process which began about 12,000 years ago.

The initial effects on humanity were detrimental: hundreds of generations afflicted by oppression, instability, malnutrition and bad teeth. A great many of humanity's biggest unresolved problems stem from its effects. But it also created opportunities. Big ones.

The second transition got going about 300 years ago and is now in full swing. Its first obvious manifestation was the Industrial Revolution. But that was just one in a series of related developments (which include the spread of world-changing technologies, a huge expansion in material wealth and dramatic increases in literacy and life expectancy), which are still playing themselves out.

We have a major problem in interpreting this second – current – transition: we're too wrapped up in it to have perspective.

To illustrate what I mean, think about what it was like to live through the initial development of agriculture. Prehistoric humans didn't wake up one day and decide to invent farming. Its adoption took the form of a series of individual steps, across thousands of years, involving small changes in subsistence from one generation to the next.

At certain stages during that process some of the people involved (presumably) grasped that their lifestyles were (slightly) different from those of their parents. But it's only with the depth of hindsight now available that we understand what was going on: humanity was swapping a way of life which had been stable for a million years for a completely different one, irrevocably. As for the ultimate implications – cities, civilisation and the rest – you can be sure those first farmers didn't have the slightest clue.

Similarly, the true nature and implications of this second transition are impossible to identify because we're slap bang in the middle of it. Global society is exceedingly dynamic. We're rushing forward into an unknown future, but we have no idea what it's going to look like. What is human civilisation turning into? What will it be like in another 12,000 years? What, in later ages, will historians make of all this?

We're not even in a position to know which aspects of this transformative period are genuinely significant. Is it the great increase in life spans? The increase in knowledge? Is it the change from rural to urban living as the norm for humankind? The spiralling sophistication of computers? Could it be some aspect of bourgeois culture which we have failed, thus far, to grasp the deeper significance of? Or maybe all those things are just the prelude to something else. Maybe we stand at the threshold of an even more profound set of changes in the human world.

We just don't know. But, in the shadow of Chartres Cathedral, it's something about which I came to an opinion. I believe that the most significant thing about this current transition we're living through is that this is the moment the human race is coming to understand its own context.

*****

Here's the thing: intellectually, we all understand that these twenty-first-century post-industrial societies we inhabit are a chapter in a larger narrative. We understand that humans are a species of carbon-based life form which came into being via a process of evolution by natural selection and which is travelling down an unprecedented and uncharted path (civilisation). Yet, when people consider the world around them, that larger context is generally ignored.

For example, in the Newtown of that Australian winter of 2006, the main gripes of the educated, bohemian crowd within which I found myself were the environment and the (then) government of Prime Minister John Howard.

Mr Howard was considered an evil good-for-nothing because he was economically and socially right-wing and had sent troops to Iraq. The fact that he was in charge was interpreted as a sure sign that the country was under the control of a corrupt establishment with a nefarious agenda.

I don't have anything in particular to say about the merits or otherwise of Mr Howard's government. The observation I do have is that, not only can we now evaluate our political systems beyond the strictures of such black and white tribalism, we now understand why humans are tribal in the first place and can assess those political systems (and their inadequacies) in terms of the 12,000-year dynamic of which they are the current (and temporary) expression. As for our politicians, we can now deconstruct their behaviour right down to the twists of the double helices inside their every cell.

Discussion about the environment was dominated by the climate change issue and peopled with good guys (including Al Gore and Greenpeace) and bad guys (including oil companies and George W. Bush). It's incredibly healthy that we're having those discussions. But not only can we have them, we can be realistic about the context in which we're having them, that is: seven billion monkeys running around on the surface of a planet, organising themselves through socially constructed abstractions (such as businesses, lobbying organisations and political parties) and struggling to make their civilisation environmentally sustainable.

Many areas of human interest, including lots of the really significant ones (such as humanity's relationship with the environment, the existential elements of religious belief and everything about the process of globalisation), make much more sense if you think about them in terms of that wider context. Not just the problems of a bunch of humans in their twenty-first-century societies, but a phase in the story of a species of hyper-intelligent tool-using social omnivores trying to build a technological civilisation from scratch, without an instruction manual.

Getting people to think about what's happening to the world in that context is a lot harder than you might think. Our conceptual systems – our very language – evolved in the pre-industrial, pre-scientific age. We understand the dynamic of our world in terms of vast time frames, but fail to assess it accordingly.

I think it's only a matter of time before that changes. When it does we'll see that most of the issues over which we agonise are the inevitable consequence of the historical context in which we find ourselves. Fate has laid down certain challenges for humanity, but there is every reason to believe that they can be overcome. All of them.

*****

Increasingly, these ideas were pouring into the big black book, where the essentials of my thesis were, by this point, taking shape. They also began informing the email diary.

My instinct was to point out dots and invite people to connect them. What I found, to my increasing frustration, was that the moment you mention God, people pigeonhole you into a predetermined set of positions (atheism, agnosticism or theism) which in my view are largely redundant. When I wrote about Angkor's temples or India's economic history there was a presumption that I was making standalone throwaway comments. I wasn't.

That was how I came to realise that, if I wanted people to understand what I was getting at, I was going to have to spell it out. So, from my home at 119 Australia Street, I drew up plans to find a corner of the world where I could do that systematically. That path led me to South America and, ultimately, to the book you hold in your hands.

70: The Newtown Zeitgeist
21 July 2006

The house vibe has gone from strength to strength of late. Every time I come home I am sucked into some fascinating new discussion about life, death, art, music, books, the world and what it's all about. I have taken to dispensing my newly acquired whale knowledge and covering the fridge in articles I feel everyone should read. We've adopted an excellent volunteer-run local radio station (FBI) and spend lots of time discussing its superb DJ sets. Then, when the others are out, I tune into the BBC World Service and listen for the news.

Adam's drama school recently put on a triumphant Hamlet and he's been educating me on literary criticism and Australian theatre. He's also acquired a magnificent dressing gown (Kmart is the rumour) in which he swans around the house. It makes him look almost exactly like Hugh Hefner. I'm thinking of getting one too.

Eden's life presses forward with soap-operatic drama. He's commenced a degree in renewable energy engineering and rushes around Sydney cooking up troublemaking schemes. Every couple of days or so he'll announce with great solemnity that some female or other is the most beautiful he's ever come across. He returns late at night to relay his adventures over the kitchen table, full of infectious energy, eyes darting about, furiously eating honey and yoghurt with a spoon.

A previous tenant at 119 Australia Street held a subscription to the *Philadelphia Trumpet* from which we now benefit. It's an ultra-radical, fundamentalist Christian-Jewish publication and its positions include: all Muslims are evil and California suffers earthquakes because it's under a curse. Its main source for these assertions is the Old Testament. The standard of journalism is poor.

Chuck the Python update: our in-house diamond python is normally the most leisured of creatures. However, when presented with a juicy rodent it turns out that Chuck is able to move, quite literally, faster than the eye can see. It's really quite shocking. Eden has started keeping dead mice in the freezer.

Days since leaving London: 421
Typical weight of a

Common dolphin:	70–110 kilograms
Strap-toothed whale:	1–3 tonnes
Humpback whale:	25–30 tonnes
Bowhead whale:	58–98 tonnes
Blue whale:	98–118 tonnes

Eat vegans – stop cows' pain. – Graffiti, Newtown

71: The Nymph, the Armenian and the Maori
1 August 2006

I first met Zoe Joyce in April at the Sydney Opera House. She's petite, Welsh and obviously highly amused by this whole 'being alive' malarkey. On further investigation it turns out she's been through life at the sharp end, grew up with travellers and first met her dad when she was in her twenties. Some people feel sorry for themselves when life is hard. Others emerge wiser, stronger and more determined. I like those people. I really like Zoe.

She's become a trusted confidante and a key part of my inner Sydney family. We've had two key moments of clarity. The first was dinner on King Street when we swapped life stories and then, during a freak power cut, danced cheek to cheek in candlelight while listening to Frank Sinatra through her iPod. The second was an evening where we went back to Australia Street, put on cowboy hats and sang along to Johnny Cash's 'Ring of Fire'. She's disconcertingly attractive, extremely gregarious and spectacularly good fun.

Zoe had already told me about Kiko, so when I saw him one evening, I walked straight over, shook his hand and introduced myself. That's how I learned that we have similar ideas about good manners. Kiko is ethnically Armenian, but grew up in Georgia. When nationalist tensions were turning nasty in 1994, he and his entire family split the country in the middle of the night. There followed a headlong rush across eastern Europe until his grandfather's passport mysteriously disappeared near Budapest.

This landed them a two-year stint in a Hungarian refugee camp. The camp was full of exiles from the Yugoslav Wars, and the Bosnians and Croats lumped Kiko's family with the Serbians (due to their Orthodox religious convictions) in their in-camp inter-group squabbles. During a visit from the Canadian immigration minister, Kiko provoked him into stating publicly that non-Yugoslav refugees could also apply for asylum. That brought the home run of Canadian citizenship and peace in Ottawa.

This life story has left Kiko with a music collection which ranges from Russian folk to American rockabilly and so many original things to say that visits to his flat are becoming a regular feature of Newtown life. One morning Eden and I were playing air guitar in the kitchen when we received an invitation to head over. There we sat on Kiko's balcony and listened to Bob Marley in the sun, when a stupendously powerful hailstorm crashed over the city. The Prodigy's 'Firestarter' went straight on the sound system as the ice roared around. Electrifying.

Said storm was eerily predicted by Kiko's flatmate Steve. Steve is a New Zealander of Maori descent and full of Polynesian knowledge about weather and navigation. He recently took up paintbrushes after a 20-year break and creates colourful landscapes and nudes (based, to his regret, on imagination). I've been among the first to witness Steve's emerging creative dynamic and am officially following the man's work.

Days since leaving London: 432
Population of

Wales:	2,958,876
Armenia:	2,900,000
New Zealand:	4,200,000

It isn't necessary to have relatives in Kansas City in order to be unhappy. – Groucho Marx

72: Preachers and Millionaires
14 August 2006

Since returning from India my living expenses have mainly been provided by the Nosh hospitality agency. They send me to jobs across the city, providing opportunities to observe all sorts of interesting corners of Australian society.

I did one gig serving coffee for a Christian sect in a marquee behind the Opera House. When I arrived at nine o'clock on Monday morning they already had their guitars out and were breaking into spontaneous 'hallelujahs'. The walls were covered with Israeli flags and colourful banners suggesting mystical 'gates' hidden in corners of the Middle East.

This was definitely not a subculture I'd normally be exposed to and I made sure I listened to as many of the preachers as possible. I wasn't personally convinced that they were articulating a sound, well-informed and internally consistent spiritual belief system. Nonetheless, while their ideas were fanciful, everyone there was sincere, unpretentious and extremely polite.

I was a little uncomfortable about two dinners at the United Grand Lodge of New South Wales (the Freemasons), but the gig turned out to be a cinch. I took the opportunity to snoop around and read their literature. The first crowd was 100 per cent male, 100 per cent white and 80 per cent obese. The food was pub-style chips and steak. During the second dinner, a visitor from Barbados made a speech reporting that they were 'almost there' in persuading the younger English prince to join up. I found that rather sinister.

I got requested for a private dinner at the home of one of Australia's 100 richest, who needed somebody reliable, with expertise in looking after drunk people, to mix cocktails for him and his chums. The mansion was awesome. It included two bars, an underground garage full of BMWs and Mercedes, a lift servicing all three floors, prime harbour views and a bewildering array of boys' toys.

On arrival the client showed me exactly how he liked his caprioskas mixed: one and a half freshly squeezed limes, two tablespoons of sugar, crushed ice, then – wait for it – 'three shots for a woman, four shots for a man', and I looked on – wide-eyed – as he dumped four shots of Absolut into the cocktail shaker. Fair play, dude.

Half the guests had drunk two of those bad boys before the entrée. By the middle of the main course he'd already ripped the stockings off one of the girls. My tip was a $100 bill.

Days since leaving London: 445
Estimated typical weight of Argentinosaurus, the biggest dinosaur known: 73 tonnes
Weight of the biggest blue whale ever accurately measured: 187 tonnes
Number of humans that could stand on the tongue of a blue whale: 50

Don't pray in my school, I won't think in your church. – US bumper sticker

73: Human Flotsam
16 August 2006

Sydney, being the glamorous, international place it is, draws people in from across the world. Notable expat communities include the Italians (we can thank them for the coffee), the Chinese (inexorably on the rise) and the Brazilians (think: highly trained scientists working as cleaners). Being a traveller is a widely understood pigeonhole and backpacker culture (characteristically twentyish, middle class and mildly adventurous) is as visible here as anywhere outside of the world's great beach Meccas.

I regard this human manifestation of the current planetary coming together (also known as globalisation) as extremely positive and look forward to seeing what kind of synthesised world society emerges. Given this mixing-pot environment, the hospitality world is full of wanderers, long-term transients and people who've never known where to settle down.

Whenever I work at Parliament House, Bernard makes sure we polish glasses together. He was brought up in Vienna during its occupation by the four Allied powers (he reports that the Americans were easily the best) and still bears attractive Germanic inflections in his accent. He came to Australia in the 1960s as a professional football player, when the prospects for young men were brighter here than in post-war Europe and footballers had normal salaries. His native-born son is a managing director earning ten times Bernard's salary (he's very proud). Employment law changes have prompted his imminent retirement and he received a shiny trophy for his efforts. Bernard's family in Austria run a famous vineyard and, as one of the team, he gets a key. He's relishing the prospect.

I spent a short period waiting tables with Paul, who is eloquent, opinionated and camp. Paul taught me about the culture of international hospitality (yes, there is one) in an endearingly snobbish manner. ('The Australian chefs rate themselves among the world's best,' he scoffs at their naivety.) In the evening Paul takes on the persona of Paula, who dresses more garishly, plays guitar and works the cabaret circuit. Paula's career is taking off after a well-deserved break. Paul will soon be leaving his day job.

Timo, an easygoing boss, was married in his native Helsinki to his first (Australian) wife. They were only supposed to come here for a couple of years, but when it came time to return she refused ('Bitch,' he said). By then a baby daughter meant he couldn't bring himself to leave. Twenty years later he's still bitter about it.

Days since leaving London: 447

If at first you don't succeed, skydiving is not for you. – Anon

74: Dispossession
25 August 2006

On Friday night the gang went downtown to celebrate Zoe's birthday. We danced until sunrise. Saturday morning found us all in the yard at 119 Australia Street sitting around a fire. The sun was bright, the sky was blue and the air was bracing. It was the start of a beautiful day. Everyone was drunk. I had no idea what the time was.

Edward was an old friend of Zoe's from the UK. I'd never met him before. He chose that moment to start shooting his mouth off. His subject of choice was Australia's indigenous (also known as Aboriginal) peoples. They've been in the papers recently. Edward had clearly been thinking about them. He declared that indigenous children should be taken away from their natural parents and put in special schools to provide them with (and I quote) 'role models'.

Adam and Glen are both sanctimonious lefties and were, not unreasonably, outraged. Things turned nasty. Voices were raised. Fingers were pointed.

Racially charged rows are not an ideal way to wind down after all-night parties. To keep the peace, I stepped in, cornered Edward, and made him talk to me about it.

Australia's indigenous peoples have had a rough couple of centuries. It's been a bleak and chaotic period in their history, and modern Australia agonises over how best to assist indigenous communities torn apart by 200 years of humiliation and social vandalism. By the mid-1960s, all Australians of indigenous descent had been given the vote. Since then there's been a gradual attempt at reconciliation via the dispensation of money and land, and the acknowledgement of past misdeeds.

Yet, across this continent, indigenous communities remain plagued by alcoholism, low self-esteem and an inability to shape their own destiny. News of deprivation within them periodically bursts across the front pages, generally accompanied by a great deal of public hand-wringing. The spectrum of emotions their plight elicits ranges from sympathy and guilt to patronising racism. A certain class of people – people like Edward – look down their noses at them and despair that they might never be able to manage their own affairs.

What is often conveniently forgotten is that for tens of thousands of years, the indigenous peoples of this continent managed their affairs very well indeed, thank you very much. For 30 millennia they lived in societies which were successful, self-actualised, culturally sophisticated and exceptionally stable.

The earliest indisputable date for the settling of the Australian mainland is 33,000 BCE. By way of comparison, the Americas were settled about 12,500 BCE and the British Isles most recently about 12,000 BCE. Before European ships arrived in the eighteenth century, the level of cultural and linguistic diversity on this continent was as great as that between England and China.

But they were caught out by geography. Due to the physical isolation of the Australian continent, its indigenous societies were not in contact with the crucial developments on Eurasia that led to technological civilisation: agriculture, and the wheels, cities and gunpowder which followed. When the British arrived to settle in 1788, the indigenous populations faced a military-industrial machine thousands of years beyond them and, within two centuries, their societies lay shattered and their homelands buried beneath the shining cities of the Australian coast.

My interest in the subject was sparked in an Istanbul bar listening to three (other) Australians discuss their continent's indigenous peoples. When I arrived I was eager to connect with people of an indigenous background. It's much more difficult than you might imagine. They're still exceedingly marginalised. It took me a while to get to know some of them well.

One of my learning experiences during this journey has been to recognise how much of what people are about comes from their parents, or whomever surrounds them as children. There is a magic that is passed down through families and a spirit across generations, not just through genes, but also subliminally, via the interaction of our minds, from ancestors we never met, via those who did.

Here's a thought experiment: you and a few hundred thousand of your peers are transported 2,000 years into the future. There you are forced to live in a hi-tech world evolved beyond the one you know by several epochs. That world is regulated by a set of abstract ideas which to you, with your twenty-first-century world view, are alien, counter-intuitive and weird. To complicate matters, you are not initially invited to integrate yourselves into this world. First you and your community are dehumanised, have your legal and civil rights curtailed, and are subjected to 150 years of violent and murderous racism.

How long do you think it would take the cultural fabric of your community to adjust to that situation? How many generations might it be before your descendants were in a position to take advantage of it?

Edward wasn't in a place to grasp my macrohistorical musings on that bright Newtown morning. He just saw communities riven by alcoholism and child abuse, felt vaguely superior and thought they should be more like him. At least I stopped a fight breaking out.

The fate of Australia's indigenous peoples may seem far from the central dynamic of world events, but I think it's a test case for us all. How long will it take to rebuild vital, self-possessed communities? Can a people brought to the brink of oblivion climb back? To what extent is humanity capable of transcending its past?

I wish them luck. For now they remain a marginal people, overwhelmed by a rising power and on the wrong side of history.

Days since leaving London: 456

Life expectancy
  Indigenous Australian males: 56.9 years
  All Australian males: 77 years

They are far more happier than we Europeans ... They think themselves provided with all the necessities of life and that they have no superfluities. – Captain Cook

Musings
The Long Now

There are some who think human history would be more exciting if an island called Atlantis had once slipped beneath the Atlantic, or if aliens had helped the ancient Egyptians build the Pyramids. The reason people think history would be more interesting if those things were true (which they're not) is because they haven't grasped how extraordinary the actual truth about their world is beginning to look, or the captivating nature of the patterns now emerging.

Anthropologists, geneticists, linguists and archaeologists are piecing together the events which brought us here, reconstructing the plotline of humanity. That plotline consists of a vast weave of human dramas which took place across one hundred millennia with a cast of 100 billion humans, each generation in turn entering this stage, playing its part and returning to dust.

In order to understand my ultimate thesis – as to how we interpret what's happening on this planet – there are two chunks of information about that plotline you're going to need. The first is about agriculture and the effect it had on human society. The second is how we colonised this world. Not the European colonisation of the last millennium, but the original one back in prehistory.

*****

Agriculture changed everything. It was the great watershed in history which transformed the human world.

Agriculture emerged in the Middle East about 10,000 BCE and fully agricultural societies were established in the Fertile Crescent (modern Iraq and the Levant) from about 7000 BCE. Agriculture then spread across the planet, transforming it from one filled with hunter-gatherer peoples into one filled with farmers. With the exception of a few groups living in marginal areas of savannah or rainforest (for example, the Kalahari bushmen and New Guinea tribesmen), that process came to an end around a hundred years before this book was written.

Once you start farming it's almost impossible to go back. Historically, populations always grew with the food supply. Because agriculture produces more food than hunting and gathering, populations grow proportionally. Once a society has adopted agriculture, within a few generations its population is too large to be fed any other way. It's called the ratchet effect. The human race was – and still is – trapped into farming.

Agriculture made life worse, not better. People in hunter-gatherer societies eat a well-balanced diet which is low in fat and high in protein. They live low-stress lives, don't have to work very hard and get lots of leisure time. People living in traditional agrarian societies spend most of their lives working, rarely have enough food, have dull, poorly balanced diets and are more or less guaranteed to suffer periodic famines.

The archaeological record shows that once agriculture became the main method of food production in a region, people lost about two inches in height, had more diseases and worse teeth than their hunter-gatherer ancestors. They also almost certainly lived shorter lives. Humans did not evolve to be farmers, so it's not surprising that it doesn't suit us.

Combine harvesters and artificial fertilisers are very recent developments. When humanity invented agriculture, that meant subsistence agriculture. The life experience of the vast majority of people between the invention of farming and the past two centuries was one of grinding toil, endemic disease, bad food, periodic famine, almost no material possessions and only the slimmest prospect of a more interesting life.

In addition, the whole political apparatus of history with which everyone is familiar – countries, kings, warlords etc. – is entirely a consequence of agriculture. Before agriculture, people lived in tribes. Life wasn't equitable, but social hierarchies were immeasurably flatter than they subsequently became. It was agriculture, the food surplus it created and the ability to support non-food producers which led to grand inequalities in human societies being instigated, reinforced and then institutionalised. A great deal of our subsequent religious, social and cultural history has been about the efforts of entrenched elites to make those inequalities appear natural, which they're not.

We are all members of a species that has just gone through a baptism of fire. In most parts of the world it lasted several thousand years.

*****

Humankind's colonisation of planet Earth – the second chunk of information I need to share with you – happened even earlier in prehistory.

Humans belong to a primate family called the hominids. The hominid family evolved in Africa 4.5 million years ago and includes several other species, including *Homo habilis*, *Homo floresiensis*, *Homo erectus* and the Neanderthals. Various branches of the hominid family have been wandering around Africa, Europe and Asia for a million years. They're all extinct apart from us.

We *Homo sapiens* also evolved in Africa, from *Homo erectus*, about 200,000 years ago. From there we colonised not only Europe and Asia, but also the other continents. Here's how it happened.

About 60,000 years ago a group of humans crossed the Red Sea from Africa to the Arabian Peninsula. From there they began spreading out. They first made their way along the coast of the Indian Ocean to Indonesia and Australia, then throughout the Middle East and Central Asia, from there into Europe and East Asia, across Siberia, over the Bering Strait, into North America and all the way down into South America.

Every habitable region of Africa, Asia, Europe and Australia had humans by 30,000 years ago. We crossed into North America about 12,500 years ago and had reached the southern tip of South America by 10,000 years ago. That left only the Pacific islands, which were colonised one by one from East Asia after about 1600 BCE. The last major landmass to receive human inhabitants was New Zealand, which the ancestors of the Maori people reached 1,000 years ago, thereby completing the colonisation of planet Earth.

Five hundred years after that, European ships began joining all those people together and mixing them up. Five hundred years after *that*, in one bohemian corner of that mixed-up world, I landed an interesting new job.

75: Only the Broadminded Need Apply

31 August 2006

I've landed a job in a drag club.

The venue is called the Imperial and consists of a bar, a cocktail bar, a nightclub and a cabaret club. It's owned by Newtown's lesbian mafia. Part of *Priscilla Queen of the Desert* was filmed there. Tourists occasionally come in and take photos.

On my first day I was given a tour of the Aladdin's Cave of wardrobe rooms upstairs and taken to meet the drag queens – Mitsy, Freda and Vianesse – while they got ready for the evening's show. There I had the unforgettable experience of standing in a room full of bulb-rimmed mirrors, shaking hands with a fortyish half-dressed Australian man with false breasts strapped to his chest. 'Hey girls, this is Peter. He's from England.'

In the main bar multicoloured streamers stretch from the centre of the roof to every corner. Below them, two pool tables act as social mixing magnets and old lushes perch on stools looking for action. On the wall a screen plays videos from the juke box (they dig Madonna). Late at night, men wander in dressed as women, while women dress in PVC catsuits, ball gowns and nurses' uniforms. Odd, confused-looking characters dance madly with themselves in corners.

I work at the bar while the girls, dressed as Valkyries, do the cancan on stage, 20 feet to my left. My immediate co-workers are Kat (short with a huge smile) and Troy (sarcastic and bitchy). They grumble about each other. I think they're both great.

Everyone else does the complicated things such as cutting up lemons and dealing with trouble. My job is to stay behind the bar and lift everyone's spirits. The gay boys love me and provide a stream of compliments about my beautiful eyes and gorgeous smile.

Fabulous, darling.

Days since leaving London: 462

I feel the same way about disco as I do about herpes. – Hunter S. Thompson

76: Newtown Lifestyle Scenarios
16 September 2006

Using the hospitality industry to get under the skin of Australian society is now paying dividends. I'm currently the in-house daytime hospitality dude for a big international law firm called Baker & McKenzie. They're lovely people to work for and the pay is great. The interesting thing is to do a day shift there, then a night shift at the Imperial. Those days run as follows …

I'll run a seminar until mid-afternoon at Baker & McKenzie's 30th floor offices, then leave dressed in my waistcoat and tie before heading to Victoria Park to sunbathe and swim. After an hour in the pool it's up the hill to one of Newtown's coffee shops to hang out and read.

I've just finished John Stuart Mill's *On Liberty*, in which he sets out the intellectual justification for the moral and economic freedom of individuals from the state (or anyone else). His thinking is diamond-studded. I'm sold.

Following coffee it's back to Australia Street to change from a waistcoat and tie into a vest top and jeans, then down to the Imperial for the graveyard shift. After nodding to the bouncers, I follow a beer-stained corridor to the main room and pandemonium. As for that job, let's just say the pay is OK, the tips are great, and when Kylie kicks in at 4 a.m. it's like something from another world.

Spending my days working at a posh downtown law firm and my evenings flouncing around behind the bar at a seedy drag club is exactly the sort of experience I came to Australia for. However, I'm just about done with the anthropology. I will shortly be dismantling Base Camp Newtown and busting a move out of Sydney. Watch this space.

Days since leaving London: 478

Afrikaans word of the day: 'waterponie' meaning 'jet ski'

77: Twenty-Three Hours
22 September 2006

Twenty-three hours ago I left work in a tower high above the harbour and let a bus ferry me west. At the pool I sat on grass and stretched myself into leisure before crawling laps for an hour and letting my mind fly free. By the time I'd meandered up the hill to Australia Street, Eden had rich salads piled ready and kangaroo flesh was sizzling on the barbecue.

Jess and Gemma, the students next door, came over in their summer dresses. We all feasted together before stomping into the night, a happy four, to a candlelit courtyard and beer on tap. There acquaintances from my time in Sydney came and went with greetings and high spirits as I said my farewells. Ten days to go.

Eden and I giggled like boys as we returned to our lair, where food called again. We had eggs and salad and sauce while debriefing, bouncing ideas and connecting our thoughts. I was ready to fade away when I received an unexpected call. 'Which number are you?' It was Zoe Joyce. The Welsh Nymph was approaching.

Minutes later she was with us, a burst of new life, full of balls and beans. Eden went to bed and we were left alone to a more serious tone. That's when she gave me the low-down, the update, the latest episode from her saga. Kiko has fallen in love with her, then fallen out with her.

The next morning my brain emerged healthy, happy, alive, alert: awake. It was 10.30. I drew back the curtains and we refuelled on sausages and sunshine. Then Zoe and I went to the pool.

There we sat in the sun, worked on our melanin and swapped stories about the people in our lives: how we came to know them and where they all are now. I jumped in, swam a kilometre and we talked some more. I told her about how glad I was that I'd met her and what a great day it had been. Then she went off on her next mission. I dived in again, opened my eyes under the water and felt so happy to be alive. It's three o'clock. I've just had 23 of the best hours of my life.

Days since leaving London: 484

> *The air was soft, the stars so fine, the promise of every cobbled alley so great that I thought I was in a dream.* – Jack Kerouac

Musings
Salad Days

That was the night I met Kerry.

By September, with spring on its way, tons of great people around and the multicoloured melting-pot madness of the Imperial filling my evenings, Newtown had turned into a bohemian wonderland. But what I really wanted was a girlfriend.

Strictly between you, me and anyone else who reads this book, I tried it on with Zoe Joyce twice. Once when we danced cheek to cheek to Frank Sinatra during the power cut on King Street and once after her birthday when she looked so gorgeous I couldn't help myself. She said 'no' both times. I was disappointed, but I didn't take it to heart. If I'm *completely* honest I also propositioned Georgia once too. She didn't fancy me either.

Many of my correspondents didn't like it when I wrote about sex in the diary. But they were 10 of the most affecting and emotionally intense days of the trip. So I wanted to say it.

78: Fully Rock 'n' Roll
27 September 2006

I met Kerry across the bar at the Imperial after complimenting her Charlie's Angels top. 'Nice T-shirt,' I said. 'Nice face,' she replied. It was clear at once that she was a young lady of considerable taste. The next time she got a drink she asked if I was gay. When I told her I wasn't she asked if she could give me her number. I called her. That was on Friday, 10 days before I'm due to leave Sydney. Talk about rotten timing.

Kerry and I have a lot in common. She sings, writes poetry and knows how to throw a party: she orchestrated the last few post-Mardi Gras bashes (16,000 bodies apiece). Kerry lives in a stunning flat above King Street cluttered with piles of paper, mannequins and photos from around the world. We haven't spent much time sleeping.

I wander around it, glass of wine in hand, as dawn's first glimmers break across the city and she reads T. S. Eliot to me. Kerry is more than able to handle the myriad of stuff which swirls around my head nowadays, so I've been pouring it all out. We've also been watching Japanese porn, trying on hats, discussing her pet fish and going on cake-finding missions. We sat through *Finding Nemo* four times. What a great film. What an amazing chick. Now I'm having trouble with the idea of leaving.

> *Only my blood speaks to you in my veins,*
> *And there is such confusion in my powers.*

Eye-opening things that happen at the Imperial: the bouncer guarding the entrance is massive, mean-looking and almost certainly armed. A faded scar runs from his right ear to his forehead. He's bent over a book. Feeling cheeky, I ask what he's reading, sure it must be a martial arts tome.

Cue big cheesy grin: 'It's about a wizard detective, this is book three!' Appearances can be deceptive.

Days since leaving London: 489

Musings
A Muse at the Last

Kerry was clever, beautiful and darkly, compellingly sexual. She was exactly what I wanted and what I needed. But when you're about to leave the city and then the continent, 10 days isn't enough time to decide to stay with someone, or ask them to come with you. By then I already had my ticket to South America. It was one-way.

I spent every evening with her until I left. The more we talked the more interesting she became. By the end my head was filled with the smell of her, the feeling of her smooth belly, the turn of her thigh and the sight of her slip beneath low-cut jeans. At the end I'd become covered in bruises and bite marks. From the moment I left on my walkabout, I was hankering to be back with her.

79: Revelation Space
29 September 2006

I'm going to hitchhike across Australia. The idea came from Eden. My goal will be the city of Cairns in this continent's north-eastern quadrant. I've purchased a new tent, a black marker and a pad so I can make signs telling potential lifts where I'm going. Assuming I make it to Cairns in one piece, I'll return here in mid-November when I'm booked on a flight across the Pacific.

Revelations that happen in Newtown: the guy in the electric wheelchair with the on-board thrash metal stereo turns out to have been able to walk all along. He's just lazy. His name is Slasher. I have an eye-witness account of him getting up from his chair, punching somebody, then sitting back down again.

In the months after arriving in Australia, I seriously considered leaving and going straight back to Asia. The thing which, more than anything else, kept me here was seeing through the dynamic of my friendship with Eden. We first met when I was hosting one of my late-night Istanbul gatherings. He snuck in at the last minute, just as I was bolting the door. I nearly threw him out. Then he started talking.

The two of us share a vision about what's important in life and a sixth sense when looking for trouble. Generally I'm the practically minded, strategic one while he's the blue-sky thinker, pusher of boundaries and chief mission-taker. Typical Istanbul scene: 'Eden, go to the room with the big eastern European blokes and the hot chicks. Bring back all the women and leave all the men.' He doesn't always succeed, but he'll always have a go.

Some of our best times have been of late, pottering around 119 Australia Street as the days grew warmer, or at night across the kitchen table, sitting and deliberating about what it all means after I'd wandered in from late shifts with bottles of wine. With Eden one can discuss anything.

Two weeks ago he found a perfect rainbow refracted onto our bathroom wall by one of the mirrors. He came and got me from my desk so we could look at it together. I think rainbows are the universe giving away something about itself, hinting that there is a magic behind its madness and a logic behind its primordial rage; giving us a clue that if we were to conduct a few simple experiments, that magic might start unravelling itself.

On that particular sunny afternoon, Eden and I spent half an hour discussing rainbows. A shared vision, the opening chapter of another story and a friend for life.

Days since leaving London: 491
Years since the life of
The Universal Common Ancestor of all life on Earth: 3.8 billion
The common ancestor of
    Humans and mice: 100 million
    Humans and gibbons: 20 million
    Humans and Neanderthals: 780,000
Eve, the most recent female ancestor of all the humans alive: 150,000

80: Walkabout
4 October 2006

On my penultimate shift there was little to do. The Nosh posse were nattering away. I had my head in the clouds. One of the girls was trying to get my attention ... 'The only reason England has got where it is is because of Jonny Wilkinson.'

I look at her sternly. Deathly pause. 'Charles Darwin?' I offer. No response. She didn't grasp the earth-shattering force of my wit. It was definitely time to get out of Sydney.

Leaving was like a mini version of leaving London 16 months ago (disposing of material things, negotiating bureaucracy etc.). Eden made it clear we were going to have a party. I thought it best to cooperate. It took most of the week to prepare the house.

He organised the decks, amp, and 400-watt speakers from our mate Wozza. The patterned UV decorations I set up in the living room/dance floor didn't work particularly well, but the 25 metres of fairy lights in the umbrella tree in our yard went down a treat. Renata found us a professional Czech DJ. DJ Shwa was small, unassuming, right off the plane from the European festival season and knew his craft.

There was nearly a fight between Brian the Irish fashion designer and Renata's boyfriend. Chuck the Python escaped; a permanently hungry constrictor snake being just what one needs on the loose at a time like that. The cops turned up at 5 a.m. They were very sweet.

The party was a focal point for the amazing final weeks in Sydney and a great way to mark my leaving. The sun was rising as we entertained the remaining hard core of guests in the yard. It had been a long weekend. I was tired. Eden, as usual, refused to stop.

Sounds on Sunday is an outdoor dance party which gets going at noon and ends at midnight. Only my sense of honour dragged me down there. As it turned out, Eden was right. It was glorious. No one in attendance had slept. Even the cloakroom guy looked squiffy.

It was dark by the time I got into a cab and split for Kerry's flat (she'd been at Sleaze Ball, the sordid version of Mardi Gras). I wanted to spend all my last nights with her. We watched *Muppet's Treasure Island*, lying on her bed together and giggling at Kermit the Frog's one-liners.

As for 119 Australia Street, Zoe has moved in to replace me. The community will continue. On my last evening I had supper with Adam, Eden, Zoe and Kerry. All my favourite Australian people in one place. Then I got the hell out of Dodge.

Days since leaving London: 495
Australians in my survey who claimed to
know all the words to 'Waltzing Matilda':   100%
Those who could produce them when challenged: 0%

In the very beginning everything was resting in perpetual darkness; night oppressed everything like an impenetrable thicket. – The Great Father Myth of the Aranda People (Central Australia)

Above: The Viaduc de Millau (mail 9)   **Below:** The Danube in Serbia (mail 23)

Above: The Blue Mosque and Obelisk of Thutmose III (mails 29 and 30)

Below: Street art (mail 49)

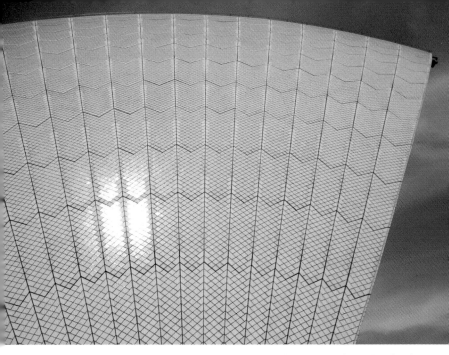

Above: Opera House (mail 51)   **Below:** Mausoleum (mail 59)

Above: Agra Fort (mail 59)   **Below:** Volcan Arenal (mail 92)

Above: The view from the Eyrie (mail 95)   **Below:** Laguna Quilotoa (mail 108)

Above: The Andes (mail 116)   **Below:** Salar de Uyuni (mail 118)

Above: Foz do Iguaçu (mail 123)   **Below:** Ilah Grande (mail 125)

Christo Redentor (mail 127)

Part 7

Magical Mystery Tour

On Hitchhiking

When someone picks up a hitchhiker, a transaction is taking place. As with all good transactions, both parties gain; one of the things the hitcher gains is some transport, while one of the things the driver gains is the feel-good factor from doing someone a favour. But the main thing both of them gain is a more interesting journey. That's the unspoken deal taking place. During my six weeks travelling north from Sydney, I did everything I could to always keep my end of that bargain.

In that Australian spring of 2006, when I said to people in Sydney that I was about to hitchhike across the country, the first thing they told me was how dangerous that was going to be. The second thing they told me was the story of Peter Falconio.

Peter Falconio was an English tourist who disappeared in the outback in July 2001 while travelling with his girlfriend Joanne Lees. The case attracted worldwide public and legal attention and, on 13 December 2005, a man called John Bradley Murdoch was convicted of his murder. Mr Falconio's body has never been found.

The third thing people told me when I said I was going hitchhiking was the plot of a horror film called *Wolf Creek*. The film depicts a madman kidnapping, torturing and then murdering two screaming young women in Australia's wilderness. It was taboo-breaking, unusually grotesque and, after going on general release on 3 November 2005, enjoyed considerable commercial success. Insofar as I can tell it hasn't got anything to do with hitchhiking, but I was told the plot seven times in the space of the ten days before I left Sydney.

Part of *Wolf Creek's* marketing was the claim it was a true story. It wasn't, but the form of some of the murders was loosely based on the Backpacker Murders that took place in New South Wales in the early 1990s.

The Backpacker Murders were carried out by the serial killer Ivan Milat and involved at least seven local and international travellers losing their lives. All the victims were repeatedly beaten, stabbed and shot. Some of them had been hitchhiking when they were abducted. Mr Milat was caught and, on 27 July 1996, sent to jail after being given seven life sentences.

When a car stops, you have to make an instant assessment as to the safety of getting into that particular vehicle. That's one of the things that makes the experience so interesting. But the main thing

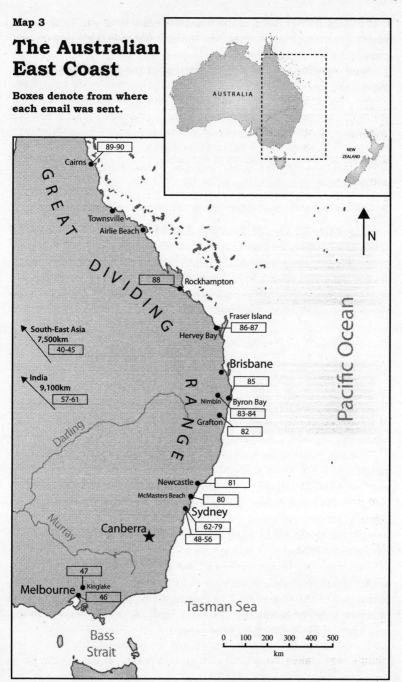

Map 3

The Australian East Coast

Boxes denote from where each email was sent.

AUSTRALIA

NEW ZEALAND

N

89-90

Cairns

G R E A T

Townsville

Airlie Beach

D I V I D I N G

88   Rockhampton

South-East Asia
7,500km
40-45

Fraser Island
86-87
Hervey Bay

India
9,100km
57-61

Brisbane

85

R
A
N
G
E

Nimbin   Byron Bay
83-84
Grafton
82

Darling

Newcastle   81
McMasters Beach   80
Sydney
62-79
Canberra ★
48-56

Murray

47
Melbourne   Kinglake
46

Pacific Ocean

Tasman Sea

Bass
Strait

0   100   200   300   400   500
km

that makes it interesting is the fact that every time you hitch a ride you're guaranteed an intense and entirely unpredictable one-on-one interaction with a completely new human being.

Here were the common characteristics of the people who stopped to pick me up:

1) Male.

2) Driving alone.

3) Had hitchhiked themselves in the past.

4) Well above average social skills.

5) Confident personality types (several were ex-soldiers).

It took me 21 rides to cover the 2,634 kilometres from Sydney to Cairns. Only twice did I wait more than 30 minutes for a lift. It was to prove a highly rewarding way of exploring the continent's east coast. As for the psychopaths who allegedly roam Australia's highways, I reasoned that getting picked up by one was statistically unlikely. I was more concerned about the bees.

81: Rivendell
8 October 2006

If you really want to understand someone you need to meet their family. My first stop heading north was McMasters Beach on the Central Coast where I stayed with Eden's mum, Sue, and his sister, Grace.

Sue and Grace live in a sprawling wooden Scandinavian-style compound perched on a hill above several acres of lawns, trees and gardens. Along one side of the building is a broad veranda, where one can drink coffee, take a spot of lunch or look out upon the lush semi-tropical surroundings. The main communal space is a hall containing a table, which effortlessly sits 12, and an almost decadent lounging area. It's a perfect place for just sitting and thinking.

Sue runs an efficient, informal and homely household. She has a collection of Japanese earthenware and a vast larder of healthy produce and is one of the best cooks I've ever met. She treated me to a mouth-watering series of beautifully presented feasts, filling my body with the nutrients it will need for the journey ahead.

Grace is trying to get her boyfriend to do what she wants, spending lots of time being bored and generally being 18. She makes a mean French toast for breakfast and looks exactly like her older brother who, she informs me, has always been the golden boy.

I stayed for five days of good food, rest and refreshment. In the afternoons I would cycle to the beach, scribble in my notebook and follow long tracks through cliff-top heather to the blue edge of the Pacific. There I'd gaze over the ocean, or south towards the far-off towers of the city I'd just left, dimly visible in the far distance.

On my fourth day Sue's boyfriend Paul turned up. He's strong-limbed, addicted to the outdoors and has a swarthy complexion which betrays his Gallic blood. Paul took me sea kayaking on the Brisbane Water and as we paddled out around tree-filled islands, he told me about his life, his daughter and her boyfriend. He also made the following two observations about hitchhiking: 'When you hitchhike, *people* are your transport and you're relying on your social skills not only to get around, but also to keep you safe.' What an interesting way of thinking about it.

That evening we all attended the opening of a local music festival where Sue's choir sang *a cappella*. They were followed by a no-nonsense, four-piece English folk band dressed in top hats and attitude, who played fiddle and mandolin, and harmonised clear baritones to stories of romance and highwaymen. After cheering them on, I wandered outside into night fields filled with bonfires, fire stick twirlers and the rich smell of spring. Breathe it in.

Paul dropped me beside a service station on the Sydney to Newcastle expressway this morning. After a five-minute wait I was picked up by Pat and Bruce, who were driving back from Sydney airport after dropping off some colleagues who were going to Kampala to build a roof on a school. I was sceptical that it could possibly be cost-effective or carbon-efficient to fly Australians to Africa to build roofs on schools, but seeing as Pat and Bruce were driving me to Newcastle, I chose not to second-guess them. What's more, they were upbeat, raised my spirits and, after several wrong turnings, dropped me right at Heidi's door.

Days since leaving London: 499

Travel only with thy equals or thy betters. If there are none, travel alone. – The Dhammapada

82: Heidi and Shane
11 October 2006

I first met Heidi through Georgia in Newtown some months ago when the three of us went disco dancing. She made an immediate and powerful impression on me. A visit to her house in Newcastle, 150 kilometres up the coast from Sydney, was my second stop heading north.

A few years back Heidi lived in London with a high-powered-lawyer boyfriend. She worked at Holmes Place – a posh gym in Kensington – and was briefly personal trainer to Claudia Schiffer. Later in life she career-changed into business and now jet-sets between California and Adelaide for an organisation establishing a new healthcare discipline called Spinology, which focuses on the relationship between the vertebrae and the spinal column.

Heidi has a no-nonsense, pull-your-socks-up attitude to life: productivity is a virtue and there's no time for wasters. Boy, was she an achiever. She's also blonde, drop-dead gorgeous and proudly drives a cerulean blue V6 Toyota Vienta. 'Her name's Maxi,' she growled, turning to me as we made ready to drive into town on my first night, one knee-high boot revving the engine and a twinkle in her big brown eyes.

Yowzers.

I stayed at Heidi's for two days. We talked almost non-stop. The day after I arrived we drove through fields of Shiraz, Sémillon and Pinot Noir to the Hunter Valley. It's one of Australia's most famed wine regions and we stopped at idyllic-looking vineyards, where gregarious winemakers regaled us with talk of oak-fermented casks and honey-nut flavours. That evening I read Heidi my favourite poem, by Khalil Gibran, about how the way we seem to other people is a garment that we wear, while the real action takes place inside the unapproachable confinement of the mind. In return she gave me one of Gibran's books: *The Prophet*. I'll be reading it.

Yesterday morning Heidi dropped me on the Pacific Highway next to the Hexham Bridge. There I was picked up by Bo. 'Bad spot to get a lift, mate,' he announced sagely as I got into his car. Bo had spotted me on his way to work, turned around at the next junction and come back to get me. For the following 15 minutes he plied me with hitchhiking-related advice before dropping me at the approach to a roundabout where the cars were already decelerating. He said that I'd get another lift from there very soon. I got one straight away.

Keenan was also on his way to work – as an outdoor activities teacher for disadvantaged kids. He loved outdoor sports and had studied education, so was well suited to his role providing underprivileged children with life-enhancing experiences. Keenan talked of how the environment that surrounds one as a child makes an indelible impression on the personality and believed that it took real strength of character to find peace after a bad start in life. I guess some of us are lucky.

Keenan dropped me by some roadworks where the traffic slowed and, after 10 minutes, a huge brown pickup truck with a meaty-looking roll bar pulled up. It was towing a trailer full of surfboards. The guy driving it was called Shane.

Shane was part-Maori and proud. His vehicle was covered in handprints like the ones Indigenous Australians put on the walls of their sacred places and he would beep and wave whenever we passed indigenous folk. 'If your grandparents came from Europe you can't call yourself *Australian*,' he reasoned in outrage.

Among Shane's business ventures was a plan to integrate Maori art with twenty-first-century architecture, fusing two creative traditions into something modern and globalised. He was already agent for several indigenous artists and enthusiastically showed me his design book.

Shane was an instinctive and enthusiastic capitalist ('If it flies, floats or fucks: lease it.') and had recently returned from a spell in Dubai. He was full of praise for the city state's entrepreneurial expat culture, telling me stories of palm-tree-shaped islands, vast man-made harbours and the tallest structures yet built by men.

All of this came between him explaining how he was learning to fly helicopters, trying to recruit me as a UK sales agent and swerving whenever we passed roadworks to knock over a few traffic cones 'because all council workers are lazy'. Then, after I'd bought him lunch, he told me about all the women he'd fallen in love with. At least two of them took houses off him.

We drove up the sunny New South Wales coast, nattering away for six hours, then sang at the tops of our voices to *The Joshua Tree* before he dropped me at a campsite near Grafton.

Last night I slept under a pawpaw tree while dreaming of shining cities which spring from clean white deserts of crushed shell and coral. I awoke at 10 a.m. to yet more stunning weather, took a cool, refreshing shower and am drinking coffee in the sunshine as I write this.

Days since leaving London: 502
Dubai, population
1822:	1,200
2005:	1,204,000

Seeming is but a garment that I wear. A care woven garment that protects me from thy questionings and thee from my negligence. The 'I' in me, my friend, dwells in the house of silence. And therein it shall remain. Unperceived, unapproachable. – Khalil Gibran

83: Sunrise on Nimbin
13 October 2006

The day after meeting Shane, I hitchhiked to Nimbin. It took me three lifts to get there.

The first lift was with Bill, who was going to collect his aunt from the hospital. Bill had five grandchildren, did a tour in Vietnam and hitchhiked a lot himself back in the 1970s. He'd recently taken some entrepreneurial risks and had his fingers burned. We talked about how self-image relates to money and how money relates to status. Bill had lost some of all three due to his latest business venture. 'There are definitely more good people than bad people in this world,' he told me, 'but there's some nasty, unethical bastards out there.'

The second lift was with Malcolm, who picked me up on the road into Lismore while on his way to deliver a table. Malcolm was driving a ragged, but solid-looking, blue van and asked question after question about where I'd been, while his black and white border collie, Star, observed me curiously from the back of the vehicle.

My final lift that morning was with Thomas, who was driving to his job as a nurse at the local clinic. Thomas was originally from England's north-east, but came to Australia for a year and never left. He'd spent his first eight months here in a rainforest community, where they lived without electricity and other trappings of civilisation. 'The parties were great but the personal hygiene was appalling,' I learned. Due to his job, Thomas had seen first hand the drug-crazed antics that go on in Nimbin. 'Don't eat the cookies,' he warned, dropping me on its main street.

Here's the deal: in 1972 venue scouts from the Australian Union of Students struck an accord with the Nimbin Progress Association of the village of Nimbin, in the north-eastern corner of New South Wales, to hold a festival. The following year saw a music and cultural event lasting 10 days between the 12th and the 23rd of May, during which the attendees celebrated free love and marijuana, registered outrage at the Vietnam War and rejoiced in the dawning of the Age of Aquarius.

The event had a permanent effect on the village. Many of the festival goers stayed to set up communes, and in this way an unassuming banana-growing and dairy region had its culture transformed. One feature of that transformed local culture is the widespread cultivation, selling and recreational use of cannabis.

The village itself is tiny, with a crowded main street on which pot is openly traded and where the facades of buildings are painted with flamboyant depictions of marijuana leaves, ganja fairies and cannabis-oriented frivolity. I'm staying on a forested hill 10 minutes out of town called the Rainbow Retreat. It's a stunning campsite. Features include a rambling bush kitchen, an authentic teepee ('that's our spiritual area') and several multicoloured 20-year-old VW vans dotted around the surrounding fields, covered with signs urging one to 'give peace a chance' and 'make love not war'.

The place is run by Doug, an old-school Aquarian, and his Japanese helper, Kin. They have very unstressful jobs. On one wall of the main building are portraits of John Lennon, the Dalai Lama, Che Guevara and an unidentified Indian guru. Che is on top.

By 8 a.m. the sun is so strong that I'm forced out of my tent to stand beneath the orange-blossomed tree under which I'm camped and take in the songs of the kookaburras. Then it's down the hill to the creek, where I cool off with a family of duck-billed platypuses.

During the day I chill out around the campsite while, in the background, Kin breaks out riffs on his electric guitar. Then, in the afternoon, I walk barefoot into town to buy newspapers and food. At dusk I go into the forest to collect wood for the evening's fire while trying to avoid the snakes that live there. Then I drink Hunter Valley wine, express myself in my notebook and read about how the North Koreans have just exploded a nuclear bomb. That's very bad news indeed.

I visited Nimbin's Hemp Embassy (where they advocate the legalisation of marijuana) and had a chat with the bearded fellow running the place and his impish, grey-haired wife. The two of them took the view that drugs prohibition is confused, illiberal and wrong. They argued that it's led to the corruption and militarisation of large sections of the world's police forces; given tens of billions of dollars to the world's most thuggish people; and placed the distribution of dangerous and easily abused substances into the hands of an irresponsible and criminalised fraternity.

I've been exposed to quite a lot of hippie-style alternative culture over the years. I always attend the Greenpeace lectures at the Glastonbury music festival and read *The Green Anarchist*, my favourite anarcho-periodical, whenever I get the chance. As a movement it's been one of the most colourful cultural and intellectual phenomena to come out of the twentieth century. Its achievements include some of the era's best music and acting as the incubator for environmentalism, which has since become such an essential element of our global conversation.

One of humanity's less far-sighted instincts is the impulse to enforce conformity. It's an impulse that feigns to be about respectability but that's really about control, and it's misguided. The human endeavour wouldn't work if we all thought the same, and the world is stronger because people believe, and do, unconventional things. As for this unique community at Nimbin, it's colourful, well bonded and highly inclusive, and they sure know a thing or two about weed.

Days since leaving London: 504
Nimbin

Population:	352
Unemployment rate:	18.1%

[the test has come] at a stirring time when all the people of the country are making a great leap forward in the building of a great prosperous powerful socialist nation. – North Korean Government announcement

84: God Systems
14 October 2006

Terry was camped away from everybody else because he found bongo drums annoying. Every day, down near the creek, I'd find him cross-legged and meditating beside his tent. He'd been on the road a long time and sported an impressive beard. Yesterday morning he got me alone in the Rainbow Retreat's bush kitchen and started telling me what he'd learned about the world. Once he got into his stride it was impossible to stop him.

Terry made some remarkable claims about the electromagnetic spectrum and kept using the word 'energy' in different contexts (without being able to define it). He claimed that there are 'seven dimensions' (one of which is 'nuclear', while the others are 'light') and believed that humans didn't evolve, but were rather 'manifested' from a design based on primates.

Further to this, he claimed that we are all God in the sense that the fundamental architecture of the universe consists of a population of 'spirits' expressing themselves through humankind. A spirit called Ramtha, 'The Enlightened One' (who formerly lived on Atlantis and now communicates with the human race through an American lady), is in the process of helping us understand these truths. Most of his information came from the internet.

To be fair, my summation probably doesn't do justice to the complexity of Terry's particular spiritual cosmology. It was elaborate and highly involved and he'd obviously thought about it a lot.

While I hesitate to compare Terry's thinking with that of the world's most illustrious religious traditions, for me his ideas shared a weakness with the stories in the Bible and the Qur'an. From the priorities they assumed to the issues upon which they dwelt, they were manifestly the product of human, rather than divine, hands.

The campfire tales of Genesis; Qur'anic images of the saved, sitting post-Final Judgement, in garden-like heavens; 35,000-year-old 'spirits' 'guiding' us to 'enlightenment' – all these ideas may be attractive to the unimaginative and easy to relate to, but they are also simplistic, scientifically incoherent and hopelessly human-centric.

To give him his due, Terry was a man at peace and I suppose people have different words for things. Nonetheless, I concluded that clinging to medieval world systems was preventing him from considering how extraordinary reality actually is.

I'm in constant awe of our species' creative powers, but nobody could have thought up a cosmic explosion of hydrogen and helium atoms that stewed into a universe which dances with stars and galaxies, or a billion-year parallel evolution of interdependent life forms building up a planet-spanning biosphere. It's just too crazy, and the truth is more spectacular than any fiction we could write.

Days since leaving London: 505

We inhabit a universe where atoms are made in the centres of stars; where each second a thousand suns are born; where life is sparked by sunlight ... where the raw material for biological evolution is made by the explosion of a star halfway across the Milky Way ... a cosmos of quasars and quarks, snowflakes and fireflies. How pallid by comparison are the pretensions of superstition and pseudoscience.
– Carl Sagan

Musings
Earth Systems

In my experience when you ask people what they mean by the word 'God' their answer basically constitutes a reduction to a noun such as 'force', 'power' or 'being'.

To us humans, thinking about an idea like 'God' in terms of a noun like 'being' comes naturally. Our mythology and art are full of beings which are non-human, such as aliens, dragons, fairies and conscious computers. We therefore easily grasp the concept and presume that we have a handle on how such entities might think and act.

But, of course, no one has ever met an *actual* alien, dragons and fairies are figments of our imagination, and no computer which could reasonably be regarded as conscious has yet been built. We therefore have no information as to how such things would actually think and act, or what about the world they would regard as interesting, significant or noteworthy.

I think one of the fundamental problems we humans have when assessing our world views is that we don't have anything radically different to compare them against. As a result we have no idea how arbitrary our basic cognitive architecture for thinking about the universe is.

The only non-human thinking beings that humans have ever encountered are Earth's other animals. At least some of those animals are probably clever enough to possess world views to which we might, theoretically, relate. Dolphins and chimpanzees most clearly possess intelligence and consciousness which is (in form if not in magnitude) comparable to our own. Whales and elephants seem to have a level of human-style consciousness and some would argue that dogs, and a few of the other higher mammals, are conscious.

Among the non-mammals, one or two species of bird (crows, for example) appear to be self-aware and some species of squid and octopus are apparently quite brainy. It's even within the realms of possibility that ant and termite colonies can think in a way which could be characterised as consciousness, although in a wacky hive-mind sort of a way that we're (so far) completely unable to relate to. Don't even get me started on bees.

But our ability to communicate with any of those other intelligent and (arguably) conscious animals is exceedingly rudimentary. We've yet to work out even really basic things about whale songs, and we're a long way from being able to say to a whale: 'We think we're a bunch of animals on the surface of a planet. What do *you* think?'

There's a further big problem in assessing our world views: in a world teeming with information we only perceive a very limited amount of what's happening around us. The human eye picks up only a tiny spectrum of the electromagnetic radiation entering the eyeball. Our sense of hearing only monitors the air pressure at our eardrums, and our senses of taste and smell provide (at best) an idiosyncratic chemical analysis of the matter on our tongues and in the air at our nasal membranes.

If these limitations weren't severe enough – not only do we humans have nothing non-human to compare our world views to and not only do we perceive what's happening around us in a very limited way, but we also spend almost all of our time interacting with other extremely similar beings, with similarly limited sensory systems and almost precisely identical world views.

None of this encourages us to be objective about ourselves. It encourages the creation of boxes which we then, collectively and resolutely, think inside.

Humans relate to each other, and each other's behaviour, reasonably well. Another human who came across me for the first time could probably make sense of the stuff I get up to (going on bicycle rides, writing travel diaries) and the things I regard as noteworthy (girls, food, sunshine etc.).

Humans *broadly* relate to the other animals on Earth. A human coming across a dolphin – a being from the same branch of the same tree of life that shares most of the human's genetic code – might not be able to guess what the dolphin is thinking, but it could probably hazard a fairly intelligent guess as to the sorts of things the dolphin would be interested in (fish, water temperature, other dolphins etc.).

But if one were to meet, say, an intelligent extraterrestrial – a creature from a different branch of a different tree of life from a completely different planet – you can forget everything you've seen in the movies, because the information we have about how such entities would think and act, or what about the universe they would consider to be noteworthy, is exactly zero.

And when we talk about an idea like *God* (who I don't think anyone would argue is a life form from a tree of life with limited sensory data about anything), *He* would interact with the universe in a way that was different from dolphins, termites, humans, bees or aliens. Radically different.

*****

When the Book of Genesis describes God it describes Him as 'walking in the garden [of Eden] in the cool of the day'. When the stories in the Qur'an describe Him, they describe Him providing flowing springs in garden-like heavens where humans can drink and frolic forever. When Terry in Nimbin thought about God he imagined Him living in Atlantis and 'channelling' through American women.

These are all projections. They are examples of human beings looking out upon the infinite and seeing a reflection of themselves. They are not seeing the universe as it is. They are seeing the universe as *they* are.

We're hard-wired to think about and to perceive the world in a very specific way. Being clear about those inbuilt preconceptions is one step along the journey of reaching beyond them. In doing so we can set out world views which account more honestly for the underlying nature of these intriguing *Homo sapiens* who use sound and ink patterns to paint pictures in each other's minds. And of the particular mind which is reading these words right now.

85: The Byron Bay Experience

18 October 2006

On 14 October, after four days and three nights in Nimbin, I took the *Happy Coach* to the coast. Fred the driver (dreadlocked with a well-developed patter) put the Rolling Stones on the stereo as we rocked through rolling green countryside and down to Byron Bay, an iconic east-coast destination famed for hedonism, adventure sports and its beautiful natural environment.

The crescent-shaped bay has about seven kilometres of coastline, with the town at the southern bowl and Cape Byron (the Australian mainland's most easterly point) at one end. I'm camped above Clarke's Beach and have spent the past three days wandering along the silvery sand, swimming in the silvery sea and hanging around my camp. It's been pretty chilled, apart from one occasion when a jumbo-sized wolf spider crept nonchalantly inside my tent to join me.

Now that I'm on the road again I've decided to make myself look more distinguished through the medium of facial hair. The bearded-Jesus look

I tested in France last year, while scholarly, caused some people to treat me like a frivolous hippie. While floating in the Pacific and pretending to be an Irrawaddy dolphin the other morning, a solution occurred to me: extended sideburns. I am growing my 'burns' forthwith, convinced that a hairier visage will add to my gravitas.

The other issue I've been wrestling with is what name to give my new tent. It's only two weeks since I left Sydney and I'm already feeling a strong urge to hold conversations with inanimate objects. The tent is the obvious conversant, but talking to a tent without a name might make me look like a nutter.

The tent requested an indigenous moniker and, while inspecting wild flowers on Cape Byron, I came across the word 'Nguthungulli' (nag-uth-an-GOO-li), which means 'father of the whole world' in the Koori tongue. Nguthungulli the Tent feels much better now he has a proper title.

Last night, while wandering west along the beach under the stars, I came across a bonfire with a small crowd of people gathered around it. One man was playing cyclic melodies through a didgeridoo while four others with drums beat out intricate tribal rhythms and three pretty girls wearing blue face paint danced theatrically beside the flames.

Spellbound, I took a pew beside a weathered, shaven-headed and roguish-looking fellow watching proceedings from the edge of the bonfire's light. His name was Jed.

Jed, who shared several cans of beer with me, had plenty to say for himself. We proceeded to have a long, rambling conversation while his crew of dancers, drummers and didgeridoo players capered around us. After some time we ended up discussing spaceships, a subject about which he knew a great deal.

'The problem with space exploration,' he told me, 'is getting there. After 50 years of rocket design, putting a kilogram of mass into geostationary orbit still costs US$11,000.'

'OK.'

'Now look here, cobber, you can come up with the best space technology you like, but that basic limiting parameter means you'll never conquer the final frontier without a shift away from chemical rockets as your workaday launch system.'

'I see.'

'And *that's* why you have to build a space elevator,' he said, pointing a finger to the sky to emphasise his point, 'a work of mega-engineering that leads right up to a counterweight in geosynchronous orbit. A thread from Earth to the stars.'

'Golly.'

'Then we can *really* start putting people into space,' he concluded. I was overjoyed by his subject matter and attitude, but know one or two things about spaceships myself and immediately began playing devil's advocate.

'Why can't we just use robots?'

'Forget it. Not exciting enough.'

'Dude, next year the New Horizons probe sling-shots past Jupiter at 82,000 kilometres per hour. Nine years later we'll have close-up, high-definition pictures of *Pluto* taken through one of the largest silicon-carbide telescopes ever flown. Don't tell me that's not exciting, and you can't do that shit with humans.'

'Look, mate,' he shot back, 'we have to colonise space so we may as well get on with it.'

'Why do we have to colonise space?'

'*Mate*,' he said, getting right in my face, 'the dinosaurs died out because they didn't have a space programme. If we don't get into space then sooner or later we'll get thwacked by a rock. Mankind can last 100 million years. Let's go for it.'

'So the monkeys can survive where the lizards failed?'

'We're not monkeys, we're apes. Get your bloody primate classifications right.'

'You say potato, I say pot*a*to. You get my point. We're just another species. "Monkey" is more poetic.'

'Stupid bloody monkeys. Get bloody everywhere,' he shouted, widening his eyes, throwing his arms out and spilling beer over his forearm. '*Did* you know,' he went on, passing me the can and leaning forward so we were eyeball to eyeball, 'that the Murrdi people of central Queensland have a dreamtime legend telling of how the area around the lakes of the Atherton Tableland were once dominated by eucalyptus trees?'

'I categorically did not know that,' I replied. 'Tell me about dreamtime.'

'Y'see,' he replied, 'the Abos believe there are two streams of time. There's your objective day-to-day time and then there's the infinite *spir*itual cycle,' he swung his arms up with the word *spiritual*, '*more real than reality itself* and of which the patterns of the world we see around us are only the echo.'

'Crazy.'

'Anyway,' he went on, 'the Murrdi myth-tellers claim that the area around the volcanic lakes of the Atherton Tableland were once covered in eucalyptus trees, not wet tropical forest like they are today.'

'I see.'

'And it turns out that this is *true*. The area *was* covered in eucalyptus trees, but back in the Pleistocene era. Do you know when that was?'

'When was the Pleistocene era?'

'Bloody *ten thousand years ago*, mate. Do you know what that means?'

'What does that mean?'

'It means the stories of the Murrdi myth-tellers constitute an accurate oral tradition stretching back *at least* ten thousand years, twice as far as any other written or oral history outside the continent of Australia.'

'I'm completely with you. That's utterly mental.'

'Much better than Christian mythology.'

'I take it you're no Christian?' I asked, passing back his beer and gesturing to the Celtic knotwork and Eye of Horus tattooed on his forearms.

'Nah. Brought up Catholic. It's bollocks. Priests are definitely monkeys. If we can send robots to Pluto we can drop ancient drongo superstition.'

'Is that what it is?'

'Mostly, and an opium for the people so the bastards who run everything can lord it over civilisation.'

'Ah-ha, *civilisation*,' I exclaimed. It's rare I get to talk about spaceships and civilisation in the same conversation, let alone with a cartoon-like Antipodean pagan astronautics specialist. 'OK. What *is* civilisation?' I asked him.

'Mmm, good one. The biggest collective mind game ever devised?'

'Is it a side effect of agriculture?'

'Nah, ants have been farming fungus for millions of years. Ants are definitely not monkeys. Goddam monkeys, bunch of dickheads.'

'What is it then?'

'A way for dickhead monkeys to destroy the Earth?' he ruminated, staring into the fire. 'Dunno. Strewth, wadda *you* think? Cut the questions and gimme answers.' He turned to face me, unblinking through the rising light. 'G'won then.' Momentarily I had nothing to say.

'It's a pattern within a pattern,' I came out with after a long pause. 'We're running around doing our thing like other animals, just in a more elaborate way. There's no difference between a bird's nest and a city except in scale.' I was speaking in a stream of consciousness. 'But as it gets more complicated, sub-patterns appear. Farming gives you craftsmen. Craftsmen give you writing. Writing gives you computers. Computers give you virtual reality. New constellations of complexity, and a bunch of apes …'

'Monkeys.'

'Whatever, a bunch of monkeys find themselves faced with a question: is it possible to run a technological civilisation on a planet?'

'That's a big question, mate.'

'Because maybe it just can't be done.' I was waving my arms and talking very fast. 'Maybe no matter how hard we try, something about the way civilisation is unfolding will undo us. Imagine, though, if we dreamed up civilisation and it *worked*. Monkeys on a spinning rock, millions of kilometres from a star-shaped fusion engine, full of dreamy urges to build ever more magnificent towers until they reach right up into the sky, crawling from the mud to construct this glittering civilisation – this, this *emergent* phenomenon …'

Right at that moment whoops began going up around us. The drumming had intensified and, snapped from my thoughts, I realised that our surroundings had changed colour. Jed stood up, raising his arms. I stood too, dizzy-headed. Everyone was cheering. I turned around to see a great shard of light burning over the horizon. The face of the sun. Morning had broken.

The bonfire crew, surrounding us, were all leaping in euphoria. One drum still banged away. A shared moment. It was so vivid. They all looked so happy.

But there are times when you join the party and there are times when you go back to Nguthungulli the Tent and write stuff down in the big black book. I decided to leave them to it. As I started back to Clarke's Beach, Jed peeled off and ran over to bid me farewell. 'I love your style, dude,' I said as he gripped my hand. 'I absolutely and completely love your style. Have an amazing life.'

'Same same, mate,' he said, 'and remember, it's a beautiful world full of incredible people. Make the most of it.'

'I'll do what I can.'

Walking back to my camp, still wrapped in the moment, I pondered Jed's statement that the human adventure might last millions of years. I like the idea. I reckon it's worth a go.

Days since leaving London: 509
Tons of hydrogen converted to energy in the sun every second:
5,000,000
Years before the sun runs out of fuel and goes red giant:
5,000,000,000

[the divide is between] those who are interested in the world and its multiplicity of forms and forces, and those who merely subsist, worrying or yawning … The world is full of light and life, and the true crime is not to be interested in it. – A. S. Byatt

86: Six Rides North
20 October 2006

After three days in Byron Bay I packed up my stuff, walked to the western end of town, then hitchhiked to Queensland.

I was picked up by Ken, who was going to Brisbane to collect his four-year-old daughter for the weekend. Ken lived in a bus and told me the story of how he'd once bought a horse on a whim, having never owned or ridden a horse before. As he had nowhere to put the horse he'd ridden it to a nearby field and bought that on a whim too. Ken was deliriously in love with his new girlfriend. He still had the horse.

Ken drove me all the way to Brisbane, where my stylish and beautiful ex-Newtown flatmate Chantel now lives with her man Kris. Chantel and Kris' house is on stilts in the Queensland style, with a gargantuan shed out back and their car in a garage underneath.

Following the obligatory barbecue, I spent a day ambling along the walkways on the Brisbane River's South Bank. The walkways were sheltered by gunmetal barriers on which purple flowers grew and wound through verdant tropical gardens and past wooden, Chinese-style temples. In the evening Kris drove us into the hills above the city, from where we looked down upon Queensland's capital, sprawled languidly in its night-time landscape.

After two days of carpets and soft beds at Kris and Chantel's stilt house, it's now back to just me and Nguthungulli the Tent. This morning Kris dropped me beside the Bruce Highway north of Brisbane. From there it took me four lifts to reach Hervey Bay.

The first lift was with John, who was going to meet some of his mates for the weekend. John had just returned to Australia after 11 years abroad, most of which he spent in Amsterdam growing drugs. His new business was a company that sent people text messages offering them the chance to win prizes. The prizes weren't very good and John was a bit sheepish about it. I assured him that it sounded perfectly ethical, certainly more respectable than growing pot.

My second lift was with Robert. Robert was rather strange and it was never clear where he was going. A few silent and awkward minutes after

I got into his car he turned to me, furrowed his brows, looked intense and enquired conspiratorially, 'What do *you* know about the New World Order?'

Almost relieved, I began asking questions.

The New World Order (also known as the Illuminati) is a malevolent organisation that Robert believes sits behind the thrones of the world's great nations, controls the weather from secret installations in Russia and Alaska and plans to take over the planet. The Rockefellers and Rothschilds were mentioned in appropriately hushed tones. Robert explained that he too sometimes tries to hitchhike, but that 'for some reason I can never get a lift. What do you think I might be doing wrong?'

Dude, where do I *start*?

My third lift that day was with Carlton, one of the most engaging conversationalists I've ever met. Carlton was working as a local government consultant and we discussed Paul Keating (good), Gough Whitlam (very good) and John Howard (bad). Carlton had married young and picked the wrong woman. The divorce was still fresh. His post-divorce sex life was 'average'.

My final lift on the way to Hervey Bay was with Joe, who picked me up at Maryborough in his bouncy gold pickup truck. Joe was returning from Brisbane, where he'd been looking at trikes. Back in the day he'd been a Melbourne-based rock promoter touring Debbie Harry and Blondie. When it came time to live on a beach he'd surveyed the entire east coast looking for the right one. Hervey Bay, he assured me, was the best place in the world and a perfect spot for morning tea and beach yoga.

Joe dropped me at the town's beachfront campsite early this afternoon. I'm pitched beside Godewyn and Brandy, two Dutch stoners, and Donnie and Millie, a retired couple with all the camping equipment money can buy. Donnie and Millie live in a tent the equivalent of a palace, with a table, chairs and several internal rooms. They've been giving me beer all afternoon, which is absolutely splendid.

Days since leaving London: 511
Country in the world with the most beaches: Australia (circa 7,000)
Annualised economic growth, Queensland, 1992 and 2002: 5% (the highest in Australia)

Hawaiian word of the day: 'pu'ukaula' meaning 'to set up one's wife as a stake in gambling'

87: Appetite for Destruction

25 October 2006

I've been on a whale-watching excursion with a tour agency from Hervey Bay.

Our vessel was a 60-foot catamaran that set out from Urangan Pier at the bay's edge. We spent four hours sailing across calm, dark blue waters following two pods of humpbacks who were preparing to head south into the Antarctic Ocean after a season of mating. The largest female came in at a cool 35 tonnes, making her easily the biggest animal I've ever seen.

The boat was subject to strict rules regarding how close it could get to the whales and when it could turn on its engines. In fact, the whole expedition was carefully orchestrated to ensure minimum whale stress and discomfort. This is extraordinary given that, just a few decades ago, other boats were hunting those very same whales towards oblivion.

The nineteenth and twentieth centuries' near destruction of the world's great whale populations is an iconic example of how irresponsible the human race has been to the rest of the Earth's ecosphere. Commercial whaling has been going on for centuries, but the big rorquals (blue whales, humpback whales, fin whales and sei whales) have swimming speeds of 30–50 kilometres per hour, too fast for traditional whaling boats to handle. What's more, if you kill them, they sink.

The crucial technological developments came in the 1860s, when Norwegian Svend Foyn built the first steam-powered whaling ship armed with the first exploding harpoon-firing cannons. At that point humans could start going after the big heavy whale species which had eluded all of our previous hunting techniques. By 1929 vast factory ships were hauling 100-tonne rorquals on board for mid-ocean processing. By the 1960s supercharged electric harpoons were causing instantaneous whale death.

One by one, the world's great whale species were hunted to the precipice of extinction. When moratoriums on commercial whaling came into effect in the late twentieth century, some of the biggest and most majestic animals which have ever lived had nearly been snuffed out. We came to our senses only just in time.

The day after meeting our aquatic brothers and sisters, I did a two-day tour of Fraser Island, a gigantic 120-kilometre sandbar beside Hervey Bay that was created through thousands of years of wave action. The island is covered by rainforest and dotted with freshwater lakes. My tour group, populated by mischievous Germanic ladies and a wandering post-retirement fellow named John, explored the island in an amphibious all-terrain bus. Our ex-policeman guide talked us through Fraser Island's history and that of the Indigenous Australians, all gone now, who once named it K'gari – paradise.

It is instructive to note that when the ancestors of those original Australians first set foot on these lands, they found a pristine continent full of animals of a size now rarely seen outside Africa: giant kangaroos, two-tonne wombats and marsupial tapirs as big as horses. Unfortunately, while being a two-tonne wombat means you're safe from almost every other animal that exists, ten blokes with language and spears will take you down every time. Within a few thousand years of that first wave of humanity reaching these shores, almost all the mega-animals were gone.

The near extinction of the great whales last century was part of a pattern. Up until quite recently this planet we all live on was inhabited by lots of big, interesting land animals. But as humans colonised the world in the past few tens of thousands of years, they ate anything too slow to run or too big to hide. In the 1800s, when we finally gained the means to take a pop at the previously unassailable great whales, we nearly exterminated them in little more than a century.

It's sometimes argued that all this is symptomatic of an irredeemably dark and destructive aspect of human nature. I don't think it is.

Humans are animals too. We evolved in a harsh and brutal world and within that world we've become a globe-bestriding super-predator. Having a ruthless and violent streak is presumably a precondition of reaching such a position.

The prehistoric hunters that eradicated Australia's megafauna and the whalers who mindlessly exploited all that floating blubber didn't understand the wider context of their actions. But we do, and there's another aspect of the human psyche which is able to subdue those wild impulses of overkill. There's a long road ahead before human-induced species loss is halted, but arguments as to the principles have been settled.

As debates regarding how we manage our relationship with the ecosphere intensify, there is much talk of the bleak futures we must avoid. Let's also remember the bright ones we can look forward to, if and when we get things right. One hundred years ago humans were visiting unthinking butchery upon planet Earth's whales. Today teams of tourist boats tentatively shadow humpbacks across tropical bays, desperately hoping for a smidgen of their attention.

This may not be a perfect situation, but it's definitely progress.

Days since leaving London: 516

Blue whales killed in the Arctic Ocean during the 1930/1931 hunting season: 29,400

Reduction in Earth's blue whale population between 1864 and 1966: 99%

Estimated global blue whale population in 2002: 5,000–12,000

> *We learn history not in order to know how to behave or how to succeed,*
> *but to know who we are.* – Leszek Kolakowski

88: Queenslanders Are Peculiar
27 October 2006

Devo looked like a cross between Santa Claus and ZZ Top – large-framed, a massive beard and covered almost entirely in tattoos. On picking me up outside Hervey Bay he immediately began talking about his vasectomy.

It was a success, but the really stressful thing, apparently, was having it reversed. After the operation the doctors told him to lie still for two weeks. He nearly made it. Then he described exactly what he did to his new wife afterwards, actually making me blush. Many years later the two of them moved to the coast so that their (five) grandkids could swim in the ocean.

Devo dropped me at a lay-by outside Bundaberg and, that evening, I camped beside the road. The next morning two figures appeared from the adjacent camper van, walked straight up to me as I packed up my camp, and began talking.

The shorter of the two was called Kevin. Kevin had some of the most unhealthy-looking teeth I've ever seen (mostly missing, and the broken remainder all shades of brown and grey). He was a naturopath (a practitioner of an alternative medical system emphasising natural remedies) and his companion was called Beatrice. She was formerly Kevin's secretary, but more recently his wife. They'd been married four days.

As I deconstructed Nguthungulli the Tent, Kevin launched into an explanation of how 'mainstream' doctors had it all wrong and how his natural remedies offered a much more effective set of public health solutions. I was informed, for example, that *any* kind of poison can be neutralised by the simple application of charcoal to the wound.

'So what's your view of science generally?' I enquired.

'Well there's science, and then there's "*true* science",' he replied. 'I've been studying it for years.'

'Oh really? Where precisely?' I asked.

'All over the place. Mainly on the internet.'

'I see.'

Kevin went on to tell me about the hidden codes in the Bible which predicted the whole of history, that particular insight coming from a video he'd only watched half of. I listened patiently, smiled brightly, enthusiastically asked questions, then waved the two of them off in their campervan, on a quest to know more of the world so very different from my own.

After an eggs and bacon breakfast at the local café, and a rendition of 'Show Me the Way to Go Home' by the roadside, I was picked up by Colin and Veronica. They were driving home to Rockhampton after visiting friends in the south. Veronica was originally Chilean, and had been a medical student in Santiago during General Pinochet's 1973 coup. Colin was a hard-headed businessman type and told me about how clean energy was the investment opportunity of the moment. Globally US$60 billion in venture capital is going into it this year, apparently. We also discussed Paul Keating (bad), Gough Whitlam (very bad) and John Howard (good).

Colin and Veronica had met shortly after the break-ups of the first marriages, which had given them both children. The two of them had been neighbours and got talking over the fence one day. They'd relocated to Queensland quite recently and were sprucing up the state's cultural life by investing in a social venue to bring the right sort of people together. The three of us talked for the 300-kilometre drive to Rockhampton, then they took me to the best pub in town, introduced me to the owners and wouldn't let me pay for any drinks. Life was good. Shiny, happy people.

Rockhampton – city of cowboys and sawdust – is where ex-Newtown housemates Adam and Chantel both originally hail from. Two hours after arriving I was picked up by Adam's brother Brett and taken back to McGowan clan central. There, for the past two days, Joyce and 'Crocodile Bob' McGowan have been treating me just like one of their own. I sleep in the 'rumpus room', where there's a dart board on the wall and a foosball table in the corner. Twice a day we sit down to family meals and, in the afternoons, Bob and I sit on the balcony, drink beer and shoot the breeze.

Adam had predicted that the two of us might have a few disagreements (me being a liberal European neo-hippie and Bob a hard-grafting old-school Queensland fellow). As it happens my view that Indigenous Australian societies are the victims of historical circumstance did differ from his. But he took the time to seek out my thoughts and basically Bob and I are on the same page about what's important in life – people, community and love.

I must also admit that I find it impossible not to feel deep admiration for the fact that Bob and Joyce have kept an amazing marriage going for decades, particularly given that I can't even organise myself a proper long-term girlfriend.

Rockhampton is the beef capital of Australia. All over the city there are statues of bulls celebrating this fact. Around here, therefore, if one is young, drunk and possessed of an ironic brand of humour, the game is to steal their testicles as trophies. Rockhampton's town council has a full-time employee replacing the balls of stone bovines. They've even employed an architect to design hacksaw-proof genitals. It's that kind of town.

This morning Brett and I drove into the countryside to check out some really big carnivorous lizards. The cowboy-hat-wearing guide at the crocodile farm was jaunty and full of reptile-related facts and figures. The big male crocs (Baku, King Wally, Rocky and Mr Stumpy) were the most interesting: 1,000-kilogram armour-plated monsters that solve problems through extreme violence. Fantastic.

Days since leaving London: 518
Number of cows within 250 kilometres of Rockhampton: 2,000,000

Deal seriously with serious matters and gracefully with lighter ones.
– Cicero's fifth rule of conversation

89: 1,000 Kilometres, No Dramas
4 November 2006

Outside Rockhampton I was picked up by Zane. As his car stopped, I, as usual, used that moment to assess the driver. Something about his manner sounded a minor alarm. However, I was still 1,000 klicks from Cairns, and Zane, on his way to spend the weekend with his brother, was heading 400 in my direction. I decided to go for it. That was a good decision. Zane turned out to be very interesting indeed.

He was working as a carpenter at one of the opencast desert mines where they tap Australia's vast mineral wealth. Driving north we passed huge, snake-like goods trains pulling coal-filled wagons down dedicated tracks. The tracks lead to enormous ports on the east coast, where they ship the stuff out as fast as they can to feed the bellies of Chinese and Indian industry and satisfy human civilisation's craving for fossil fuels.

The world's globalised commodity markets transfer that addiction straight into an Australian mining sector without enough labour in its harsh desert workspaces. That means sky-high wages and lots of bored, lonely men earning six-figure salaries – a recipe for gambling, drugs and prostitution.

Zane was conducting a tempestuous love affair with a hairdresser in Rockhampton. He spent his bucks on her, while she provided the emotional support he craved. Sometimes he didn't treat her right, and they fought a lot, but Zane's heart was definitely in the right place. He was saving for a long sailing trip and hoped that she would join him.

At one point he stopped the car to go to the boot and show me one of the books she'd given him. It was Milan Kundera's *The Unbearable Lightness of Being*. 'I just love her black ass,' he said, shaking his head and staring into the middle distance. He told me stories of rows, literature, money and his deep, abiding sexual hunger for her. I silently approved at the depth of his passion.

As Zane and I struck north, the surrounding plains became drier and drier while, to our left, the ragged peaks of the Great Dividing Range marked the western horizon. Periodically we'd pass farmsteads or flocks of feral camels. I meditated on the shimmering desert, the kilometres rolled by in their hundreds and Otis Taylor sang the blues.

My next lift, Chris, was returning a hire car to Cairns. Chris' job was to deliver cars across Australia. He'd been to every town on the continent I could name and seen more of this country than anyone else I've met. He didn't have any immediate family, though there was a sister he occasionally stayed with. It was a lonely life about which he spoke with honesty and humility. He told me that he'd once planned to explore the rest of the world, but something always came up and he didn't think he'd get around to it now.

Chris detoured 50 kilometres out of his way to drive me to the gates of the campsite at the coastal town of Airlie Beach – travellers' centre, busy marina and gateway to the nearby Whitsunday Islands. It was buzzing.

Over the next four days I explored the islands in a boat (think: Irish backpackers, drinking games and a snorkel), ate fresh barramundi with a couple of touring Germans and threw rugby balls with my neighbour Dave, who lived in a van and built resorts for millionaires on nearby Hamilton Island.

The campsite was dotted with fruit trees and, every night, a colony of bats would congregate in them (*woomp* went their wings), squawk noisily and throw figs about. At one point Dave got out his 10-million-candle-power torch and shined it right in the bats' faces, just an arm's length away. They were enormous, but arrogantly uncaring of our curiosity: crushing fruit between their teeth, sucking out the juice, then letting the drool-sodden pulp fall down through the branches.

On my last night in Airlie Beach, Dave came back with two bottles of cheap sparkling wine and a couple of (exceedingly tacky) green perspex champagne flutes. I sat in his camping chair, bubbles tickling my nose, while he told me how, this year, Earth's population passed six and a half billion. He thought this was a dangerous development, wildly comparing us to the monkeys in Stanley Kubrick's *2001: A Space Odyssey*, who run their hands over the mysterious black obelisk and unleash forces they don't understand.

I questioned both the quality of Dave's sparkling wine and that of his Stanley Kubrick analogy – pointing out that ultimately the monkeys path is a more interesting one after their black-obelisk moment. Following a night of conversation beneath raucous fruit bats, I retired to Nguthungulli the Tent. There I dreamed of champagne bubbles sparkling behind green perspex and of monkeys, stimulated by black obelisks or by abstract shapes on pages.

Heading north once more I was picked up by Dain, who was going to help his kids go through his recently deceased ex-wife's stuff. They'd been separated for some years and he said that it was only after her death that he'd realised how much his children still needed him. Dain talked of the previous day's fishing with his grandson and the big catch they'd made. On dropping me on the road north of Prosperpine, by a track that led to the house, he said that if I was done hitchhiking for the day I could follow that track for a warm bed and fish supper.

After 20 minutes I was just about to take up his offer when I heard a voice behind me. A silver station wagon had pulled up and a man was leaning through the window. 'Vood ju like to come with aas?' he asked.

Well, of course I would.

David Schneeberger works in a bank in Bern and is travelling with his Czech girlfriend Regina, a dark-haired beauty with a passion for ice hockey. David follows English football with as much fanaticism as all but the most hardened England fan and goes crazy for heavy metal music. 'Sometimes I juus freak out and start headbanging,' he mused.

Like me, David and Regina were concluding an adventure, having just spent three months driving anti-clockwise around Australia. They'd started in Cairns and were about to finish the loop. We reached Townsville that first evening, ate dinner together, played on the shore-front swings and slides, then drank café-lattes by the ocean the next morning.

Yesterday afternoon, as we drove north once again from Townsville, David and I argued about economics. He said that, without the guiding hand of community control, capitalism runs amok. I took the view that, while communal systems of organising economies may be well intended, they are inefficient because they have no way of handling the information problems.

Basically he, the Swiss banker, wanted more regulation and government intervention, while I, the pilgrim hitchhiker, was in favour of global free markets. It's a topsy-turvy world.

The three of us arrived in Cairns at eight o'clock last night. Job done. No dramas.

Plan update: I've booked five days' diving on the Great Barrier Reef. After that I'll return to Sydney (by plane this time), bond with my Newtown posse one last time, say goodbye to Australia, then fly across the Pacific to the Americas and the final stage of this pilgrimage.

Rock on.

Days since leaving London: 526
Wingspan of a fully grown fruit bat: 5 feet
Human civilisation's primary energy consumption (billion billion joules per year) in

1900:	22	1990:	320
1950:	70	2000:	355
1970:	189		

Congratulations, it's a Viking.' – Marketing slogan for Cryos, a Danish sperm bank

Musings
World Systems

Every night on my way up the east coast I was pouring out my heart into the weather-beaten and black gaffer-tape-reinforced notebook I carried, but since visiting India, I'd stopped writing poetry.

By this point I was on a mission. The notion I'd absorbed during my travels was that there's an approach to thinking about the world – a modern approach – which is ready to be synthesised by someone with the interest, time and head space. So that's what I'd do.

*****

Imagine a party. Now imagine that somewhere in that party, on a tray, is a glass of champagne full of bubbles. Now imagine sticking (bubble-sized) brains in those bubbles and asking them what they thought about their world. They'd probably come up with lots of bubble-related issues to talk about, such as who was the biggest bubble and which bubble sparkled the brightest. If they started talking to each other, no doubt it wouldn't take long for bubble politics to emerge.

From the point of view of bubbles in a champagne glass, which bubbles are the biggest and brightest are matters of note. But the *really* interesting thing is the party swirling around them. At this moment in history humans are at the point of perceiving the glass and the party, while still thinking stubbornly like bubbles.

For example, the east coast of Australia is an environmentally aware region in an environmentally aware nation. When I hitchhiked along it the issue on everyone's lips, just as in Sydney, was climate change.

Here are two narratives for thinking about that issue.

Narrative One

For more than a century, people have relied on fossil fuels for their energy needs. Burning such fuels releases carbon dioxide, which is a greenhouse gas (i.e. it traps heat by forming a blanket around the Earth). As carbon dioxide stays in the atmosphere for many years, concentrations of it are building up and global temperatures are rising.

As a result humanity is sitting on a ticking time bomb and has a short period of time in which to avert a major catastrophe. This is one of the greatest, if not *the* greatest, problem facing the human race. Our failure to tackle it decisively could soon send the planet into a tail-spin of epic destruction involving extreme weather, floods, droughts, epidemics and killer heat waves beyond anything we have ever experienced.

Narrative Two

Humans are a species of hominid thrown up by Earth's biosphere. The evolutionary processes which gave rise to them caused their line to develop hands, tool use, large brains and sophisticated culture. Twelve thousand years ago those characteristics allowed humans to start producing food via the technique of agriculture.

That, in turn, set in motion a chain of events which caused human technology to improve inexorably until, at the end of the eighteenth century, they started to build machines powered using the fossilised organic matter in the Earth's crust.

That, in turn, helped drive an enormous increase in humanity's command of the physical sciences such that, by the late twentieth century, humans realised that the waste gases their industry and transportation systems released affected the constitution of their planet's atmosphere which, in turn, had side effects.

That realisation came as a shock. Humans had not previously understood where the forces of history were driving them to, nor the effects their actions had on the Earth's meteorological rhythms. Theories were soon postulated, computer models cobbled together and everyone began arguing about what to do.

I believe that the second narrative is a much more complete way of thinking about what's happening (with greenhouse gases and climate change) than the first one.

I also believe that the reason climate change is thought of as the overarching threat of the twenty-first century (rather than the inevitable consequence of being a civilisation-building tool-using species on a planet with fossil fuels) is the same reason champagne bubbles that one day realise that they're floating in a glass in the middle of a party might initially panic – because they're subroutines in a system which they're only just beginning to comprehend.

A century and a half before this book was written, humans began to grasp that life forms evolve across generations and that, over time, species subdivide into new species. At the time, Herbert Spencer coined the phrase 'survival of the fittest' to describe this newly grasped process.

But 'fittest' is a subjective idea. The ancestor of the tapeworm was an animal that ran around and had legs, but it evolved into an egg-laying parasite which could only exist in the guts of other species. The reason we think about a phenomenon like evolution by natural selection in terms of an idea like 'survival of the fittest' is because we're thinking about it from the inside.

Earth's biological systems throw up sets of differently designed beings in every generation of every species. Those beings are born into a dynamic environment, so what survives (i.e. constitutes 'fittest') is ceaselessly changing. In addition, any animal born into an ecosystem alters it – resulting in a permanent feedback mechanism which helps keep the flavour of Earth's biosphere in flux.

There's a modern twist. Human activity is intensifying that feedback loop. In addition to affecting other species on the planet, civilisation changes so fast that it constantly introduces new variables affecting who has children. That, in turn, affects the direction civilisation will take.

We're not currently in a position to design equations to model how particular new technologies and cultural trends alter human breeding patterns. But in a world where human action changes the environment, the environment changes who breeds and people inherit the traits of their parents, evolution will be never-ending.

Such processes led to every mental and physical attribute of the animal reading these words. For example, you were taught to use tools (knifes, forks, loo paper) by your parents (or whoever brought you up). They were taught by their parents, and so on. But if you follow that line back to the first thing ever to use a tool, it wasn't human. It was one of your non-human hominid ancestors.

And yet because the appendages at the ends of that ancestor's forearms were so well suited to basic tool use, and because being able to use basic tools made them slightly more likely to breed, a two-and-a-half-million-year feedback process of greater manual dexterity was set in motion which led to the shape of the hands holding this book right now (which are, as you can see, brilliantly evolved for advanced tool use).

It's more straightforward to think of oneself as a member of a static species that evolved, rather than the momentary expression of a constantly churning biosphere. But thinking about oneself as that momentary expression – a single revolution in the circle of life – is not only more complete, it's more fun.

Until recently humans had little information regarding what they were and how they came to be here. The frameworks we'd built up for thinking about the world were limited in a direct reflection of that limited knowledge. But now that we can assess our situation stripped of the assumptions implicit in human discourse since prehistory, everything starts to look even more beautiful.

*****

By November 2006 I was already emailing out the diary in the knowledge that it would only fully make sense once bound together with these musings. But scribbling away in my tent was never going to nail the job. Going to the Andes had been Susie's idea. In the end that self-imposed isolation was to constitute an acceleration, rather than the culmination, of the path I was on. However, before going to Quito I first returned to Sydney and, before that, I went diving.

90: Finding Nemo
9 November 2006

If I was going to show the sharks who was boss I needed a dive buddy who wouldn't freak out when faced with an apex-level predator at 20 metres underwater. I therefore teamed up with a capable, Viking-like and up-for-it Finnish architect named Kai.

We prepared for our dive trip with a two-day refresher course in Cairns, then took a speedboat to the *M. V. Kangaroo Explorer*, a 25-metre catamaran which permanently wanders between dive sites above the Great Barrier Reef and hosts a diving colony of 50 people.

Life on the *M. V. Kangaroo Explorer* involved watching sunsets, sharing time on deck with Kai and the gang and swimming around the boat with sun-blanketed water stretching to every horizon. Three times a day there was the camaraderie of climbing from the latest dive site to de-equip, rinse wetsuits and discuss what we'd seen. It was the perfect finale to my east coast hitchhiking adventure.

In addition to the salt water, boat life involved full immersion in the world of diving-obsessed characters who make their living on it. 'I used to be a financial direc-*ta* but then I discovered *doi*-ving,' drawled Ronaldo, the ginger-haired, ruddy-faced South African, whose only role seemed to be to induce people to do ridiculous things underwater and then selling them the DVDs.

Kai and I spotted our first (black-tipped reef) shark while snorkelling on the first afternoon. I immediately duck-dived and set off in pursuit. I was only yards away when the fish realised I meant business, flicked its tail and made good its escape. Cheeky li'l rippa.

Back in the barbarian-like 1960s they actually attempted the extermination of the reef's shark population by paying cowboys tax dollars to take pot shots at them from helicopters. After exterminating so many species down the ages, we went after the sharks more or less for the hell of it. Our faltering progress towards ecological enlightenment comes none too soon.

Other aquatic fauna encountered included two other species of shark, a couple of hawksbill turtles, an angry blue fish which wriggled its bum and mock-charged when I approached the square foot of coral on which it lived, and an incy wincy clown fish hiding among the waving fronds of its tentacled home.

Found him.

Since announcing my project to make myself hip through facial hair I've been subjected to a barrage of rude words from correspondents across the world. I ended up caving in to this long-distance peer pressure, taking out a razor and reducing my beloved burns to more respectable dimensions. However, in order to ensure I maintain internal stylistic integrity, I have purchased a hat sporting the words 'Aussie Aussie Aussie' in green and yellow lettering around the rim. I regard my new headwear as constituting a devilishly ironic, post-modern statement. Everyone else says I look like a plonker.

Days since leaving London: 531
Scuba divers killed by sharks on the Great Barrier Reef, ever: 0

Life is crazy. Don't let that stop you from enjoying it. – Peter F. Hamilton

91: Australasian Exit Strategy
16 November 2006

So there I was: half-naked, wearing my new Aussie-plonker hat and sitting in the middle of a music festival with the Oz-crew sprawled merrily on the slope around me. Kerry was on fire; Brett was visiting from Rockhampton; Adam had finished his first year of drama school; Eden and Zoe were stripped off and swapping hats; and everybody was in blistering form.

I had returned, bronzed and triumphant, from my hitchhiking expedition two days before the Newtown 2006 Dreamfest, an annual community event held just 100 metres from 119 Australia Street. Despite a shaky start on the continent, things had worked out. But the time had come to continue east. Two days later I was due to fly to South America.

After leaving the Great Barrier Reef I had five days before crossing the Pacific. Here's what happened:

Day one: Wake up in Cairns at four in the morning with a fever and stomach cramps. It seems I swallowed something dodgy with the salt water. Two hours later, while walking from the airport terminal to my Sydney-bound flight, I vomit yellow bile onto the grass verge. The chief air steward ponders whether to allow me on board. I hold myself together, turn the charm to maximum and he lets me fly. Phew. Four hours later I wake up in Sydney feeling happy again and, at 119 Australia Street, Eden and Zoe burst from the door with cameras, affection and cups of tea. Chantel and Kris are down for the weekend's U2 concert. They announce their engagement. Hoorah.

That evening I make a keenly anticipated reunion with Kerry at the newly refurbished Bank pub on King Street. I'm burning with desire and she looks astounding. I throw my arms around her, then we walk arm in arm down King Street to her flat. There I tell her all that's happened to me and, bursting with blood and hormones, ravish her until morning.

Day two: I return to an Australia Street bathed in sunlight, where Eden and I drink dark-red cocktails with breakfast. That afternoon we drive to Bondi Beach with our friends Jarred and Rachel (he's an actor, she's in costume – basically a couple of luvvies) to look at the Sculpture by the Sea exhibition. Blow-up pink plastic anemones and squat surrealist figures are dotted among the coast-front rocks. Around them Sydney's beach culture is flowering into summer.

Day three: The Newtown Festival. The whole suburb goes ballistic for 24 hours. Thousands of happy, smiling people, live music and one eccentricity after another. In the dog look-alike competition Johnny Depp (a border terrier, replete with pirate uniform) sees off Batman and Arnold Schwarzenegger to win best in show. King Street is a whirlwind of parties.

Day four: I spend the whole day with Kerry at her flat, drinking in the last of her. We join Adam, Zoe and Eden that night for a final meal on King Street. At the evening's end we link arms and take photos of ourselves. Goodbye everyone.

Day five: I say my final farewell to Kerry at 8 a.m. before walking down King Street, to Australia Street, for the very last time. Then Eden drives me to the airport, we drink coffee in the sun, we embrace and I go to board my flight. That's it then.

The immigration guy gives me a goofy grin and says, 'No worries.' I realise how much I'm going to miss the Australians. The next thing I know the plane is taxiing down the runway and a chapter of my life is vividly coming to a close.

Now I'm on a new continent reflecting on everything which has happened and all the people I've met. It's only now that all the things I want to say come to me. But it's too late. We're separated by an ocean of water, and suddenly life seems so short.

Days since leaving London: 538
Days spent in Australia: 308

> *When we make a friend another had gone;*
> *Should a woman's kindly face*
> *Make us welcome for a space,*
> *Then it's boot and saddle, boys, we're*
> *Moving on.*
> – Banjo Patterson

Part 8

On Bread Loaf Mountain

92: Trans-Pacific
22 November 2006

Crossing the Pacific took 12 hours, during which we flew over the International Date Line, arriving in California five hours before leaving Australia. In Sydney, it had been a beautiful summer's day of clear skies and beating sun. Los Angeles was grey, concrete and raining.

United States border officials have a mean reputation and an obsession with bureaucracy. They insist that everyone writes the details of a hotel on the forms they brandish, even if you have nothing booked. I wrote 'Hotel California, Dark Desert Highway'. No one noticed.

It was early morning and I was flying out that night; so I caught a bus into town, ate some food in a diner, found a hostel, then flopped. Eighteen hours later I was on a plane to Costa Rica.

Here's the deal: my Sydney-based travel agent had informed me that for US$10 airport tax I could stop in Central America for as long as I wished. I opted for seven days. When boarding that Costa Rica-bound plane I knew two things about the country: where it was and that it famously has no army. I didn't have any idea what I'd do with my week there, so I chatted up the girl next to me, borrowed her guidebook and formulated a plan.

I picked two places to visit: Volcán Arenal, Central America's most active volcano, and Monteverde, a village in the central highlands. My flight landed in the city of San José. It was small, lacklustre and a bit grubby. I split town the next day and headed for the mountains.

Travelling north I met two Swiss pixies on the bus. Their names were Manuela (tomboyish good looks and a dusky Bavarian complexion) and Rachel (buxom and smiley, with curly dark-red hair). By the time we arrived at Volcán Arenal I'd joined their gang.

We checked into a wooden alpine-style lodge at the volcano's base, then hired bicycles to help us explore. At the market we purchased an outrageously large carrot to go with our picnic. The girls pulled out said vegetable at several opportune moments that day in order to make the following gags: 'What an enormous carrot you've got,' (penis gag); 'Look at the size of my great big vegetable,' (penis gag); and 'What's up, doc?' while raising eyebrows and suggestively pretending to chew on the carrot (blow-job gag masquerading as a Bugs Bunny gag).

Later that day I tried to impress the two of them by singing in the rain as we made our way across Volcán Arenal's slopes. Rachel is a policewoman, but before becoming a policewoman she was a pastry chef, and before becoming a pastry chef she was an opera singer. She responded to my crooning by belting out 'The Queen of the Night Aria' from the ruddy *Magic Flute*, utterly putting me to shame.

As for Manuela, she's currently working as a travel agent in San José and she has an extremely optimistic attitude to life. Manuela believes that exploring the world should be about more than just self-indulgent fun and that there's a firm relationship between how you deal with the universe and the way it treats you in return. She'll go far.

After two days with the pixies I took a four-by-four out of town, crossed a lake under the circling eyes of some local raptors, then caught a bus which wound up through coffee plantations to the highlands. Monteverde ('Green Mountain') is an ecotourism Mecca that sits among Costa Rica's cloud forests (i.e. a forest where it's cloudy and it rains all the time). The day after arriving I packed a bag, donned my waterproof, then wandered off alone to bond with the trees.

My towering leafy companions were high, mighty, ancient, wrapped in moss and draped in vines and completely dominated their forest kingdom. Overhead, their crowns were lost in grey-green mist. Below, tangled root systems extended above the ground, forming dark nooks and crannies where tarantulas and scorpions made their homes, emerging at night to hunt. I sang songs as I splashed about in hired wellies all day, exploring the root-straggled paths, goggling at the jumbled Jurassic-style undergrowth and daydreaming about the elves and goblins I felt must surely live there. It was one of the best days I've ever had.

I arrived back in San José last night. As the bus switchbacked its way into the valley, I pored over my Quito guide and Spanish notes, absorbing information as fast as I could. This morning, I'm on a plane to Ecuador.

Days since leaving London: 544

	Costa Rica	Ecuador
Population	4,075,261	13,547,510
Life expectancy at birth	77.02 years	76.42 years
GDP per capita	US$11,100	US$4,300

To me, nature is sacred. Trees are my temples and forests are my cathedrals. – Mikhail Gorbachev

93: Welcome to South America
1 December 2006

I'm in Quito, mountain capital of Ecuador, in the north-west corner of South America, right on the Equator. The city is built into a valley running north–south through the Andes; precipitous slopes, along with eight volcanoes, form the backdrop to my new life. The Old Town, where I've based myself, is enchantingly South American: packed with whitewashed churches, sumptuous colonial plazas and a splendid Gothic-Hispanic basilica.

There are loads of guns. Seeing that as far as I'm aware Ecuador is in no imminent danger of invasion, one wonders who they might be used against. The whole place has a sense of edgy danger. During the day, old men sit around and bemoan government corruption. At night, the threat of violent robbery means one must be very careful.

On my fifth day in the city it was the final round of the country's presidential election. There was a major security operation. Police stood around in teams, gas masks fixed ominously to belts. Soldiers in jackboots guarded the main intersections. They did a good job of looking serious, although I caught one typing out a text message when he thought nobody was looking.

The two candidates were Rafael Correa (leftish, called George W. Bush 'a dimwit') and Alvaro Noboa (banana tycoon and Ecuador's richest man). The atmosphere during the vote was civilised. The quality of the media coverage was excellent.

Correa won.

I'm going to base myself in Quito for two months. I've taken an apartment, enrolled in Spanish classes and cleared my reading list of everything but South Americana.

In order to ensure contact with the outside world during the coming period of relative isolation, I've joined a travellers' organisation called South American Explorers. Membership gives me access to its tranquil neo-colonial clubhouse (wood panelling, a library, free coffee and a pet kitten), which is a marvellous haven from the city's bustle.

The crowd there is diverse and impressive: biologists drawn by Ecuador's enormous biodiversity; anthropologists working with tribes in its jungle; grad students on secondment from the USA; and environmental consultants working for the oil companies. 'My clients think I'm an ecoterrorist, the environmentalists tell me I'm the devil,' said one.

During the last two weeks of hotels and country-hopping I've been repeatedly asked my profession in the forms one has to fill in. 'Naturalistic Pantheistic Neo-Hippie' won't generally fit. I've therefore started to record myself as 'Global Muse'.

Days since leaving London: 553

Quito's elevation above sea level: 2,850 metres
Date of last eruption of Pichincha, the closest volcano to Quito: 23 August 2006

> *Chocolate without cheese is like love without kisses.* – Ecuadorian proverb

Musings
A Global Muse

Moments of transcendent ecstasy and all-encompassing oneness with the rest of the universe are all very well, but they are spontaneous, and ephemeral. Capturing those moments – systematically deconstructing, articulating and recording them in a way that is complete and internally consistent – requires patience, discipline, head space and time.

The 18 months between leaving London and arriving in Ecuador had filled me with inspiration and mental energy. I was in Quito to focus that energy. The rationale for going there was to put myself in a place where nobody knew me and there were no distractions, in order to get some things off my chest about what's happening on this planet.

I was in Quito to write stuff down.

I'd set myself two months. There was no time to waste. During that first week I checked into a hotel, explored the city on foot, joined South American Explorers, answered an advertisement for an apartment, viewed the apartment, then moved in.

My new living arrangements were rustic. So the morning after moving in, I went to the shops, bought a job lot of cleaning products, then spent a day sweeping the place out and scrubbing its floorboards on my hands and knees. I then tried out 20 different internet cafés (to test them as office spaces), took a bunch of books out of the library and joined a language school.

I'd gone through a complete cultural sphere change: a new city, a new country, a new continent and a once-in-a-lifetime mission. It was *really* exciting.

Then, to top it all off, at the end of that week I learned that a brand-new human being had appeared right in the middle of my family.

94: Uncle Peter
5 December 2006

I have become an uncle.

My big sister, Ruth, and her tall and handsome other half, Richard, have produced a daughter. Polly Eliza Oberg was born on 25 November 2006. She does not know this yet, but she is now my niece. This is the most exciting thing that has ever happened to me. I'm feeling very emotional about it.

'Uncle Peter' not only takes his new responsibilities seriously, he goes further and has developed a wildly inflated sense of his own importance with respect to this new project, unilaterally declaring himself chief godperson in absentia. I intend to commence young Polly's spiritual education the moment I set foot back in the UK.

First, however, I have six months left to conclude this pilgrimage.

In order to complete my set-up-a-life-in-Quito phase I've joined a local gym. It's laughably third-world and dilapidated, but Sam, who runs and owns it, is a cool guy. Pride of place in the weights room goes to a huge poster of Che Guevara and Fidel Castro striding purposefully, shoulder to shoulder. Faded pictures of a buffed-up 1970s Arnold Schwarzenegger adorn the walls alongside images of scantily clad ladies draping themselves across Lamborghinis (intended, I assume, to offer encouragement to the patrons).

I'm now doing four hours of Spanish lessons a day. Reuben, my teacher, is young, thoughtful and bossy. He doesn't allow me to speak English in his presence so as to prime my brain for the Latin tongue. Reuben tells me his woman troubles. You see, he's got one, but he's thinking of ditching her because, although she's extremely hot, she's also crazy and irrational.

Chicks, tsk.

Elkin and Ramone, two Colombians running a café where I sometimes eat lunch, have been complimenting me on the clarity of my English compared to that of those damnable Yankees. Naturally, I lap up this sort of thing. They adore it when in return I note that their accents are more agreeable than those of the Spanish themselves – comments which are met with vigorous nodding, enthusiastic back slapping and all-round comedy lisping at the expense of the Iberians.

Days since leaving London: 555
Number of hummingbird species native to Ecuador: 140

Spanish word of the day: 'amanecer' meaning 'dawn'

95: The Eyrie
7 December 2006

Quito has two city centres: the Old Town and the New Town.

The New Town is filled with modern restaurants, travel agencies, internet cafés and foreigners. South American Explorers is based there and it's where the gringos hang out.

Down the road, Quito's Old Town is classier, cheaper and one of the world's most picturesque urban centres. Its Centro Histórico is based around the Plaza Grande and flanked by the Presidential Palace, the Archbishop's Palace and the Cathedral. Off to one side is a hill (and local landmark) called El Panecillo ('The Little Bread Loaf'). At the hill's summit is a statue of the Virgin and built against its side, among a jumble of corrugated iron roofs and shanty-style box houses, is my apartment.

The apartment has four rooms: kitchen, bedroom, bathroom and rumpus room. These are joined by a balcony containing a table, two benches, a pot plant and room enough to swing several cats. That balcony sits above a courtyard, on the other side of which (and below) live Nella and Henry – my landlords and newly adopted Latin American family.

Nella is Dutch, speaks six languages and works as a guide leading tour groups into the Amazon. Henry is Ecuadorian and an artisan, plays harmonica in a band and, when not indulging his new English brother with ad hoc Spanish lessons, sits in a workshop beneath my balcony making jewellery out of amethyst and silver.

The apartment comes with a stereo. I have two CDs: one is Peruvian pipe music I bought from some street musicians at the Plaza Grande, the other is an astonishing fusion of Spanish guitar and hip hop mixed by Japanese DJ Mitsu, which was given to me when I left Sydney. I'm spending my time gazing out over the Andes, writing in my big black book, conjugating Spanish verbs and dancing around, all by myself, in my new hilltop home. Hip hop, I've come to understand, loves me 100 per cent.

The eyrie is an elevated location in a city built onto the side of a mountainous valley at nearly three kilometres above sea level, so the views from my balcony are utterly and comprehensively spectacular. When I went to look at the apartment during my first week here, Nella described it as 'a good place to dream'. She hit that nail right on the head.

Days since leaving London: 561

Population of

London:	11,624,807	Sydney:	4,199,190
Istanbul:	11,332,000	Quito:	1,397,698

We are at the very beginning of time for the human race. It is not unreasonable that we grapple with problems. But there are tens of thousands of years in the future. Our responsibility is to do what we can, learn what we can, improve the solutions, and pass them on. – Richard Feynman

Musings
A Good Place to Dream

I'd started attending church.

Quito's Old Town has a lot of beautiful churches: dark and serene stone temples, built among the ashes of the Spanish Conquest. Two-thirds of the way down the hill between my apartment and the gym lies the Monastery of San Agustín. It has a nave filled with pensive saints and an atmosphere ripe for contemplation. So, every day, I would stop there to clear my head.

My personal experience of studying the Abrahamic scriptures had persuaded me that they were not the deliberately inspired product of divine wisdom, intended to set out eternal messages for humanity. They seemed too clearly human projections and clung too impulsively to capricious ideas such as 'revelation' and 'miracle'.

Jed from Byron Bay would have used such things to explain away religion as the residue of ancient foolishness: superstition and mysticism no longer sufficient for a species growing in confidence and self-knowledge. But that is not my view. Sitting within the soothing confines of San Agustín I did not, in my heart, believe those traditions to be misguided.

Debates concerning whether 'God exists' are filled with semantic misunderstandings – words which everyone uses and about which everyone understands different things. Is one talking about a dude in the clouds? An all-encompassing supernatural 'force'? Or an omnibenevolent dictator who controls the universe?

I'm of the view that positions such as theism and atheism fail to embrace how different tomorrow's ways of thinking might be from those of today. I'm not against faith, but I think it might be time to start being more imaginative about what one is having faith in.

You see, I'm not just an optimist about the human condition. I'm an optimist about the very nature of reality, about the underlying fabric of the space–time continuum of which we're all expressions.

If one were to accept that we're a species of carbon-based life form which evolved on this planet, that spiritual belief systems are one of our collective features and that social institutions (in the form of the organised religions) have grown up around those belief systems, then the core question is: what underlying phenomena are those social institutions an expression of? Why, *ultimately*, have these humans built this church?

Thinking constructively about that sort of thing means stepping outside the boxes one is normally trained to think inside. So, if you locked yourself in a South American hill shanty with a talking tent for a couple of months, it's the sort of thing you could probably take a pop at.

96: The Latin Family
15 December 2006

Since I arrived in Quito, Nella has spent nearly all her time leading expeditions in the Amazon. On the rare occasions she isn't in the jungle, then, in the main room of the house she shares with Henry, there's invariably a pile of equipment that's either being unpacked from the last trip or prepared for the next one.

Nella rarely stands still and she talks very fast. Her conversation (monologues really) takes the form of a stream of consciousness made up of plans, half-plans and snatches of information deemed relevant that millisecond – continuously jumping into its next subject before finishing with the one before. The most interesting thing is just to let her roll.

Yesterday I stopped at their house for an hour (Henry was away, they'd had a fight) while she made me coffee and a sandwich. As she bustled around the kitchen she provided a commentary on herself bustling around the kitchen (first the toaster was believed to be working, then it wasn't, then it was again). Meanwhile she peppered this debate with herself about the functionality of the toaster with anecdotes from her day. She'd met a friend on the street (he was a musician and had lived in Portugal, she mused); it was near the opera house (cue: translation of opera into Dutch) while she was leading a tour group; said group were Canadian-Jewish, wanted to see everything (which was impossible, she interrupted herself to point out) and (I was informed) were off to the Galapagos the next day. By the time the sandwich landed in front of me it had occurred to her that I'd be in Peru next year. That provoked a machine-gun explanation of the places I simply had to visit and her friends I could drop in on. Concentrating hard I could just make out place names. Within a minute she'd filled a side of A4 with destinations and email addresses, which I was served with my coffee.

Nella also comes with a shock of curly blonde hair and a big fat work ethic; all in all, quite a girl.

However, the lion's share of my non-Spanish-learning human contact in Quito has been with Henry and, as my language skills have improved, we've found much to discuss. If he's still awake when I return to my apartment after an evening of writing, I pop in for a chat. On several occasions I've talked long into the night with my *hermano ecuatoriano* ('Ecuadorian brother'), as I insist on calling him.

Like many Ecuadorians, Henry is frustrated by his country's inability to take control of its destiny. In the past five decades many countries around the world have seen their economic fortunes transformed. Ecuador isn't one of them.

And yet, apart from the odd (minor) tiff with Peru, Ecuador has been at peace for generations and has vast natural resources, including lots of petroleum. So what's the problem? The Ecuadorians have a long list of people they like to blame. High on it are the oil corporations, corporations in general, politicians and, inevitably, the good old Americans.

In recent years Henry has gotten himself a nice Dutch girlfriend and settled down to make beautiful objects, but he has a colourful past. He tells me about the antics of his youth, the rock bands he's played in, his old lovers (scattered across Colombia and Brazil) and his kids (the same). Sometimes, when it's late and he's in a melancholy mood, he tells me about the Conquest.

Days since leaving London: 567
Proportion of world's population living on US$1 or less per day:

1981	40.6%	1993	25.6%	2004	18.4%

Gaelic word of the day: 'giomlaireachd' meaning 'the habit of dropping in on mealtimes'

97: Guinea Pigs and Peanut Sauce
23 December 2006

Guinea pigs have been an important element in Andean diets for 7,000 years. Their consumption is a tricky cross-cultural food issue. Some people (from countries where they're usually kept as pets) find the sight of their paws and teeth sticking out (after they've been spit-roasted) unnerving. The native word for them, Cuy ('cooi'), presumably derives from the cute squeaking sounds the furry little fellas make before you cook them. *Kwee kwee*.

I finally spotted one on the menu while out to dinner with Marisol, who works at my adopted English-language bookshop in the New Town. The bookshop is run by Mark, an Essex boy, and it's a meeting place for an element of Quito's Anglo-American expat community, who are uniformly male, middle-aged, obese, physically unattractive and (one can only assume) sexually underperforming. They're all married to Ecuadorian women in their twenties. Get the idea?

Every day this particular crowd assembles in Mark's bookshop in order to carry on their favoured topics of conversation – namely complaining about:

1) Ecuador

2) The Ecuadorians

3) Ecuadorian women

Marisol, who witnesses these conversations on a daily basis, is a level-headed sort who sees the funny side. She also reports that Mark is an excellent boss.

My dinner with Marisol was one of three nights out following two weeks of hermetic existence during which I put in long stretches typing up notes at the internet café and only spoke to Henry, Reuben and (briefly) Nella. As Christmas loomed, I thought I'd better try being sociable. That involved excursions to the Mariscal.

The Mariscal – centre of Quito's New Town – is a classic example of the sort of ghetto found across the world due to current discrepancies in global wealth: relatively rich expats congregating in one part of a relatively poor country. If you want to party you go to the Mariscal or, as the taxi drivers refer to it, 'gringoland'.

In the clubs the music shifts between contemporary pop/rock and the obligatory salsa. These guys know how to salsa, so if your skills aren't up to scratch, be prepared to look silly. Take it from one who knows. They're also international places where younger Ecuadorians of both genders practise 'gringo hunting'. Such an environment attracts a colourful assortment of criminals and dodgy characters. It's exciting, dangerous and very seedy.

As for my guinea pig dinner, I ate mine with avocado, potatoes and peanut sauce: high in protein, low in cholesterol and hits the spot with a 2005 Chilean Cabernet Sauvignon. Yum.

Days since leaving London: 575
Value of assets you need to be one of the

richest 50% of people on Earth:	US$2,161
richest 20% of people on Earth:	US$14,169
richest 5% of people on Earth:	US$150,145
richest 1% of people on Earth:	US$514,512

Spanish word of the day: 'descarado' meaning 'cheeky person'

98: Man on Hill
5 January 2007

I've received some good news. Just before New Year I heard from my friend Sue Harrison, who (as I learned while cycling across France in 2005) lost one of her legs during the terrorist attacks in London on the 7th of July of that year. She's relearning to jog, is back working part-time as a nurse and has been made ambassador for a charity doing research into limb regeneration. Apparently, salamanders can regrow lost limbs, so they're studying them in the hope of one day doing the same for humans. In this world of ever-increasing miraculousness, no doubt we'll get there eventually.

I just received a second email. Sue and her superstar boyfriend, Mike, spent Christmas in a holiday cottage, then New Year's Eve at a Fat Boy Slim gig on Brighton beach. They're to be married. This is an unquestionably marvellous development.

On Bread Loaf Mountain the festive season has been subdued. I invited Marisol over for Christmas dinner in an attempt to organise a sit-down community thing. Unfortunately, she ended up out of town and Nella was away, so in the end it was just me and Henry. We had a small plastic Christmas tree, a bit of glitter and matching Santa hats.

I cooked pasta and chillies, which we ate on my balcony. Then we both went to bed early. As Christmases go it was low key, but the view was amazing and it's one I'll always remember.

A week later, on the final afternoon of the year 2006, I walked to the Plaza Grande to phone my family in England, to find that the Old Town had emptied of traffic and filled with street football and roadblocks manned by monsters. Halfway down Bread Loaf Mountain, I was accosted by a ghoul and forced to dance before a crowd of rowdy onlookers. The ghoul was drunk and it tried to get money off me.

Heading to the New Town that evening my taxi was held up by a zombie drag queen accompanied by one of the Muppets. They wanted money too. It was strange. I even saw Shrek. He was shorter than I'd imagined.

I spent that night with the gringo crew from South American Explorers. We stuffed effigies with newspaper and dragged them into the throngs of the Mariscal, where they were burned in great pyres as fireworks exploded overhead and a street party raged around. Out with the old.

It's a funny thing to have spent six weeks in a place like this, overlooking the mountains, far from anyone who knows you. You can think, then write, then think, then write. You can let your mind wander into the internet during the day, then sink into books in the evening. It lets you float over the valley, glass in hand, taking lungfuls of fresh air, meditating on a far spread of buildings in the morning then a sea of white points at night. Above are the stars, patterns in the sky, waiting to be connected.

Days since leaving London: 588
Current best estimate of the number of people who've ever lived:
106 billion
Proportion alive today: 6%

Science word of the day: 'paleozoogeography' meaning 'the study of the distribution of prehistoric animals and their relation to ancient geographic features'

Musings
A Day in the Life

New Year's Eve 2006 was my last night out in Quito.

During my first four weeks in the city, Reuben and I had done one-on-one Spanish training four hours a day, five days a week. Completing my daily homework then took an additional three hours.

It's an intense schedule, but you learn Spanish very quickly.

After that I suspended the language classes and went into full-time hermitage. I'd see Henry every few nights and, occasionally, Mark and Marisol at the bookshop. Apart from that it was just me, Nguthungulli the Tent (who at this point was living in my backpack in the corner) and a lot of dreaming. The days ran as follows ...

I'd wake up late and, after breakfast on the balcony, make my way down the staircase from my apartment to Henry and Nella's courtyard, then down a further stairway to the street and (always) blazing Andean morning. Picking my way through the garbage on the pavement I'd walk across the valley to the Plaza Grande. On its far side, at the Monastery of San Agustín, I'd sit and contemplate before descending to the Plaza La Marin and my very own clapped-out third-world gym.

After pumping iron with Sam and the gym homies beneath the watchful gaze of Arnie, I'd eat lunch then take a tram to the New Town. The best internet café in Quito was on a road called JL Mera in the Mariscal. I'd be there by the early afternoon, then begin working.

Here's how you write a thesis about human civilisation, in a developing country, using internet cafés.

First, pick the right café. Essential features include a USB connection, a printer and good coffee. Things to avoid include rowdy atmospheres, slow computers and primitive word processors. Next, don't underestimate the time required. Writing such theses doesn't involve an hour here and an hour there. It involves 10-hour stretches at a computer, patiently working out how to present complex ideas in the simplest, most elegant way possible, then repeatedly reading through each bit of text until it's as good as you can get it. Finally, you mustn't become distracted. Quito has a lively gringo subculture and plenty of intriguing South American women. Don't get involved.

I spent those days in Quito alone, from afternoon through to evening, with my big black book propped up beside the monitor, recording, crystallising, dividing and subdividing my thoughts. Then I'd save what I'd written onto a USB stick and email it to myself for safety.

The internet café on JL Mera closed at 10 p.m. At that point I'd pay my bill then walk two blocks to the corner of Reina Victoria and J Calama, where there was an internet café which stayed open until midnight. I was invariably one of the last people there.

After they kicked me out I'd return to the Old Town by taxi and climb back up the stairs to my apartment. There I would drink wine, look out over the sea of lights below and immerse myself in books.

The most affecting thing I read during that period was a blow-by-blow account of the Spanish Empire's sixteenth-century conquest of the Incas. It's emotionally shocking stuff and, inevitably, it began pouring into my email diary. First, however, I decided to give my correspondents some background.

99: Paleozoogeography
11 January 2007

After a month cooped up in my apartment studying South Americana, it's time to share.

Twenty million years ago North and South America were separated by a sea. In that sea the waters of the Atlantic and Pacific freely mixed and, beneath its waves, two plates of the Earth's crust were moving against one another, the Pacific Plate sliding under the Caribbean one. That slow-motion tectonic collision caused the sea's floor to buckle, throwing up a line of underwater volcanoes. After five million years some of the volcanoes broke the surface and sediment from the adjacent continents began filling the gaps between them. Within two million years a land bridge had been created.

The formation of the Panamanian isthmus bridging North and South America rerouted Atlantic and Pacific currents and, by extension, the entire planet's oceanic and atmospheric circulation: re-sculpting rainfall patterns, landscapes and ecosystems. It also caused the two continents to start swapping species.

The technical name for the biodiversity event that was set in motion is the Great American Interchange. Animals, plants and freshwater fish from both continents began migrating between them. Racoons, llamas and sabre-toothed cats went south. Armadillos, porcupines and terror birds made the trek north.

The interchange was asymmetrical: northern species did better in the south than southern species in the north. The main reason for this was that North America had been sporadically connected to Eurasia (and thence Africa) via the Bering Strait, so northern species had effectively evolved over a bigger area than southern ones. They were therefore the products of a larger, more competitive, evolutionary arena.

That meant that they were a little faster and a little brainier and had slightly more efficient nervous systems. Within a few hundred thousand years, most of the big South American animals had been replaced by North American ones.

Three million years after that, Earth's ecosphere threw up a new mammal species in Africa. It used tools to manipulate its environment and language to articulate ideas. It also used culture to regulate and innovate its group behaviour, an ability which allowed this tropical African species to move, generation by generation, between habitats, continuously finding new ways to exploit food resources.

The prehistoric humans of the time didn't think about it that way. They were just getting on with their lives. And yet by the end of the last major glaciation they'd made it all the way to Siberia.

At that point sea levels were lower than today and Alaska and Asia were joined. The first Americans hugged the coast in their primitive boats and used an ingenious harpoon technology to hunt game in that savage north. When the climate warmed and the ice sheets retreated they followed the animals they hunted and went south.

Once established in North America there was nothing to stop them. They quickly spread across it and down through the Panamanian isthmus, following the same route as those other invaders three million years earlier. In the end it took about two thousand years for that small group of Siberians to fill both continents.

They reached Ecuador from the endless jungles of the east: one of the last branches in a tree of colonisations that took one hundred centuries to wrap this world in humanity and lay the foundations for the domination of the planet that would follow.

I've started talking to my tent again. I'm not sure if this is a good thing. I'm having trouble sleeping and have been thinking about the bees a lot. It's been over a year since they launched one of their periodic and unprovoked attacks. I'm concerned the bees may be plotting some sort of all-or-nothing surprise offensive.

Days since leaving London: 594
Difference between sea levels at the height of the last Ice Age and today: 130 metres

I've wrestled with reality over 35 years, and I'm happy, Doctor, I finally won out over it. – Jimmy Stewart

100: Native American State Formation

14 January 2007

Right now the weather in Quito runs like clockwork. In the mornings the sun burns your skin; in the afternoon clouds blot the sky and drench everything. Then, after dark, mist fills the valley beneath Bread Loaf Mountain and obscures the city below. After getting home every night I tell Nguthungulli the Tent how my day has gone and what I've been writing about, we compare the tasks completed with the to-do list prepared the evening before, then I sit on the balcony watching the lights go out beneath the Andes.

One of the intriguing features of the human endeavour is that, even though everyone has been making it up as they went along, everyone has come up with similar ideas. At least five separate human groups independently stumbled into farming, the development which set us on the path to the world you see around you. One of those original farming groups lived in the Andes, and among their contributions to posterity were the domestication of the llama and potato. Domesticating potatoes probably didn't seem very revolutionary at the time.

Like everywhere post-agriculture, Andean societies became more hierarchical, less stable and more innovative. Pottery and weaving were invented (on this side of the Atlantic) around 1800 BCE. The first metal employed was gold, around 1500 BCE, followed much later by copper. By two thousand years ago Andean societies were demonstrating the early features of state formation. South America was becoming a land of kings.

The first sedentary people of Ecuador were called the Valdiva. They lived on the coast and created earthenware statuettes of women with exaggerated breasts. Then there were the Machalilla, who deformed their own skulls by elongating their craniums with stones. Subsequently, there were the Cañari, who came from the south and had a fierce reputation; the Caras, who lived beside the Pacific; and the Quitus, after whom this city is named.

They'd all descended from the same group of Siberians who'd crossed from Asia 12,000 years before and who were, in turn, descended from a group of Africans who'd left Africa about 47,000 years before that. One corner of a continent-spanning tapestry of peoples, warring, interacting, advancing and evolving.

Then, from the south, came the Incas.

Days since leaving London: 597
Year planet Earth's population reached

1 billion:	1802	4 billion:	1974
2 billion:	1927	5 billion:	1987
3 billion:	1961	6 billion:	1999

Year planet Earth's population currently projected to peak: 2075

Only barbarians are not curious about where they come from, how they came to be where they are, where they appear to be going, whether they wish to go there, and if so, why, and if not, why not. –
Isaiah Berlin

101: Plonkerman and the Incas
21 January 2007

On learning I had a tooth problem Henry enthusiastically directed me to the university, where apparently they sort you out for a cool five bucks. I tried to conceal my horror at the suggestion that I let some half-trained five-dollar dental student near my teeth with a drill and anaesthetics. Forget it.

I instead opted for a reassuringly expensive gentleman with his own practice. As he was about to get stuck in, his assistant thrust a stuffed Bugs Bunny into my hands (to squeeze). 'Is this going to hurt?' I asked.

'Sí,' he replied. I was brave.

You can imagine my delight when it dawned on me that, in Spanish, the phrase 'hasta la vista' is both conversationally acceptable and grammatically correct. I now deliver it at every opportunity with a cheesy grin, a thumbs up sign and the suffix '… baby'. It works particularly well when I'm wearing my Aussie-plonker hat.

While the Incas weren't the first imperial people to dominate pre-Colombian South America, their empire was the most spectacular the continent had then seen and it isn't unreasonable to think of their civilisation as a golden age. It was an age characterised by ancestor worship, the building of a vast road network, efficient public administration, a complete absence of money and an endearing propensity to hold enormous drinking parties.

They'd exploded out of their motherland around Cuzco (in Peru) in the fifteenth century, conquering all before them and welding South America's peoples into the largest empire of the western hemisphere. When they arrived in Ecuador they were at the height of their power.

The locals put up a fight, but the Incas were relentless. They massacred thousands of Cañari in one infamous battle, dumping the corpses into Laguna Yaguarcocha ('Lake of Blood'). One by one, the local peoples succumbed. Quito fell in 1487.

Tupac Yupanqui, the Inca emperor, then fathered a son by a Cañari princess. That son, Huayna Capac, went on to succeed his father and, in turn, had two sons: Atahualpa, who grew up in Quito, and Huascar, who grew up in Cuzco. Inca power had reached its zenith. Huayna Capac, considered a god by his people, was master of the known world.

Then everything started going horribly wrong.

Smallpox killed the emperor. It had arrived on South America's northern coast with the first Europeans, then travelled across the Colombian jungle tribe by tribe, before sweeping into the empire and decimating its population. On his death bed the emperor divided his lands between his sons. It was a bad decision. Predictably, they went to war.

That was just when a bunch of pale-skinned, bearded strangers riding outlandish four-legged animals appeared in the north. By the time Atahualpa had won the civil war, the Spanish were making their move. They had not come in peace.

Days since leaving London: 604
Population of the Inca Empire at its height: 12 million

Do not be lazy, do not lie, do not steal. – Inca Commandment

102: Insomnia and the Clash of Civilisations
23 January 2007

As January draws to its close I'm spending all my time at the computer or musing away on Bread Loaf Mountain. My insomnia has raged completely out of control. I've stopped fighting it, spending the nights wild-eyed, scribbling away and feeling the hip hop.

Nguthungulli the Tent reckons I'm cracking up, but he underestimates my mental stamina. The Jolly Pilgrim has learned to show no weakness. I insult Nguthungulli in Spanish in order to demonstrate my superiority over him. Stupid tent.

If you want to understand history in order to better appreciate the human condition, it is unhelpful (and a touch absurd) to take sides in ancient conflicts. The past is complicated and tragic. The challenge is to make sense of it, not to make judgements. However, as one who has just spent three weeks plagued by insomnia and immersed, night after night, in the grizzly details of the Spanish Empire's conquest of the Andes region, you're going to have to indulge me on this occasion. It's unbelievably dreadful.

The conquistadors didn't comprehend the real significance of their 'discovery' of the Americas in 1492: first contact between advanced human civilisations which had evolved independently for millennia. It was a unique and unrepeatable event. The Spanish adventurers who devastated this region 500 years ago understood the context of what they were doing in a very narrow way and they were motivated by land, status and gold.

Tragically, the native peoples of the Americas didn't understand the monstrous scope of what was befalling them until it was too late. In the Andes, pre-Conquest political and military authority was firmly in the hands of the Incas and their initial reaction was horribly bungled. The Inca leaders naively delivered themselves into Spanish captivity, where they were abused and then murdered. The Inca heartland fell with hardly a weapon raised in its defence.

It was the Spanish campaign to capture Quito in 1534 which saw the first concerted military resistance. By then gold-hungry Spaniards were pouring into the region and the rape of the country was under way. Quito was evacuated and razed before it could fall into the hands of the fiendish invaders. The defending armies then fought a series of battles through the surrounding valleys, but Spanish military superiority was overwhelming.

After Rumiñahui (the Inca general) surrendered, Benalcázar (the Spanish commander) had him tortured in an attempt to find more gold. Marcas de Niza, the Spanish chaplain, reports that the Inca accepted his fate stoically, behaved with great composure and left Benalcázar with '… nothing but his greed'.

Days since leaving London: 606

103: The Black Legend
24 January 2007

Following the Conquest, the events which unfolded in the Andes region were the stuff of nightmares.

Under the Incas and their predecessors, the valleys and coastal areas of what are now Ecuador, Bolivia and Peru had been organised to support the region's large population (think: agricultural terraces, irrigation systems and store houses). After the Conquest, the invaders immediately fell out over land and treasure, and plunged into a protracted series of civil wars. The maintenance of that sophisticated civil infrastructure was therefore ignored and it collapsed, leading to widespread famine.

Churches were built over all native temples and the symbols of indigenous culture were systematically destroyed. Priceless Inca art was fed straight into Spanish furnaces so as to be more easily divisible among the soldiers. The native artistic heritage is lost to posterity.

Native people were stripped of legal and civil rights and forced into an encomienda system of indentured labour that was basically slavery. Torture was routinely employed as a tool in coercion. Untold numbers died due to overwork, undernourishment and the random and horrifying violence meted out by Spanish immigrants. Most of the death, however, was at the hands of the microbes which had been stewing in Eurasian populations for the 10,000 years they'd been separated from their American cousins, and against which those cousins had no immunity.

The native women were used as chattels. Sexual violence against indigenous women reached such a pitch that the Inca institution of marriage broke down and was replaced by a system of public prostitution. The conquistadors developed a 'cape test'. If they hit a girl on the head with a rolled cape and she remained upright, she was considered old enough for sex.

Before the invasion, the native population had lived in a society that was stable, well organised and deeply conservative. The profound cultural shock of the Conquest, and the pandemonium it unleashed, caused that society to break down at a very fundamental level. Birth rates collapsed. Many people, unable to cope, lost the will to live or simply killed themselves. Mothers murdered their own children rather than let them live under the new realities. Reports reaching Spain at the time record large-scale infanticide and suicide.

Population loss reached catastrophic proportions. Within decades of the European arrival local populations were a fraction of pre-Conquest levels. In the worst-hit coastal plains contemporary accounts report losses of 95 per cent. One of the most populous and orderly regions of the world had been laid to waste.

At the deepest level there are only two periods in the human history of Latin America: pre-Conquest and post-Conquest. It was in this manner that the current period was born.

Days since leaving London: 607

> *... by what right or justice do you keep these Indians in such cruel and horrible servitude? On what authority have you waged a detestable war against these people who dwelt, quietly and peacefully, in their own land?* – Antonio de Montesinos

104: Macrohistory
25 January 2007

Immersing myself in the story of the Conquest has not been just an exercise in contemplating one of humanity's darkest hours. It's rarely so apparent how societies are moulded by their history.

The level of technological development in the civilisations of the Americas at the time of Christopher Columbus was broadly comparable to that of the Akkadian Empire – that was the empire founded by Sargon, the first great warlord of recorded history, in the Middle East around 2300 BCE. Sargon was the guy who conquered Sumer.

The Americas were not reached by us humans until about 70,000 years after we'd gotten into Eurasia, so it's not surprising that civilisation here was at an earlier stage of development. In addition, the civilisations of the Americas didn't enjoy many of the advantages of the Eurasian ones, crucially, that the great powerhouses of technological innovation (the Middle East, India, Europe and China) had been feeding off each other's developments for millennia. So after 1492, when the conquistadors crossed the Atlantic and started to look around, they had guns. The Amerindians were still working on the wheelbarrow.

The only reason one can believe that the societies of South America and Mesoamerica (Mexico) were subdued by such tiny numbers of invaders is the fact that it actually did happen. Pizarro, who destroyed the Inca Empire, started with 168 men. Cortez, who initiated the conquest of Mesoamerica by defeating the Mexica (also known as the Aztecs), had 530 men. Both empires contained populations in the millions.

Let us never forget the apocalyptic scale of what followed. Whole peoples ceased to exist. Entire societies collapsed and the survivors were reduced to a cruel servitude beneath the weight of a foreign yoke. When Columbus arrived, the best estimate is that the population of the Americas was about 54 million. In the following years it was reduced to maybe 10 per cent of that and would take 400 years to recover.

The following centuries under the Spanish and Portuguese empires did not constitute a rebirth into a new golden age. The technological advantage that enabled the Conquest was not used to lift up the conquered. Instead, after quenching their thirst for golden trinkets, the conquistadors instituted medieval and race-based social and economic systems which have held back this continent's peoples into modern times. It's a state of affairs from which they're only now rising.

The Eurasian takeover of South America was not really a Spanish–Inca conflict. The Incas just happened to be the dominant Andean group in the century when contact was established, while the Spanish happened to be the Eurasian group at their military and naval apex. If contact had been established 200 years later, some other empire would have been ripe for plundering.

The Conquest was more properly the subjugation of one whole tradition of culture by another. The Amerindian peoples had been collectively engaged in a process of step-by-step advances, continual learning and dynastic survival of the fittest, which characterises the progress of human societies over long time frames. They were just 4,000 years behind the Eurasians, engaged in the same process, on the other side of the Atlantic.

For the original Americans that process came to an end in the sixteenth century. When the elite who ran the Inca Empire were swept away, they were replaced not by another product of Amerindian culture, but by alien rulers who marked themselves apart by their race. Half a millennium later, modern Ecuador's political and business elite are of predominantly European ancestry. Meanwhile, on a socio-economic ladder where race and power remain inextricably linked, those of predominantly Amerindian ancestry remain at the bottom. I can report that they're really pissed off about it.

Cortez and Pizarro may have had guns, germs and steel on their side, but they were not invincible. Forgive the melodramatic nature of the analogy (and aliens are not, repeat not, going to take over our planet) but I'd like to think a similar fate couldn't unfold for this twenty-first-century civilisation: that a hundred blokes with ray guns couldn't rock up, exploit the squabbles we were obsessing over that decade, then subjugate the lot of us in a few short years.

I'd like to think that our civilisation now is too self-aware, too dynamic and too adept at identifying and dealing with problems. I'd like to think.

Days since leaving London: 608
Earliest known date of utilisation of bronze in
    Eurasia: circa 3500 BCE (Iran)
    The Americas: circa 1200 CE (Peru)

The annals of former generations are lessons to the living: a man may
look back upon the fortunes of his predecessors and be admonished;
and contemplate the history of past ages and be purged of folly. –
Tales from the Thousand and One Nights

Musings
The Catalyst

It seemed appropriate to shoot my mouth off about it at the time, but the story of the Eurasians and the Amerindians was only one thread of the thesis I was weaving on Bread Loaf Mountain. Although it was not a luxurious period of my life, for raw romanticism and inspiration those two months in Quito couldn't be faulted: the tink-tink of Henry's silver hammer echoing around the courtyard below, the rustic flat, the stupendous views, the tent, the mountains and the hip hop.

It's probably the maddest I ever went. Following 19 months on the road I was extremely homesick and very much in my own world. On leaving Quito I was looking forward to hanging out with gringos again, but when the time came I was initially flustered. It wasn't like I could tell the people I met what I'd been up to in Quito, or the things which afterwards occupied my mind.

Because those final months, wandering around South America after leaving Quito, was when it really started to flow. I'd worked hard on Bread Loaf Mountain. By the time I left, I'd written masses of material and felt satisfied. But in hindsight it was where I gave structure to a mental landscape which could only subsequently be filled in. When I set out those ideas – that way of thinking about the world – in the final sections of this book, I'm going to take you through it just as it happened.

I didn't see the end coming. From an unhappy place in Sydney, to the side of a mountain in Ecuador, I'd kept following a path and one thing just kept leading to another. Then, when I reached the magic island in Brazil, unexpected and unplanned, it all clicked into place. That's how it happened.

Before I tell you about it, there was one final adventure in Quito. It took place in the Women's Prison.

105: Quito's Women's Prison
27 January 2007

Yesterday I paid a visit to Quito's Women's Prison with South American Explorers. I had no idea what to expect.

Locking 800 women in one building is not conducive to the creation of a stable, well-ordered social environment, but on initial appearances there was nothing depressing about it. I entered into a haven of frenetic activity: washing was hanging from balconies, food was being fried or boiled in corners and kids were running about. Everyone seemed imbued with great purpose.

However, on talking to the inmates it became clear that being locked in a third-world prison was a taxing experience. People react to it in different ways. Most of the inmates (and 100 per cent of the gringos) are there for drugs offences and the place is soaked with narcotics. Many inmates use them as a way of dealing with the stress. I was introduced to two German girls who apparently used to be quite normal. A three-year incarceration had taken its toll on their teeth, health and minds. They weren't normal any more.

Then there was Zoe Savage, a young Irish journalist, who told me how she'd come to be there.

Four years earlier Zoe was running orphanages in Africa, bringing up a young family and living life with gusto. She flew to Ecuador to do a story at the urging of a trusted contact. That turned out to be a mistake.

When she arrived the contact failed to materialise, the story didn't check out and strange things started happening. After a few days she and her team decided to split back to Europe. At the airport the police dogs made a fuss. The cops searched their bags and found nothing, but the dogs wouldn't shut up. Nobody noticed when the camera crew slipped away to go to the toilet. That was half a decade ago. They haven't been seen since.

When one of the police slipped a knife into the seam of her bag, it came out covered with white powder. Then they broke open the cameras. They were stuffed with cocaine. Zoe got eight years.

Zoe is a dynamic, iron-willed and media-savvy type, and the big guns came out in her defence. Guns don't come much bigger than Oprah

Winfrey, who flew to Quito to do a live broadcast from the prison (they wouldn't let her in). Following four years in jail, Zoe remains a legal football in the mess that is global narcotics policy and one of the less deserving victims of the inglorious War on Drugs.

In her time at the prison, she's written two books and started the foundation of a school for its children. She was a dedicated and charming hostess for the morning and a genuinely amazing human being. After listening to Zoe's story, as the tram returned me to the city I felt a powerful sense of elation and incredibly lucky to have crossed paths with her.

I'm leaving Quito in five days. For my next trick I'll be going back to basics and hitting the South American backpacker circuit. My plan is as follows: first explore the Ecuadorian Amazon, Andes and coast. Then travel down the west side of South America and up the east side. That basically equates to: Peru, Bolivia, Chile, Argentina, Uruguay, Paraguay then Brazil. My final destination will be a haven on the Caribbean coast where two old friends await. Then this journey will be complete.

To conclude my potted history of this region: following the unimaginable trauma of the Conquest, it took until the seventeenth century for population levels to stabilise. Ecuador's people then began the long (and still incomplete) process of building a hybrid society.

Ruling the Americas from capitals in Europe was never going to be a sustainable system. When the sweep of independence came in the nineteenth century, it was a mirror image of the sixteenth-century conquest: the areas conquered last were the first to rise up, ultimately converging on Peru.

Independence for Ecuador was won by the legendary Venezuelan liberator Simón Bolívar. The decisive battle was fought on 24 May 1822, when Field Marshall Mariscal defeated the royalists at the Battle of Pichincha and took Quito. Ecuador was then briefly a part of 'Gran Colombia' (Bolívar had dreams of uniting South America) but, in 1830, the Ecuadorians got their own country.

Good on 'em.

Days since leaving London: 610
Value of global illicit trade in
Firearms: US$1 billion   Humans: US$32 billion   Drugs: US$320 billion

Spanish word of the day: 'sobreviviente' meaning 'survivor'

106: On the Road Again

1 February 2007

I've spent my final week in Quito doing Spanish-language cramming to prepare for the adventures ahead. This morning I returned to Quito's Women's Prison. I needed to see Zoe Savage again before leaving.

I took some requested supplies for her school, a considerable amount of high-quality news media and a mobile phone. Taking mobile phones into Quito's Women's Prison is against the rules. Nonetheless, Zoe needed one, so I hid it at the bottom of my bag. The prison guards sniffed it out, confiscated it, told me off (with pointed fingers and raised voices), then briefly threatened to arrest me. Naturally, I talked my way out of trouble.

Zoe, who had witnessed two knife fights since I visited last week, took me to meet some of the prison's wackier characters. The most striking was an elderly lady who turned out to be the institution's head loan shark and chief drugs kingpin. At an unprepossessing five feet, and with serious dental issues, you'd never have guessed her lofty criminal underworld status. She came across more as a smiling grandmother than mafia godmother, but she charges 100 per cent interest a week and if you piss her off, she'll kill you.

Zoe and I later made our way to a burger bar on the main concourse being run by a young Colombian cocaine smuggler serving food next to a stereo blaring salsa. She and I made friends and, after I'd finished my meal, she turned up the volume and asked me to dance.

So that was how I came to dance salsa with a beautiful Colombian cocaine smuggler in the main hall of Quito's Women's Prison in front of a hundred female prisoners while they leaned over the balconies, wolf-whistled and shouted at me, in Spanish, to take my clothes off. It was the maddest moment of my life so far. Those inmate chicks dig me.

Zoe Savage is one of the most impressive people I've met during this adventure. We had a long chat in the afternoon and I left her with some of what I've been writing in Quito, which isn't the sort of thing one gives to just anybody. In return she made a promise to meet up when she's a free woman.

Electrified once again by her company, I rode the tram back to the city to see Reuben for a final Spanish lesson, then returned to the Old Town one last time. In the square at the foot of Bread Loaf Mountain a stage had been set up. A band wearing grey jumpsuits were singing about how happy they were to be young and from Ecuador while a crowd danced, merry and smiling, in the afternoon sun.

It took me two hours to pack up the apartment. As the taxi pulled up, Nella helped load my bags while Henry watched from across the street. I realised I hadn't said goodbye properly, so I ran over, threw my arms around him and gave him a big hug. Then I got in the taxi and went to the bus station.

Days since leaving London: 615

What is the feeling when you're driving away from people, and they recede on the plain till you see their specks dispersing? – it's the too huge world vaulting us, and it's good-bye. But we lean forward to the next venture beneath the skies. – Jack Kerouac

Musings
The Thesis

Every now and again it is instructive to stop what one is doing, close one's eyes, clear one's mind and meditate on the now: that feeling of the blood pumping through your veins, the tingling in your nerve endings, the sensation of being alive ...

I'm a happy guy. Whatever reasons of nature or nurture incline some people towards optimism (and others pessimism) predisposed me to having a relatively sunny disposition. To be honest, ever since overcoming the awkwardness of adolescence, I've enjoyed almost everything about being alive, even the humdrum bits.

Don't get me wrong: lack of sleep makes me grouchy and I'm no better than anyone at coping with serious loss or heartbreak. But generally, I think being alive is amazing. What's more, I'm an optimist about the human condition and the trajectory of human affairs. I genuinely feel, deep in my heart, that our collective future will ultimately be bright and that there is something wonderful going on here on planet Earth.

There's more to it though: I have an *intellectual conviction* that those things are true. The more I learn about global society, and the narrative which has brought us to where we are, the more I believe that we, as a species, are fundamentally on the right track.

I'm in a minority in holding this view.

As I travelled around the world I observed a great deal of negativity in the global zeitgeist. There is a widely held belief that, because we have so many problems, we are doomed; and that, because so many people act in ways we deem to be irrational, or evil, the world is in decline. That assessment simply does not fit with my understanding of what is happening on this planet, and I believe that there are two reasons the world is misinterpreted in this way.

The first is that individual reasons for dissatisfaction are confused with existential ones: it is assumed that, because so many bad things happen, something essentially bad must be going on.

It's true that life is very hard. It is full of discomfort, frustration, suffering and pain and takes place in a baffling universe pervaded by injustice and pointless cruelty. In addition, we have to deal with the fact that we're mortal: fated to lose our looks and have our minds deteriorate. Then, one day, we'll die. There's nothing we can do about it. Bummer.

But this isn't *heaven*. This is Earth. That's what being alive is like. One shouldn't take it personally.

The second reason is that people overestimate the magnitude of our problems. That's because they fail to see them in context. Twelve thousand years ago humanity entered a new chapter in its story, a chapter which is forcing us to face a completely unprecedented set of challenges. We, as a species, are engaged in a complicated and arduous learning process for which there is no road map.

We've got a lot of problems. Some of them are quite frightening. That's probably always going to be true. But there are no insurmountable barriers between ourselves and infinity. If we keep our heads about us, and a sense of proportion, then there is absolutely nothing to stop us from going to the stars.

But we need to start thinking bigger.

During the final two sections of this book, I will outline my interpretation of humanity's current circumstances, subject by subject. At this point broad generalisations about peace and love don't really cut it so, to explain what I mean, I'm going to have to go into some details.

Four qualifiers to what follows:

1) My interpretation of what's occurring on this planet constitutes the thesis of a user of its facilities. It does not constitute a scientific hypothesis.

2) I'm talking about the wood, not the trees. I am not professing specific solutions to the world's problems. My point is that those problems make more sense, and appear less overwhelming, when seen in context.

3) My interpretation is based on a certain value system. I'm not going to spell that value system out for you. You'll figure it out. Basically, I'm in favour of peace, love and brotherhood, and against ignorance and boringness.

4) My thesis is informed by several disciplines, primarily: history, anthropology, evolutionary psychology, economics, environmental science, genetics, theology and physics. To the best of my knowledge my factual assertions are broadly mainstream (or at least defensible) within the relevant fields.

One of the extraordinary things about this current age is that the universe, and the way we experience it, is being subjected to systematic study. Lots of interesting insights are being thrown up by that process. We, as citizens of the world, should not see it as separate from our lives. We should be assimilating those insights into our world views and attempting to understand what they mean for us.

*****

That's what I tried to do: explore the world as thoroughly as I was able, then make my own sense of it; combining the cerebral with the experiential. I drew much inspiration from the experience.

The most intense part of the process that was catalysed on Bread Loaf Mountain took place on the island of Isla Grande. It's one of the most exquisite places I've ever been.

On the day before we left, I went alone to a beach on the far side of the island. The beach is called Praia Lopes Mendes and faces straight out across the Atlantic. It is one of the most beautiful beaches in Brazil.

I arrived late. As I walked down through the forest I saw a bank of cloud approaching from across the ocean. At the sand's edge, I hid my clothes beneath a tree and waded in. I swam out a long way, past the violence of the breakers and into the deep beyond where you are lifted up and down by mountainous swells as giant wave fronts roll in from the east.

An enormous V of sea birds sailed above my head towards the shore just as the clouds' arrival cast a slate backdrop behind the island's perfect green mountains. The distant beach cleared of humans. I was alone. When the rain fell on my face, it was warm.

I floated there for a long time, feeling the blood coursing through my body and the rapture of being alive. Thinking. A thing of beauty is a joy forever. This is it. You only live once. You only get one chance to try to understand.

So try.

Part 9

Global Deconstruction

Global Musings I
The Species-Wide
Monkey Tree

First, some perspective ...

Once upon a time, life on Earth wasn't as interesting as it is now. Back then it was all sponges sitting on the floors of the primeval oceans and jellyfish floating around in them. Don't get me wrong; I haven't got a problem with jellyfish, but they're clearly not as exciting as tigers.

Then life went through a step change – the Cambrian Explosion – and the scope of what it could be set off along all sorts of interesting tangents.

Six hundred and ten million years after that, one of those tangents arrived at a line of beings we call the hominids. The hominids possessed hyper-advanced minds of unprecedented faculty and potential, and one purpose to which they applied those minds was the systematic use of tools – something for which they found lots of intriguing applications.

One million years later, a particular species arose from the hominid line. *Homo sapiens* were clever to an unprecedented degree, turning their intellects to the colonisation of the world, the building of uniquely complex social structures and the dramatic upgrading of their technology. Following another 130,000 years, as the polar glaciers underwent one of their periodic retreats, *Homo sapiens* invented agriculture.

That game-transforming innovation led to a radical restructuring of their society and set in motion a chain of events that would give rise to all we know as recorded history and civilisation.

With the passing of a further 12,000 years, the pace of change accelerated once more. Human industry expanded suddenly and dramatically, leading to a population explosion and throwing almost every aspect of human life into flux.

And *that's* where we come in.

*****

Before setting out my interpretation of what's happening now, there are four really basic things about us, and how we relate to the world, which I need to point out.

1) The human brain – the medium through which we experience reality – is an evolved organ. Everything we want out of life, our entire value system, all the things we regard as important (or irrelevant) and the way we think about time and space are entirely governed by that evolutionary heritage.

2) The physical context in which the human mind currently finds itself (technology, cities and a global civilisation) has less and less in common with the one in which it evolved (spears, tribes and the African savannah). Our living environments have changed radically over the past 12,000 years. Our minds have not. That dichotomy is central to many of humanity's biggest problems.

3) Human culture and civilisation are constructs: their non-physical elements are only real in the sense that they exist in our heads. Those socially constructed, non-real, imagined elements include all our economic systems, all our social systems, all our political systems and our entire legal paraphernalia. Those things are the abstract media we've created (in our minds) in order to coordinate our activities and regulate our interactions with one another.

4) The characteristics of those systems are the consequence, not the cause, of human nature. The reason we have problems with them is because (due to what we're like) we've set them up in a certain way. There are lots of things about those systems which are commonly regarded as immutable, inevitable and permanent, but which are in fact fluid, artificial and transitory.

*****

All around the world people complain about governments, bemoaning the quality of public administration and the moral attributes of politicians. I think it's a mistake to regard those things as our real problem because, in fact, they're actually only the symptoms of something deeper.

The real problem is that (due to their evolutionary heritage) humans aren't mentally tooled up to run countries, let alone planets. How to do it remains a major practical conundrum which has yet to be fully resolved.

Our ancestors were social before they became human. Systems for organising ourselves evolved along with us. They worked something like this ...

We'd divide ourselves into tribal groups of 100–150 individuals. Each tribe then subdivided to hunt, gather and find food. Everybody in each tribe agreed who they were because they spoke the same language with the same accent and shared various cultural attributes. Within each tribe everyone struggled to be top dog and maximise the reproductive success of themselves and their children.

Neighbouring tribes distrusted each other and would periodically find excuses to engage in 'war' so that they could steal each other's land and women. When a tribe got too big it split into two tribes. After a couple of generations the people in those tribes had developed slightly different accents, which was useful because that gave them an excuse to go to war ...

Sound familiar?

No one designed those systems. Our ancestors perhaps never thought to scrutinise why they acted in that way. Ultimately, the reason was that it was the most efficient manner for a species of hyper-intelligent social tool-using omnivores to extract resources from the environment in which they evolved. All our mental foibles are calibrated to work in that context. Retrospective moral judgements aside (regarding living in a state of almost constant warfare), the system worked. It made evolutionary sense. It was stable.

Then somebody went and invented agriculture.

In the space of 12,000 years we've gone from living in tribes of a hundred to billions of people existing in one interconnected planet-wide society.

Countries of millions (or global civilisations of billions) have to deal with an array of organisational and logistical matters that are completely alien to a hundred people living as a single breeding unit on the savannah. But our recent ancestors, imbued with a ready-made set of tools for self-government, unthinkingly applied those tools to their new circumstances. It's not like they had a great deal of choice.

For the past 12 millennia, systems of government (such as they are) have been a series of thinly veiled attempts to apply primitive methods of tribal organisation to a range of situations for which they are ludicrously inappropriate. It hasn't worked very well, it still doesn't and it's never been stable.

*****

This conundrum is now resolving itself. The signs of that resolution are all around. But before I describe them I need to highlight two aspects of human nature which are central (though not exclusive) to why we've never been very good at running anything bigger than a tribe.

The first is that human beings have an obsession with status built into the fabric of their minds. Much of what we get up to is an attempt to satisfy that obsession, even though it's often dressed up as something else (such as getting rich, getting famous, or rising up the pecking order in one's own particular monkey tree).

This obsession is our genes telling us that high status improves reproductive success. Whether that's true or not in the modern world is debatable. But that's not the point. The point is that this is how we're built and that's why. To some animals, status isn't relevant to their reproductive success. To a fish – even a very clever fish – the idea of 'making it' is meaningless. But it's not meaningless to us.

There's nothing wrong with this. The desire to 'make it' drives many of humanity's most magnificent achievements – from the châteaux of the Loire Valley to the sublime Mughal mausoleum beside the Yamuna River. Our status obsession is one of the things that make us so fascinating as a species. It's unlikely that we could live without that obsession and nor should we necessarily seek to.

In the modern world, human perceptions of status are complicated by money. Money is one of those abstract constructs that exist in our heads. People become fixated on it and perceive that more money will make them happier. That's a misconception. Money is useful in lots of different ways and it's an invaluable tool for organising civilisation, but having it is about status, not about being happy.

Counter-intuitive? Picture yourself as a farmer living 1,000 years ago. Like people today, you would have wanted the best living space and material possessions. When you got those things you would have felt happier. Yet the benchmark by which you judged your standard of living would have borne no comparison to the living standards of today. Back then it was 10 to a hut, no running water and no iPods and food was a problem. The 'poorest' people in modern post-industrial societies have greater material wealth than all but a tiny minority 1,000 years ago. Conservatively, standards of living are higher by a factor of 10.

So are people 10 times happier? Of course they're not. Having a big hut is nice, but doubling its size does not make one twice as happy. The thing that feels good is having the biggest hut in the village.

Money, status and happiness are not directly proportional. Many rich people are miserable. Many high-status people are poor. It's entirely possible to be low status, poor and very happy (attributes which suggest a beautiful soul). But there's a correlation between the three that we all intuitively understand, even if we don't always admit it. Winning the lottery gives one access to lots of shiny baubles. But that's not what people get off on.

For what it's worth, I've personally tried to transcend this aspect of my character: tried to turn myself into someone who does not – at any level – care what other people think about him. It's well beyond my abilities. Maybe the really enlightened people reach that point. Maybe Jesus did. From what's said of him, the Buddha did. But I can't, and I've never met anyone who has.

*****

The second aspect of the human psyche holding back our efforts to organise this planet is the fact that we are predisposed to manipulate any system of which we're a part to our own personal advantage.

Some animals, like tigers, spend most of their time alone. The interesting things tigers do (stalking, killing, being fierce) are solitary pursuits. Humans aren't like that. Humans are evolved to live in communities and the interesting things *we* do are only possible in that context.

I, for example, travelled around the world and wrote a diary about it. But that was only possible because other people grew food, built bicycles and ran internet cafés.

As social animals we live within a network of other humans. That network is regulated by our social, economic and political systems. Manipulating other people through those systems is how we get things done. When a baby cries for milk he only dimly understands what he's doing. When a CEO orders her managers to set up a new division she understands exactly what she's doing. But they're both manipulating the same set of systems, just with different levels of awareness and sophistication.

Our minds have certain evolved tendencies which regulate how we manipulate those systems. One set of tendencies corresponds to our self-interest. We all want money, status, or sometimes just a bit of milk, and manipulate the people around us to get those things. That's fine. Society only works because people look after themselves.

But if we all spent all our time ruthlessly following our immediate self-interest, society wouldn't work at all. So we have another set of tendencies that facilitate cooperation in the intricate ways necessary to run human society. They include loyalty, compassion and a sense of fairness.

All those characteristics of human nature are balanced to work in the context of groups of maybe two hundred people. We're not mentally set up to be top monkey in trees any bigger than that. Yet those which have emerged since the dawn of agriculture are much, much larger.

*****

So what did happen when imperfect egotistical monkeys, hard-wired to manipulate systems to their own personal advantage, found themselves in charge of chiefdoms, city states, kingdoms and empires?

In short: they found manifold ways of increasing and marking their high status (from physical symbols through to fawning courtiers and the frantic accumulation of cash); the apparatus of government was used as a vehicle for improving their reproductive success; all societies became based on exploitation; and the logistical matters which arose with civilisation were subverted to the narrow interests of the ruling classes. A whole range of justifications were then invented (and generally declared immutable) to explain why things simply had to be that way.

Such has been the basis of human government until the very recent past. The kings and princes of old didn't think of themselves as status-obsessed primates, but that's what was really going on. As fellow humans, we easily relate to why they acted in the way that they did.

If the ants or termites (or for that matter the bees) had to organise a global civilisation they'd probably take to it naturally. We don't and, for thousands of years, we've been stumbling along with what are, in effect, proto-governments. It would have made everything much easier had we had rulers and public administrators with no vanity or selfishness. But humans don't come in those flavours.

Remarkably, though, following 12,000 years of war, despotism and chaos, these post-agricultural monkey trees have started to sort themselves out.

If you've got a problem with the political leaders of today, just remember how bad things used to be.

The earliest states were parasites on their people, looking for any excuse to perpetuate and legitimise themselves. At the dawn of civilisation, conquering the neighbouring city state meant killing all the men and enslaving the women. In the early post-agricultural empires the leader was considered a god, public policy was whimsical and warmongering for the sake of egotism standard practice. Essentially, they didn't have a clue and were crudely applying tribal models of organisation to the new-fangled world in which they found themselves.

The first attempt to attack the situation intellectually was made in China 3,000 years ago. Someone came up with the brilliant idea that rulers should rule due to their personal attributes, not just birth, force of arms or divine ordination.

Revolutionary.

From that point on the human race has been engaged in a slow, excruciatingly painful, multi-generational learning experience. The main lessons have come from the chaos and suffering caused by poorly functioning systems. Progress is constantly hampered by the evolutionarily derived urges of the people at the top of the tree, and quite a few of those only halfway up. A big part of making civilisation work has been about finding institutional methods of taming those urges. This learning experience has been by nature piecemeal, with each development resting upon the one before.

An elementary step was separating the state from the property of the ruler. A more sophisticated step was imposing constitutional constraints on rulers, which, in turn, led to the idea of explicit agreements between rulers and the ruled. Making rulers answerable to their community initially meant making them accountable to narrow vested interests (for example, a king to his barons), but it was a step along a road which led to universal suffrage.

Akbar the Great was promoting reason as the highest value of the state by the sixteenth century. Mathematics and rationality were introduced into government under leaders such as Louis XIV of France and Frederick the Great of Prussia, in the seventeenth and eighteenth centuries. Innovations such as the separation of powers specifically address an underlying flaw in the aptitude of humans for running large political enterprises; that is – no one can be trusted with too much power.

Until recently, the main option for upgrading political systems was violent revolt. It's not an efficient method of redesigning one's public administration. More practical (and less disruptive) methods – such as elections – developed over time. It's all blindingly obvious in hindsight. But getting there is a long-winded evolutionary process, taking place across millennia, involving the slow accumulation of better customs and more effective ideas.

The techniques required to run a pan-planetary civilisation could never have been deduced logically from suppositions about human nature. They've had to be pieced together, painfully and messily, from experience.

*****

Remember, what's *really* going on is that a bunch of highly intelligent hominids are running around on the surface of a planet and, as the past few thousand years have gone by, they've gradually been killing each other with less abandon and collaborating more intelligently.

Our progress since those ancient Chinese political scientists started to think outside the box has more properly been the steady refinement of the abstractions we use to organise ourselves and play out our games of status and prestige: finding ideas that work, then finding ways to make them stick.

There's nothing immutable about the abstractions we use today and there's no reason to believe that they cannot continue to be improved upon.

*****

In the early twenty-first-century world of my journey the quality of public administration varied a lot. The richest parts of Europe, North America, Australia and East Asia (with their highly developed policy-making apparatus, competing centres of power and massive logistic abilities) probably represent the best large-scale management of its affairs that humanity has thus far achieved.

Many regions (South America, for example) have time firmly on their side. Fifty years ago military dictatorships were the norm, but the long-term trend has been firmly towards social emancipation and democracy.

In other regions, governments are often still not far removed from primitive tribal systems: little more than criminal enterprises under the veil of governmental legitimacy, where the state is an instrument of exploitation passed from father to son.

If you happen to live in an early twenty-first-century country with a really catastrophic government (for example, Burma or North Korea) it probably isn't much comfort to know that you're being suppressed by misguided primates locked into doomed systems of tribal governance in a preposterous hangover from prehistory. But that's basically what's happening.

It's a shame. The human race has spent painful millennia learning best practice. The sooner those lessons are applied, the sooner we can get on with the next, more interesting, phase in our history.

*****

Despite the much-discussed inadequacies of our political leaders, governments in the better-run parts of the world have become active and competent in a way that would have been unimaginable two centuries ago. They have begun to turn themselves into genuinely accountable servants of the people. However, anyone who lives in one of them (for example, Britain) understands how imperfect they still are.

Systems remain biased towards the rich and powerful. The state remains a servant to itself as well as the people. The public sector is inefficient. Politicians keep starting foolish wars. In addition, modern forms of democracy have specific flaws. They're capricious. Populist rhetoric often triumphs over logic. As countries become better run, politics becomes dull. People, being fickle, become disengaged. What's more, there are some things these relatively advanced forms of government are still learning to do, like making trade-offs across generations on matters such as pensions funding and climate change.

But democracy is a milestone, not a finishing line. Becoming a democracy, or even a 'mature democracy', does not represent some ultimate form of political organisation. Being accountable to the populace is a feature of proper government, not the complete answer.

The most enlightened governments in the world today are still just a few steps removed from command-and-control despotism. It would be a mistake to suppose that just because modern governments are so much better than ancient ones, a dimension of human history is reaching its conclusion. We can still get much better at this.

Some who live in the mature democracies refuse to vote on the basis that all competing political parties are flawed, and all politicians two-faced. That position is extremely short-sighted. If you're waiting for an honest, principled, technically capable and morally unpolluted government-in-waiting before you vote, then you were born at least a thousand years too early.

You're voting between competing elites of imperfect monkeys. Deal with it.

*****

There was never the remotest chance we could go directly from hunting and gathering to an efficiently managed, just and fair global civilisation. Organising a planet is complicated. Working out how to do it takes time. We're on a journey. The world you see around you is a phase within that journey. It's a phase that cannot be skipped. But this is the groundwork, not the endgame.

Map 4

Central and South America

Boxes denote from where each email was sent.

········· **Route of journey**

107: Ecuadorian Comedown
6 February 2007

I was almost hysterically happy to be on the road again, barely containing my excitement in the taxi from my apartment to the bus station. Once there I boarded an overnight coach bound for the Amazon basin and, exhausted, fell asleep almost at once. We'd dropped two kilometres vertically by the time I woke up, nine hours later, in the rough-and-ready frontier town of Lago Agrio. At that point my stellar mood evaporated.

I've never had an altitude-sickness reaction before, so it caught me completely off guard. My ears needed popping but, despite my best efforts, for the first time in my life I couldn't pop them. I'd clearly become acclimatised to my mountain home. There commenced a pounding three-day headache, which put a serious downer on what followed.

I'd booked onto a forest trip from Quito and, that morning, joined three serious-minded Spanish ornithologists (Javier, Orlondo and Salvador) and a slight lady with cropped hair from Pennsylvania called Selma. Together we boarded a dilapidated minivan that took us down dirt tracks for two hours to the bank of a river, where the road ended, the jungle thickened and a pig-sized tapir wallowed in the mud. There we boarded a sleek motorised canoe, which zipped us downstream for a further four hours to an isolated camp, deep in the rainforest.

The camp consisted of a clearing containing one grand wooden structure with a pitched roof but no walls, and a smaller structure off to the side – reachable only via a rickety wooden walkway – where the washrooms were located. All the buildings were on stilts (to keep them away from the poisonous things crawling around the forest floor) and we all slept in hammocks (to keep us away from the things which made it up the stilts).

For the next three days we explored the jungle from that camp – hiking through it by day, investigating at night using torches, swimming in the river one afternoon and then, the next morning, going piranha-fishing in the very same spot. I'm pleased to report that we didn't catch any piranhas.

My Spanish ornithologist chums were obsessed by spotting big animals. The broody-looking black caimans we saw from canoes one evening were a matter of great excitement. A troop of cute-looking, white-bellied spider monkeys that went swinging through the canopy above us during one walk prompted a hundred long-lens photos. Other fauna encountered included pink river dolphins, an eight-foot green anaconda (Chuck the Python wouldn't have stood a chance) and a host of ridiculous creepy-crawlies, from nine-inch cockroaches and alien-like stick insects to evil-looking, ghost-white spiders.

Personally, I found the intensity of the ecosystem more interesting than its individual creatures. A million and more species living in an interdependent web of life. A vast symbiosis of beings, interacting and unknowingly relying on one another. Not entirely unlike us humans.

Selma had just finished a degree in environmental chemistry and, on my third and final night in the jungle, the two of us sat under adjacent mosquito nets and talked in the flickering light of a candle (in which one brave moth-like creature noisily committed suicide). With the twitter of the jungle and the smell of life all around, we discussed the phenomenon of ecotourism: an industry which makes it advantageous to understand and preserve habitats; a perfect fusion of environmental and economic rationalism; and a textbook example of how six and a half billion humans might live in harmony with nature.

A boatman came to collect us this morning and, after four hours on the river, we were dropped at the end of a different dirt track at the jungle's edge. Following a short wait we were picked up in a four-by-four by a round-faced local man called Estafen, who drove us back into Lago Agrio. As I sat next to him, and stood by his side on the diesel-scented raft that ferried us across one river, Estafen told me what he thought about the oil majors.

Estafen had a lot to say about those companies and, with a head pounding from another wave of reverse altitude sickness, I struggled to follow his impassioned Spanish narrative.

Lago Agrio was built in virgin forest after oil was discovered here in the 1960s. Many of the oil-extraction techniques employed have damaged local ecosystems. Waste products haven't been properly disposed of, there've been a number of spills and several sections of rainforest have been despoiled. Many locals and environmentalists point their fingers at the US company Texaco (now Chevron), which founded the oil industry here. Chevron points its finger at Petroecuador, the state oil company which controls the industry now. Estafen talked of toxic waste, water pollution, soil contamination and cultural upheaval. Lawsuits continue to fly.

As we bumped along the dusty roads I looked out through the grubby window of Estafen's vehicle at the oil installations we were passing, thinking about a young civilisation still finding its feet, carelessly tearing an inheritance of hydrocarbons from the Earth and just waking up to the consequences.

We got back to Lago Agrio this afternoon. I've just eaten a dull meal of brown rice and chicken and I'm waiting for the bus that will take me back into the Andes.

Days since leaving London: 620
Age of planet Earth: 4.567 billion years
Appearance of the first land vertebrates: 395 million years ago
Appearance of the first trees: 360 million years ago

Spanish phrase of the day: 'retrato grande' meaning 'big picture'

Global Musings II
Gaia Theory

The human race has a problem in its relationship with the environment. That problem is an intrinsic consequence of running a technological civilisation on the surface of a planet and it's one we were destined to face since long before perceiving it. Now that we do perceive it, and everybody's talking about it, we should start being more realistic about the historical context of those discussions.

All life forms exploit their surroundings to get what they need to survive. Daisies need sunlight, squirrels need acorns, whales need krill. We humans, however, have always been rather more ambitious about what constitutes our needs and, for 100,000 years, those ambitions and their side effects have been inexorably increasing.

By the time behaviourally modern humans were spreading across the globe after 60,000 BCE, already no other animal could stand against us. We'd become the invincible global super-predator. Snuffing out species. Re-ordering food chains. Distorting ecosystems.

Agriculture increased our impact on the world to a new scale. Watercourses were redirected, forests cleared and marshes drained. Systematic land alteration on a massive scale. The face of the world artificially reworked.

The Industrial Revolution intensified our influence once more as we twisted minerals into artefacts, scorched fossils into electricity, shaped rock and clay into cloud-skimming edifices and began constructing the physical trappings of this grand civilisation of ours.

The stage for this drama has been the surface of planet Earth, the climatic and biological systems of which are fantastically complex, poorly understood and intertwined through an assortment of mysterious and subtle feedback mechanisms. Everywhere those systems are being modified by the new-fangled civilisation sitting among them, and every day that civilisation grows larger and more elaborate.

To set our environmental situation in fundamental terms: this universe, and in particular this planet, is set up in such a way that once a species of hyper-intelligent tool-using omnivores (with apparently bottomless ingenuity and imagination) gets going, their activities are *bound*, sooner or later, to reach such a magnitude that they freak out the constitution of the planet on which they live.

*****

We didn't choose to be here. The long chain of technological innovations that brought us to this point was not premeditated. No one sat down and planned the invention of agriculture or the Industrial Revolution.

However, now we're here there can be no turning back. We don't have the option of returning to our pre-agricultural days of hunting, gathering and living off nature's rhythms. Population densities far exceed levels that can be nourished through such practices. Hunter-gatherer peoples live at average population densities of less than one person per square kilometre. Population densities in the heavily populated regions of the world are now well over 100 people per square kilometre (and reach 800 people per square kilometre in places like the Ganges plain).

With this in mind, some have sometimes suggested the Earth has more humans than she can sustain and that a population crash is both inevitable and necessary. As one with an optimistic view of the problem-solving panache of humankind, I think we can come up with a more creative way forward than that.

In essence we've naively constructed a civilisation that is not environmentally sustainable. Now we have to re-craft it into one that is. It's an enormous job, but in the early twenty-first century of my journey it was well under way.

Off the Australian east coast, whales that had recently been hunted towards oblivion were being fawned over from tourist boats. In the Amazon, ecotourism was turning conservation into tourist dollars. Businessmen, politicians and environmentalists were wrestling to define rules for resource extraction while, in Quito, consultants struggled to interpret them. North American students were studying the chemistry of ecosystems. Venture capitalists were investing tens of billions of dollars to pin down the science of renewable power and the business models to exploit it. In 20 years global warming had gone from an obscure environmentalist concern to a signature issue of international politics, and, across the world, a debate about energy was beginning to rage.

A technological civilisation is not anathema to environmental sustainability, even if it has a growing economy. It's true that the character of our civilisation's hardware and logistics over the past few centuries has meant that the size of economies has been proportional to their environmental side effects, but it won't always be that way. The nature of tomorrow's economy will be radically different from today's and, ultimately, its size is a subjective thing. Economic growth doesn't have to mean ever-bigger factories. A firm of lawyers generates more economic output (and a lot more hot air) than a polluting mill, even though it has lower carbon emissions.

There'll always be physical parameters constraining some things, such as the amount of fresh water and certain elements available, but using such resources elegantly and effectively has only just commenced. The logistics of civilisation can, in the future, become efficient in ways so far undreamed of. One day we may establish companies that use geothermal energy to make recycling machines from recycled materials and have very low carbon emissions indeed.

Changing civilisation so that it works in harmony with the environment isn't impossible, it's just a very big problem.

*****

Right now everyone's talking about climate change. It's come to light that dumping large volumes of heat-trapping gases into the atmosphere for 200 years may have affected the atmosphere. This is causing a lot of angst.

First of all, let's not forget just how *extraordinarily* inconvenient this is. Carbon dioxide (CO_2) is the basic waste product of nearly all our energy and transportation systems. At this point in history, expanding the capacity of those systems will dramatically improve the life quality of billions of humans. In addition, reducing carbon emissions requires a planet full of self-absorbed *Homo sapiens* to act in a coordinated way that is against their immediate best interests.

Given all that, achieving such reductions was always going to be extremely difficult and involve long, protracted and acrimonious global arguments about what to do (precisely like the arguments now raging).

Ultimately, what are the possibilities?

Around 18,000 years ago, what is now London stood at the foot of an ice sheet that stretched to the pole. Scotland, directly to the north, lay under two kilometres of the stuff. Sea levels were 100 metres lower than they are today.

Around 74,000 years ago, a supervolcano exploded on the Indonesian island of Sumatra, throwing 3,000 *cubic kilometres* of rock into the stratosphere, turning South-East Asia into a giant firestorm and blanketing India with a metre of ash.

Around 130,000 years ago, hippopotami found it warm enough to splash about in the River Thames, where glaciers, and one day London, would later stand.

If you go back tens of millions of years you come to the great extinction events: gargantuan meteorites slamming into the planet, consigning it to millennia of ecological pandemonium at a time.

Stuff like that happens. The Earth gets over it.

The worst-case scenarios of climate change go something like this: the Siberian tundra releases its methane stores into the atmosphere, global warming spirals out of control, the Greenland and Antarctic ice sheets melt (a process which takes centuries) and sea levels rise by tens of metres over that period.

If that happens (and it might), it will be extremely unpleasant. Some of the richest, most heavily populated and fertile parts of the world (including most of the really big cities) will be inundated. Billions of people will be displaced and there will be a prolonged period of global chaos and disruption. But it will not constitute the end of the world, or even the end of civilisation. It will just be really nasty.

So we're in a race. The magnitude of our civilisation inexorably increases, while we continuously look for ways to mitigate its side effects, so Earth doesn't squish us. The effort we put into running this race will be a key test of our mettle as a species and heavily influence how much fun the next few centuries are going to be.

But, whatever fate awaits humankind, one million years from now Earth will be a place of forests, lakes and animals. When we talk of destroying (or saving) the planet, we're taking ourselves too seriously.

*****

Human civilisation has reached a bottleneck. It's a bottleneck that became an historical inevitability centuries (and probably millennia) before this book was written and which we've been plodding unknowingly towards for all of that time. We've now entered a period of history during which our relationship with the environment is unstable. It is a period that will see some level of climate change, ecosystem disruption and species loss. What is unknown is how long and traumatic this period will be.

CO_2-induced climate change may (or may not) turn out to be our environmental Achilles' heel. But even after it's eventually brought under control, there will be other mechanisms for environmental catastrophe waiting in the wings that we don't currently perceive.

We're nowhere near understanding all the long-term effects of running a technological civilisation on the surface of a planet. Three hundred years ago, who would have guessed that an overarching problem for humanity would soon be to manage the machinery of civilisation so as to limit the release of certain gases? We didn't even know CO_2 *existed* until the eighteenth century.

This learning curve will probably take centuries (at least) to climb. Most of the environmental sciences are at a nascent stage. Our understanding of them will seem laughably primitive in the lifetimes of people already born. The terms we use to make sense of these problems – terms such as carbon footprint, global warming and sustainable development – are the opening syllables of a conversation that has only just begun.

Even once we've re-crafted our civilisation to work in harmony with Earth's ecosphere, we will stand only at the threshold of yet further challenges. For this is a world on which solar cycles, ice ages and mobile coastlines are an implicit part of the gig. CO_2-induced climate change is not our great collective environmental challenge – it's one in a long line of complicated learning experiences.

*****

One curious feature of humankind's prehistoric colonisation of Earth was that when we reached the continents that had never seen hominids before (Australia and the Americas), the big animals ('megafauna') on those continents almost immediately became extinct.

The elephants of Africa and horses of Asia had evolved alongside us (and our forebears, *Homo erectus*) so they knew to be wary of humans. But when the first people arrived in the New World, with their huge brains and highly developed hunting technologies, the giant wombats and horse-sized tapirs were all dead before they'd learned to run.

To the prehistoric Australians, killing that last giant wombat (which could probably feed a family for a week) must have seemed like a brilliant idea. What they didn't understand was that, with a few leaps of the imagination, those wombats could have been harnessed and ridden, or attached to ploughs. It took tens of thousands of years before the extermination of the megafauna returned to haunt their descendants, but return to haunt them it did.

The first Australians weren't stupid, but there were lots of really important things they just didn't understand. The same is true of us. We should prepare for the future with that ignorance in mind.

Once you've killed every great whale in the sea, nothing similar is going to re-evolve any time in the next ten million years. Once an ecosystem completely vanishes, so do the species which rely on it. Many of the matters over which we humans fret are not, in the grandest scheme of things, a terribly big deal. Others are a very big deal indeed.

Even 1,000 years from now, the hell those foolish twenty-first-century humans put themselves through because sports utility vehicles (SUVs) pushed their ego buttons may just be one more calamity in this epic multi-generational drama of ours. But every species consigned to oblivion is a facet of the world which cannot be remade, even in the most distant future of humankind, no matter how many times the seas rise and fall. In attempting to attain a sustainable relationship with our host planet, let's take the long view. There are uncounted generations to damn us for what's destroyed.

*****

There's a more complete way of thinking about what's happening.

The Earth's biosphere has been increasing in sophistication and intensity for three billion years. But it's only in the past few hundred million that the strikingly complex big organisms (birds, mammals, reptiles etc.) got going.

One of the most arresting bits of data I've ever come across is that, even though median animal brain size hasn't increased since the Cambrian Explosion (cockroaches were always dim-witted), the brain size of the biggest-brained animals has doubled roughly every 34 million years over that time. That's true even if you ignore us especially clever hominids.

Humanity should see itself for what it really is: an ecological phenomenon. One more experiment in life thrown up by the Earth in her never-ending inventiveness. It's the blend of tool use, social minds and language she's selected for us which are the real genesis of the environmental conundrum we now face.

But if an ecosphere as majestic as this one was always fated, sooner or later, to throw up such an ingenious tool-using species, and such a species was predestined to face such an environmental conundrum, then the depth of destiny which brought us here can be measured in millions, rather than thousands, of years. So, by ensuring that Earth's other manifestations of life pass through this bottleneck alongside us, we can really show history what we're made of.

108: The Mission
13 February 2007

Six days ago I arrived at the Andean town of Latacunga, capital of Cotopaxi province. The town is about 350 kilometres south-west of Lago Agrio and 89 kilometres south of Quito. Its population is predominantly indigenous and mixed race, its market is a riot of colours and smells, and the giant volcano after which the province is named looms, brooding and silent, in the near distance.

I'd intended to start exploring the mountains on my second morning. However, I was accosted by a teacher called Adriana looking for a native English speaker to spend a couple of hours with her students. At first I resisted, but Adriana was extremely persistent and had a too-charming smile. I ended up going for it.

It turned out to be a school run by the police. The kids, aged 6 to 16, wore military-style uniforms with name badges sewn above their left breast pockets. In the headmaster's office there was a long cabinet lined with brightly polished child-sized black helmets replete with over-the-top white plumes. Shortly after I arrived, the whole school turned out for a parade in which everybody stood in straight lines and barked things in unison.

'Spending a couple of hours with Adriana's students' turned out to mean giving five classes, back-to-back, with zero preparation. I haven't taught formally for 10 years, so I had to wing it – wearing my most colourful shirt, waving my arms and hamming it up.

The seven-year-olds were the most amusing. In hindsight I shouldn't have shown them the game where I picked them up and swung them around while roaring. After that a crowd of the little tykes followed me around for the rest of the day, calling out 'Peeta' and trying to climb on my back.

In the end I didn't leave until one o'clock that afternoon, so it was later than expected when I caught a local bus bound for Laguna Quilotoa.

Laguna Quilotoa, about 30 kilometres west of Latacunga, sits within the caldera of an extinct volcano at 3,854 metres above sea level. The lake is two kilometres across, bright green and encircled by a 500-metre-high ridge. It's utterly spectacular. Arriving full of reckless gung-ho I pressed on with my original plan to walk the entire seven-kilometre circumference that afternoon.

Foolhardy.

After an hour of vigorous trudging I was enveloped by a wall of cloud, lost sight of the ridge, took a wrong turn and ended up on the volcano's outer slopes with no idea of how to get back.

Whenever I'm a little lost I draw solace from the fact that Christopher Columbus, on seeing the Sierra Maestra in Cuba, thought he was looking at the Himalayas. *That's* lost. Nonetheless, on attempting to find a way back my spirits were depressed and enthusiasm dissipated by the onset of another crushingly horrible altitude-related headache.

As the temperature and my energy levels plummeted and evening approached, it dawned on me how unfortunate it would be to get caught outside at nightfall at nearly 4,000 metres. An inner alarm made me press through the enveloping lethargy, haunted by the thought my grand project might reach an ignominious end on that wind-swept mountainside. I stumbled miserably back to the shack I was staying in just as the light failed. The family who owned the place gave me a huge pile of blankets. I slept under all of them.

The next day I awoke with all-over body aches and a general feeling of nausea. All I needed before leaving was a cup of tea and a place to sit, but the lakeside village was exceedingly rustic and such things were not to be found there. I ended up putting on all my warmest clothes and collapsing on a patch of grass – one arm flung across my eyes – until the once-a-day bus drove by.

When it arrived there were no seats, so I stood in the aisle next to a tall gringo in a faded grey jumper, who cheered me up by listening indulgently to my story of a difficult day. He was an Italian photographer called Davide and had come into the mountains in search of a religious mission fronted by a renowned and aged Italian priest by the name of Father Gigi. That afternoon we checked into the same hotel at the next village, Chugchilán. Then, in the morning, Davide and I went in search of the mission.

It took 40 minutes of walking and talking before we arrived at a busy and well-ordered compound of whitewashed buildings, which swarmed with young boys. On one wall was a fresco of Padre Gigi and, off to one side, a small church, where the man himself was hearing a long line of confessions.

One of the people running the place – a heavily built man with a thick black beard – came to say 'hi', and, recognising each other's Italianness, Davide and he immediately began waving their hands and talking excitedly. The man gave us a tour of the grounds, where food was being distributed from giant metal pots and elegant wooden furniture was being constructed in pristine workshops. Then he fed us brunch.

Brunch consisted of succulent white cheeses and warm home-baked bread, the likes of which I've not seen since arriving in South America. As for the coffee, you have to have experienced the local sub-Nescafé with powdered milk to understand my glee when they produced real ruddy espresso served in actual espresso cups. Gotta love those Italians.

Our hosts were seriously increase-the-peace Catholics, who'd set up the mission 25 years earlier to work on behalf of the region's Amerindian poor. To begin with they'd concentrated on social work, but after a few years had refocused their efforts on what they'd come to regard as the area's underlying issue: its chronically underdeveloped economic state. This part of the world does not have anything approaching an ingrained tradition of market capitalism and the problem, the mission's workers report, is teaching innovation. When they'd demonstrated how to build a mozzarella factory, the local people all started building mozzarella factories.

It was a blunt reminder of how the different communities of Earth are all at different phases in equally complex processes of social and cultural evolution. In Chugchilán one of those communities is reaching out to another across a gulf opened by thousands of years of history, with hope, faith and the best will in the world. Good luck to all concerned.

Davide went with the infectiously energetic 75-year-old Father Gigi who, shortly after shaking my hand, left for another village to perform further religious duties.

I spent the rest of the day walking alone through lush meadows filled with pink and yellow flowers, then sat beneath a copse of pine trees that clung to the edge of the precipitous valley above which Chugchilán sits. With a vista of greens before me I mused upon the Amazon, the Andes and the current tapestry of peoples in this world.

Now I'm back in Latacunga. This evening I catch a bus beneath the cloud-wisped immensity of Cotopaxi and head for the coast.

Days since leaving London: 627
Number of times

    Latacunga has been destroyed by earthquakes: 4
    Cotopaxi has erupted since 1738:   50

I believe in God, only I spell it Nature. – Frank Lloyd Wright

109: XXXIII
17 February 2007

I'm in Canoa, a village on Ecuador's north-western coast, full of palm trees, hammocks and incredibly chilled-out people.

The overnight bus from the mountains dropped me at nearby Bahía de Caraquez three days ago. From there I took a ferry to the town of San Vicente and then a sweaty local bus to Canoa itself.

Just as the bus was pulling up, an elfin-looking girl with tanned skin and a stargazer lily tattooed on her left shoulder popped her head over the seat in front of me and stuck a packet of biscuits in my face. 'Cookie?' she asked. Her name was Victoria. We got talking.

We ended up talking all the way from the bus, along a dusty footpath, to the beach, accompanying the gang she'd arrived with. There's Rose, a blonde Dutch 20-year-old student, who's spending some time in South America following her first year of university, and Ryan, a thoughtful bearded fellow from Oregon, who's come to Ecuador to study permaculture. As for Victoria, she's just decided to spend her life working in ecotourism. What a splendid idea.

Ryan led us to a beautifully arranged European-run joint called the Hotel Bambú. It consists of a collection of scattered bungalows and a sprawling restaurant, where they serve banana pancakes and an array of elaborate fruit-based cocktails.

Canoa has a long, wide and perfectly sandy beach in front of a line of relaxed bars and surf shops. A few hundred metres to the north there are caves which can be explored at low tide. If you walk there in the morning hundreds of teeny-weeny crabs flee in panic at your approach, from the sand where they've been feeding to the holes in which they hide from gulls and the big people.

Within hours of arriving I'd become part of a beach-based community made up almost entirely of North Americans from the Canadian city of Vancouver and west-coast US states of Washington and Oregon. Everyone is a big-time environmentalist. No one votes Republican.

For me, the core of this community are Rose, Ryan and Victoria. The four of us share a ramshackle dorm at the top of a creaky wooden staircase, above a washing area containing two huge mirrors. At least twice a day Victoria and I find ourselves post-swim, staring into those mirrors, complimenting each other on how gorgeous the sand, salt and sun are making us look.

Ecuador, it turns out, is a hotspot for permaculture. Ryan's been teaching me all about it: a philosophy of agricultural systems design which mimics the relationships found in natural ecologies. Permaculture techniques seek to replicate the way, in nature, a web of connections allows diverse populations of plants and animals to survive efficiently and productively.

It was developed in the 1970s, driven by a desire to reduce reliance on industrial farming methods and *engage* nature rather than bend her to our will. If industrial farming allowed us to feed the seven fold expansion of Earth's population over the past two centuries, then the next phase of human agriculture – the one that will bring us through the long haul to sustainability – will draw upon ideas such as these.

Apart from listening to Ryan's permaculture lectures, activities with the gang have included burying each other in the sand, wading into the Pacific while the sun sets, and filling watermelons with vodka then using straws to suck out the alcohol-saturated juice. The main topic of conversation is how much fun we're having.

After my long isolation in Quito, all this witty, joyful and intelligent company has brought me right back into the cut and thrust of human interaction. Canoa is turning into one of the highlights of my life and has therefore been a perfect spot in which to spend my birthday. Ryan made sure everybody knew, so a fuss was made of me and I even got presents. I'd intended to send this email yesterday – on the actual anniversary of my birth – but, on obscure palm-tree-lined beaches on the outer fringes of civilisation, sometimes all the internet connections go down at the same time without any explanation as to why.

I try not to ask too many questions, or let it get me down.

Days since leaving London: 631
Days since I was born: 12,062

> *A man told me to beware of 33. He said: 'It was not an easy time for me'* – Jarvis Cocker

110: Curious Happenings during Carnival
19 February 2007

Now I'm road-tripping the backpacker trail, I've begun the process of re-ethnicising myself through the purchase of beach jewellery. I currently sport a string of thick wooden beads and a necklace on which a Hindu mandala hangs. It goes with the territory and my deeply satisfying new beach tan.

Spiritual architecture update: since leaving Quito I've read two books dealing with ideas regarding God.

1) *In Search of Personal Peace* by the American evangelical Billy Graham. It was a gift from Zoe Savage and the last thing she gave me as I left

her cell in Quito's Women's Prison. Zoe told me to read it then leave it on a bookshelf somewhere on South America's west coast. In the book, Reverend Graham sets out the born-again Christian world view and argues that the Resurrection of Jesus Christ is an undisputable historical fact.

2) *Contact* by the twentieth-century astronomer and scientific communicator Carl Sagan. It's the only work of fiction he wrote and, in it, he imagines a pre-universe intelligence which has built an unambiguous sign of its existence into the fabric of reality.

Professor Sagan (who for me does the more satisfying job of touching upon the infinite) points out that the ancient creeds which talk of miracles never even worked out that the small twinkling things one sees at night are the same as the blindingly bright thing one sees during the day, just farther away.

Recognising that the sun was a star is exactly the sort of thing those Middle Eastern holy men could have guessed without mathematics, telescopes and the paraphernalia of modern comprehension. All they required was a medium-sized leap of the imagination and a smidgen of divine guidance. But it was beyond them. By attempting to pronounce truth in stone they failed to grasp that (for fallible beings like us) keeping a standing invitation open to the world to try to prove you wrong is the most certainty attainable and the only way of attaining it.

Carnival began on our third day in Canoa. Water balloons were suddenly being thrown at everyone, an almighty beach party erupted and my North American associates redoubled their dedication to the 24-hour-party lifestyle. We've been dancing by the water in the evenings, drinking cocktails with the sand between our toes, then throwing ourselves into the breakers by moonlight.

Yesterday morning I had my chance to make a move on Victoria. I messed it up. It was early, post-party, and we were alone together at the north end of the beach. She was leaping barefoot from rock to rock telling me how wonderful the dawn was, while I followed with rather less grace. Then we sat together as the sun rose and the tide came in, but even after everything I've done during the past 21 months I still wasn't brave enough to kiss her.

Earlier that evening something crazy happened. I was sat in the thick of the action, drinking rum with an introspective Canadian man. I never got his name. All I remember is that he was youngish and weathered, with a thick blond beard and a pleasant girlfriend.

We were talking about the cultural differences between peoples. I was saying that individuals from the various regions of the world basically approach life in the same way and that perceived variations between them are largely illusory, stemming from our proclivity to focus on the few things which differentiate us.

He leaned across the sand towards me. Around us, the full force of carnival was raging: a white noise of a thousand thoughts being exchanged and explored; a human machine that was more than the sum of its parts, hissing with the sound of intellectual fuel being mixed, integrated and reconstituted. 'But aren't even more basic differences also illusions?' he said matter-of-factly. It's funny how those moments come along. One step and then another.

'What kind of differences?' I asked.

'Well, like the difference between me and you.'

I wish, I wish, I wish there was a way I could map what happened to the neurons in my brain in the minute after he said those words.

Days since leaving London: 633

Global Musings III
The Ghost in the
Machine

Human civilisation faces a lot of big scary problems. What's more, the current ones (climate change, resource depletion, global poverty etc.) are just the beginning. As civilisation matures over the next few centuries it will become more complicated. As it becomes more complicated, the problems it faces will become more challenging and the solutions less obvious.

Civilisation didn't come with an instruction manual and no one is going to solve these problems for us. We therefore need a systematic mechanism for pinning down the solutions. That problem-solving mechanism will have to be methodical, robust and flexible because it's going to have to deal with some very difficult questions.

Take the most often-discussed contemporary big scary problem: humankind's relationship with the environment; or, more precisely, the related series of problems including deforestation, species loss, ecosystem loss, pollution and climate change.

Sorting this stuff out is going to be tricky. Earth's climatic and biological systems are extremely complicated. There's a mountain of data about them which we're only just learning to interpret. The price of getting things wrong is high, many of the relevant sciences are new and the cost–benefit decisions are fiendishly complex.

What's more, different sections of human society disagree – sometimes vehemently – as to how we should proceed. Who's right? That, at least, is clear: no one. No one has the answers to those sorts of questions.

*****

In thinking about how we proceed under such circumstances it's instructive to step back from ourselves and consider the underlying mechanics of how a planet full of fallible humans works out anything really complicated from scratch.

What I'm going to say next may initially seem obvious. Bear with me.

First, everybody talks to each other. Those conversations take place within and between families, internet groups, academic institutions, newspaper offices and political organisations. That process throws up ideas, some of which will be good, and some bad. It won't initially be apparent which are which, so they will be debated. Ideas that ultimately turn out to be beneficial will come from different sources: some will come from hard-core environmental activists, others from no-nonsense capitalists and a few from travelling hippies who talk to bicycles. Promising ideas will spread, be subject to closer scrutiny, refined and synthesised.

Some ideas will then be implemented. Ideas tackling our environmental problems will involve things such as energy generation, waste disposal and economic best practice. Implementing them will involve changes to lifestyle, new legislation and (occasionally) massive, publicly funded endeavours. Implementing some ideas will be expensive and difficult (e.g. imposing an international carbon tax) and others straightforward and free (e.g. turning more lights off).

That process of implementation will provide lessons: some ideas will work, some will fail and some will backfire. Ideas that work will be built upon. On the whole, good ideas will spread. Generally, we won't be aware of where an idea was initially proposed. Yet, in the long run, we will all benefit from each other's inspiration and learn from each other's mistakes.

As civilisation develops it will become better disposed to the generation and dissemination of new thinking: literacy will continue increasing towards 100 per cent, information will become more widely available and more of the world's people will be brought into the conversation. More people means more ideas. Better-informed people means better ideas.

Our knowledge base and capacity to collect and interpret data will both constantly increase. Some of that new information will refine our ability to act, some will confirm what we already suspected and some will disprove fundamental assumptions. Received wisdom will be challenged and re-challenged. Measures that initially looked trivial will turn out to have been foresighted; ones that seemed foresighted will turn out to have been naive.

We'll get a lot of things wrong. In the case of our relationship with the environment, some of those things will cost many lives and be bitterly regretted. For example, it's possible we'll fail to act decisively on carbon emissions, only to face catastrophic sea level rises. Or we might spend precious resources reducing such emissions, only to ultimately realise that we misunderstood the data. Only time, debate and trial and error will tell.

Progress will be through small steps and there'll always be scope for improvement. But we *will* make progress and, as time passes, elements of human activity that affect the environment (which is quite a lot of them) will be modified, re-modified, overhauled and occasionally discontinued.

This process is ongoing, never-ending and the only method via which the human race will generate and implement solutions to its environmental problems or, for that matter, to any of its other big problems.

*****

Think of it as a machine.

Each human is a node. Any medium of discourse between humans is a connection between nodes. The whole arrangement of nodes and connections – the pooled knowledge and collective consciousness of the human race – takes the form of a matrix.

Ideas – flashes of inspiration – are generated within individual nodes. Those ideas are then passed through adjoining connections into the matrix to be filtered and refined. Ideas initially judged to be promising are passed more widely around the matrix to be subjected to closer, and more detailed, scrutiny. This filtration process causes some ideas to be discarded and others retained.

The application of ideas generates learning experiences, which are then reabsorbed by the relevant nodes and fed back into the matrix. Ideas which are demonstrated to work will spread throughout the machine, at first haltingly, then faster as they prove themselves more fully. Each learning experience helps to stimulate the next generation of ideas, and enhances the machine's ability to analyse ideas under scrutiny in its matrix.

The quality of the machine's raw materials is determined by how well informed and free-thinking people are. The efficiency with which ideas are sifted and synthesised relates to the energy of debate and how many people apply themselves to it. The effectiveness with which good ideas are chosen and implemented relates to our judgement and willingness to adopt new inventions, scientific concepts, social norms, or whatever. The rapidity with which lessons are learned and applied correlates to the openness of our societies and how accountable our institutions are.

The machine is the only rational and coherent mechanism for generating, refining and implementing solutions to the big problems faced by humanity. It's a babbling, confusing, messy, argumentative thing, but it does the job.

The more complicated human civilisation becomes, the more important it will be that the machine operates efficiently. To ensure that happens we should be clear-headed about the level of certainty (about anything) available to imperfect beings (like us) in a mysterious and inscrutable universe (such as this one).

First, accept the big picture. We have no idea what the future, its challenges or the solutions to those challenges will look like. Many of the things which ultimately turn out to be true are going to be unexpected and counter-intuitive. Industries, schools of thought and branches of learning currently undreamed of will one day be developed to help us deal with, and make sense of, this astonishing universe. The seeds for many of those things will come from right over on the left field. We therefore *need* people to think outside the box, challenge assumptions and go against the grain.

Second, the wider and more diverse the spectrum of inputs, the better. People with different cultural backgrounds, life experiences and genetic predispositions will have insights into different sorts of things. The more globalised dialogue becomes, the more productive it can be. Attempts to restrict the machine via censorship are short-sighted, counter-productive and wrong.

Third, everything must be (and stay) up for discussion. No one is (or will ever be) in a position to predict where the good ideas will (or will not) come from. The machine doesn't work if everybody believes the same thing and the truth loses from the silence of those who take exception to it. Autocrats may boast of protecting their flocks, but it is not the wisdom of the heretic that's retarded by the imposition of orthodoxy.

Finally, remember, nobody has all the answers and nobody has been anointed to speak the truth. If anybody tells you they've got it all figured out, they're wrong. If you're ever tempted to think *you've* got it figured out (and if you were king for a day you'd sort out all our problems), don't be. You're as fallible as I am. You'd only make things worse.

*****

There are deep-seated reasons why dictatorship, tyranny, or rule by self-selected cliques cannot work. The reason conventionally given is that power corrupts and absolute power corrupts absolutely. Those things may be true, but even if our mythical benevolent dictator was the wisest, most compassionate and incorruptible person who had ever lived, their reign would still be doomed to malfunction and failure.

No matter how impressive we may be as individuals, all humans are fallible. We all have some matters on which we will brook no compromise, we're all wrong about some of those matters, and we are, each one of us, the worst judges in the world regarding which ones. The moral conundrums, conceptual challenges and logistical complexities that humankind is set to face in the coming centuries are orders of magnitude beyond the capabilities of an imperfect status-obsessed primate, even if he's a really nice guy.

Any system of government founded on the basis that a self-selected individual, or group of individuals, is in a position to decide how to tackle those complexities is, sooner or later, going to run into a wall.

At this point in history several such self-selected groups of humans are attempting, with various levels of success, to dictate the affairs of parts of the world over which they hold sway. Half the planet lives in the shade of such monkey trees, but such arrangements are not sustainable. Over the long term, running a country along those lines does not and will not work. Not because of the various moral considerations, but because of the underlying realities of being billions of fallible animals on the surface of a planet – realities that we're all locked into, whether we like it or not.

There's only one strategy open to us in navigating a path for this pan-planetary civilisation we've inadvertently constructed: tapping the massed energies of our collective planetary psyche. Nowhere is that more relevant than when assessing governments. There is only one rational system available for their ongoing evaluation and improvement: frequent peer review by their fellow humans.

*****

Over the last few centuries this has been gradually dawning on everybody. How long it will take to implement systems of democracy across the world – another 100 years or 1,000 – remains to be seen. But the complexity of our problems is going to keep increasing, as will the price of getting things wrong. Now those problems have entered the realms of planetary climate management, haphazardly chosen *Homo sapiens* just making up the answers really doesn't cut it any more.

In many parts of the world this has, in principle, been accepted. Free speech is (in theory) unchallenged. The executive branch of government is elected and broadly reflects the mood of the machine. Deliberation is sophisticated and inclusive and takes place through numerous accessible media. As a result, new challenges are rapidly identified and innovative ideas are efficiently generated and implemented.

Yet it never fails to astonish me how emotional people get about politics, the ugly hyperbole it inspires and the hate-filled exchanges that take place between people who just happen to disagree about certain things. If the machine is going to work, ideas need to be tried out that some people will disagree with. Sometimes it will be you (or me) that disagrees with what is being done. Sometimes you (or I) will feel very strongly about it. It's not supposed to be a smooth process. It's supposed to involve argument, disagreement, mistakes and self-correction.

But twenty-first-century political debate doesn't have to include the demonisation of the people who don't agree with you. That's true even if they're politicians and even if you *really* don't like what they're doing. We are all part of, and rely upon, a collective decision-making mechanism which nobody is in a position to maintain on their own.

Nourishing that mechanism's vibrancy is an unending process. Humanity will always need to be introspective about what it's doing and why. People are never going to stop being fallible and all creeds and philosophies become stale without the fray of argument.

Being realistic about all that, and obsessing less about the small real differences between us, would leave the human race better positioned to discuss what does and does not work about civilisation and what we're going to do about it. Because, at this point in history, as literacy and free speech spread, and the internet stretches its filaments across the globe, the potential of this planetary psyche is only at the threshold of coming to be realised. A structure is falling into place for a planet-wide deliberation of unprecedented scope and promise.

*****

There's a more complete way of thinking about all this.

All human minds share an almost identical design. In addition, we all go through the same basic sequence of experiences: birth, life and then death. Yet, despite that, our tiny differences in experience and mental disposition give rise to a plethora of ways of looking at, and thinking about, the world. It's that *range* of understandings, and their interplay, which allows humanity to tackle something as enigmatic as the cosmos.

The rhythms of our genes, and the way multiple generations of those rhythms have caused our brains to work, mean we're *built* to think of ourselves as individuals. But in doing so we're acting like those champagne bubbles in a glass, which argue over who is the more sparkling while ignoring the swirling party, and overlooking their own essential nature.

Sometimes, when we perceive each other to be enemies or rivals, we're actually acting as the instruments for something larger than ourselves.

No individual, benevolent or otherwise, is in a position to navigate our collective path or come up with the answers to the big questions before us. Those answers are embedded – dispersed in chaotically arranged fragments – within the brains of the people of planet Earth. The only way those fragments can be drawn out and assembled is by us all, collectively, breathing life into the planet-wide matrix of which we're a part. A multi-billion-node hive-mind. An immense babble of humans all talking to each other. Somewhere in that white noise, we will find our answers.

111: Beach-Hopping
27 February 2007

Following the joys of Canoa I decided to head for another beach.

I split town the day before my Ecuadorian visa expired, spent 15 hours going bus to bus, then crossed the Peruvian border at midnight. It was 2 a.m. when I was dropped by the roadside at the surfer town of Mancora. Carnival was still in full swing. I walked along the main parade knocking on doors, but there were no rooms left in town.

Rocking up in Peruvian villages at 2 a.m. with nowhere to sleep in the middle of carnival isn't the sort of thing that fazes me nowadays. I've got Nguthungulli the Tent, so I can always find a secluded spot and pitch up. However, Francine and Manco, the beautiful Swiss-Peruvian couple I got talking to, were convinced I was about to get robbed and insisted I sleep on a mattress in the backroom of their restaurant. Angels.

As I carried my bags inside, two of Francine's friends, Teresa and Sara, walked by. Realising I was new in town they asked if I needed to sleep straight away or if I wanted to go to a party.

Whaddyareckon?

Down at the beach the festivities were in full swing and the energy was infectious. Things rapidly got out of hand. One minute we were drinking rum on the beach. Then we were at a club. Then we were back at their place.

The place Teresa and Sara were renting was an extremely sparse concrete arrangement with no furniture. The three of us sat on mattresses – Teresa on one, and Sara and I on the other. There were two candles providing light. As soon as we arrived Teresa pulled out a fist-sized see-through plastic bag full of white power. 'For you, baby,' she told me, flaring her nostrils, 'it's free.'

We then proceeded to get heroically wasted by candlelight while the two of them, speaking very quickly indeed, filled my head with their worlds. Sara was studying economics in Cuzco. She was from a well-to-do family on the coast and came to Mancora to hang out during the holidays.

Teresa was the more vocal of the two. She was a chef working near Lima and when she learned I'd eaten Ecuadorian ceviche (a citrus-marinated seafood dish traditionally made in Peru) she expressed her outrage with the phrase '*Ecuadorian* ceviche? *My pussy*', along with descriptive hand movements. Teresa went on with this sort of stuff for about an hour. Then she fell asleep. At that point Sara put one hand under my shirt, another under my chin, kissed me on the neck and whispered in my ear, 'Bring the mattress. We'll go to the next room.'

Five hours later I stumbled, naked, ecstatic and dizzy-headed, into Teresa and Sara's back garden. I hadn't had a moment's rest. The garden was enclosed by a brick wall, behind and above which could be seen the looming face of a small red cliff. A few scraps of grass were growing through the concrete and there was a simple outdoor toilet. This part of the world is just south of the Equator and just north of the desert. It was approaching 40 degrees Celsius. I looked down at the taut and swollen muscles of my limbs and abdomen, then at the sweat beading every square inch of my body, then up, towards the pounding sun, as it cascaded its heat energy down upon me. Then I closed my eyes.

Welcome to Peru.

After gratefully collecting my bags from Francine's restaurant that afternoon, Sara helped me find a guest house with a room. I spent the next four days in Mancora having long sessions of animalistic, drug-fuelled sex, punctuated by the odd hour floating in the Pacific watching sea birds perform mid-air acrobatics and dive-bomb the local fish.

After four days as Sara's concubine and plaything she got bored of me. One night she disappeared with her friends and didn't return. So, in a minor huff, I split Mancora the next morning and caught a tuk-tuk south to the next beach along, Los Organos.

Los Organos is more civilised but much less exciting than Mancora. There's hardly anyone here. I'm staying at a beachfront hotel and have been reading Peter Benchley's *Jaws* in between trips into the water. I made sure I did a night swim like the chick that gets eaten at the beginning. Nothing tried to chomp me.

Plan update: from Los Organos I'll be following the arc of the Peruvian coast south. Lima is about 1,000 kilometres away and Nazca is 500 beyond that. From Nazca I'll head inland to Cuzco and the Sacred Valley. But, before any of that, I'm going to pay my respects at the place where the world changed, Cajamarca.

Days since leaving London: 641
Planet Earth (1993–2006)

Population growth:	18%
GDP growth:	91%

Better the tyranny of Saddam than the chaos of the Amerikan. – Baghdad graffiti

112: Checkmate
1 March 2007

I'm in Cajamarca, five hours into the mountains from the coast and the town where, in the year 1532, the Spanish and the Incas had their first fateful encounter.

Atahualpa, the Inca Emperor, had conducted his preparations perfectly – drawing the foreigners right into the heart of his empire. The Spanish were 100 kilometres from the ocean and any possibility of reinforcements. On the hills above them was Atahualpa's army: 40,000 warriors, battle-hardened from the civil war, armed and ready for a fight.

Nice one, Atahualpa.

With Mesoamerica largely subdued, the Incas were the only force in the western hemisphere with the resources and organisation to stem the Spanish takeover, or at least force some sort of compromise. But, of course, they did not know that.

If one could talk to Atahualpa with the benefit of hindsight one might say: 'If you attack now you can win. Throw everything you have at this expeditionary force, take their weapons and horses, take prisoners, learn their ways and you might – just might – be able to take control of this situation. If you do there is a chance you might be able to spare your people some of the horror that will follow. Defeat this small band and you'll have a fighting chance. This chance won't come again. Take them out now.'

But that's not what he did.

Francisco Pizarro, the Spanish leader, invited Atahualpa into Cajamarca on the pretence that he wanted to talk. Atahualpa went, with his entourage, unarmed. Mistake. Pizarro may have been illiterate, but his ruthlessness knew no bounds and he was not in Peru to talk.

As Atahualpa's entourage entered Cajamarca he was met by Vicente de Valverde, the Spanish priest. Vicente told the Inca that he'd been sent to reveal a new religion to him. Atahualpa was unimpressed, throwing Vicente's Bible to the ground.

That was when Pedro de Cadia, Pizarro's gunner, fired his artillery straight into the massed ranks of the Inca's unarmed entourage, and the Spanish, hiding in the surrounding buildings and not in the slightest bit unarmed, attacked with everything they had.

After the massacre Atahualpa was famously ransomed for a roomful of gold and two rooms of silver. Then, when the ransom had been paid, the Spanish murdered him anyway. The Incas had utterly lost the initiative. They would never regain it.

The Spanish ploy may sound audacious, but they were simply applying a formula they'd learned in the Caribbean. Pizarro had cut his teeth in the Americas taking part in the extermination of the Arawak Indians. Surprise seizure of the local ruler during a friendly parlay was a run-of-the-mill tactic known to paralyse initial resistance among peoples who still considered their leaders gods (as the ancestors of the Spanish also would have done millennia before).

After Cajamarca things got really nasty for the Native Americans. The conquistadors went on to make good their plans for the lands they'd found, and they had not come in peace.

I spent an afternoon wandering around Cajamarca alone, walking through tile-decorated streets lined with whitewashed buildings, then visiting a gallery where three paintings, in turn, depicted Jesus Christ turning water into wine, undergoing crucifixion and ascending to heaven. After that I sat in the square where the first massacre took place, looked up at the green mountains rising above the city and thought about the generations of anarchy, social dislocation and war that were set in motion there. Finally, I visited the ancient stone building where Atahualpa was kept prisoner.

A sign hangs there. It reads: 'ÉL CAMBIÓ LA HISTORIA DEL MUNDO' (he changed the history of the world).

It's instructive to note that all the Spanish protagonists mentioned above met their ends in the orgy of violence that they initiated. Here were their fates:

Pedro de Cadia, who fired his field gun into the Inca's unarmed entourage, died at the Battle of Chupas during one of the post-Conquest civil wars. He was executed by his own commander for 'not firing his cannon sufficiently vigorously'.

Vicente de Valverde, the priest who confronted Atahualpa with Christianity, spent his final days fleeing Peru by ship to Panama. He ended up stranded on the island of Puná, where the natives, also unimpressed by his religion, ate him.

Francisco Pizarro and the other architect of the Conquest, Diego de Almagro, fell out almost at once over gold and territory. De Almagro was garrotted by Pizarro's brother in 1538 and, in the predictable revenge attack, De Almagro's supporters broke into Pizarro's palace in 1541 to murder him.

As the great conquistador fell to the ground, he made the sign of the cross in blood and begged for forgiveness. But, rather than hear the confession of a dying man, his attackers smashed an urn full of water into his face and screamed at him to 'confess in hell'.

Days since leaving London: 643
Time it took the Spanish to hunt down and destroy all the mummified Inca kings: 27 years

From books, the Spanish knew of many contemporary civilizations remote from Europe, and about several thousand years of European history ... literacy made the Spanish heirs to a huge body of knowledge about human behaviour and history. By contrast, not only did Atahualpa have no conception of the Spanish themselves, and no personal experience of any other invaders from overseas, but he also had not even heard (or read) of similar threats to anyone else, anywhere else, anytime previously in history. That gulf of experience encouraged Pizarro to set his trap and Atahualpa to walk into it. – Jared Diamond

Global Musings IV
Weaving the Current Tapestry

The Spanish capture of the emperor Atahualpa was a turning point in world history. It led to the political domination of the Andes region by a European people and the marginalisation and disenfranchisement of the original Native Americans in that region. Earlier in my journey I had come across an even more extreme case of such disenfranchisement: the indigenous peoples of Australia.

These are both examples of a broader phenomenon. Disparities in economic and political power between people from different ethnic backgrounds are a striking feature of human society in the early twenty-first century. Such disparities manifest themselves both between different ethnic groups within the same region and between regions of different dominant ethnicities.

This phenomenon is bound up with the great patterns of the human past – patterns to whose fortunes we've all been hostage. During this current (extremely enlightened) epoch, those patterns (and the causes which drove them) are actually quite well understood. If one's interested in why our world is the way it is and where it's going next, it's worth deconstructing what happened.

*****

Eurasia – the single landmass made up of Europe and Asia – is more suited to the development of agriculture, and technologically advanced civilisations, than the rest of the world. For the purposes of the historical theatres I'm about to describe, Africa north of the Sahara was part of that Eurasian world.

The ultimate reason Eurasia and North Africa are better suited for agriculture and civilisation is that, in prehistory, those areas were home to most of the plant and animal species that happen to be suitable for domestication (i.e. the wild ancestors of wheat, oats, barley, cows, sheep, goats etc.).

This fact of biogeography was compounded when the original Australians and Americans wiped out most of the large mammals on those continents which might one day have been domesticated. As a result, agriculture got a few thousand years' head start in Eurasia.

Civilisation develops as a consequence of agriculture. Hunter-gatherers have more fun than farmers, but they never build pyramids.

As agricultural societies can accumulate a surplus of food, they can divide their labour between people that grow food and people that do other things, like build pyramids and invent stuff.

That division of labour allowed by agriculture therefore allowed civilisation. It also led to a step change in technological progress. Humans invented lots of things before all this (such as clothes, wigwams and bows and arrows) but the really world-transforming stuff (such as writing and mathematics) requires agriculture and the civilisation which sometimes goes with it.

As agriculture got a (huge) head start in Eurasia, so did civilisation and the resulting technological progress. Thousands of years ago Eurasia was already dotted with lots of big, impressive civilisations in China, India, Europe and the Middle East. Ever since their inception they witnessed a steady stream of inventions and technological developments.

Next, because of geography, the Eurasian civilisations continually fed off each other's developments. We divide Europe and Asia into two continents for historical reasons. But it's all one landmass and, back to the deepest eras of human prehistory, it was thoroughly connected with North Africa via the Sinai and the Mediterranean sea routes. So once something was invented in one place, sooner or later it spread. The Romans and Han Chinese of 2,000 years ago were rarely in direct contact, but ideas were slowly floating across Eurasia between the two cultures.

For example: paper was invented in China in 105 CE. It took 600 years to get to Central Asia, reached Baghdad by 795 CE, Egypt around 900 CE, Islamic Spain later that century and Germany by the fourteenth century; and, in 1495 CE, the first paper mill was built in England. That might seem unimaginably slow by twenty-first-century standards, but the point is that the idea diffused across Eurasia eventually. Meanwhile, in Australia, they still didn't have the wheel.

None of the technologies that gave the Spanish their crushing military advantage over the Amerindians in the sixteenth century (horses, steel and guns) were Spanish developments. Horses had been domesticated in Central Asia around 4000 BCE, steel use grew out of Middle Eastern iron production after 900 BCE, while the first guns were developed in China in about 1280 CE. Spain was not substantially more advanced than its neighbours in Europe, but it was heir to an 8,000-year-old tradition of Eurasian technology to which the Amerindians had no access.

Technology wasn't the only thing the Eurasians were swapping. Infectious diseases need minimum populations to sustain themselves. Hunting and gathering groups traditionally had relatively low levels of infection because they didn't live in units big enough for diseases to establish themselves. But the herd animals we tamed did. It was our close proximity to those animals during the first millennia of agriculture that gave their germs the opportunity to mutate and infect us.

The major microbial killers that have spread death through Eurasian populations down the ages were the direct result of animal domestication. The common cold originally came from horses; measles, smallpox, diphtheria and tuberculosis all came from cows; and flu, would you believe, we originally got from pigs, via ducks.

*****

Five hundred years ago European ships circumnavigated Africa and crossed the Atlantic. That marked the beginning of a chapter in human history – lasting about 400 years – during which the human race went from being geographically divided to living in a single global society. With the exception of North Sentinel Island and a few tribes in Amazonia and New Guinea, that joining-together is now complete.

Before that watershed, because of their head start in civilisation and technology, Eurasian societies had large, well-organised states with high levels of political and technological sophistication. In those spheres they were about 4,000 years ahead of South America's most technologically advanced cultures and 8,000 years ahead of the Australians. That's a big difference.

There's a widely held perception that groups native to Europe were ahead of the rest of Eurasia. That's true up to a point, but the European advantage was ephemeral in time scales longer than 200 years. China was the traditional powerhouse of Eurasian civilisation. The Middle East was particularly influential between the seventh and thirteenth centuries and the Ottoman, Mughal and many other empires went through periods of political ascendancy. The main reason people perceive European societies (and those they spawned) as being ahead is that we happen to stand at the end of two centuries of European dominance.

From the Mongols to the British, different Eurasian groups have always gained short-term advantage over one another. Europe's nineteenth-century Asian empires are just the most recent example of that. Europe's brief domination of Asia may have been traumatic (for the dominated) at the time, but the fabric of Asian societies was never torn apart like those of Australia and South America.

The wild card in this Old World/New World model is sub-Saharan Africa. The sub-Saharan peoples lacked the trappings of high civilisation, but they had steel and all the Eurasian diseases. The nineteenth-century European imperialists may have ushered in political volatility, but they never displaced African populations, or imposed upon them the particular fate that was to be suffered by the peoples of the New World. For when the world began coming together after the fifteenth century, catastrophe immediately began overwhelming those New World populations.

Contact was heralded by a wave of mass death as the infections that had been bubbling away in the Old World since the domestication of animals hit them all at once. Europe's colonising powers then used their overwhelming advantages in technology and political cunning to ruthlessly subjugate the survivors. That process enshrined political and economic advantages that have been maintained ever since.

*****

The most complete way of understanding the harrowing events which unfolded when the Spanish conquistadors reached America and the British colonised Australia is in terms of evolutionary psychology. The British and Spanish colonisers were animals motivated by an agenda set out in their genetic code and they acted precisely as that agenda dictated. The Native Americans and Australians occupied a vast ecological niche on their home continents from which they were brutally displaced by their Eurasian cousins.

In the sixteenth-century Andes the all-male Spanish expedition came across a densely populated, well-organised, hierarchical agricultural society which they could easily dominate. They reacted by sweeping away (then supplanting) the native elite, killing or enslaving the men and impregnating as many of the women as possible. This was probably broadly in line with their reproductive interests, as evidenced by the large number of Latin Americans in the world.

In eighteenth-century Australia the British found a continent well suited to their agricultural techniques. The native peoples of the time were without any central organisation, generally non-sedentary, thinly dispersed and using Stone Age weapons. Any resistance they might mount against an empire that was an inheritor of 8,000 years of Eurasian military technology and at the threshold of an industrial revolution was ludicrously inadequate.

The British effectively had a free hand. They therefore shot the natives, stole their land, declared the survivors less than human and instituted a century and a half of ghastly cultural sabotage, which undermined the fabric and dignity of what was left.

Of course, at the time, the Spanish and British didn't see it like that. They saw what they were doing in terms of the socially constructed cultural and political abstractions through which they regulated, and made sense of, their lives.

For example, Indigenous Australian societies did not use (or need) a system of land ownership. Humans owning land is an abstract cultural construct, useful in some periods and places. The British, viewing the world from an eighteenth-century Eurasian perspective, took such systems for granted. They therefore imposed one and assigned all the land to themselves.

The British colonists further convinced themselves that certain physical differences between them and the Indigenous Australians indicated that they were separate species (which they weren't) and that the native peoples were of an intrinsically lower mental faculty (which wasn't true). They then used these things as their rationale for denying the native peoples legal and civil rights, and murdering them to suit the colonist's convenience.

The Spanish who took over the Americas from the sixteenth century had an even more elaborate narrative for what they were doing. They convinced themselves that they had access to a set of religious truths, bestowed by infallible wisdom, to which the Amerindians were not privy. They also convinced themselves that what they were doing was divinely ordained (which it wasn't). The Amerindians, even more naive about the context of what was going on, rationalised the Armageddon overtaking their societies on the basis that the gods were against them (which they weren't).

None of this is very nice, but such is the story of our species. The British and Spanish were not the only colonialists of the previous millennium. A virtually unlimited number of sins can be found in the history of any branch of the human race.

Even the sort of mass population replacements that made Australia white and South America Latin have gone on many times in prehistory. For about four thousand years after 3000 BCE, Bantu farmers from (what is now) Nigeria and Cameroon colonised huge swathes of southern Africa, displacing the Koisan hunter-gatherers who were its original inhabitants. From about the same time, two enormous migrations expanded out of southern China (the Austroasiatic expansion into South-East Asia and the Austronesian expansion into Indonesia, the Philippines and eventually Polynesia), replacing earlier populations with the ones we know today.

Delving even further into the tides of prehistory you come to the great Indo-European expansion that largely repopulated India, Iran, Central Asia and Europe between 6000 BCE and 4000 BCE and left them with the vast Indo-European language family they have to this day.

*****

So here we are. Seven billion hyper-intelligent social tool-using omnivores living on a planet. The weaves of human history have brought us to this current tapestry. Now we're all mixed up and we've all got the same diseases.

Yet the inequalities instigated by that uneven history remain entrenched. For example, the descendants of the Native American peoples of the Andes region remain frustratingly unable to achieve economic, social and political parity with the descendants of those who overtook them (despite the sincere and best efforts of capable and well-meaning Italian missionaries). In my experience there are two mechanisms that cause such inequalities to be propagated across generations – one external, one internal.

The external mechanism is discrimination. When in a position to distribute jobs, money, land or whatever equates to power in the context of a particular society, people favour those they perceive as being part of their in-group. We're never short of ways to divide ourselves up – a surname, accent or shared cultural background will suffice. However, the most emotive reason is discrimination on the grounds of race.

Technically, humanity possesses no internal racial divisions that biologists would define as races in another species. Our genetic uniformity is one of our remarkable features. There is more genetic diversity within a single tribe of chimpanzees than between all the humans alive. Nonetheless, over the years certain physical differences – notably skin colour – have been used as the basis for group definition and discrimination.

But even when discrimination is stripped away, there's another mechanism causing power relationships between groups to propagate across generations: an internal mechanism which defines how a group is set up to advance its interests in the world.

Take the example of the group which has suffered the most profound cultural dislocation that I came across during my pilgrimage – the indigenous peoples of Australia.

Australia is an advanced, well-informed and extremely wealthy society. It has a technocratic government with plenty of material resources to throw at problems. What's more, it is keenly aware of the predicament of its native peoples and genuinely eager to address the problem.

Even so, large sections of Indigenous Australian society remain a deeply disenfranchised, racially defined underclass tragically torn by drug abuse, criminality, a lack of self-determination and a general inability to function as healthy, self-actualised communities. Why?

There is a spirit running through us. We are each imbued with the intangible spirit of the culture, subculture and family from which we arose. That spirit consists of the assumptions we take for granted, the abstract ideas with which we're instinctively familiar and the status within the world we've been conditioned to expect. It is part of the deepest training our brains receive, it's highly specific to the context in which we grow up and it is absorbed subliminally during our formative years from the community that surrounds us, principally from our families. Its character is fashioned by that community's past experiences and through it we are all something of our ancestors.

Take the example I know best: me. I'm a product of late twentieth-century western European culture. There are certain cultural, political and economic concepts I understand thoroughly, for instance money, land ownership, the law, the idea of national government and how capitalist economies work.

It's not just that I intellectually grasp these ideas; I *instinctively* understand how they regulate the world I live in. I grew up in a culture where they've been implicitly accepted for centuries and in some cases millennia. They were being drummed into my mind from the day I chanted my first nursery rhyme or heard my first fairy tale.

My brain is very specifically trained – in thousands of subconscious ways – to take advantage of a world in which they are important. I learned about them from my parents and the people surrounding me as a child, via a long and drawn-out process of nurturing whereby one generation of minds shapes the next one.

I'm also self-possessed and a little full of myself. That's not just because of my genes. My mum and dad are like that. Their parents were probably like that, and we all come from a proud, self-confident society – Britain – that's used to getting its own way. Because of all that I'm mentally in a place where I think I can get away with cycling across continents and cocky enough to write a book about it.

I'm lucky. The rules of this twenty-first-century world happen to have been set by people with a very similar cultural background to me. But the cultural spirit of an inhabitant of a self-confident, twenty-first-century post-industrial world is radically different from that of a farmer living in an agrarian society, a member of a hunter-gatherer community, or an individual who is part of a racially defined underclass which has suffered two centuries of repression and humiliation.

*****

On Fraser Island on the Queensland coast there were three tribes, who'd lived there for 5,000 years. Contact with the outside world was sporadic. The British established a penal settlement in the area in 1824. In 1842 the area was opened to free (white) settlement. Shortly afterwards, the massacres started.

In 1870 the remaining natives were confined to a Christian mission and told to become Anglicans. That mission was then closed, then opened again, then moved when white settlers complained about its location. At that point the remaining natives were moved to a concentration-camp-style institution, where they suffered endemic malnutrition and dysentery until, in 1904, they were forcibly deported 500 kilometres away to a place with which they had no cultural or historic connection whatsoever. Of the 2,000 inhabitants of 50 years earlier, there were 117 left to get on that boat.

It's difficult for someone like me to relate to where one is at mentally and culturally when you, your parents, your grandparents and everyone you are close to has lived out their lives within those sorts of parameters. I imagine not in a zone to go cycling across continents.

Before the arrival of the Europeans, Australia's indigenous peoples had spent millennia training themselves to deal with the hunter-gatherer world in which they lived. Every aspect of their culture was tuned to manage the day-to-day challenges implicit to thriving in such a context. Their societies had survived for 30,000 years so they were clearly very good at it.

A radically different world, regulated by weird and counter-intuitive rules, was then imposed upon them. They were not initially invited to take advantage of that world (that option didn't arrive until the 1960s). First they had to suffer 150 years of exclusion and oppression. The self-actualised and (one assumes) proud indigenous societies that flourished in Australia for tens of thousands of years are now gone.

There are forces at work in humanity that cannot swiftly and easily be redirected by social programmes and good intentions. The Indigenous Australians spent more than 30 millennia tuning themselves to flourish in one context, then 200 years being dragged through the nightmare of another. In consequence their story is passing through a bleak and grief-soaked chapter.

Their plight is an extreme example of a universal phenomenon. Different groups have suffered various levels of cultural dislocation over recent centuries. Those experiences have left some communities in a position to take advantage of this modern world and others not so well positioned.

Australia's indigenous communities live on the fringes of Australian society. Yet Chinese immigrants (from a country with a two-thousand-year tradition of bourgeois culture) turn up and immediately start their own businesses. Meanwhile, in Britain, first-generation immigrants from India's elite Brahmin caste have children training as doctors, while Afro-Caribbean immigrants (whose recent ancestors were slaves) take a generation longer to reach the same point. All humans, and all human societies, are moulded by their historical context.

*****

Here's what happened ...

Given 60,000 years and a few thousand generations, humans settled the entire planet using primitive technologies. Different groups were then separated for millennia. By the time ocean-going ships started binding our species back together, technological and power differences had emerged. The more powerful groups, motivated by greed and ignorance, then exploited that situation in a way that temporarily entrenched those differences.

This book happens to be written a few centuries after the creation of a single global society, but before the imbalances resulting from 60,000 years of separation have evened themselves out.

It's one more dimension of the period of flux we're passing through. For things to have panned out differently, quite a lot about human nature and the geographic realities of planet Earth would have needed to have been different. It's hard not to conclude that this situation was inevitable.

But that's not the same as saying it's going to be permanent.

113: The Matriarch
5 March 2007

At the Hostal Santa Apolonia in Cajamarca I met Beat, an ex-captain in the Swiss Army (no, he didn't get a penknife), who was in Peru to visit a girl he'd met over the internet. I dragged him around the town's archaeological museum then the two of us ate Italian food, found a club and spent the rest of the night boogieing to 1980s music with two local lasses, Janet and Roxana.

Janet works as a DJ at Cajamarca's radio station. She's thirtyish with a cute face and brown bowl-shaped hair. Roxana has big dark eyes, long black hair and an air of inscrutability about her. She is, I eventually surmised, a witch doctor. We hit it off and, the day after our disco session, the girls took me into the mountains to stay at Roxana's house.

It was a 40-minute drive up from the valley, passing farms and ridges thick with conifers. Cajamarca is 2,750 metres above sea level, so Roxana's house, which is well above the valley, must be at three kilometres. It's more of a compound than a house, with two long wings either side of a tiled courtyard containing an elaborate marble fountain. Two mean-looking dogs guard the place. At the end of one wing is a small tower, with a water tank and solar panel on the roof and a kennel underneath. The gardens contain fruit trees and cacti, and back onto a small field of maize. In the surrounding hills sheep graze placidly in fields of sturdy red and green grasses. What the place lacks in electricity it more than makes up for in tranquillity and staggering views.

That first evening I was sent into the forest to collect fuel under the luminosity of a perfect full moon. Then the three of us sat around the fire, surrounded by the smell of wood smoke, and talked until midnight. The next day we went for a walk.

After an hour of hiking we came to the house of Genevieve, a local matriarch and old friend of Roxana's. Genevieve has seven children and seventeen grandchildren and lives in a sprawling hilltop home in which chickens run about and guinea pigs are kept in long straw-filled cages. She was extremely welcoming and, after giving me a tour of her spacious but simple home, we took tea together.

'So tell me, señora, have you ever met an Englishman before?' I asked (in Spanish).

'What's an Englishman?' she enquired.

'A man from England, of course,' I informed her.

'I don't know of England,' she responded. 'Is that the same as America?'

Genevieve was kind enough to invite me to be guest of honour at a formal family lunch the next day. So, the following afternoon, Janet, Roxana and I hiked back through the mountains to her house once again.

The meal was eaten with three generations and chickens underfoot. We sat on long wooden benches while the food was cooked in huge iron pots held above open fires and against a wall coated with the soot from decades of cooking.

Every stage of the multi-course extravaganza that followed enjoyed an elaborate commentary from Roxana as to its particular cultural significance. As the ritual progressed a bottle of Cañazo (the local firewater) appeared, to be passed around in solemn ceremony. Then, after the food, a bag of coca leaves was produced ('An important Inca tradition,' I was informed) and we all chewed away while Roxana regaled me with tales of the herb's cure-all properties.

Personally, I didn't feel that the second bottle of Cañazo was strictly necessary. However, in the interests of Her Majesty's good name I went along with it. We were well into bottle number three ('A good digestif,' I was assured) and Genevieve, Janet and I had begun to dance around the courtyard when one of Genevieve's granddaughters appeared with a suspiciously wicked-looking knife and asked me if I wanted to see the testicles cut from a live pig.

I was not clear-headed at that point and it took some moments to establish that she wasn't joking. Apparently, it fattens the things up. This I had to see.

The chief ball-cutter was an older señor wearing a cowboy hat, who had just walked 11 kilometres through the Andes in sandals to cut the balls off that pig. He was keen to teach me Quechua (the old Inca tongue) and kept referring to me as 'gringito' (which roughly translates as 'amusing young white fellow').

The pig castration took place in the yard behind Genevieve's house. Roxana and Janet stayed away from the action, instead watching me, from a distance, with some amusement. I looked on – eyes wide and arms hugging myself in horror while the señor and the granddaughter held the poor thing down. It put up a struggle (well you would, wouldn't you?). There was a load of squealing and quite a bit of blood. Afterwards, the clearly disgruntled pig walked oddly.

Days since leaving London: 647

Quechua word of the day: 'upiachu' meaning 'cheers'

114: Pyramids, Mud Bricks and Third-World Capital

11 March 2007

After leaving Cajamarca and the mountains, my next stop was the city of Trujillo, a bustling place of colonial mansions and streets laid out in the grid pattern of a planned town. It was my base for exploring the archaeological remains left by two of the region's pre-Inca imperial peoples.

The culture we call the Moche dominated northern Peru from around 100 CE to 700 CE. The most significant monuments they left are the Pyramids of the Sun and the Moon, mud-brick piles just outside Trujillo, recently uncovered from the savannah and notable for their enormous size and colourful frescos.

Unfortunately, I was grabbed at the entrance by Daphne, a student guide who railroaded me into a free tour. The tour involved dragging me between certain places (with a couple of portly Brazilian gentlemen), then getting me to stand there while she read out statements written for people with no idea what they were looking at. It was annoying; nonetheless, the site is hugely impressive.

The Pyramid of the Moon is a complex of platforms and terraces reminiscent, I'm sure, of the mud-brick ziggurats constructed in Mesopotamia 3,000 years earlier. The Pyramid of the Sun is 340 metres long, 136 metres wide, 41 metres high and covered with stylised images of exotic spiders and bloodthirsty sea monsters. From its summit, the tumbled ruins of the ancient city stretch away for hundreds of metres. It was on that summit that the ancient Moche would dope up selected warriors with hallucinogenic cactus, then tear out their beating hearts for the pleasure of the gods.

Moche civilisation finally collapsed in the eighth century, after half a millennium of political dominance, when they found that they were unable to control the weather through human sacrifice.

Seven hundred years later another group of empire builders, the Chimu, made their home in these same lands. The re-creation of their faces in a local museum showed them to be a square-jawed people and clearly the direct ancestors of Trujillo's notably handsome modern population. The Chimu spoke a language called Quingnam and, for two centuries before the coming of the Incas, theirs was the chief state of Peru.

Chimu cosmology held that humankind was the result of a divine mating between Rem (the Moon God) and Huis (the Earth), and that all people are descended from four stars: the 'noble' people from the two greater stars and the 'common' people from the two minor ones; conveniently justifying social stratification on the basis that it has a divine origin. How elegant.

The Chimu capital – Chan Chan – was the largest pre-Columbian city in the Americas and the biggest mud-brick settlement that has ever been built. Obviously a guy like me just had to see something like that. The day after visiting the pyramids, I headed over.

Chan Chan's ruins are spread across 20 square kilometres and the bus that took me there drove past colossal mud walls and fallen mud houses for a mile before we arrived at the abandoned metropolis' centre. Undisturbed by pesky tour guides I spent a dream-filled afternoon wandering through the abandoned streets, watching archaeologists at work and communing with the ancients.

That was my last afternoon in Trujillo, so afterwards I thought I'd pop to the coast and have a look at the ocean, which was just five kilometres away. Wandering along the waterfront at the fishing village of Huanchaco, I was hailed from a rooftop by a cheerful-looking fellow with an American accent and a Stetson. 'Come have a beer with me,' he yelled.

'Where you from?' I shouted back.

'*Teee*xas,' came the reply. Two minutes later I was on that Huanchaco rooftop with South American Sam (as he deemed himself), his two lady friends (Sylvia and Jackie) and an ice-cold Budweiser.

Sam was an ex-US Air Force captain (B52, tail gunner, twin barrels, 7,400 rounds a minute, serious hardware). He was spending his retirement on alcohol, fast women and a beauty boutique for his Peruvian girlfriend, Jackie. As country music blared from his radio Sam entertained me with stories of jungle adventures involving indigenous shamans, drug-induced apparitions and brutal, uncontrollable diarrhoea. Then, in case I needed any more evidence that you never know what you're going to get from people, as I rose to leave he began reciting raw and earthy poetry that he'd composed himself.

> *…I come back down the road some day,*
> *I'll cry about my choice that made no sense,*
> *travelled under an unknown sky,*
> *never letting life pass me by …*

I got back to Trujillo tipsy and later than expected, collected my stuff from the hotel, then ran for the bus that would take me south along the Pan-American Highway.

The next morning (three days ago) I woke up in Lima, Peru's enormous capital city and home to one-third of its people. I'm staying in

Miraflores, a ritzy beachfront suburb of clean streets, swanky restaurants and supermarkets stocked with luscious first-world-quality cheese, meat and wine.

The first item on my agenda was the Museo de la Nación. Unsurprisingly, the chief museum of Peru is fantastically well stocked with treasure. I drowned myself in several millennia's worth of artefacts until my feet ached. Next I went to the Catedral de Lima, where I visited the tomb of Francisco Pizarro, the man who lit the touch paper of the Conquest. Upon his tomb is carved a resting marble lion. The lion is black. Shadows weigh down.

Outside, in the palace-flanked Plaza de Armas, I was accosted by two young ladies, Mariella and Valentina, who insisted that I join them that evening in the suburb of Barranco. I was promised that there would be dancing and found their offer to be irresistible.

Valentina, a firefox with a Chinese mother and a Peruvian-Italian father, was the leader. Her gang included Julio, a heavily set language teacher, and Rafael, an engaging family man who ran a restaurant and was setting up his own mobile-phone-leasing business.

Valentina, Rafael and their crew whisked me bar to bar around the city, periodically bumping into other groups of up-for-it young socialites on their own nights out. Then, as the evening drew to its close, they took me to a club with 1950s rock memorabilia on the wall, where a beautiful young woman in knee-high black PVC boots sang, 'Come on baby, light my fire.'

Most of my time in Lima, however, has been spent in my hotel room. I've been looking out over the city's sun-drenched rooftops, writing in my journal and thinking about the rich labyrinth of Andean civilisations, ancient and modern, I'm passing through.

Modern Peru returned to democracy in 1980 after 12 years of military dictatorship. There followed a period of internal conflict driven by fighting between the government and a Maoist insurgency group known as the Shining Path. That conflict resulted in 69,000 deaths between 1980 and 2000, three-quarters of them Native American-descended Peruvians living in the highlands.

Alberto Fujimori (president between 1990 and 2000) ended the insurgency, brought hyperinflation under control and liberalised the country's economy. Since then macroeconomic stability, peace and high mineral prices have allowed the government to attack poverty and child malnutrition through food aid and increased social expenditure. This bustling metropolis – Peru's industrial and financial heart and accountable for 45 per cent of its GDP – is at the hub.

I'm *completely* impressed by Peru. The moment I crossed the border from Ecuador the difference was obvious. It's much more dynamic and self-confident than its smaller northern neighbour. In Ecuador people explained how their problems were the fault of the politicians and the Americans. In Peru everyone tells me about the businesses they're starting and what they're going to do with their life.

Right now Peru's economy is growing at nearly seven per cent a year and, with numbers like that, countries stop being 'developing' within time frames measured in decades. This current generation of Peruvians feels like a transformative one. So I look out over Lima's rooftops and meditate on this land, its people and the logistics of civilisation.

Days since leaving London: 653

GDP growth, 2006:		Population:	
Ecuador	2.8%	Quito	1,397,698
Peru	6.4%	Lima	8,472,935

There must be farmers to produce food, men to extract the wealth of mountains and marshes, artisans to produce these things and merchants to circulate them. There is no need to wait for government orders; each man will play his part, doing his best to get what he desires. So cheap goods will go where they fetch more, expensive goods will make men search for cheap ones. When all work willingly at their trades, just as water flows ceaselessly downhill day and night, things will appear unsought and people will produce them without being asked. For clearly this accords with the way and is in keeping with nature. – Ssu-ma Ch'ien (written circa 100 BCE)

Global Musings V
Civilisational
Logistics

The human race needs a game plan. Before I go any further, let me spell out what I think that game plan should be.

I believe we should attempt to establish a global civilisation which is inclusive, socially and economically just, provides for the material needs of all men and women, minimises organised violence and human suffering, does not catastrophically destabilise the ecosphere, and in which all humans can live dignified, self-actualised lives and – to paraphrase the late Bill Hicks – explore space, both inner and outer, together, forever, in peace.

It can be done. No law of nature stands between us and that goal. But it isn't going to be easy. Civilisation cannot simply be redesigned to achieve such a bright future. It's a multi-generational task.

Nevertheless, we have all the tools we need to move forward and there's every reason to hope that, right here on this planet, within foreseeable time frames, we'll have a world without poverty, where governments are representative, people are free and our relationship with the environment is stable.

That will mark the conclusion of the adolescence of human civilisation.

*****

Harmonious and stable global civilisations require certain physical and non-physical facilities. A key task, therefore, is to organise our logistics properly.

In the opening years of the twenty-first century, six and a half billion humans live on the Earth. At the time of my journey demographic projections held that Earth's population would reach nine billion (and then peak) in the second half of that century. All those people are going to need a stable food supply, housing, amenities from water to waste disposal, complex educational and healthcare arrangements, access to a global transport infrastructure and a wide array of physical artefacts.

A large and growing portion of humanity already has those things. But that isn't good enough. We all need them – all six and a half billion and more of us.

Let's never lose sight of what an eye-wateringly colossal logistical task that is. It's going to involve serious amounts of teamwork and well-thought-through systems for organising ourselves – systems designed in a way that's realistic about human nature and based on a pragmatic assessment of the challenges before us.

*****

A huge and dynamic branch of learning deals with the study of such systems: economics. I've never liked the word. It sounds like a subject that's only of interest to accountants and businessmen. It shouldn't be. Economics describes the set of conceptual systems we use to organise the operational parts of our civilisation.

Consider three economic ideas with which anyone reading this book will probably be familiar: money, loans and interest. If you think about what those things *really* are it quickly becomes very complicated and kind of weird.

- 'Money' is an immaterial quantity that exists in the human mind and which is sometimes given physical representation by bits of metal, paper or electronic switches (i.e. it's a made-up thing).

- 'Loans' are a component part of an immaterial quantity that exists in the human mind which 'belongs' to one such being (or one of their institutions) but is in the possession of another such being or institution (i.e. it's an even more made-up thing).

- 'Interest' is the rate at which an immaterial quantity that exists in the human mind which belongs to one such being or one of their institutions, but that is in the possession of another such being or institution, notionally enlarges itself based on an accord reached between the two parties (a legal contract) which is, in turn, regulated by a convoluted system of ideas (the law) haphazardly built up over generations and which is, itself, a complete abstraction (i.e. it's an outrageously made-up thing).

None of these things are real. *They don't actually exist.* They're a covenant we've made between ourselves because *acting* as though they exist is incredibly useful. The abstract store of value that is 'money' evolved from ancient systems of barter into today's global language for the communication of goods and services. Social constructs such as 'loan' and 'interest' are money's increasingly sophisticated syntax, morphology and tenses. Together they allow us to do something profoundly counter-intuitive: coordinate the activities of billions of people spread across a planet.

Imagine the following scenario: that all six and a half billion of us just appeared on this planet one day with all the expertise we needed to manage our affairs (people were already skilled up to build houses and bicycles and act as doctors, farmers and engineers) but without any conceptual framework through which to organise those activities. How would we decide who builds houses when and where, what things engineers construct, how doctors systematise curing people, who gets a bicycle and the million other organisational decisions needed to run a viable civilisation?

Take one of those million tasks: the production and distribution of potatoes. Growing and distributing potatoes on a planet-wide basis is a mind-bendingly complicated thing to do. Each potato needs to be individually planted, fertilised, grown, transported, stored and processed.

Every one of those potato sub-stages involves thousands of people working in a coordinated way while taking lots of complex potato-related decisions. There are many ways to fertilise a potato. Which is best? Then there are questions like: How should potatoes be moved? How many potatoes should each person have? If there aren't enough potatoes, how should they be rationed?

When you get down to it, global potato management is an extremely tricky business. Standing on that planet, head spinning with potato-related problems, you'd have no choice but to come up with a system, and that's basically what happened.

We did not, however, sit down at a big conference and consciously design our potato management systems (or any of our other economic systems) in a way that would allow humankind to live together in peace, love and harmony. As a species, that's not really our style.

The process of system design was, instead, an organic and piecemeal affair. It took place against the background of human history. Or, in other words, everybody competing for resources, struggling for influence and stabbing each other in the back – things that, as a species, are very much our style. As a result, the set of economic concepts currently in use (from capital to companies to consumption) are associated in peoples' minds with the circumstances under which they were developed (lots of exploitation), how they've been applied historically (lots of injustice) and the economic shape of the world they partly created (lots of inequality).

That background gives those economic concepts negative connotations, which often blind us to how effective some of the ideas we've stumbled upon actually are. I believe that, in fact, many of the concepts which regulate our economic systems resonate deeply with an underlying logic as to how oodles of apes swarming across a rock in space *should* best organise themselves.

*****

At the moment the most dynamic parts of the global economy are organised through the medium of 'companies'. Companies aren't real except in our heads, but they're extremely useful. They allow us to demarcate particular elements of our civilisational logistics in order for them to be individually assessed and organised.

Companies facilitate disparate groups of people to work in a coordinated way, with a functional command structure, towards a complex outcome. If companies didn't exist, there would definitely be a need to invent them. Because the economy is too complicated to be comprehended in its entirety, breaking it into chunks means we can assess what does and does not work, one chunk at a time.

We make those assessments based on another conceptual tool: profit. Profit is an unfortunate word for an *extremely* useful idea. It's associated with evil capitalists because those are the sorts of people who came up with it. Yet it plugs into the mechanics of our civilisational logistics in a really profound way.

The fact a particular chunk of the economy generates 'profit' is not just some dastardly money-making scheme (though it may be that also). It tells us something deep about the way that chunk of the economy interfaces with the rest of it. Given the chunk's internal systems, the assorted inputs and outputs, and the various bits of money washing around it, does that chunk, in the end, spit out cash? If it does it's making a profit, and if it's making a profit it fits into the indecipherable rhythms of our civilisational logistics in a way that makes sense. The economy *wants* it.

Something may *sound* like a good idea (let's move potatoes using jet skis), but is it *really* a good idea (does moving potatoes using jet skis make a profit)? Whether an element of our civilisational logistics is profitable disciplines whether it should exist, or should exist in its current form. It's a rational way of making a mind-bendingly complicated judgement call. Does this system *really* work? Does it make sense? Is it profitable?

*****

'Property' (an ethereal link connecting a human and a thing) is an outlandish idea we all take for granted. Take land ownership: the idea that a human 'owns' a piece of the Earth's surface is like a flea saying it owns the dog, but hell, if it helps the fleas work as a team, good on them. The principle of free private property is not fundamentally sacrosanct. It's just incredibly handy.

Humans owning things incentivises them to manage them properly. If I 'own' my iPod, I'll look after it. If anyone can use it, it'll soon get broken. It's the same with companies. It's not really important who owns the companies which grow, distribute or sell the potatoes. The important thing is that I can get potatoes.

When a human dreams up an idea for a new chunk of our civilisational logistics and wants to have a go (can space tourism, moving potatoes on jet skis or generating energy using wind turbines be made profitable?), that human 'owning' that chunk is an arrangement which means that they are motivated to make it functional. People who own potato distribution companies are, on the whole, better placed to make tactical and operational decisions around potato distribution than anybody else.

Which chunks of the economy deserve more attention, or more energy to pep them up, is the role of another human conceptual achievement that exists at an even higher level of abstraction: the financial markets.

Think about what a 'market' (for petroleum, capital, housing, labour or whatever) really is. Take the potato market. The potato market takes account of: the number of potatoes planted, the weather around potato farms, potato transport costs, potato storage costs, how fashionable chips are that season, and thousands of other potato-related variables. It then gives you a number: the price of a potato.

It's a giant abstract information mechanism that summarises a whole corner of the economy. It taps into, and assimilates, the labyrinthine factors affecting potatoes, then provides succinct data upon which rational potato-related decisions can be made. I don't need to understand the various problems affecting the growth and distribution of potatoes that day – that's the problem of people who work in those bits of the economy. I just need to understand one thing: the price of a potato. I can then make a rational choice based on sound data about whether I want to buy one.

Markets aren't just *any* information mechanism. They actually interface with, and reflect something about, reality. They have a bad reputation in some quarters, but any facet of our civilisational logistics described using them gives us information about that facet which we have no other way of accessing. The financial markets perform that task for entire segments of the economy. They're a vast insubstantial instrument for assessing which bits of it are working, chunk by chunk.

Because the wheels of those financial markets are manned by so many rich and irritating people, it's often forgotten what an awesome conceptual achievement our global financial system is. In the grand scheme of things the size of an investment banker's house isn't very important, but allocating resources across the globe in a logical way is very important indeed.

Individual investors may be greedy, vainglorious and overpaid. But remember, the money only exists inside the limited confines of their status-obsessed mammalian brains.

Think of them as tools.

*****

Eighteen months before I sat in my Lima hotel room and scribbled about potatoes, I'd had an epiphany beside a willow tree at the edge of a Serbian wheat field.

On 8 August 2005 the upper house of the Japanese parliament rejected a bill set before it by Prime Minister Junichiro Koizumi to privatise Japan Post, the country's post office. Mr Koizumi responded by calling a snap election on the issue. The election took place on 11 September and Mr Koizumi won resoundingly. Fifteen days later, on 26 September (the day before cycling into Belgrade), I lay inside Larry the Tent, wine cup in hand, and read about it.

Here's the deal: Japan Post not only delivers letters, it's also Japan's main depository of household savings. Being the chief savings vehicle for the world's second-biggest economy is a really big deal. A three-trillion-dollar deal, to be exact.

Ensuring three trillion dollars of capital is rationally allocated is a major concern for the Japanese economy. Should it be used to build roads, potato farms or PlayStation factories? With Japan Post in government hands those decisions ultimately lay with politicians, who lend money to farmers because they have an effective political lobby.

The alternative was to cut the funds to the political interest groups, liberate the cash from the hands of the state and let the markets allocate it. The job of a banker is to get investment decisions right. A banker lends money to a farmer because he judges him to have a more robust business plan than, say, someone who wants to build a PlayStation factory.

In essence, does Japan get new farms because it needs them, or because building them is in the interests of certain political lobby groups?

Three trillion dollars of financial energy. The rational management of humanity's resources. The proper allocation of capital. The penny dropped.

*****

The end result is what matters. If an ant colony builds a good nest, what individual ants are thinking isn't necessarily important. We should judge the operational bits of our civilisation based on things like whether we grow enough potatoes, they are distributed properly and everyone has enough to eat. The mental tricks we're using to coordinate ourselves are peripheral.

Humans, as it happens, are self-interested, status-obsessed animals that think as individuals. The bits of intellectual paraphernalia we've developed reflect humanity's internal temperament and the circumstances under which we dreamed them up.

At this point in history we've reached the stage of figuring out the basic conceptual tools that allow billions of bipeds to cooperate to do mind-bendingly complicated things like produce and distribute potatoes. The challenge now is to apply those conceptual tools systematically and fairly, because they *are* our tools, not our masters. I'm not suggesting that we run civilisation based on the profit motive, or that we don't collectively (and democratically) manipulate the global economy through regulation and taxes. The goal is improved human welfare and an even more interesting world.

But remember, it's *very* easy for humans to invent justifications for making up rules which are really about advancing (what they perceive to be) their own economic interests. Once politicians start directing economies they are predisposed to do irrational things while persuading themselves that they know best, which they don't.

Take a simple scenario. There's a town. It contains bicycle shops and potato shops. One day the town's residents begin consuming fewer potatoes and riding more bicycles. The appropriate way to adjust the town's potato and bicycle distribution systems is by having fewer potato shops and more bicycle shops.

The response of free and open economies is coordinated by workers, owners and investors in those shops, who get new jobs, find new businesses or switch investments. How might a central authority, with imperfect information, manage what is basically a change in tastes for potatoes?

What such authorities often do is subsidise potato production via bicycle sales, which is silly. No central authority is in a position to determine how many potato shops a town needs, let alone make the really big decisions such as which industries to expand, technologies to pursue or ideas to invest in.

It may not be to our taste that the forces shaping our world are so impenetrable, but they are. Limited animals are no better at controlling economies than they are at dictating the affairs of countries. Maybe, in some far-off future, we'll have supercomputers so awesomely powerful that they will be able to manage such problems. While we do not, ideas such as companies, markets, property and profits provide a robust conceptual architecture for coordinating the economic transformation through which this world is currently passing.

I'll get onto that economic transformation shortly. First, however, there's one further feature of the collective psychology of billions of people organising a planet (which has recently come to light) that I need to point out: our appetite for economic expansion appears to be open-ended and it appears to be driven by our obsession with status.

Once a society has risen out of penury (defined at about US$10,000 per person per year at the time of my journey), average happiness doesn't rise with material wealth. Norwegians are not happier than Australians, even though they're richer. What makes people happy is having more money than their immediate neighbours. People are 'happier' with material wealth equivalent to $25,000 per year in a context where everyone else has $10,000, rather than $50,000 where their neighbours have $100,000.

The phenomenon of open-ended economic growth may well constitute a gargantuan misfiring of our collective genomes, spinning us into a meaningless game of ceaselessly greater 'wealth'. There may, in the future, come a time when practical matters such as feeding and housing everyone have been thoroughly dealt with. At that point economic growth may become, in large part, a question of fussing over frivolous baubles – working frantically to acquire shinier baubles than one's neighbours while still feeling anxious and unfulfilled.

A world of fabulously wealthy but despondent people is going to raise some pretty profound questions. However, for the time being we need to follow this path, because even if not everyone needs a private jet, everyone needs a house.

And saying that a global economic transformation is essential for building a harmonious planetary civilisation isn't the same as saying it's the meaning of life. If people want to spend their lives fussing over baubles then they should be allowed to. Personally, though, I would encourage everyone to think less about material things. I believe more satisfaction would be gained from life if people spent less of it amassing treasure and more of it embarking on world-spanning pilgrimages of cosmic exploration.

But that, of course, is only my opinion.

115: Ancient Horizons
13 March 2007

After three days in Lima things were getting too hot to handle. Valentina was becoming over-friendly and I suspect she had designs on my hand in marriage as the means to a UK passport. She picked the wrong pilgrim for that kind of caper. So, on my fourth afternoon in the Peruvian capital, I caught a taxi to the bus station and broke south. My next stop was one of the places I had to see before I die: Nazca.

The town of Nazca lies in the deserts of southern Peru, and its famous Lines were made by a people who inhabited the region's river valleys between 200 BCE and 700 CE. The Nazca Lines were created by moving dark pebbles from the pale earth upon which they rested. As it's one of the driest places on the planet the designs have endured for 1,300 years. People had understood for centuries that there were patterns on the desert floor. However, it was only in the 1930s, with the first plane flights, that someone noticed the 90-metre monkey.

Disembarking from the bus with me yesterday evening was a blond-haired European fellow who looked disoriented. I took him under my wing and, after getting rooms in the same hostel, we went for dinner. Sebastian is Dutch and having his first big adventure. He is also six foot five, has a surname which means windmill and is fluent in four languages. His Spanish is already ahead of mine, even though he's only been here eight days.

Nazca's tourist infrastructure is entirely dedicated to flying people over the desert. Early in the morning on the day after we arrived, Sebastian and I were taken to the airfield, shown a half-hour documentary about the Lines, then loaded into a single-prop aeroplane. As the ground fell away, images began appearing beneath the horizon.

What took me aback was the scale of it. It's not just that there's a few interesting animals picked out on the desert's floor – there are *thousands* of glyphs, lines and pictures covering hundreds of square kilometres. They range from the straightforward (it's clearly a hummingbird) to the surreal (it's clearly a pair of hands emerging from a blob). As we banked left, then right, over the great plain of thousand-year-old abstract art I wondered at this enthralling fragment of the craziness that went on during prehistory.

A scientific consensus as to the Lines' purpose has yet to be reached. Crackpots and passing neo-hippies are therefore free to offer suggestions. Mine is that the designs are the remnants of an elaborate and fiendishly complicated board game, probably played out over a number of generations and with lots of interesting rules.

However, no matter what was going through the heads of the ancient Nazcans, I'd bet my bottom dollar that at least some of them understood that creating 46-metre images of spiders on the desert's floor was fundamentally just a really cool thing to do. In this universe (where we're all ephemeral) and in this world (where we're all destined to spend most of our time thinking about food, status and the wellbeing of our children) opportunities to create something that will speak to our distant descendants are few and far between.

Maybe less far-sighted individuals among the ancient Nazcans asked, 'Why bother?' With 1,300 years of hindsight, it's all so blindingly obvious.

Days since leaving London: 655
Size of some famous Nazca figures

Giant astronaut:	14 metres
Giant whale:	68 metres
Giant condor:	135 metres
Giant pelican:	285 metres
Length of the longest Lines:	15 kilometres
Area covered by the Nazca Lines:	650 square kilometres

You know it might just be this one anonymous glory of all things, this rich stone forest, this epic chant, this gaiety, this grand choiring shout of affirmation, which we choose when all our cities are dust; to stand intact, to mark where we have been, to testify to what we had it in us to accomplish.

Our works in stone, in paint, in print are spared, some of them for a few decades, or a millennium or two, but everything must fall in war or wear away into the ultimate and universal ash ... 'Be good of heart' cry the dead artists out of the living past. Our songs will all be silenced – but what of it? Go on singing. – Orson Welles

Global Musings VI
Planetary Wealth
Gradients

When talking about the economic shape of the world and its inequalities, I find that people almost never mention the big picture.

Here's the big picture:

For the 12,000 years since farming began spreading around the world, the overwhelming experience of the overwhelming majority of humans was one of subsistence agriculture. Economic growth was exceedingly haphazard. Economic theory and macroeconomic management were practically non-existent.

Translated into early twenty-first-century money, historical income (across the whole world) was about $400–$450 per person per year (somewhere between $1 and $1.50 a day). That's approximately the average income today in extremely poor sub-Saharan countries such as Chad or Malawi.

Between 1000 CE and 1800 CE, global economic growth averaged (with a lot of ups and downs) about 0.05 per cent annually. By 1800 CE (just as the Industrial Revolution was kicking off) average income per person globally had increased to the equivalent of $650 per person per year, still under $2 per day. With the exception of a very small elite, everyone in the world was still living a lifestyle that would today be characterised as abject and grinding poverty.

Then everything started to change.

Two hundred years later, in 2000, average income was more than $5,000 per person per year, or $13 per day. Not only was the average human seven and a half times richer than 200 years earlier, but there were also seven times more humans. So the size of the global economy had increased more than fiftyfold.

To frame those miraculous two centuries of wealth creation in terms of your family, all that happened in about ten generations.

That's the big picture.

*****

When people discuss global poverty and inequality it is often noted that some parts of the world are very rich, while others are very poor. But a far more complete way of thinking about humanity's economic geography is that the whole world was exceedingly poor until quite recently, then some parts of it became rich. That wealth creation was unequal, but given the complex and uneven nature of history it would be extremely strange were that not the case.

At the moment the world is characterised by big wealth inequalities and capitalism is the ascendant economic philosophy. The first of those facts is sometimes blamed upon the second. I think that's a mixed-up way of looking at the situation.

It's unsurprising that the humans in the regions which ended up richest are using the most efficient organisational systems, or that the elites in those regions are among the best trained to take advantage of them. Many of the rich people in question don't advocate capitalism out of high-minded intellectual idealism. They advocate it because they're already rich, commonly due to the circumstances of their birth. That good fortune has left them empowered to take advantage of the status quo. Their underlying agenda is the maintenance of their elite status.

What's more, many of the rich capitalist regions of the Earth do not act so as to spread their agreeable economic state (despite often claiming otherwise). *Their* underlying agenda is the maintenance of their political ascendancy.

None of that changes the mechanics of how a multitude of primates on a rock best work as a team. Economic liberty and free markets work for solid practical reasons, even if that isn't always obvious from the way they're applied. There's a logic to them, beyond mere functionality, which taps into the realities of how a planet of fallible humans best arrange their affairs in accordance with their own nature and limitations.

All the regions of planet Earth that became materially wealthy over the past two centuries did so using broadly the same set of conceptual systems – allowing individuals to create wealth by pursuing their own economic interests. Britain did it in the eighteenth century. Europe and America did it in the nineteenth century. Japan and bits of East Asia did it in the twentieth century and China, India and loads of other places were doing it when I wrote this book.

Charity doesn't turn poor countries into rich ones or build a sound and self-perpetuating logistical infrastructure in a region. If you really want to help some part of the world develop economically, the best thing you could do isn't send money there, or join a non-governmental organisation (NGO). The best thing you could *possibly* do is introduce a new bit of its civilisational logistics which interfaces with the rest of the economy in a meaningful and sustainable way: by starting up a business and trying to turn an honest profit.

*****

The economic globalisation taking place during the end of the twentieth and the beginning of the twenty-first century is about tearing down the imaginary barriers that stand between us and rubbing out the lines we've drawn in the sand. Billions of people cooperating is not a zero-sum game. Many regions of the planet were poor when I went on my adventure, but it doesn't have to be that way.

At the time this book was written, the post-World War II economic reality of a billion rich people and lots of poor people had already been replaced by an emerging reality of a billion rich people, four billion people getting rich and a billion who are not. Those regions of low growth and severe poverty are heavily concentrated in sub-Saharan Africa and certain parts of Central Asia (like Afghanistan). In 'developing' economies outside those areas, long-term economic growth per person per year increased from 2.5 per cent in the 1970s to 4.0 per cent in the 1980s and 1990s. In the opening years of the twenty-first century, economic growth in those economies had accelerated to 4.5 per cent.

During the years of my journey (admittedly the tail end of one of the most significant bursts of economic growth planet Earth had ever seen) world economic growth stood at:

2005	4.6%
2006	5.1%
2007	4.3%

For the 'developing' world the figures were:

2005	6.5%
2006	6.9%
2007	6.4%

Those numbers are stunning and game-changing and represent an era of wealth creation unprecedented in all of history. With numbers like those, the experience of each generation will be dramatically different from that of the one before, and absolute poverty can be brought under control within foreseeable time frames.

*****

Shortly after my pilgrimage a recession would begin. Because the global economy had been growing so smoothly for so long, it would catch a lot of people off guard.

Remember, what's *really* happening is that a bunch of highly intelligent hominids are running around on the surface of a planet and learning to organise the logistics of a global civilisation through socially constructed abstractions, which they've dreamed up from scratch. Highly intelligent hominids are no more naturally disposed to organise global economies than they are to govern countries or to manage planetary climates.

At this point in history we're learning to do all three at the same time. It's tough. Sometimes we stumble. We've stumbled before and we'll stumble many times in the future. There was never the remotest possibility that the future economic reality of human civilisation would be smooth, three per cent growth rates.

Because expectations are always being ratcheted upwards, we agonise over whatever economic realities we see around us. In the extremely rich parts of the world (such as the one I grew up in), people whose great-grandparents could barely afford shoes complain about the cost of private nurseries. But the average human at the beginning of the twenty-first century still owns wealth incomparable to nearly every other human who has ever lived during any previous period of history.

What's more, the efficiency with which we move resources, exploit new technologies and organise our logistics continues to get better all the time. The wealth and technical expertise of tomorrow can utterly eclipse those of today and this process can take us wherever we decide to go.

*****

It's vital that our current economic expansion continues. Civilisation cannot be made harmonious or stable without it. There are at least three reasons for this.

The first is to make poverty history. Large sections of the human race live in penury and die from hunger and water contamination. Average global living standards have to rise, and they have to rise a lot.

The second is to control population. The number of humans Earth can sustain is unknown, but it is not infinite. If the global population were to rise indefinitely, physical parameters would eventually kick in to limit it. That could be unpleasant. Lifting people off in spaceships is not an option because there is nowhere to take them. The global population must therefore be stabilised. One feature of the human psyche that's been recognised in the past century is that societies stop growing in population once they reach a certain material wealth. This removes a basic limiting factor to a harmonious world and it is one of the most extraordinarily convenient things about human nature that has ever come to light. If everyone is rich (and I'm talking in absolute, rather than relative, terms) then Earth's population will stabilise. So everyone must be rich.

The third reason is that there are technological barriers still to be crossed before civilisation becomes sustainable, and economic growth drives scientific and technological progress. Standing still technologically is not an option. A flagship example is the energy crisis. Human civilisation's energy use increases by about two per cent a year, fossil fuels are finite and forever is a long time. We can only afford to spend $10 billion on an audacious attempt to build an experimental fusion reactor because we've got lots of spare resources.

The underlying economic and population trends affecting human civilisation are that global poverty is decreasing, the breadth and depth of scientific and technological progress has never been greater and birth rates are falling across the globe. The only parts of the world where population growth remains out of control are poor and/or war-torn.

As the scale of our material wealth and technical expertise continues to increase, a lot of things are going to start becoming possible. Only when everyone has enough food and somewhere to live can we get stuck into the really interesting things we could be doing with all this money.

Space elevator, anyone?

116: The Seat of the God Emperors
21 March 2007

Sebastian was heading my way so, out of a (possibly misplaced) sense of camaraderie, I agreed to share a bus out of the desert and towards the Sacred Valley. Sebastian wanted to take the cheapest available bus. For 'cheapest available' bus, read '15-hour-nightmare-with-no-loo-stops' bus. The next morning we arrived, haggard and a bit smelly, at the city of Cuzco, formerly the capital of the Inca Empire.

Once again, Sebastian wanted to stay somewhere cheap. And once again, out of misplaced camaraderie, I agreed to join him. The hostel he picked was full of naive young Europeans who'd never been abroad before and an obese American called David, who had lived in Peru five years, hardly spoke Spanish, and solemnly intoned that South Americans couldn't be trusted and that 'anyone who's lived here more than three months will agree with me'.

After a few hours, the whole embarrassing arrangement was seriously cramping my style. I therefore showed Sebastian where to find the local office of South American Explorers, moved to a more expensive hotel and went out on the pull.

A couple of hours later I'd been kidnapped by two half-Inca ladies called Ximena and Anotella, who were in town for their holidays. Anotella had just graduated and landed a job at a Lima bank, while Ximena was working as a jewellery retailer and was a decade younger than her two brothers. 'I was the "oops",' she smirked, shrugging her shoulders.

Anotella and Ximena were troublemakers, telling me of a recent adventure in Bolivia, where they'd gotten stuck without money, then persuaded a diplomat at the Peruvian Embassy to give them $100 to get home. They were certainly experts at getting me to pay for stuff and pursued me through the city's energised club scene for two expensive days of very little sleep and far too much alcohol.

Cuzco – in addition to being the seat of the Inca god emperors, a first-class colonial gem and a great place to go clubbing – is also the stepping-off point for South America's most famous ancient site, Machu Picchu.

It's a testament to the scale of the post-Conquest transition that it took 400 years for anyone to notice 'The Lost City of the Incas'. The current thinking is that the settlement was a retreat for the Inca elite, which was abandoned when Cuzco fell to the Spanish. It is not believed to have been a place of particular religious or political significance during the pre-Columbian period.

It was therefore only after 1911, when it was brought to world attention by the American explorer Hiram Bingham, that Machu Picchu came into its own: becoming a key global destination for explorers and adventurers, and turbocharging the Peruvian tourist industry. The trick is to visit the site via the famous Inca Trail – a four-day hike through the Andes, which makes use of parts of the old Inca road system and culminates in a dawn arrival above the lost city.

Ximena and Anotella prepared me for the trek by taking me out, getting me to drink a bottle and a half of tequila with them, and then only letting me sleep for two hours. I was not of a clear head the next morning when I arrived at the coach for the 5 a.m. kick-off.

My Inca Trail buddies were 16 top-notchers, each worthy of a chapter in this diary. They included: Graeme, a Scot from Edinburgh, who needled me ruthlessly with 'all English people are morris dancers' gags; Emma, an engaging Canadian air traffic control person, who directs planes above the Arctic Circle; and Emma (another one) and Nicole, two hot, mad-for-it Sydney chicks.

The altitude was punishing during the highest parts of the trek and at four kilometres above sea level everyone went a little space cadet. Nonetheless, those hard climbs were put in perspective by the local fellows, running past carrying packs the size of washing machines, and made easier by the vistas of spectacular white-capped majesty every time one looked up. But it's the first sight of the lost city – ghostlike through the morning mist – that's burned into the mind and spirit.

There are 140 structures and features at Machu Picchu, covering 13 square kilometres. They include rock-cut stairs, towers, sanctuaries, storage buildings, plazas and cemeteries – all built without mortar, some so perfectly that a blade of grass will not fit between the stones. There's a temple to Inti, the sun god, and the Intihuatana, the only pre-Columbian ritual stone not smashed by the Spanish when they were desecrating the Inca religious sites. The Intihuatana is 1.8 metres tall, with a pillar and pedestal carved from a single block. At the equinox it casts no shadow.

However, the ruins, while outstanding, are not Seven Wonders of the World material in and of themselves. The thing about Machu Picchu is the setting. The Incas, you see, had the good taste to build it on top of a mountain.

On every side knee-trembling precipices give way to gigantic valleys, beyond which tower mile-high pinnacles of vertical granite. Cloud banks sweep past, alternately hiding and then revealing the surrounding witchery of the jungle and, in the unfathomable drop below, the Río Urubamba roars its way through the rock. Llamas amble about nonchalantly. 'Dramatic' doesn't quite do it justice.

After exploring the site I climbed to the top of the hill that rises behind it, spread my arms over the great citadel and thought about all that has happened to me during my month in Peru. I have to admit that I've found the Peruvians slightly overwhelming, with their big dark eyes and wild, unpredictable ways. What incredible people. What an amazing country.

Days since leaving London: 663
Height above sea level of

Machu Picchu:	2,430 metres
Cuzco:	3,399 metres
Highest point of the Inca Trail:	4,200 metres

Quechua word of the day: 'yuyanapaq' meaning 'to remember'

Global Musings VII
The Current
Tapestry

Machu Picchu stands as testament to the heights to which Native American culture rose before it was rudely and violently caught on the wrong side of history and quashed by invaders from the east.

Patterns going back tens of thousands of years conspired to shape those events. Given 60,000 years and a few thousand generations, humans settled the planet. By the time ocean-going ships began binding our species back together, technological and power differences had emerged. Motivated by greed and ignorance, the more powerful groups exploited and entrenched those differences.

Temporarily.

Because just as history pushed us apart, now it is pushing us back together.

Maybe I'm biased. Before starting my trip I'd spent eight years living in London, which, in the twenty-first century, is possibly the most cosmopolitan place ever to have existed. My first big stop was Istanbul, currently the nexus for a political and cultural unification of historic scale. In the following two years I met more than a thousand people from six different continents. I'm sure I don't need to spell out that, as far as I'm concerned, we're all basically the same.

I therefore find it genuinely difficult to believe that the themes which will ultimately define the future of the human race are going to be characterised by a competition between the minuscule differences in human traditions which are otherwise almost entirely identical.

Sociologists have apparently been predicting for a hundred years that divisions based on race and ethnicity are set to lose their relevance. The proclivity to divide ourselves into groups is powerfully built into the human psyche, and skin colour will always be an obvious trait for it to latch onto. Race may well remain a powerful social force. But in my experience, attitudes to it are evolving.

The backlash against overt discrimination in the West is the tip of an iceberg. Globally, at the time of my adventure, racism was the norm rather than the exception, but everywhere I went the current generation was less prejudiced than the one before it.

In Britain and France, those who remember a world dominated by a Europe with an inflated sense of its own importance do not think about race and ethnicity with as much sophistication as the younger generation who grew up within the multiracial, transcultural realities of today.

In the Andes, socio-economic status is closely tied to race but it's mixing up fast. The people of Cuzco are all very proud of their glamorous heritage, very determined to take advantage of this modern world and everyone's got an email address. Bolivia and Peru both elected Amerindian-descended presidents in the first six years of the twenty-first century. That's a watershed.

It will be a long time before a person of indigenous background becomes prime minister of Australia, but the generation of Anglo-Australians I met were unquestionably more enlightened than their great-grandparents who shot people for having black skin.

The Indigenous Australian people's struggle to synthesise their cultures into ones that can take advantage of the realities dumped upon them by history will probably take well over another century. Four decades of relatively enlightened social policy and sweeping away legal discrimination are steps along a road. Empowering people is not as simple as giving them the same rights as everybody else, but it's a start. The Indigenous Australians have been through a grim period during the last 200 years. Nevertheless, they've survived and are now in a position to move beyond the ruinous hand which fate has temporarily dealt them. History, finally, is on their side.

Integrating a planet of quarrelsome mammals is a big job. It takes time. But in a world where people are basically the same, the trend will be towards equality between groups as the internal cultures of those caught out by the imposition of the modern world adapt to take advantage of it. The underlying pattern of global events will – over the long term – empower them to transcend their historical baggage.

The millennia-sized technological differences which gave rise to those power disparities are a thing of the past. They were the result of a long separation of peoples, which is not about to return. Inventions no longer take a thousand years to cross Eurasia.

Right now, in Dubai, European expats have huge wealth, while South Asian labourers struggle for little. European descent equals relatively rich; South Asian descent equals relatively poor. That's the way the world's been of late. But 2,500 years ago the ancestors of those expats lived in huts, while those of the construction workers lived in a society that was undergoing possibly the greatest spiritual enlightenment of all time.

Evolution has implanted a status obsession in our minds, along with a predilection to think of ourselves in terms of tribes. But there are grander games for us to play than competing for ephemeral cultural ascendancy, or for the honour of squatting at the crown of our species-wide monkey tree. A lot of difficult and unforeseen stuff is going to happen in the next 2,500 years and we are, whether or not we like it or admit it, a single pan-planetary self-contained species, we're in this together and we stand or fall as one.

117: 100% Bolivian
26 March 2007

Things that go wrong in Bolivia:

1) Crossing the Peruvian border to find that Copacabana, by Lake Titicaca, is the first town since Cambodia without an ATM. I am saved from a life of exile by £10 that Eden dropped me in an Istanbul nightclub 16 months ago (and which has been lying at the bottom of my rucksack ever since). I ritualistically starve myself for a day in order to save money.

2) The $2 bus from Copacabana to La Paz drives off with my rucksack on the roof but without me. I give frantic chase with a local *taxista*, who rips me off on the fare. We get stuck behind the obligatory tractor as said bus disappears over the horizon. I pull out my hair while chase buddy is sanguine. But then, he doesn't have all his worldly belongings on a one-way trip to an unknown Bolivian shanty.

3) After chasing down my runaway backpack, I arrive in La Paz with excruciating tooth pain. The poorest country in South America is not an ideal location for dental work. The US Embassy leads me to Jorge: rotund and jolly, with a state-of-the-art-looking surgery. His disarmingly attractive assistants, Luisa and Dana, make faces at me while I lie prostrate. Jorge actually takes a call on his mobile while pushing bits of metal into my gum. I leave pain-free and cheerful.

Bolivia is the whipping boy of South America. Since gaining its independence in 1825, more than half of its territory has been swallowed by its neighbours. From 1879 to 1883, it fought the War of the Pacific with Chile, culminating in the Chilean annexation of the entire Bolivian coastline (along with its valuable nitrate and copper deposits). In 1903 Brazil persuaded the (then) Bolivian province of Acre to cede to it (along with its rich rubber plantations) and, between 1932 and 1935, Bolivia fought a war with Paraguay, resulting in it losing three-quarters of the Chaco region (which turned out to have none of the anticipated petroleum that 100,000 people had died fighting over).

La Paz, Bolivia's mountainous capital, sits in the bowl of a broad canyon at between 3,250 metres and 4,100 metres above sea level – a kilometre higher than Quito. Because the city is so cheap I've gone for a swish room, with a desk and an en suite bathroom, at a joint called the Hostel Maya. Outside, the district of Rosario is crisscrossed by steep cobbled roads lined with poncho shops. The streets are full of a swirling street life and guys selling Andean trinkets and dirt-cheap cocaine.

I can't stop writing. The month in Peru has left my head in a whirl. I've been keeping myself to myself in the hostel, piling into my notebooks, scribbling away, drawing upon patterns.

People, however, keep approaching me. On my first night two local girls (Cinthia and Mauge) grabbed me out of the crowd and offered me a night out (declined), a tour of the city (declined) and their email addresses (accepted).

Yesterday, while dining on the set menu lunch in a food-hall-style café, I was approached by a lively British couple eating chips at the next table. The man, Jamie (a well-built fellow with long white hair and a thick Glaswegian accent), asked if I knew enough Spanish to get directions to a bus stop (no problem) and the lady, Annie (mischievous-looking with a northern-English drawl), soon piled in.

Annie and Jamie let out their house on the island of Jersey two and a half years ago and they've been exploring the world (Australia, China, India, Africa and South America so far) on the rent money. Insofar as I could tell they'd basically been skipping between the planet's most beautiful locations and making merry for the whole 29 months. They're the kind of people who go out for dinner on a Sunday afternoon, then end up at full moon parties. Lust for life. Top marks.

Finally, while visiting the Church of San Francisco in the city centre, I was approached by a New York journalist called Noelle, who was passing through Bolivia on her way to interview one of the economic advisers to Hugo Chávez (the Venezuelan president). She was full of outrage at the world. As we walked back up the canyon she talked of a recent trip to India to visit Tibetan colleagues.

'The Tibetans have been brutalised for fifty, fifty-five years, close to six decades, and everyone stands aside.'

'Mmm, it's kind of awkward with China and all ...' I started to offer as we trudged into Rosario.

'*China*!' she exploded, interrupting me while panting in the rarefied air. 'Disregarding human rights, threatening Taiwan and the US can't wait to climb into bed with it.'

'And sell it Treasury Bonds,' I quipped.

'The world's biggest economy will soon be an autocracy, where the citizens have no rights and torture and state executions are rife, and all we do is to buy their cheap plastic toys.'

'But isn't the world coming together and isn't that a good thing?' I asked.

'But look at the *way* it's coming together,' she pleaded, 'the West doing business with corrupt oligarchies whose only goal is to make money. Is that really what we want? Is it? *Is it?*'

I didn't have time to tell Noelle what I really wanted and I didn't get the impression she was all that interested. Pilgrimages should be about listening not talking, and I try not to dictate the agenda of conversations. Nonetheless, I couldn't help thinking that if she could see just a little bit deeper and a little bit further she wouldn't find everything so scary.

Days since leaving London: 668
Number of years Bolivia has been a republic: 181
Changes of government during that period: 192

> *Spanish phrase of the day: 'enfermedad de altitud' meaning 'altitude sickness'*

Global Musings VIII
Dragon Renaissance

In the early twenty-first century, when I undertook my journey, the ripples of China's economic and political rise could be seen everywhere. The biologists who would shortly be helping me escape Bolivia's desert were Chinese Americans. In Quito, the language schools were full of Chinese diplomats learning Spanish. In Queensland, freight trains trundled by, loaded with coal for Chinese furnaces, and the earliest drafts of this book first took shape in a Sydney internet café run by a Chinese man called Joe.

Across the world, everybody was talking about it. In a Genoese campsite, two Belgian executives predicted that it would undermine the economies of Europe. In an Istanbul café, an American postgraduate assured me that it would spark war with his country. In Agra, a German professor spent dinner soothsaying a China-inspired plunge in Western living standards and, in La Paz, Noelle – genuinely terrified – followed me up the canyon's side, telling me China's rise would cast a shadow over the century which had just begun.

These are classic examples of a positive development being seen in a negative way because of a failure to think about it in context. I think China's current metamorphosis is one of the most profoundly encouraging things ever to occur, and a sure sign of human civilisation's intrinsic vitality.

To appreciate that point of view, one has to understand a tiny slice of Chinese history, then take a step back.

*****

Chinese civilisation has exceptionally rich cultural and intellectual traditions. For two and a half millennia it's been a dynamo of human progress, supplying many of our most important innovations. In fact, during most of recorded history, China was Earth's most technologically and politically developed region. As recently as 1800 China had the world's largest economy, its industry was among the planet's most advanced and Beijing was Earth's biggest city. Then, from the mid-nineteenth century, a series of cataclysms plunged it into a dark age from which it is only now recovering.

The decisive event was a war known as the Taiping Rebellion. In the 1840s Hong Xiuquan, a Christian convert, received a revelation.

God (allegedly) told him that he was the younger brother of Jesus and that it was his mission to save the world. In 1850 Hong and his associate Yang Xiuqing (former firewood salesman and 'Mouthpiece of God') initiated a war to overthrow the Manchu emperors.

The Taiping Rebellion was one of the most catastrophic conflicts in history. For 14 years a gargantuan war raged across south and central China. There was slaughter and starvation on a colossal scale. The final death toll was between 20 and 30 million people: nearly half the global body count from World War II a century later.

While the Taiping Rebellion was under way a series of other hugely destructive civil wars exploded across the country, including the Panthay Rebellion from 1855 to 1873, the Nien Rebellion from 1853 to 1868 and the Hui Minorities' War from 1862 to 1877.

Concurrent with all this were the opium wars. At the time there was massive global demand for Chinese tea, porcelain and silk, but European industry could produce little the Chinese economy needed. British merchants therefore began smuggling opium into the country to redress that trade imbalance. The Chinese government first attempted to stop them in 1839. In response the British launched the First Opium War, in which they forced China to import the drug and annexed Hong Kong. In 1856, with the immense carnage of the Taiping Rebellion in full swing, the British and French launched the Second Opium War, in which they captured Beijing and burned the Summer Palace.

The destruction caused by those 30 years of bloody conflict that tore across China's richest provinces was exacerbated by a sequence of natural disasters. In 1855 the Yellow River changed course, leading to a decade of catastrophic flooding. Then, in the 1870s, the North China Famine killed 13 million people.

The compounded effects of these wars and multiple catastrophes meant that, between 1850 and 1873, China's population fell by 60 million.

In 1887 the Yellow River broke its banks (again), leading to one of the worst floods of all time: 130,000 square kilometres were inundated, between 900,000 and two million lives were lost, two million were left homeless and a major epidemic was triggered. Then, in 1894, war erupted with Japan.

The First Sino-Japanese War was a defeat for the Chinese. It culminated in Japan compelling them to pay a massive forced loan and annexing several bits of Chinese territory, including Taiwan.

Germany, Britain, France and Russia all then took advantage of the situation by annexing their own bits of China.

These humiliations provoked a nationalist backlash to remove the foreign powers (the Boxer Rebellion). Europe and Japan responded by raising a joint army which, in August 1900, sacked and looted Beijing. China was then forced to accept an array of punitive concessions and, most cripplingly, surrender part of her tax base. It would take 50 years of disintegration, factionalism and another vast war to escape those bonds.

The 1931 Yellow River Flood was the deadliest natural disaster of all time. Between one and four million people died. Then, at the end of that year, Japan invaded Manchuria. This marked the beginning of a 14-year attempt by the Japanese to take over the country. A full-scale invasion was launched in 1937.

The Second Sino-Japanese War (which was fought entirely on Chinese soil and eventually merged with World War II) resulted in 20 million Chinese casualties, 95 million Chinese refugees and economic damage to China equal to 50 times Japan's GDP. When it ended in 1945, China had to endure yet another civil war before finally emerging as a unified nation (minus Taiwan) in 1949.

There followed an excellent example of why an imperfect, self-centred animal is not well placed to attempt the coordination of immense economies or dictate the affairs of hundreds of millions of people. Chairman Mao presided over both the madness of the Great Leap Forward (the most lethal famine in the history of the human race, with 30 million deaths) and the self-mutilation of the Cultural Revolution.

China has had the largest economy in the world for 18 of the past 20 centuries. But, since 1850, it has suffered the biggest famine in history, the biggest natural disaster in history and two of the deadliest wars of all time.

To understand China as a scary poor country with a nasty government that's suddenly becoming alarmingly rich and powerful is to completely miss the historical context of what is happening. The reforms initiated by Deng Xiaoping from the 1980s, and the extraordinary events which have followed, constitute a renaissance. It is long overdue.

*****

The momentum and confidence of China's rise may seem remarkable to people like Noelle. But there are rhythms at work in human societies that are not easily measured and which operate on time scales longer than a single lifetime. China is heir to millennia of advanced civilisation in a way other 'developing' countries (for example, in sub-Saharan Africa) are not. Only India (which is also starting to transform) and the Middle East (which for the most part, at the time of my journey, was not) can claim comparable traditions.

Those cataclysmic wars of the nineteenth and twentieth centuries, the natural calamities that accompanied them and the European and Japanese exploitation of that situation may seem like settled history. But the current dynamic of world affairs is very specifically shaped by those events.

The China which emerged from those black 130 years was not a prosperous, self-confident state with an accountable and progressive government. It was demoralised, impoverished and presided over by a corrupt and repressive dictatorship.

It's extremely unfortunate that those things are true. It is also unfortunate that my recent ancestors flooded China with opium to solve their trade problems and that Japan went through a phase of intense militaristic imperialism in the twentieth century of which China bore the brunt. But it's no use pretending that the last two centuries of history didn't happen.

It would be great if China could organise a one-step transition to a free, open, materially wealthy and self-assured society with a democratically accountable government. But it's difficult to envisage how such a step might, even in theory, be taken.

The richest societies in the world today have set new benchmarks for order, justice and civil rights. It is in everyone's interests that China joins them in that happy state as soon as possible. Every society that got to that place followed a path. None of those paths were entirely pretty. China is progressing along its own as fast as it might plausibly do so. Given the way it was laid low, tolerating its mischievous ability to make cheap products that other people want to buy seems a small price to pay.

*****

All men are brothers. Recent history has left us trained to think in terms of, and identify with, competing political units. We need to stop doing that. A billion poor frustrated Chinese people with nuclear weapons was never a stable or morally appropriate state of affairs, and there is only one endgame that should be acceptable to anybody.

China's economic miracle is probably the greatest human development story of all time. When I wrote these words China's economy had been growing at 8 per cent a year for three decades and its rate of absolute poverty had decreased from 64 per cent to 10 per cent. Five hundred million people had been lifted out of poverty in a generation. That is one of the most incredible things which has ever happened.

None of this is much comfort if one is a Tibetan monk. But whatever course China pursues, a political arrangement where a self-selected government clique dictates the affairs of an increasingly highly educated, internet-savvy, globally aware and tax-paying citizenship isn't sustainable beyond the medium term.

As for how the Chinese people manage that next phase in their history, I wish them well. But the construction of a harmonious global civilisation requires a China that is happy, healthy and fully on board as quickly as possible. While the last 200 years didn't leave the fabric of Chinese culture well placed to make the most of this new world, the last 2,000 left it very well placed indeed.

118: Mad Dogs and Englishmen
2 April 2007

After four days in La Paz I climbed aboard yet another Andean bus and headed to the Salar de Uyuni in the south-west of the country.

Fifty thousand years ago, the Salar de Uyuni was a lake inhabited by fairy-tale megafauna (six-metre ground sloths with foot-long claws and the mass of a bull elephant) of a sort that covered this world before our ancestors colonised it, demonstrating that with abstract thinking, language and Stone Age weapons there was no other life form they couldn't take out hands down. The sloths got wiped out and the lake dried up. It left 10 billion tonnes of salt.

We drove through the surrounding deserts in four-by-fours. Tornado-shaped rocks, flamingo-filled lakes and Martian stone fields filled an endless procession of valleys. Distant groups of guanacos and llamas wandered watchfully through their vast and dreamlike home. We reached the salt flats at sunset. A thin film of water from the season's rain reflected a perfect vision of the silver moon and golden sky above. I couldn't believe how beautiful it was.

Unfortunately, our drivers (whose characterful performances were made less endearing by their ambiguous relationship with truth) loaded my backpack onto the wrong jeep. I spent four dusty days chasing it down, *Wacky Races*-style, culminating in my being abandoned in the middle of the desert, with the wrong backpack, on a plateau five kilometres above sea level with no food or money. I strive not to let the little things get me down, but trust me, at the time it was stressful.

My 36-hour escape routine involved hitching a lift with three biologists, hijacking a rangers' station, a 40-minute walk across the desert in the pounding midday heat, and burning up beside a dusty track (scribbling furiously in my notebook and listening to Bob Dylan's 'Like a Rolling Stone' through my battered iPod), hoping that a vehicle would pass by.

After five hours one did. I flagged it down. It was driven by Hugo, who agreed to take me back to what passes for civilisation in those parts. I then spent nine hours in the passenger seat of his jeep as we travelled between great sheets of multicoloured mountains and back to where I'd started.

After recovering my luggage and telling the guys at Juliet Tours that they were a bunch of penises, I undertook yet another marathon day-long sand drive across the desert to the Chilean border. I crossed it yesterday morning to find an actual road. From there it was an hour's drive down from the mountains to San Pedro de Atacama. Tarmac ain't never looked so good.

Days since leaving London: 675

English word of the day: 'gambol' meaning 'to frolic freely in the plains and forests'

119: Dharma Bum
4 April 2007

On gratefully arriving, sunburned and exhausted from six days in the desert, I found a campsite and pitched Nguthungulli the Tent next to the thick trunk of a mammoth pale-green conifer. I moisturised my sunburnt face 13 times that afternoon, and spent two hours cleaning my body and laundering my sweat-drenched clothes. Then I went to the local shop, bought a huge picnic, ate it all and slept for half a day.

San Pedro de Atacama is a small, pristine settlement, with streets that look like the set from a spaghetti western and a whitewashed Iberian-style chapel. It's right at the edge of the driest desert in the world and, whichever way one looks, red cone-shaped mountains command the background. Oliver and Nick, two English fellows camped next to me, are packing expensive-looking racing bicycles. They've come to Chile to have a two-week cycling adventure in the high plateaux. Pussies.

I've been on the road for more than 22 months. I err on the side of keeping quiet about this but, travellers' conversations being what they are, I'm occasionally asked the direct question. When that happens I deliver an abridged summary of my pilgrimage. As anyone who's been following what's been going on in my head for a while can imagine, it's kind of difficult to explain.

Only a fraction of the equipment I left London with is still with me. I now have a singlet from France, a hoody from Istanbul, a pair of glasses from Bangkok, boots from Sydney, a bag from Byron Bay, trousers from Quito and a hat from Canoa (I misplaced the Aussie-plonker one in the Andes). I've still got my original star chart.

It's been a year since I saw anyone who's known me for more than a few months. This has taught me that there is a level of interaction one can reach with other human beings after two days, another level after a month and then a more intimate level. There are some things of which this hobo's life leaves one starved. I'm feeling pretty lonesome.

I am, however, holding it together, unlike Nguthungulli the Tent, who is going off the rails. Last night the Jolly Pilgrim and he were enjoying a bottle of the local Merlot (soft and fruity with good elbow) when Nguthungulli began taking a series of ridiculous positions that were clearly intended to provoke me. He is a juvenile tent.

Sometimes Nguthungulli the Tent talks to himself. The local people give him funny looks when he does this. I remind Nguthungulli that if he mumbles in public people will think that he is crazy. Nguthungulli fails to heed my warnings, or to acknowledge my clear victories when I set clever logical traps for him then laugh at his stupidity. Revenge is my fruit salad.

I worry about Nguthungulli the Tent. I also worry about those other infernal tricksters: the bees.

Days since leaving London: 677

> *Franz Ferdinand found alive – First World War a mistake.* – Graffiti in the loo of this internet café

120: Mendoza Red
13 April 2007

Two days after emerging wild-eyed and unshaven from the Bolivian desert, I ran into a charming Spanish-Chilean couple called Cesar and Daniela. Daniela was from Santiago and Cesar, her Spanish boyfriend, was a student in Madrid.

After we'd spent a night hanging out together in San Pedro they invited me to visit the holiday home of Daniela's family at the coastal town of Cachagua (just north from Santiago) for Easter. It was 1,000 kilometres to the south and well away from anything in the guidebooks. They gave me a three-line address. I told them I'd find it.

I arrived two days later to discover that Cachagua was extremely upmarket and Cesar and Daniela's crew were well mannered, well dressed and well-to-do. There was red wine, proper cheese, a beach, a barbecue, a pool and loads of hip hop. This time the hip hop was in Spanish.

It was at Cachagua that I encountered the limits of my Spanish language abilities. When confronted with an entire room of full-speed, slanged-up Chilean hipsters, I go all kangaroo-in-the-headlights and clam up – something I rarely do in English.

I was dropped in Santiago four days ago. I spent a couple of afternoons hanging out in its cafés and playing chess with old men in its parks. Then, on the evening of the 10th of April, I boarded a bus that would take me across the Andes for the very last time, to Argentina and the city of Mendoza, capital of its chief wine-producing region. I spent the following day swimming in the local pool and wandering around Mendoza's wide, leafy boulevards, then, that evening, everything went mental.

I'd met three Irishmen – Byrne, Aiden and Robert – on the bus out of Santiago and, in the evening of that second day in Mendoza, I joined them for dinner along with their friend Sally, who was in Argentina teaching English to local adults. The restaurant had burgundy hardwood furniture, multi-hued light boxes and washrooms decked out in black granite with sleek chrome fittings. There were five cuts of beef on the menu. The Malbec was soon flowing.

We ate, drank and gossiped through three rich, buttery and calorific courses. The Irish boys told us about Liverpool Football Club and their adventures in a Santiago coffee shop where all the waitresses worked topless. Sally, meanwhile, who became increasingly tipsy, described some of the juicier details of the sexual encounters she'd enjoyed with her students.

Inevitably, we ended up piling into cabs and going to a club. Once there I found myself drinking caipirinhas with a seedy, long-haired man from Buenos Aires called Diego.

I'm certain that when I arrived Diego was with his girlfriend, but the next thing I knew the two of us were on the dance floor with two amiable and breathtakingly attractive ladies called Julieta and Isabel. They were both 19 years old and working as dancing teachers. Isabel wore low-cut jeans and a tight vest top; Julieta a short skirt, a black waistcoat and designer black-rimmed glasses. Basically, imagine your wildest fantasy of what a 19-year-old Argentinian dancing teacher might look like.

I was dancing with Isabel. Diego was dancing with Julieta. All three of them were breaking out moves I couldn't handle: getting down and shaking it while I clung to my caipirinha and looked like an uncoordinated wally. All the time, Diego was getting in my face when the girls weren't looking, pinching his fingers and hissing, 'You have to kiss eet.' I was feeling a bit English about the whole thing, but on Diego's repeated urging planted a cheeky one on Isabel's cheek. An awkward second followed.

The next thing I knew she had her hands behind my neck and was snogging my face off on the dance floor. I was so taken aback that, after she'd finished with me, I stood momentarily disoriented as the sound of the Rolling Stones thundered around us. The next thing I knew Julieta had grabbed me around the waist and put her tongue down my throat. *What*? Then they started to take turns on me. Diego tried to get some of the action but they ignored him. I couldn't believe what was happening. Two elegant and perfectly spoken Argentinian dancing teachers were casually using me as their man doll on a Mendoza dance floor to the tune of 'Honky-Tonk Woman'. It was the best thing that had ever happened.

After an extended out-of-this-world experience the girls pulled me to the edge of the dance floor and looked expectant for a while before going to powder their faces, leaving me in semi-shock, head spinning, still clutching my caipirinha. Just then I was tapped on the shoulder and turned around to see a black-haired, confident-looking woman with a crooked smile, looking me straight in the eye. 'You're coming with me,' she said.

Grace was a sassy, sexy, on the ball, quick-witted Canadian chick. The two of us spent the next hour in the corner of the club talking about everything. I can't even remember the details, just that she was beautiful and clever and marvellous and that it was love at first sight. Then the club was closing and everyone was leaving. She told me she wanted to see me again and that I had to memorise her email address. It was Grace dot something at Yahoo dot com. But I can't remember. Damn that eleventh caipirinha.

I woke up yesterday morning – on a bunk in a hostel on my own with a hangover – in disbelief that I'd let Julieta and Isabel go and failed to write down Grace's email address. Horrified at squandering two opportunities of a lifetime in one evening, I forlornly packed my things and went to catch the coach to Buenos Aires.

The coach was air-conditioned and spacious, with two decks and an on-board attendant, who distributed bottled water. I had my own double seat and, as my head cleared and the green fields of the Cuyo region rolled by, I spread out my newspapers and contemplated.

When I crossed the border between Bolivia and Chile I changed cultural spheres. Ecuador, Peru and Bolivia (the heartlands of South America's old indigenous high civilisations) form a distinct cultural region. The Southern Cone countries of Chile, Argentina and Uruguay form a separate one. They're more economically developed and the Latin Americans here tend to be more Latin and less American. Chile and Argentina are modern, self-confident places which are both currently dealing with the darker aspects of their twentieth-century past.

Chile's recent political history was dominated by the presidency of General Augusto Pinochet Ugarte. In the late twentieth century the country became a Cold War football, leading to the polarisation of its politics and the election of (USSR-backed) President Salvador Allende. President Allende was deposed in a (US-backed) military coup in 1973 and General Pinochet, who led the coup, was president until 1989. The lives of everyone above young adult age in Chile were deeply affected by his premiership and it's an exceedingly touchy subject. That's because it raises a very real moral dichotomy.

On the one hand, General Pinochet's government set Chile's previously shambolic economy on course to become the highly developed one I just passed through. On the other hand, he was also a complete bastard who replaced a democratically elected government with a nasty dictatorship, ordered thousands of extra-judicial killings and tortured people who disagreed with him.

Argentina had an on-off relationship with dictatorship and political violence for large parts of the twentieth century, but moved decisively to democracy in 1983. It was famously the tenth-richest country in the world in 1913 but its economy has had several ups and downs since then and, in 2001, it suffered a major economic crisis from which it's presently bouncing back.

Meanwhile, in the news, one-third of the way around the world in Iraq, a truck bomb has blown up a bridge over the River Tigris and a man wearing an explosive-packed vest has detonated it in a cafeteria beside the country's parliament. Hearing of such things causes my thoughts to diverge, so I fell asleep last night as my coach headed into the Pampas, thinking about Chile, Argentina, Iraq and this messy, complicated, interdependent world. When I awoke this morning, I was in Buenos Aires.

Days since leaving London: 686
World's fastest growing major economies, 2006

China:	+10.5%
Venezuela:	+8.8%
India:	+8.5%
Argentina:	+8.5%

Current American casualties in Iraq: 3,248

How vast these Orbs must be, and how inconsiderable this Earth, the theatre upon which all of our mighty designs, all our navigations and all our wars are transacted is, when compared to them. A very fit consideration ... for those Kings and Princes who sacrifice the lives of so many people, only to flatter their ambition in being masters of some pitiful corner of this small spot. – Christiaan Huygens, 1690

Global Musings IX
The Mechanics of
the Planetary
Adolescence

I'm a news junkie. I find the story of humanity – unfolding in real time – so intriguing that I never tire of keeping an eye on its details, and I kept my eyes on those details all the way through my journey. But that isn't what went in my diary and I'm not writing all this down to record the fleeting things of this world. However, in order to give a true account of my pilgrimage, there is one affair, current at the time, which deserves special mention.

Between 27 May 2005, when I set off from London, and 8 June 2007, when I returned, I, like so many others, followed the ongoing catastrophe in Iraq with increasing alarm. I was attached to an intravenous drip in a Croatian infection hospital when Abu Musab al-Zarqawi declared all-out war against Iraq's Shi'ites; down and out in Sydney when the Golden Mosque at Samarra was blown up; high in my Ecuadorian eyrie when Saddam Hussein was executed; and on an overnight bus to Buenos Aires when I read about truck bombs destroying the al-Sarafiya bridge over the Tigris. From Croatian doctors, to Turkish producers, to Ecuadorian taxi drivers, everybody was talking about it.

With hindsight it's possible to imagine a response to the mass murder of 11 September 2001 where the United States of America single-mindedly hunted down and brought to justice Mr Osama bin Laden, then immediately marshalled the resources of twenty-first-century civilisation for the rejuvenation of long-pummelled Afghanistan. It was not to be. Instead the reputations of some of the world's most progressive peoples became stained, hundreds of billions of dollars were squandered, hundreds of thousands of Iraqis were sent to their graves and Osama bin Laden was to spend a decade unpunished. Meanwhile, North Korea got the bomb.

There are various narratives to describe what happened.

I've never been face-to-face with an 'Islamic extremist' so I should probably be careful in claiming to know what they believe, what their goals are, or how they think they might achieve those goals. I tried hard during my journey to get hold of al-Qaeda literature. The only substantive document I got my hands on was a jihad manual, which I read in a Bolivian internet café while surrounded by Israeli backpackers (not a comfortable experience). The manual didn't have anything profound to say, although it did quote passages from the Qur'an in peculiar contexts – particularly some of the things it says about what happens when you die.

Islamic scripture is explicit about the relationship between heaven and Earth. Reality is a vehicle. Its purpose is to choose who (following the Day of Judgement) gets to sit on couches, discuss wholesome matters and drink flagons of pure drink, for eternity.

Is it possible that the fabric of existence was set up – in a literal sense – to pick which humans go to drink from flagons for eternity? Is it within the realms of the possible that, under prescribed circumstances, killing other humans reserves one a spot? Is it within the outer realms of the possible that the infallible creator of reality sponsors one group of humans against another in their earthly, limited and short-sighted squabbles?

Personally, I don't think it is.

A different narrative holds that the most powerful and important nation state of the early twenty-first century was, in the year 2001, attacked by implacably evil psychopaths, who sought to murder its people without reason. Those who hold to this narrative might describe the backlash that followed as a 'War on Terror' in a contest between good guys and swivel-eyed baddies.

Yet another narrative – one widely espoused at the time of my journey – holds that elements within the American military-industrial establishment used the crisis precipitated by the 11th of September attacks to declare pre-emptive wars, cut back civil rights and further their reprehensible and dastardly economic and political agendas.

While it is understandable why one might hold either of these views, or the many shades in between, I believe that a more complete narrative than any of them is this: there are billions of imperfect, evolved, fallible monkeys; they live on a giant ball of rock that is hurtling through space; they don't have an instruction manual; and they're trying to organise a planetary civilisation without any external guidance. As a result, human history has been chaotic and uneven, the world is a complicated and confusing place full of mutual incomprehension and irrational hatred, and some of the resulting conflicts take bizarre forms.

When a small group of unemployed ex-college students flew aeroplanes into the World Trade Centre, the political establishment within the United States had to fashion a response to an emotionally charged, complex and unprecedented crisis. In attempting to form such a response it allowed its policy to be influenced by populism, prejudice and a search for real or imagined enemies. The train of events which followed soon became thoroughly entangled with the extant politics of the day.

One of the things this episode highlighted is how limited our ability to respond to emotionally charged, unprecedented crises remains. One of the best adjusted and most well-resourced political systems ever achieved ruinously mismanaged its response and, as a result, the dawning century will be a shade darker than it might otherwise have been.

But the gnat of al-Qaeda having a pop at the juggernaut of the West never represented one of the great obstacles to human progress, or constituted a coherent alternative political and economic vision as to how we, as a species, might proceed.

It's a distraction.

The human race faces a number of fundamental tasks and it will stand or fall (as one) by the proficiency with which it tackles them. Those tasks include the eradication of poverty, the investigation of the physical world and the management of our relationship with the environment. Those things will remain our fundamental tasks no matter how many wars are declared on abstract nouns, no matter how many narcissistic criminals dream of re-establishing ancient Caliphates they only dimly understand and no matter how many lives are lost in the crossfire.

*****

Most of the must-solve conundrums humanity faces – such as sorting out our logistical and environmental problems – are built into the mechanics of being a species of fallible animals trying to organise a civilisation. Owing to the events of recent history, a further such conundrum has come to light. Scientific and technological developments in the past few hundred years have placed us in a position where we must, within a few centuries, construct a robust planet-wide political architecture.

The twentieth century saw the introduction of mechanised war machines, two world wars, the industrialisation of genocide, and the development of nuclear weapons and their first use at Hiroshima/

Nagasaki.

The realities of contemporary geopolitics are that we divide ourselves into political units which interact within a framework crudely derived from the one we evolved with. A feature of that framework is violent competition between units, with several units now holding nuclear weapons and the number holding such weapons rising inexorably.

Under such realities it is a question of when, not if, nuclear weapons are once again used in anger and when, not if, there is a nuclear war. Will it be a hundred years? Five hundred years? A thousand? Then, once the first step upon that dark path has been taken, the next question will be the frequency of such occurrences. Forever is a long time. This is not a sustainable situation.

Like so many of those other really big problems facing the human race, it's difficult to imagine how things might have been otherwise. Humanity's predisposition for violent conflict exists with good reason. Hyper-intelligent tool-using omnivores do not climb to the top of the food chain and colonise the world without being fairly belligerent. The violently competing political units through which we're predisposed to organise ourselves were around long before anyone dreamed up civilisation, let alone its blackest blossom.

Now civilisation is global it's difficult therefore to envisage how, at least initially, this current geopolitical state of affairs might have been avoided. Burning ourselves with our new toys was also probably an inevitable part of the learning curve.

To frame human civilisation's geopolitical situation in fundamental terms:

1) A hyper-intelligent species like ours does not create a pan-planetary civilisation without being fighters.

2) A species predisposed to violent inter-group competition which creates a pan-planetary civilisation is probably destined to initially generate geopolitical arrangements characterised by war.

3) Assuming one's physics is good enough, weapons of mass destruction will, at some point, inevitably get thrown into that mixing bowl.

This is the situation conspired for us by fate. Are we up to dealing with it?

I think we almost certainly are. Two thousand years ago it would have been unthinkable that different factions within the British Isles would not periodically be going to war. Now it's unthinkable that they would. Two hundred years ago it would have been out of the question that some nation or other within Europe would not be primed to launch periodic bloodbaths against some other nation. We're very close to that point right now.

Huge tracts of the Earth are almost entirely free from the worst forms of organised violence. If it can be done across a large island or an entire continent, then there is no reason to suppose it cannot be done across a planet.

I believe we may actually have been reasonably lucky with the rhythms of our technological and political development. Humanity's most destructive wars broke loose just before the game-changing artefacts of nuclear death arrived in the mid-twentieth century. We've made it through the bottleneck of the Cold War and (despite sabre-rattling and squabbles over hydrocarbons) there are no profound conflicts of interest between the world's most powerful nation states.

This point has been reached just as we've started to get a handle on macroeconomics (so everyone's getting rich), the internet has appeared (so everyone's talking to each other) and memories of World Wars I and II are fresh enough to deter anyone from doing anything really stupid.

Given that we've probably been destined to face this grand geopolitical hurdle for the 12,000 years since agriculture was developed, the circumstances under which we face it could have been far less auspicious. If one imagines some of the hypothetical scenarios which pan out from having billions of angry anthropoids on a rock with nukes, quite a few of them are pretty unappealing.

*****

Thirty years before this book was written, the Cold War between the USA (and her allies) and the USSR (and hers) was a defining geopolitical feature of the age. Seventy years before, the struggle between France and Germany was such a feature. One thousand years before, it would have been the struggle between the Bulgarian and Byzantine empires and, three thousand years before, that between the Hittite and Egyptian empires – the two great superpowers of the age. Untold other such conflicts have given structure to the story which brought us here. Neither you nor I have even heard of most of them.

The really frightening political problems, such as the ones in Palestine or Kashmir, sometimes appear immutable. They're not. There are no eternal political problems. The phenomenon of humanity, and the emergent phenomenon of human civilisation, are dynamic things. All such problems – even the ones in Kashmir and Palestine – will eventually be disentangled. What is unknown is how much ruin that disentanglement will bring down.

If all the people in the world were to magically disappear it would take a few centuries for vegetation to envelop our cities; maybe ten thousand for the major artefacts of human civilisation to be undetectable to anyone without a metal detector and a machete; and (I was once informed by a geologist who'd read a paper on the subject) five million before the evidence of our passing constituted a thin, chemically anomalous layer beneath the Earth.

The future doesn't need us. It's entirely possible that our fossilised remnants will one day be picked over by alien archaeologists, musing on what was. But there's a wave right in front of us that's ready to be ridden and, if we don't screw it up, there's a very large carrot waiting for us.

In the meantime, if you're worried that human civilisation is too dependent on oil, or that political policymakers are prone to embarking on misguided foreign adventures in order to sate that dependency, allow me to suggest the purchase of a bicycle. You'd be surprised how far that can get you.

121: Buenos Aires Calling
21 April 2007

Buenos Aires, planet Earth's fourteenth-largest metropolitan area by population, has a gold-plated reputation as South America's premier party hotspot. On my arrival, on the morning of Friday, 13 April 2007, I drank coffee in one of the cafés in its gargantuan bus station while watching the local news. The main story was that Diego Maradona, one of the greatest footballers who has ever lived but now massively overweight, was being rushed to hospital after an apparent cocaine overdose.

I went for a downtown travellers' hostel. The backpacker scene here is fuelled by readily available high-quality red meat and red wine. It's a scene where people take siestas during the day and hit the town at midnight. After checking in I walked around town for a while, spent two hours in an internet café, joined a sports club, swam up and down its pool for an hour, ate a fat steak lunch, then went back to my hostel and to bed. I woke up at 11 p.m. and didn't sleep again for three days.

On Saturday evening I hit the clubs with Emma and Nicole, the two Sydney girls I've been in on-off contact with since we did the Inca Trail together in Peru and who happened to be swinging through town. We went to Pacha, the local cathedral to techno, and superstar DJ Timo Mass rocked the house.

On Sunday football fever gripped the city as the two titans of Argentina's Primera División, Boca Juniors and River Plate, met in their biannual clash – one of the most fiercely contested sports derbies in the world. It was a seriously massive deal. They drew 1-1.

On Monday I was introduced to the cultural institution that is tango, a highly evolved world of sophisticated protocol and bewildering social hierarchy where the women are glamorous, the men slick back their hair and mafia-style Don-like characters rule the roost.

On Tuesday morning at 3 a.m. I sat down, fuzzy-headed, at my hostel's internet connection to see an email from Maria del Pilar Rios. She's a friend of my friend Susannah Colbert, who visited me in Sydney after passing through Buenos Aires last year. The email invited me to dinner that very evening. I responded saying I'd be there, then went to get some rest.

On the night of the 17th a ferocious rainstorm crashed across town, spreading havoc in its wake, sending water spirals spinning across the streets and lacing the sky with lightning. The city looked like a chic version of *Blade Runner* from the inside of my cab, which crawled through rain-drenched avenues to the muffled sound of beeping horns. It took an hour to reach my dinner appointment.

Maria del Pilar Rios – Pilar to her friends – turns out to be a serious-minded type, who reads management books for fun and idolises Jack Welch, the legendary ex-CEO of General Electric. She lives in Palermo, a posh northern suburb, where every shop is designer and every restaurant swanky. Her apartment is an all-in-one kitchen and living room space, with patterned cushion covers, generously proportioned windows and modern art on the wall. Pilar herself is about five nine, with a conservative, elegant dress sense, long dark hair, vivid brown eyes and freckles.

We spent the evening engaged in a protracted and sprawling conversation which dwelt on how she'd looked after Susie when she broke her arm last year, the city of Mendoza (where Pilar once lived), her nephews (who live in the south) and my niece Polly. We ended up talking through the night and into the next morning.

On Wednesday afternoon I went back to the hostel, slept for six hours, gathered up my things, checked out, caught a cab back to Palermo, then, that evening, moved into Pilar's flat.

Two emotive bilateral issues mar Argentinian/UK relations:

1) Ownership of the Falkland Islands. The Falkland Islands (known as the Malvinas around here) are sheep-infested rocks in the south Atlantic (human population circa 3,000) claimed by both nations. In 1983 the two countries fought a war over them (they started it), which destroyed an Argentinian dictatorship and revived a British government. Personally, after a week here, I can't believe we were ever at war with such tasteful and entertaining people.

2) Diego Maradona's handball goal that put England out of the 1986 Mexico World Cup. I've now been informed that it was 'the best goal ever' and awarded a badge (by Pilar's friend Danny) with a photo of the crucial moment when Señor Diego clearly punches the ball into England's net.

We was robbed.

Days since leaving London: 694
Buenos Aires, population: 12.4 million
Diego Maradona
    International appearances: 91
    International goals: 34

I want to do to you what spring does to the cherry trees. – Pablo Neruda

122: Cloud Nine
29 April 2007

Leaving the world of nocturnal backpackers and frenetic dorms and moving into the apartment of a cosmopolitan *porteña* lady in a leafy Buenos Aires suburb turned out to be a decidedly positive development. As serendipity would have it, Pilar had resigned from her HR manager job the week before I arrived, so we've been spending all day every day together.

I normally sleep until about ten o'clock, at which point Pilar wakes me up after collecting warm croissants from the bakery across the street. We then drink fresh coffee with breakfast and discuss our plans for the day – invariably a whirl of afternoon tea, city tours and tango clubs.

Pilar has spruced up my wardrobe during shopping trips to Palermo boutiques. We've visited the city's immense annual book fair, been to the zoo (where it's all happening) and spent an afternoon wandering around the necropolis (city of the dead) at Recoleta. Argentina's great and good, including Eva Perón, are entombed there. We walked down its tree-lined avenues under the watchful gaze of stone angels, picking out the names of poets, admirals and racing car drivers from the weather-worn facades of sarcophagi.

Pilar's mother, Monica, with whom we've dined on a number of occasions, is a great joy. At our first meeting, at a sophisticated and funky coffee house, she leaned across the table, furrowed her brow, and asked me seriously: 'Would you like to drink beer or tea?' She was clearly my kind of woman.

Monica has loads of great stories. On one occasion the cops caught her driving too fast and issued a fine, so she went down to the station and turned on the tears to see what she could get away with. Ten years later she's still married to the chief of police. That tale came out over a lunch of succulent black pudding that melted out of its skin and was served with a big tasty sausage thing. The slab of freshly cooked cow that was the main course went down a treat too.

I took a two-day trip across the Río de la Plata to the Uruguayan town of Colonia del Sacramento. It's a fine colonial settlement of tile-and-stucco houses and winding cobblestone streets, founded by the Portuguese in the seventeenth century. In its Museo Municipal are the 40,000-year-old remains of a giant armadillo: the physical remnant of a recently vanished aspect of Earth's ecosphere.

Back at Pilar's flat, she and I have been hanging out watching her favourite TV programmes (*Dancing for a Dream*, where celebrities dance together, and *Nip/Tuck*, an American drama about plastic surgeons). My books and newspapers are cluttering up the place alongside her copies of the *Harvard Business Review* and half-empty bottles of Mendoza red. We take it in turns to make the tea.

Buenos Aires is amazing. The people are stylish, the boulevards are magnificent, the food is incredible and the buzz is hugely compelling. This is one of the most fantastic cities I have ever visited and the first place since leaving Europe where I could genuinely imagine living out my life.

But I've got a problem: I can't do that.

Exactly a year ago I set myself a task. Now I've come this far I have to finish what I've started and I can't do it in Buenos Aires. So, this afternoon, I'm leaving for Brazil.

Days since leaving London: 702

Aranda phrase of the day: 'altjiranga mitjina' meaning 'the timeless dimension of dreams'

Global Musings X
Third Millennium

It's not the world that's got so much worse
but the news coverage that's got so much better.
– G. K. Chesterton

Now I'm going to give you a bunch of numbers. They all concern what's been happening to humanity during recent history. Don't feel the need to absorb them all. My point is the trend – that, in every way which can be measured, human life is richer and more interesting than it has ever been before.

*****

Humans now live far longer than during any previous period of history. Archaeological studies demonstrate that, for most of history and prehistory, average human life spans were 20–30 years.

By 1900 life expectancy at birth for the average human had increased to 31 years. By 1950 it had increased to 46 years and by 2005 it had reached 67 years.

In 2005 the figures by region were:

Africa	52.8 years
Asia	69.0 years
Latin America and the Caribbean	73.3 years
Europe	74.6 years
Oceania (Australasia/the Pacific)	75.2 years
North America	78.5 years

At the beginning of the twenty-first century the average human life was well over 100 per cent longer than during our pre-industrial phase.

*****

From the dawn of mankind up until the very recent past, infant mortality rates (the proportion of people who die before their first birthday) were about 20 per cent. One in five people never experienced more than their first year of infancy.

By 1950 global infant mortality had dropped to 15.7 per cent. By

2003 it had dropped to 5.7 per cent. In that 1950 to 2003 period, improvements in infant mortality by region included:

China	19%	to 3.3%
India	18%	to 6.3%
Sub-Saharan Africa	17.7%	to 10.1%
The developing world overall	17.1%	to 6.2%

In 2003 the infant mortality rate in Sweden was 0.28 per cent – lower than historical levels by nearly two orders of magnitude. In the period during which this book was written infant mortality rates were far lower than at any other time since humans evolved.

*****

Famine has caused incalculable misery down the ages. However, in the past two centuries, our perpetual war with hunger has taken an unprecedented turn for the better. At the beginning of the twenty-first century agricultural productivity was higher than at any previous point in history. Food supplies were richer and more secure than they had ever been.

Between 1961 and 2002 the average daily calorie intake per person worldwide increased by 24 per cent, despite a huge increase in global population. Average increase in calorie intake by region over that 1961 to 2002 period included:

China	80%
Brazil	22%
India	17%
Sub-Saharan Africa	7%
The developing world overall	38%

Inflation-adjusted prices of food commodities declined by 75 per cent between 1950 and the beginning of the twenty-first century. Between 1950 and 1984 world cereal production increased by 250 per cent. Between 1971 and 2002 chronic undernourishment in the developing world decreased from 37 per cent to 17 per cent.

*****

The average human is now far better informed and knowledgeable about the world than ever before. From the invention of writing until the very recent past, only a tiny proportion of people could access the knowledge contained in the written word.

As recently as 1970, 46 per cent of the humans alive were illiterate. By the early twenty-first century that figure was 18 per cent. For the first time ever, well over three-quarters of the people on Earth can read. For 15- to 25-year-olds the literacy rate is approaching 90 per cent.

The number of years spent in education is steadily increasing in every region of the world. Globally, the percentage of the population of the relevant age enrolled in tertiary education increased from 6.8 per cent in 1965 to 25.6 per cent in 2001.

In addition, human knowledge has undergone a measureless increase in the past few centuries. Until quite recently, scientific and academic research was carried out by interested amateurs and a handful of genuine universities. At the beginning of the twenty-first century, a global network of dedicated institutions was systematically rolling back the frontiers of every field of knowledge.

*****

Birth rates are dropping everywhere. In 1970 the global fertility rate (children born per woman during her lifetime) was 4.47. By 2005 it had dropped to 2.55. Between 1970 and 2005 fertility rate drops by region were:

Europe	2.16 to 1.45
North America	2.01 to 2.00
Oceania	3.23 to 2.30
Asia	5.04 to 2.34
Latin America and the Caribbean	5.04 to 2.37
Africa	6.72 to 4.67

By 2005 only 14 countries in the world still had fertility rates above six children per woman. Apart from Afghanistan they were all in sub-Saharan Africa.

*****

Disease is an implicit challenge for complex multicellular life forms such as us. Humanity has been repeatedly ravaged by pandemics down the ages, which have spread untold sorrow in their wake. Until very recently, we had an extremely limited understanding of what disease was or how to deal with it.

Globally organised programmes now tackle every one of the major microbial killers. Smallpox, responsible for hundreds of millions of agonising deaths, became, in 1979, the first human infectious disease to be eradicated from nature. HIV only made the jump to humans during the second half of the twentieth century, yet within decades, not only was it well understood, but a worldwide response was under way to tackle it. In the early twenty-first century, when strains of avian and swine flu mutated to infect humans, a globally coordinated public health infrastructure immediately swung into action to contain them.

*****

Governments are becoming more dependent, accountable and rational. In 1900 no country in the world enjoyed universal adult suffrage, while one in eight enjoyed limited forms of democracy. In the first decade of the twenty-first century 44.1 per cent of the people alive lived in democracies and 18.6 per cent lived in limited democracies. In the quarter-century following 1974 (the year I was born) multiparty election systems were introduced in 113 countries.

*****

In the early twenty-first century, global homicide rates are almost certainly at their lowest levels since humans evolved. From New Guinea to Africa, 90 per cent of hunter-gatherer peoples go to war at least once a year. Around 25–30 per cent of adult males in hunter-gatherer societies die as a result of homicide. The total homicide rate in such societies is around 0.5 per cent of the population per year. That is considerably higher than the homicide rate during the notably bloody twentieth century and far higher (by a factor of more than 10) than the homicide rate in nearly every region of the world in the early twenty-first century.

Between World War II and the beginning of the twenty-first century the average number of battle deaths per year fell dramatically. The number of international wars peaked in the 1970s and fell afterwards. The total number of international and civil conflicts fell from more than 50 at the start of the 1990s to just over 30 in 2005. The number of civil wars rose until about 1990 and was falling when I wrote this book.

*****

Humanity still has an awful lot of big problems, but the early twenty-first-century world in which I undertook my adventure was the greatest golden age it has seen by a huge margin. Already we'd reached a point where an ordinary fellow with £20,000 and some attitude could go around the world for two years, pondering the collected wisdom of five thousand years of human thinking and written history. It's pretty amazing that this is true, and it's not true because of luck. It's true because of us.

There's no rule book for what is happening to the human race. There is no precedent for us to follow and no higher being is of a mind to open the clouds and explain to us how to organise this world – we're on our own, working it out from scratch. And, while the immediate objectives of this grand human adventure are arguably clear, the details of achieving them are extremely fiddly.

The health, educational, transportation and governmental systems which have so transformed and enriched the human experience over recent centuries could only have been worked out step by painful and untidy step. The business models, best practice, technical expertise and skill sets which underlie our ability to run a civilisation of such scope and complexity could only have been pieced together one generation at a time.

People who think that revolution is about men with political messages redirecting societies are kidding themselves. Real revolution is about a global community of interdependent humans working as a team and slowly getting better at it. That's the way the world changes. That's the miracle. It's a miracle heralded by everybody learning to read, everybody learning to talk to each other, the slow dismantling of the anachronistic power structures imposed upon us by prehistory, and the deconstruction, one by one, of our inherited preconceptions and prejudices.

It is a high-risk, pitfall-ridden path the human race is following, but there's no reason for the numbers at the top of this subchapter not to keep getting better. Just because we have one set of problems now doesn't mean that those are the problems we'll always have. There's no underlying reason why we cannot look forward to an era during which our traditional arch-enemies – famine, poverty, disease and war – are, for the first time, brought under control. The really interesting question – the one that nobody ever talks about – is what happens next?

History, of a certain human sort, may have a habit of repeating itself. But there is a rhythm to this story, this *thing* that we're all a part of that's of a grander scale than we humans usually think about. And that rhythm is not, in the profoundest sense, circular. It is linear.

* * * * *

The world you see around you is not defined by some grand struggle between America and Russia, India and China or radical Islam and modernity. Its fundamental patterns are not described by a clash of civilisations, a warming planet or a rebalancing from West to East.

Those things are just incidents. They are the twists and turns in a story of which economic crises, pandemics, wars, natural disasters, ideological disagreements and climate change are inevitable and implicit parts.

The human race, human civilisation and every aspect of the human world are the fine detail of a larger process – temporary phenomena thrown up by a 4.6-billion-year-old planet, with a 3-billion-year-old ecosphere, in which brain size is doubling every 34 million years.

Because we're so busy being jealous, scheming monkeys, we neglect to look down upon ourselves as a bunch of jealous, scheming monkeys having a collective experience – an experience that's extraordinary and unprecedented, a story that's lineal not cyclical, the groundwork not the endgame, a baby civilisation on an antique world.

Part 10

Pilgrim Unplugged

On the Road

I was on a high before I left London. I had a great job and a boss I respected. My relationship with my family was close and loving. I shared a big comfortable house with two dynamic young women, to which friends would habitually pop round. My support network was broad and solid and deep. At parties there was always someone to talk to. I even had enough money. Sorted?

Maybe, but having an easy life isn't necessarily the same as having an interesting one.

Fancy chasing off around the world in search of adventure and love? The moment you get on a bike and head to Istanbul, that comfort zone goes straight out of the window. After a week on the road, something in your subconscious grasps what has been given up and what is faced: five months, camped in fields, alone. That's when you hit your first bad patch.

After two weeks more you've found a rhythm, settled in and got used to your spartan new lifestyle. Then you begin to get really fit, which helps a lot, and find your singing voice.

Five months later you've had your heart broken, been hospitalised, been up, down, then up to the top of the world. During the days – a head burning with prose and numbers – you sing your way through rolling eastern European landscapes. At night you stretch out beneath autumn stars, pour out your thoughts into notebooks and giggle jokes to your bicycle, which has, by then, become your best friend. You've gone a bit mad, but you're bursting with physical and mental energy and right back in that comfort zone.

Then, one day, you're in Istanbul. In the space of two hours your life completely changes – alone in a hotel room, just another stranger in a strange land. You go to the bar, order a hot meal and try to make some friends. It's weird. Later that week you come across one of the most interesting people you've ever met. His name is Tarik. He gets you drunk and talks you into scaling the walls of the Blue Mosque. Off you go again.

Six weeks later and 'the city of the world's desire' has been the backdrop to a defining chapter in your life. Several of your favourite people have crossed Europe to visit you and you're off to the tropics to meet a girl on a beach. Too good to be true? Ain't it just.

Six weeks after that you're alone, abandoned, betrayed and being haunted by a physical deformity you thought long-conquered. The money you've spent years stashing away is slipping uncontrollably through your fingers and your grand plan is in tatters. That support network is 20,000 kilometres away, you're a legal alien in a world where everyone's got their own problems, it's February and life's a bitch.

But there's a light on the horizon – a gold-plated chance to win your heart's desire, in India. The chance comes but it all goes awry, leaving you on the wrong side of the world, with an empty feeling in the pit of your stomach and the last of your scheme unravelled. So then, stranger, what are you going to do?

You hold your nerve and *work* while cold months of gritted teeth go by. Gradually things start falling into place. By August you're living with your best friend and meeting one terrific person after another. During the days you manage events for high-powered lawyers in a downtown Sydney skyscraper. In the evenings you work the bar for drag queens at a riotous all-night club. You've got a fascinating job and a mad life and spring is coming. Revelation space, baby. Just when things can't get any better you meet a hard-bodied woman with a quick mind and a wicked edge. She moves like a cat and writes sweltering verse about persuasion, *azul* moons and the colour of the sky. Jackpot.

Time's up.

Next thing you know you're on the other side of the Pacific being interviewed by an Ecuadorian man and his Dutch girlfriend. They want to know if you're a suitable tenant for an apartment they've got to rent. The apartment has a desk, a balcony and unreal views of the Andes. Welcome to your new world. During the days you take Spanish classes. In the evenings you gaze over those mountains and seize a once-in-a-lifetime opportunity to capture a way of thinking about the world, and build a tool with which to conserve it. Within a couple of months the Ecuadorian man and his girlfriend are like your brother and sister. Then *that* phase ends and your life changes again.

Two weeks later you're on a beach with the backpacking fraternity. They're all doing their expeditions and talking about the same conventional things, but your head's in this whole other place and you can't remember how to relate to these people ...

That's what those two years felt like – stripping off one comfort zone after another and plunging into the next, entirely different, world. Each time you have to sacrifice what you've built up. Each time you initially struggle to cope. It's rewarding and character-building, but psychologically it's extremely disorienting.

And yet it was during those final months that it all clicked into place. Rocking into one South American city after another, a kaleidoscope of exotica, a whirl of dreamlike experiences, a bit like being in a book; and it was pouring out of me, every evening, mind ablaze.

*****

Pilar and I had a row. That was the real reason I left Buenos Aires when I did. It was a proper Latin-style row. She raised her voice and pointed at me accusingly. I paced up and down her apartment in righteous indignation, then stormed off to brood in a chic Palermo coffee shop.

I don't remember how the row started, or what it was ostensibly about. What it was really about was that Pilar wanted a man who wouldn't just get inside her, but who would get inside her head and stay there. Yet, despite all the mornings curled together in a half doze and the blissful evenings staring at each other across the table, my hand on her thigh, the two of us never made it that far.

When you're the green-eyed explorer from overseas, people project onto you what they want you to be. They rarely dig down and explore what's going on inside. Meanwhile, down there, my mind was bent to the creation of a tool. I was just at the beginning of understanding how much work that process of creation would involve.

The human race can start being more realistic about its own story. Someone just needs to say it – to describe the human adventure from first principles, and assess it in a way that stands in contrast to assumption-loaded and pessimistic notions of how the world *should* look. I could think of no way of doing that other than to write it down in a book. So why not a travel book? That would be my vehicle for setting out a world view worthy of this dawning Age of Aquarius.

Planet Earth is bigger than a lifetime's exploration could fleetingly touch. The trick, therefore, on a trip like mine, is to immerse oneself in the places to which fate bears you, then extrapolate from those parts of the jigsaw. Where precisely one goes is not the point. The real adventure is the one that takes place inside your head.

Global Musings XI
The Age of Aquarius

There is a cosmological imperative known as the anthropic principle. It states that any theory explaining the universe must allow for the existence of humans, because if the laws of physics didn't allow you to exist you wouldn't be reading this book.

That's clearly true.

What is also clearly true is that the universe must work in such a way that it is possible, in principle, for a species of hyper-intelligent tool-using omnivores to construct a world-spanning technological civilisation, because that's what's happened.

However, it does not necessarily follow that, just because a species of hyper-intelligent tool-using omnivores can exist in the first place, and just because such a species can go on to construct a pan-planetary civilisation, such a venture should – even in principle – be either open-ended or sustainable.

It's possible, for example, to envisage a scenario where a species of hyper-intelligent omnivores appeared on a planet (like we have), developed agriculture and thence civilisation (like we did) and underwent sufficient steps to conceive of, print and distribute books (like the one you're reading), only to later discover that their adventure was limited in some way.

The most arresting thing about the situation in which *we* find ourselves is that it appears, at least in principle, to be sustainable, unlimited and completely open-ended.

*****

The societies that we twenty-first-century humans inhabit are a phase on a continuum that snakes back into the mists of history and prehistory. Like any story, it has chapters.

From where we're standing we can see three of those chapters. During the first, the human world consisted of hunting, gathering and living off nature's rhythms. As a way of life it was stable and profoundly in harmony with the rest of the ecosphere. At the time it must have seemed normal, which I suppose it was.

Then there was a transition. Agriculture was invented and human society was transformed.

That transition inaugurated a second chapter from around 10,000

BCE, which was coming to an end when this book was written. That second chapter contained most of the unpleasant aspects of the first one, hardly any of the fun bits and a range of disagreeable new features. Life was hard. Humans were tied to the land. Our darkest urges to exploit and dominate were given occasion to express themselves. At the time it probably seemed normal. It wasn't.

Now, we're at the beginning of a third chapter. Humanity is entering a phase of bourgeois values, fabulous technology and constant flux. Human society is changing, but we have no idea what into, and it's definitely not normal.

This new chapter has presented us with a challenge: can we find a way to get billions of humans, spread across six continents with diverging world views, to live fulfilled, meaningful lives together in peace and harmony without destroying the planet?

That was always going to be tricky.

*****

We should stop always judging the state of humanity against a hypothetical standard which only exists in our heads. Humans are not peaceful star fairies. We're a species of impetuous and hormonal primate that has crawled from the mud and pandemonium of Earth's ecosystems to construct, without any guidance, a world-spanning civilisation.

Our evolutionary heritage has left us with a variety of psychological idiosyncrasies which are deeply unhelpful when one is attempting to undertake such a venture. Civilisation is forcing us to deal with unprecedented and extremely complicated tasks (such as coordinating economies and managing planetary climates) which are completely alien to minds evolved to think about food, status and sex. The solutions are having to be worked out, and refined, generation by generation and step by painful step. The industries, cultural traditions and political institutions we've developed to deal with them were not meticulously planned or carefully designed. They were cobbled together on the fly. Their quirks mirror our own.

The saga that brought us here was messy. We're carrying a lot of historical baggage. People believe, and do, really weird things. We've got some strange institutions and a lot of very serious problems. But, given how we reached this point, to wish things were different is the same as wishing you lived in a different sort of universe. The remarkable thing isn't that we're beginning to get quite good at running civilisation, but that we're managing to do it at all.

And now something new has started to happen: we're beginning to understand our own context.

Our ancestors a millennium ago didn't realise that they were carbon-based life forms who'd been generated by a billion-year process of evolution in parallel with the rest of the biosphere. When they complained about the kings who lorded it over them, they didn't grasp the mechanics of the evolutionary psychology which had hammered those behavioural patterns into DNA inside every cell of those kings' bodies. When famine tore through their societies they didn't perceive the forces of demography which were aligned to guarantee such catastrophe, nor that the pox which struck them down was the consequence of their forefathers' enslavement of cattle. When the conquistadors swept away the Incas with steel and microbes, neither side understood the great tapestry of historical forces which had shepherded them to that point.

Our ancestors were not in a position to understand the path they were following or, in most cases, even that they *were* following a path. But we are. Unlike them, we can be realistic about who we are, how we came to be here and what's happening to us now.

If one assesses humanity's situation in those terms, things really aren't so bad.

*****

Most of the major challenges our species faces are unavoidable parts of the gig when creating a pan-planetary civilisation from scratch. How exactly we'll meet those challenges are questions with which we now wrestle, but the underlying mechanics of how the human race, this planet and this universe work means that there's every reason to believe it can be done.

That, in and of itself, is kind of strange. Humans didn't evolve to run sustainable civilisations, so there's no particular reason to suppose we should be able to. Looking through the fossil record reveals no trace of earlier beings treading this path. Our situation appears to be unique.

No matter how much we love to complain about our glass being half empty, it's not like we have any alternative to being carbon-based life forms in this universe. Given that, the underlying parameters (defining how tough it's going to be to construct a harmonious civilisation which survives into the distant future) could have been far worse.

For example, we tend to see our fossil fuels situation in terms of the substantial problems it's causing us. Yet overall it was rather handy that, just when we needed an energy boost in the eighteenth century, we could make use of all that coal and oil which had been conveniently lying around in the Earth's crust (for when a bunch of civilisation-building omnivores needed something to power their steam and internal combustion engines). Despite their grubby politics and world-warming side effects, those fossils turbocharged civilisation and allowed us to power up the industrial base needed to cultivate the next generation of energy technologies. Horse-drawn ploughs and wood stoves would not have got us as far and as fast as tractors and coal-fired power stations (and they would have seen the end of a lot more trees).

Ultimately, we're lucky to live on a planet with biological and geological systems which lay down a store of easily accessible energy for when the relevant level of technological development was achieved. Global warming is the dark lining on a cloud which has been strikingly silver for the human race.

Then there's our racial problems. We think of ourselves as having big issues with race and racism. Yet, regardless of how much fuss is made over skin colour, the bottom line is that the actual racial differences between humans – genetically speaking – are trivial. But that's only because of several accidents of history. As recently as 30,000 years ago the world was full of genuinely different hominid species. Had the geographic quirks of Earth been slightly different we might – right now – live in a truly multiracial world. That would introduce moral complexities far more confounding than the ones we actually face. As it is, there's no underlying reason we cannot move forward as a single, self-contained and unified species.

Several of the psychological idiosyncrasies bestowed on us by evolution are also beginning to look rather convenient. For example, our craving for status, which has led to so much gratuitous bauble collecting, looks like it will ultimately save us. It's driving the open-ended economic growth which is, in turn, driving our accelerating technological progress, which is the only thing that's going to transform this currently non-sustainable civilisation into a sustainable one. The ants and termites might not have had the destructive wars we've had, but will they ever be competitive enough to design hydrogen fuel cells?

Then there's this paradoxical aspect of human psychology whereby (contrary to what one might expect) as societies grow richer, people have fewer children. It's already driven a demographic transition in the large majority of Earth's human populations. Yet it's possible to imagine a scenario (if humans were, for example, psychologically more akin to rabbits) where we could never learn to live without either population booms and busts, or draconian population controls. Either of those scenarios would make our potential futures look a great deal less fun than they actually look.

There's also the fact that we humans are, to put it bluntly, remarkably clever. It's presumably plausible that a species could think up farming and then the internal combustion engine, without ever having both the mental oomph for quantum mechanics and the organisational aptitude to give some of its members the head space for the required contemplation.

Now we understand more about genetics, we understand that our genetically (more or less) identical ancestors could *in theory* have been doing all the crazy stuff we do for much of the past hundred millennia. The reason the guys who painted the Lascaux Caves weren't designing space shuttles was not due to their intellectual limitations, but because there were no universities to teach them astronautics. The burning question, therefore, is what marvels lie before us that *we* just haven't got round to yet?

Our ancestors lived through a baptism of bedlam and chaos. Yet the mental peculiarities which made them do so many dreadful and foolish things – and dragged them through ages of exploitation, poverty and war – *ultimately* manufactured a situation conducive to the running of a long-term technical civilisation on a planet.

How much of that was due to luck and how much due to some sort of inevitable evolutionary conditioning that takes place when hyper-intelligent species evolve on planets, we're not yet in a position to say. But I'll tell you what I think. I think Shakespeare had it right.

Noble in reason, infinite in faculties, express and admirable in form, in action like an angel and in apprehension like a god.

Let's face it, we're amazing.

*****

Now we can see human civilisation in context, rather a lot about the general shape of its story over the past 12,000 years looks kind of inevitable.

Once we'd stumbled into agriculture, the (relatively) limited nature of the human experience during the subsequent epoch was probably more or less guaranteed by the egocentricity of humans and the realities of population growth, agricultural productivity and technological progress.

Those 12,000 years were a really difficult period to be a human. Very few people got to be kings or philosophers. For the vast majority it was the unforgiving grind of subsistence agriculture. One would never have consciously chosen such a life over the freedom of hunting and gathering which our prehistoric ancestors once enjoyed. It was a path we stumbled upon, then got trapped in. It's only with the amount of hindsight now available that it looks like an audacious and exciting move for us to have made as a species.

But the guys who slogged through those toil-filled ages (to whom I, for one, am eternally grateful) didn't know that it was going to lead to *this*: this modern world where most of us get to live for 70 years, nearly all of us can read, we've got computers and books and flying machines and, instead of just struggling to survive, we can travel across our home world and ponder 5,000 years of collected human wisdom.

In addition, as trial and error teaches us how one does, in fact, organise billions of people on a planet, we're starting to glimpse what the broad shape of a long-term civilisation will look like. There's good reason to suppose that this coming millennium will be considerably more inviting than the last one.

Law and order work better than anarchy. When people are free to follow their interests, society is more vigorous, dynamic and interesting. Governments are more effective when they're afraid of the people, rather than the other way around. Once one person (or a small clique of people) is stopped from stealing the whole cake, the cake gets larger, and a good deal tastier.

No matter how long self-selected cliques in certain parts of the world continue to kid themselves to the contrary, no human, or small clique of humans, is ever going to be mentally equipped to direct the affairs of a country. Because that's true there is only ever going to be one practical system available for governing human civilisation over the long term, and it's not dictatorship.

The mechanics of our global adolescence have also played out so as to produce this intriguing game-changing shift in the parameters constraining what is, and is not, a feasible system for organising civilisation.

Billions of monkeys don't take over a planet unless they're fighters.

Original parameter:
No fighting instinct = no planet to play with

But that feature of the human psyche now makes the status quo unstable. The make-or-break tasks we now face (such as planetary climate management and not blowing ourselves up) require, as a prerequisite, cooperative behaviour across the whole species for the foreseeable future.

New parameter:
Keep fighting = no planet to play with

There is no rule book which says that civilisation-building species reach a point where they face a choice between cooperation and suicide. There's no rule which says that systems of government which are equitable and morally realised are more practical than ones which are not. Yet, as it happens, those things do appear to be true.

But the most mystifying and glorious thing of all about this path which humanity has stumbled onto is that – if we will it so – there need never be an end to it.

*****

The laws governing how reality works are too complicated for humans to figure out by casual observation. But, once we'd realised that they could be figured out, we were mentally more than up to the job.

What's more, those laws are arranged in such a way that the conceptually easy bits (such as Newtonian mechanics) prepare you for the far-out abstract stuff (like Einsteinian relativity). If we'd had to work out the general theory of relativity as our first mental jump there's absolutely no way we'd ever have made it. But several easier jumps came first and, once we started making them, we got onto a roll.

We take technological and scientific progress so much for granted nowadays that it's easy to forget how marvellous it is that the universe *allows* such progress. We might have lived in a cosmos that was limited or limiting, but we don't. This universe not only allows monkeys to exist, but it works in such a way that, once they start talking, cooperating and working things out, their world spirals upwards and ever greater dimensions of wonder and experience open up.

Our preconceptions about where this path might be leading are largely defined by four generations of science-fiction writers. Their imaginative achievements blind us to how profoundly and comprehensively enigmatic the future is.

To set humanity's situation in fundamental terms: the laws of nature, the geographical realities of planet Earth and the psychology of humankind have conspired to generate a state of affairs which is open-ended, utterly mysterious, unlimited and becoming more interesting with every passing century. Even in my wildest imaginations I can think of absolutely nothing more beautiful, more sublime and more perfect than that.

123: Awesome Big Stuff
4 May 2007

Until the Three Gorges Dam in China powers up, the world's largest operational hydroelectric power station remains the Itaipu Dam on the Paraná River on the border between Paraguay and Brazil. As titanic works of engineering go, it's quite something.

I reached the site from Paraguay, via the dilapidated smugglers' haven of Ciudad del Este ('City of the East'): it was full of shifty-looking human mules hauling contraband to some of South America's biggest and blackest markets. Rarely have I found a more wretched hive of scum and villainy. I was cautious there.

I took a bus from Ciudad del Este to the dam. As I approached, a forest of pylons – pumping electricity across the horizons – clustered into the distance. The dam's superstructure is three kilometres long, soars to the height of a 65-storey building and contains 18 gargantuan turbines, the first of which went on line in 1984. By 2000 the power station was generating 93.4 billion kilowatts of energy every hour, providing 95 per cent of Paraguay's domestic requirements and 20 per cent of Brazil's. That's enough electricity for 30 million people and equivalent to a *lot* of coal-fired power stations.

It's hard not to be impressed by a facility which powers 1.2 countries, but up close and personal it sure ain't pretty. I went past unreal pipes and towering concrete walls and, inside, visited a 100-metre-high, kilometre-long, tungsten-lit generating hall, scattered with giant bits of engineering hardware. It was utterly science fiction.

Such a gargantuan undertaking does not come without considerable cost. The construction bill was a whopping US$25 billion (much of it illegitimate: Paraguay has eye-watering corruption issues) and, when the 1,350-square-kilometre, 220-metre-deep reservoir behind the dam was filled in 1982, it drowned one of South America's most famous spectacles: the great waterfalls of Sete Quedas.

All was not lost, however, as, just down the road on the border between Argentina and Brazil, the Foz do Iguaçu ('Iguazu Falls') remains one of planet Earth's most impressive natural wonders.

We approached by boat on May Day. Black vultures flew spirals above the solid green walls of subtropical forest on either side of the river. As the cascades appeared, like something out of a souped-up Tarzan movie, I fell into one of the uncontrollable laughing/shouting fits I suffer from when something particularly exciting happens.

Our vessel gunned right into the mass of boiling vapour at the falls' base and, in the seconds it took for the roar to overtake our boat and its passengers to become comprehensively soaked, an arc of multicoloured light appeared above us like an ancient biblical sign. Stupendous.

There are 275 separate waterfalls at Iguazu. I stayed until evening fell, clambering around the surrounding cliffs and exploring numerous sun-lit clearings, each with its own pristinely set cascade. Little racoon-type creatures bimbled about attempting to steal people's food. Lemon-green butterflies would land on me and feel about with their tongues, trying to decide if I was tasty.

The centrepiece is La Garganta del Diablo ('The Devil's Throat'): a 700-metre-long half circle, where the flow drops 80 metres into a roaring steam-filled pit from which multiple rainbows stretch their way into the sky. It had been raining upstream. Twelve thousand litres of fluid were passing over the edge every second. From the white chaos below, genies would periodically spring, raising themselves into the air and whipping sheets of vaporised liquid across the faces of we mere humans watching, like insects, from above.

Days since leaving London: 707
Itaipu Dam statistics
    Eiffel Towers you could build with its steel: 380
    Petroleum you'd have to burn daily to reproduce its generating capacity: 434,000 barrels
    Operational life expectancy: 300 years

124: The Sun Chasers
11 May 2007

On reaching Brazil I had one month left of this adventure. I therefore faced a choice. Either I could take a 15-hour bus to the interior to visit the Pantanal – the vast wetlands of southern Brazil known as the best wildlife-spotting region of the New World. Or I could say 'to hell with it' and go to the beach.

That decision became even more of a no-brainer when I met up with Annie and Jamie, the travelling couple I first encountered in Bolivia back in March (30 months on the road and four continents so far). At the time, I'd been so struck by their big-hearted vivacity that I'd said I would love to share some of my journey with them (which isn't the sort of thing I say to just anyone). We've stayed in email contact and our paths re-crossed in Brazil.

The day after visiting the Foz do Iguaçu I met them at their hotel in the town next to (and named after) the great waterfalls. For that whole afternoon, and the one which followed, we hung out by their pool, drank beer and swapped bits of life story.

Annie, a Geordie born and bred, is a small, neat fireball of enthusiasm with something of Kylie Minogue about her. She says 'just a bit of fun' a lot and has been keeping me up late every night against my better judgement. She took great relish in relating the story of how the bank she used to work for sent her on a weekend seminar to help imminent retirees cope with the lifestyle change. Everyone else sat around and worried about the future. Annie already had a three-year, around-the-world adventure with her boyfriend prepared for launch.

Jamie grew up in the Gorbals, a hard-man district of Glasgow. He told blood-and-alcohol-filled stories of growing up in the city's gangster end in the 1950s, then about how he'd moved to the island of Jersey as a young man and never looked back. He spent three decades running a building company on the island while seeing his children ensconced as lawyers and bank managers. He talked of them, their partners, his ex-wife and his beloved Rangers Football Club.

With so many life duties complete, now that he's jet-setting the world with Annie, Jamie doesn't feel the need to hold back. He has a habit of exposing his bottom in public for the amusement of anyone present and tells stories with anecdotes such as (cue: thick Glaswegian accent) '… and then ah took all me cloths orf and started roonin aboot'.

On the evening following our second day by the pool, the three of us packed up, checked out, got a taxi to the station, caught a bus to the coast, then began chasing the sun. For the past week we've formed a three-person travelling circus which has been meandering its way north-east along the Atlantic coast.

Our first destination was the poetically named coastal city of Florianópolis. From there it was a short hop to the island of Santa Catarina (on which the city half-stands), where we rented a two-bedroom apartment and spent the rest of the day drinking cocktails on the beach.

The next morning brought rain clouds so we cut our losses, packed up our stuff and took an overnight coach to São Paulo. At 8 a.m. on the 8th we found ourselves at the bus station of South America's biggest city, then went straight onto another coach which took us further along Brazil's startlingly well-developed coastline. From the windows of our vehicle we saw blue lagoons, offshore tropical islands and dense forests, all the way to the town of Darante. From there we took a four-by-four to Trindade, a fishing village with six beaches and numerous waterfalls, where we stayed in a cosy dark-wood inn.

When we arrived in Trindade it was all mangoes and sunshine so we chilled out on the sand, frolicked in the surf and dived into the waves. Then, that evening, we ate *badejo* (sea bass), sweet potatoes and palm hearts while getting drunk on Skol beer.

Jamie (I've learned) is the king of reconnaissance: zooming off the moment we arrive somewhere new and scoping out each town within hours. Annie is world champion at communicating with people without sharing a common language (employing a positive engagement strategy, lots of hand-waving and a thoroughly winning smile). It's a joy, after all this time on my own, to let my hair down with two such relaxed and sparkling fellow travellers (although, at one point, Jamie foolishly tried to help me pack my bag. I shooed him away).

On the morning of the 9th the clouds had caught us again and it rained all day, so we put on cagoules and walked up and down the shore as mist fell off the thickly wooded line of hills running parallel to the coast. Then we sat around a table in a sheltered tea house while rain battered the roof and the proprietor taught us that 'árvore de palma' in Portuguese means 'palm tree'.

Yesterday morning, with a second day of rain kicking in at Trindade and one eye on the internet meteorological maps, the three of us headed north once again. At midday we reached the town of Angra dos Ries (about 150 klicks south-west of Rio), which looks out upon the Bay of Ilha Grande and its 365 islands. From Angra dos Ries, we took a 90-minute slow boat across the bay, to Ilha Grande itself – an Arcadian paradise of sand, sea and jungle that sits right on the Tropic of Capricorn.

Annie and Jamie – ever the sun worshippers – insisted we sit on the bow of the chugging wooden vessel and catch some rays. As we made-way into the archipelago under perfect blue skies, grey air coalesced in the distance and a rainbow snaked down to land on one of the distant islets, leading to all-round whooping, digital cameras and a belly laugh from me.

The universe giving away something about itself. A magic behind its madness. A logic behind its primordial rage.

From nowhere, a downpour enveloped us. The digital cameras were hidden away and everyone ran to the back of the boat to pull out cagoules once more. Then, at four o'clock yesterday afternoon, we disembarked at the island.

And that, unexpectedly, brought a sense of completion.

This is it. I've reached my destination.

Days since leaving London: 714

Arabic word of the day: 'al-alamin' meaning 'all the worlds of mankind, the angels, animals, plants, this world, the next and so forth'

Global Musings XII
Spiritual
Architecture

This feeling of being alive – of experiencing reality through one's subjective sense of self – is a mesmerising sensation. During its most complete and beautiful moments it can be overwhelming in its intensity. What's more, this universe in which it takes place is almost *suspiciously* spectacular: global culture in its labyrinthine intricacy; the circle of life spinning down the generations; the great cosmic expansion of which it's all a part.

All in all, this whole 'being alive' business raises some pretty major questions and begs for a focus, an explanation or an interpretation as to what, exactly, is going on here.

The human psyche needs a framework through which to deliberate upon those most boundless of matters and to think about its individual place within the grandest scheme of things. I believe that the most complete way of understanding the phenomenon of religion is as the conceptual architecture which has grown up in human societies in order to provide that framework.

*****

The particular religious architecture an individual adopts is like a window. It doesn't necessarily define their relationship with infinity, but rather acts as the lens through which they relate to it. The window a person uses generally reflects their cultural background – people born in Thailand tend to be Buddhists, those in Turkey, Muslims. Anyone who is even a little bit worldly understands that it is the way a religion is practised (rather than the religion itself) which is important. Every creed contains both ethical, morally realised people and embittered destructive ones.

If religion didn't exist there would definitely be a need to invent it. It's with good reason that it's been a ubiquitous feature of human societies. As the framework through which one relates oneself to the rest of the universe, religion is central to people's sense of individual and group identity and fulfils a range of critical functions.

For example, it gives structure to the shared spiritual experiences which bind us together. It's hard to think of a more beautiful way of uniting people from across the world, and giving expression to the truth that they're part of something larger than themselves, than the

Muslim Hajj. I, for one, am all in favour of pilgrimages. Religion also provides the language and ceremony to mark life's defining moments: the great watersheds of birth, marriage and death – occasions when families and loved ones come together and think about what they're part of.

At its best, religion provides a calming and unifying force within human communities and acts as the vehicle for dispensing moral wisdom. Communities need an organised way of reminding their members about the difference between right and wrong and that thou shalt not kill. Getting everyone together to listen to a lecture about morality (one of the things going to church is about) has got to be a healthy custom. The principles of compassion, selflessness, forgiveness and 'do unto others' expounded in the teachings (though not always throughout the founding texts) of the world's great religious traditions profoundly encapsulate how to live a noble, self-actualised and virtuous life in this crazy world of ours.

It is true that religion is often hijacked as a vehicle for oppression, exploitation and, at its worst, all that war and genocide. But rather than having a specifically religious basis, I'm of the view that the evils perpetrated in its name are more fundamentally part of wider patterns of human-on-human violence and coercion. Humans are naturally predisposed to crave high status, manipulate institutions to their advantage and generally screw each other, and they commandeer whichever tools are available in order to accomplish those ends. 'Believe in [my] God or go to hell' is, at its heart, a crude attempt to provide divine justification for telling other people what to do.

*****

Humanity, human culture and the human condition are all intrinsically dynamic. As a result our religious systems are also dynamic – continually evolving along with the communities for which they act as a focus. The religious systems in use during any particular period of history grew out of, and drew inspiration from, those which came before. The characteristics of existing religious systems therefore reflect humanity's history, and spiritual experiences, thus far.

With the Abrahamic family of religions those interrelationships are unambiguous. Islam self-consciously regards itself as part of a tradition that includes Judaism and Christianity. Jesus (whatever else he may have been) was definitely Jewish, while Judaism grew out of even earlier (and now largely extinct) Egyptian and Mesopotamian religious systems. Whether one believes that any of this constitutes progress probably depends on where one was born and how religious one's parents were, but it's definitely evolution.

The religious systems we know today are more properly the contemporary expression of a constantly changing inheritance of spiritual thinking stretching right back into prehistory. One cannot know for sure how long the human race has pondered such matters, but presumably back to well before the invention of agriculture, and very probably for at least as long as humans have been behaviourally modern (60,000 years plus).

There is absolutely no reason to expect that process of religious evolution to stop now.

*****

This book is written from a point of view which implicitly accepts the validity of science as a method for understanding the cosmos. Science has become associated with lots of emotionally charged issues. Curiously, for something now so central to the human adventure, there is a popular perception of a conflict between science and spirituality, and confusion about what the scientific endeavour actually is.

This universe is not directly understandable. Lots of things about it don't make sense and the patterns that drive it cannot be deduced from casual observation. The scientific endeavour is the human race making an organised, disciplined and systematic attempt to tackle that situation.

There is not, and never has been, a conflict between science and spirituality. That conflict only exists in the minds of people who don't understand what the scientific process is or don't like some of the things which are turning out to be true. Where there *is* sometimes conflict is between the pursuit of knowledge and making things up, then claiming that they're true – a practice with a long and illustrious tradition. The essentials of the scientific method are the same as how any human (or, for that matter, anything else that learns) learns.

Brian is five. Brian has plastic toy cars and metal toy cars. Experience has taught Brian that plastic toy cars are better for hitting his big sister than his fist (initial hypothesis). One day Brian uses a metal toy car to hit his big sister (experiment). Brian's test leads him to conclude that metal toy cars are better bashing tools than plastic ones (refined hypothesis). Brian then finds his bold enquiry into knowledge provokes his big sister into beating him up (eureka moment). This opens up a new field of enquiry (what he can get away with when hitting his big sister).

The humans in white coats who roll back the frontiers of knowledge are more sophisticated in their deductive techniques than Brian and, unlike him, they're subject to peer review. But it's basically the same process. Individual scientists may be cantankerous, egotistical and annoying, but don't worry about that. Think of them as tools.

It is true that light being both a wave and a particle is only a theory. It is also true that evolution by natural selection is only a theory. But they are theories in the same way that believing the world will still be there when I open my front door is 'only a theory'. I don't *know* that the world will still be there, because I can't see into the future. I just have a mountain of experimental data consistent with that being true. Nevertheless, it's only a theory.

The fact that we've embarked on this journey of understanding is probably the most magnificent thing which has ever happened. Without it the human adventure would always have remained limited. It is the scientific endeavour which makes it unlimited. Humanity is on a quest to perceive the truth of things and investigate what it doesn't understand. The universe, expressing itself through life, is embarking upon a grand journey of systematic introspection.

*****

That journey of introspection has created a paradox in human society which remains unresolved, and a disconnect in our spiritual architecture.

The religious systems we've been using in recent millennia (particularly the Abrahamic family) made certain assertions about the existential nature of reality. They claimed, for example, that it was an elaborate prelude to an endless garden party and that an omnipotent being with humanlike characteristics was directing the affairs of the cosmos and interfering in it through miracles. With 2,000 years of hindsight, some of those claims look naive.

The undermining of those claims has, in part, undermined those religions' intellectual bases as spiritual architectures. Yet the role of religion was never really to teach the nitty-gritty of cosmology. Its fundamental roles were to provide a lens through which to think about our relationship with infinity, to provide structure to our shared spiritual experiences and to act as a vehicle for maintaining and disseminating moral wisdom. Those are roles in which it cannot easily be replaced.

Yet religion's cosmological claims (particularly with respect to ways of thinking about God) were intimately bound up with their broader role as frameworks for thinking about our relationship with infinity. In outgrowing those religious systems we have lost something. Communities and individuals *do* draw strength from religious conviction. Traditional ideas of God and faith *do* bind people together. As frameworks for understanding, at an emotional level, those systems worked.

To put it incredibly crudely, people find the idea of an all-powerful and infinite 'God' – who has a sublime master plan for creation, loves them and will send them to heaven if they're good – comforting, and the alternative sterile. So now we have this strange (sometimes obsessional) conflict. On the one hand, you have those who take a theist position (i.e. God exists), which to some might seem intellectually incoherent. On the other hand, you have those who take an atheist position, or some derivation thereof (i.e. God doesn't exist), which to others might feel emotionally unsatisfying.

This situation is ironic on a cosmic scale. What is turning out to be true is far more beautiful and satisfying than what had previously been imagined. It wouldn't really be comforting to learn that this was all a machine to choose the attendees at a garden party. What appears actually to be happening is far more interesting – and comprehensively more awesome – even if we humans aren't quite so central to it.

This paradox needs to resolve itself. The human race is on a path which appears to be unlimited and that will take us to the stars. We need a framework for thinking about our place in the grand scheme of things which is both intellectually *and* emotionally satisfying. We need to reconcile our spiritual architectures into ones that make sense of, rather than conflict with, our unfolding understanding of the truth and yet still perform the traditional functions of religious systems.

It's one of the great challenges humanity faces. It's right up there with our environmental problems, but may well take longer to resolve.

Like so many of these big tests, this one is probably intrinsic to the process when a bunch of imaginative hyper-intelligent omnivores set up a pan-planetary civilisation. When one finds oneself in a universe this spectacular, one is bound to wonder what's going on and how one fits into it. It's not just an obvious question, it's an inevitable question. Once we turned our incredible minds to it, frameworks for understanding evolved. Those frameworks included cosmological ideas which (humans being humans) were then proclaimed the infallible product of divine wisdom. When we later set about investigating what was *really* going on, some of those presumptions inevitably turned out to be incorrect. The universe was never going to be in perfect harmony with human conceits.

Contemporary debates regarding whether or not 'God exists' are really this dichotomy playing itself out – the fleeting expression of a transition taking place in the way we think about our relationship with infinity.

It's very difficult at this point in history to imagine what a resolution to this paradox is going to look like. It's hard to envisage how our established spiritual architectures – such as those defined by God and faith – will evolve to embrace the majestic narrative which we are slowly starting to comprehend. No doubt it will be a matter of evolution rather than revelation. No doubt it will be some time before a solution takes shape. No doubt that solution will emerge, fragment by fragment, from the ghost in the machine of our collective species-wide psyche.

* * * * *

Anybody who's tried to fully express themselves with respect to this topic recognises that we don't have the linguistic tools to adequately articulate ourselves regarding the most infinite matters. Human language isn't up to the job. That's why religious communication makes so much use of parable and metaphor. As the Arab sage and polymath Ibn Khaldun taught: religion serves those who need symbols to grasp the truths revealed by philosophers.

On the magic island of Ilha Grande, on the Tropic of Capricorn, where I was to stay for 11 days, I lived in a lodge high up the mountain. From that mountain one could, if one had a mind to, stand under the stars, surrounded by the nocturnal mumble of the jungle, see Brazil stretching away into the west, the moonlight reflecting off the unspeakably scenic waters of the South Atlantic, look up to see the enveloping garland of the Milky Way and think hard about what, exactly, it is that one is a part of.

While standing there I *did* feel a sense of transcendent ecstasy and a oneness with the rest of creation. One can deconstruct that feeling down to my subjective experience of a whirlwind of biochemistry taking place in my brain, but that doesn't stop it from being real, or miraculous.

The human race can aspire to more than looking only backwards at truths revealed in the distant past, interpreted by men who perceive the voice of the divine in words of Greek, Hebrew or Arabic. We can also look forwards, towards an extraordinary coming together, driven by ancient forces we're only now starting to comprehend. An epoch of awakening. A species moving beyond its adolescence, into an age that will contain as many wonders as we choose to fill it with, in direct reflection of the quality of our humanity.

The time-honoured moral and spiritual systems always reflected real things. The emotion of love we feel for our children, each other and 'God' is the immediate way our minds experience the forces – forces we don't yet have words for – which unite us, and the patterns of which we're a part. The human race is bound together as part of a greater whole. Our individual lives don't make sense outside the context of the people around us. We rely on each other to give our lives meaning. Those things are true whether or not we admit it, or choose to live in a way which embraces them, and no matter what religion we claim to belong to.

As for God, He is apparently all-knowing, all-seeing, all-powerful, at one with everything, mysterious, unknowable and infinite. He sounds suspiciously like the universe to me.

There's no rule saying He has to be completely mysterious. For three centuries humankind has been systematically unravelling the nature of reality. What's coming into grainy focus resonates with spiritual connotations that are numinous, all-embracing and – more than any of our campfire fables – worthy of being described as holy.

*****

The Flower

Thirteen billion years ago the fabric of reality came into being in an all-encompassing white flash of incomparable brightness during which everything that does, or ever will, exist appeared in a single moment of unifying oneness. From this unity at the beginning of everything the bright young cosmos expanded, not into emptiness – for before it there was no such thing as emptiness – but, as it unfurled itself, the very essence of space–time unfurled with it. As it did, the elemental stuff within coalesced into the titanic bubbles of the galactic superclusters, bursting with the majestic swirls of the galaxies themselves and filled with the fires of a zillion zillion suns.

The primeval generation of stars became spent, blazed out and belched their innards into the empty depths of space. Emergent from that elixir of stellar ash emerged a fresh cohort of child stars. With them came a six-septillion-kilogram ball of silicon and iron. An embryonic world, hurtling through the black void, bathed in the radiated power of a newborn star.

As this baby planet spun around its host, it was blitzed by gargantuan rocks and raked by ultraviolet rays, while monstrous electrical storms boiled across its surface. These, together, conspired to break open the rich molecules – deep-cooked in the belly of a vanished star – which lay across it and kindled into them the power of self-replication.

The reproductions were not perfect, but approximate. Time brought mutation, differentiation and evolution. A great zodiac of child molecules came into being. Generation by generation, their distinctions grew. The universe, and the phenomena inherent within it, had conspired to fashion life and populate a primal world with its first primitive forms which floated, uncomprehending, across that world's surface.

As the aeons rolled by, this Byzantine alchemy conducted experiment after experiment. Moulding and remoulding. Morphing into billions of species and generating a sublime interconnected multiplicity tied symbiotically to the film of gas and liquid wrapping its rocky home. New and ever more sophisticated expressions came into being until the seas teemed with fish and the land was enclosed with steaming jungles through which giant beasts thundered.

Species rose and passed away. The climate adjusted and readjusted. The Earth, on a whim, would belch forth magma, cover herself with ice or receive the suffocating embrace of heavenly suitors. As this majestic cosmic opera laboured on, ever more convoluted life forms swirled in and out of existence until, after three billion years, we came to a dynasty of primates dwelling in the canopy of the planet's tropical forests.

They possessed colour vision to perceive the forests' fruits, cunning hands to pull themselves among the branches and brains adequate to grasp the logic of a primitive social order. One day those primates descended from the boughs, snatched up the first stone tools, made their way out into the savannah and began bending the world to their will. In them, *the universe had attained self-awareness and, for the first time, the language to articulate ideas about itself.*

Humanity pressed on. Each generation passing its lessons to its children. Daughter following mother, its might increased until it had made its way to the summit of the food chain, spread itself across the globe and taken possession of all lands.

Animals were tamed, then plants, and humanity stumbled upon an audacious but perilous scheme. It would strike a Faustian bargain with destiny.

No more roving the Earth at will. Instead 12,000 years of drudgery, monotony, grinding labour and episodic famine – the price to be paid by 600 generations so a minority could turn themselves to inventing, building and crafting. A species-wide baptism to win the magic that would allow them to navigate a course through the uncharted territories of civilisation.

Now, finally, the investment is paying off. Now we can begin to reap the rewards. Now we can start to understand. Now, at last, the cosmos will unravel her enigmas.

What do we find? We find that, as we build ever more devious machines to peer into the structure of reality, and out to the distant reaches of forever, this universe is stranger and more dazzling than any of the fairy stories that sustained us thus far.

That, right now, at the dawn of the twenty-first century, is where we stand. Unintentional voyagers on a 13-billion-year one-way train into forever; held together by the crude but robust social fabric that bound together our forefathers when they strode onto those ancient savannahs; standing on the pale blue dot of paradise with an infinity of blackness stretching in all directions; each one of us an individual realisation of the cosmos expressing itself through the phenomenon of life; collectively engaged in the biggest group-mind project ever conceived; all together on a journey with no discernible end; the whole universe our oyster, no boundaries, no rule book and no game plan.

*****

That's what's really going on here. None of it requires faith in anything. It's just true.

125: The Magic Island
17 May 2007

The 193 square kilometres of the interior of Ilha Grande are entirely mountainous, with slopes coated in a thick layer of rainforest and three tiny vegetation-besieged settlements. There are 108 beaches. Electricity is intermittent. We got here a week ago. I'm having trouble getting the smile off my face.

The main village, Vila do Abraão, is named after an English pirate who holed up here back in the swashbuckling years. As you walk around town adorable miniature monkeys with white ear tufts specifically evolved for comedy chase each other around, jump between telephone wires and occasionally electrocute themselves. One often finds oneself sharing the road with football-sized crustaceans that look nervous and waggle their claws if you get too close.

Annie and Jamie are staying in town, while I'm up the hill at a place run by two dreadlocked and intellectual French hippies (one used to be a stockbroker, he fell in love with a Brazilian girl and gave up his life in Europe for her, then she left him, yada yada yada). Small white mushrooms grow right outside my door. When I return to the lodge after nightfall state-of-the-art mixing decks have miraculously appeared on the veranda above its gardens to pump deep house music into the encircling tangle of flora.

Activities on Ilha Grande have centred on stuffing my face with tropical fruits, hanging out on the beach, staying up late musing on the swirl of the night sky and going for walks across the island's forested interior.

Those walks take one beneath 130-foot palms and dinosaur-sized stands of Dr Seuss-style bamboo. On the surrounding peninsulas and islets, towering columns of the local raptors reach up a thousand feet, spinning within invisible thermals, searching for their next meal.

Petrobras, Brazil's state oil company, has a major installation on the adjacent mainland, from which petroleum is channelled to the metropolises of the country's south-east. The long, low silhouettes of supertankers can be seen cruising through the nearby waterways, in abrupt contrast to the resplendent paradise around us.

The effect of all the natural beauty, head space and walking has been enough to send the Jolly Pilgrim right over the edge. Ilha Grande is one of the most fantastic places I've ever visited. There are even bees. I've made peace with them.

Days since leaving London: 720

We have loved the stars too fondly to be fearful of the night. – Epitaph, anonymous

126: The Piper at the Gates of Dawn

21 May 2007

On day eight on the magic island, a boatful of Brazilian marines flooded into town. Boy, could those guys samba. They regaled us with sailors' songs while the bar girls taught me how to make a perfect caipirinha and everyone talked very quickly in Portuguese.

On day nine Jamie took me clubbing until one in the morning, then, unable to sleep, I stayed up through the night, synthesising threads in my mind, wandering periodically among the verdant plant life outside, while Pink Floyd filled my head with driving, psychedelic rock and sang of interstellar space, scarecrows and bicycles.

On day ten we spent the afternoon sprawled on a huge boulder at one of the beaches near Vila do Abraão. Then, towards evening, Jamie and I swam out, directly perpendicular to the shore, for more than half an hour, discussing the nature of the birth-life-death cycle, until the sky had turned midnight blue and Annie was just a spec across the mirror-smooth water behind us.

On our eleventh and final full day on the island I went for a long walk across one of its peninsulas, alone. With the chatter of birds and fragrance of woodland as my companions, I thought through all that's happened during these past two years on the road and prepared myself for the journey home.

A lot of things went through my head. They included how much I miss my family, how much I'm looking forward to meeting my new niece Polly, reminiscences about all the people I've met during this adventure, all the things I've seen and learned, and what one might conclude from it all. In addition, I pondered the fact that astronomers have made their first detection of an Earth-sized extrasolar planet among the stars – the unimaginatively named Gliese 581c lies in the constellation of Libra and is on a 100-billion-year journey around its red dwarf parent. I also gave some thought to the really big existential questions, such as why is there something rather than nothing? Why does the fabric of reality exist at all?

These are matters about which one has the opportunity to arrange one's thoughts fairly thoroughly during two-year around-the-world adventures.

I remember as an undergraduate being taught why the known universe is composed of 74 per cent hydrogen and 24 per cent helium. The 'reason' boils down to how many protons, electrons and neutrons were created in the Big Bang and how the four fundamental forces of nature happen to operate. One can then, of course, ask about the reasons for *those* things and the answers will lead you to an even more profound set of questions. But the thing that struck me at the time was that even very basic things about the cosmos have a deeper significance than simply being true.

Maybe every question we can ever frame – even 'why is there something rather than nothing?' – will, once resolved, lead to further, currently inconceivable, questions. Maybe humanity's journey of understanding will lead perpetually deeper into a universe of infinite complexity in which we come to grasp our own context with ever greater completeness.

Alternatively, it's possible that the intellectual paraphernalia we use to model reality is inadequate – that the universe (to paraphrase Sir Arthur Eddington) is stranger than we're able to comprehend and if a tremendously wise alien one day attempts to explain it to our descendants, that alien will be reduced to using metaphors about old men with beards who live in clouds.

Or perhaps the structure of human languages is insufficient to handle the really big stuff. Maybe if we one day gain a perfect theoretical understanding of everything, words such as 'meaning' and 'purpose' will be too rooted in human actualities to properly frame the questions (let alone the answers) we're attempting to express.

My hunch, for what it's worth, is that the future will be more interesting than any of those eventualities.

After several hours of walking I reached the far side of the peninsula and saw a bank of cloud approaching from across the Atlantic. So, while reprising all the songs which have sustained me through this pilgrimage, I hiked down to the ocean for one last swim.

Days since leaving London: 724

Pilgrim's word of the day: 'apotheosis' meaning 'the highest point in the development of something; a culmination or climax'

Global Musings XIII
Apotheosis

In this book I've tried to step back from the collective human experience and deconstruct it in a more complete way than it is usually deconstructed.

However, one could step back even further.

The real illusion is the one separating you from me. That's the thing which, once seen through, means everything makes more sense. The deception exists with good reason. Our minds are conditioned – *evolved* – to think about the world in the way that they do. Seeing ourselves as separate from one another is one of the boundaries which allows those minds to perform the tasks they were generated for.

But the boundary isn't real. It's an artefact.

We're like champagne bubbles, thinking about the party from their limited, glass-based, point of view.

The enlightening thing would be to glimpse ourselves entirely in context – stripped of the assumptions and social constructs which fill the human mind, as something that shared none of our perceptive limitations might see us.

Technically, that isn't the sort of thing a human like me can do. Having certain preconceptions, and a built-in conceptual architecture, are confines which come with being an evolved carbon-based life form. Nonetheless, if one were to float in the Atlantic for a while at the end of an appropriately thought-provoking period in one's life, one could probably take a pop at it.

*****

So then, there's this six-septillion-kilogram sphere of iron and rock. It's spinning around the gravity well of a billion-year-old fusion engine and it's wrapped in a film of gas and liquid. Within that film are dispersed carbon atoms. They are dancing to a tempo directed by earth, wind, fire and chemistry and, as the aeons proceed, their dance becomes ever more elaborate ...

About one billion years after the genesis of life on Earth a single-celled, bacteria-like organism entered the body of a larger such creature. Whether it was trying to parasitise the bigger cell, or the bigger cell was trying to eat it, is unknown. However, once inside it transpired that the smaller cell could metabolise the larger one's waste products. The two cells developed a symbiotic relationship – starting to replicate together, swapping a few genes and becoming, for all intents and purposes, a single life form.

A billion years after that a bunch of these symbiotic double cells became stuck together. That arrangement turned out to be to their collective advantage as, living in colonies, they could better reproduce themselves. Eventually the double cells came to depend upon the groups in which they lived and the colonies became, for all intents and purposes, single life forms. Individual cells within those symbiotic cell colonies then started to specialise – to divide their labour – and, out of that specialisation, an emergent phenomenon was born.

Multicellular life forms (such as humans) have some cells which are mortal, in the sense that they are built to eventually die; and some cells (technically, the germ line cells) which are immortal, in the sense that they can reproduce themselves indefinitely (and, in fact, have been doing precisely that for the two billion years since the germ line was formed by one bacteria merging with another on the surface of the primordial Earth).

The way such multicellular life forms work is by growing their (mortal) bodies out of the (immortal) germ line cells formed at the moment of conception. Those mortal bodies then form a shell around the germ line cells. The shell's purpose is to get those germ line cells into the next generation. Talking strictly cause and effect, a chicken is the tool by which an egg creates another egg, and a human is the tool by which the human germ line propagates itself across generations.

The name for that mortal shell is the soma: the disposable bit of a multicellular life form (and every part of it except for its immortal germ line cells). Everything about the form, characteristics and behaviour of the soma of a multicellular life form is defined by what succeeds in getting germ line cells across generations. Every one of its properties is hammered into place by that evolutionary requisite.

As the biosphere of planet Earth fermented through the aeons, the somas thrown up by different germ lines evolved into ever more convoluted shapes, including tyrannosaurs, chimpanzees and oak trees.

In very many cases the logic of evolution determined that these somas would develop sophisticated internal decision-making mechanisms (also known as brains). In some cases (specifically in the case of the germ line that eventually generated somas which were humans) those internal decision-making mechanisms became so refined, the flurry of intersecting impulses and subroutines within them so elaborate, and the internal models by which they mapped the world around them so intricate, that sub-patterns within them (which would one day be named consciousness) began to think of themselves as being self-aware.

At that point the mortal somas of which they were part began to do some *very* peculiar things.

It was once believed that the brain was an instrument for housing the self. We now understand that this isn't the case. Physically changing a person's (or an animal's) brain changes that person's (or animal's) underlying identity. The brain, it turns out, is a mechanism which generates the self.

In summary, the conscious entities (like you and me) which do all these interesting things (such as read and write books) are sub-patterns within complex biological decision-making mechanisms that are one element of mortal cell colonies generated by an immortal line of germ cells, which are actually a couple of bacteria that have been replicating together (and throwing up increasingly spectacular by-products) for the two billion years since they became symbiotically joined on the surface of the primordial Earth and are, themselves, one subdivision of a dispersed agglomeration of carbon atoms which are dancing through the film of liquid and gas wrapping a planet that's spinning around the gravity well of a 4.6-billion-year-old fusion engine.

You wouldn't normally think about yourself in those terms because your brain is built to think like part of the disposable shell thrown up by some germ line cells as their vehicle for getting into the next generation. You're hard-wired to perceive the universe from that – *extremely specific* – point of view. All the emotions that fill your world, from happiness to sadness, to pride, pain and hunger; all the things you choose to do (like showing off, reading books and thinking of yourself as mortal); and all the boxes you have a predilection to think inside (such as identifying yourself as a Buddhist or believing in money) are by-products of being an ephemeral sub-pattern in that enormous fountain of über-chemistry.

And, if being a part of all that wasn't mind-blowing enough, there's a modern twist. The intricacy of the workings of the human mind has caused the somas thrown up by the human germ line to interact in such prodigiously convoluted ways that they have begun to specialise – to divide their labour – and, out of that specialisation, an emergent phenomenon has been born.

That phenomenon (which, in this book, I've been referring to as 'civilisation') is the consequence of an extended series of inadvertent consequences. Multicellular life is a by-product of two bacteria becoming joined in the primordial soup. Brains are a by-product of multicellular life. Human intelligence is a by-product of the increasing sophistication of brains. Agriculture is a by-product of human intelligence. Civilisation is a by-product of agriculture and all of this is ultimately just one by-product of a universe of hydrogen atoms stewing for 13 billion years. Nevertheless, that pattern within a pattern within a pattern works to its own internal rhythms and *those* rhythms are not only linear (and seemingly unending) but they have, in turn, led to further inadvertent side effects.

One of those inadvertent side effects is to destabilise the planet-wrapping film of gas and liquid within which all of this is taking place. Another is to cause the non-life atoms on the planet's surface (in the form of first ploughs, then genetic sequencing machines, then ...) to begin pirouetting around the carbon atoms and joining their dance. Another – most outrageously of all – is to allow those sub-patterns within the brains of the somas generated by the human germ line to *understand* that this is what they are. Now it's on the verge of allowing them to overpower the genetics defining everything about them.

If you ever meet anyone who thinks life is boring, predictable or humdrum, rest assured: they're simply not thinking about it carefully enough.

And if you're one of those human somas (like me) who think that being alive is great; that being a member of such an express and admirable species is a pleasure; that living in a linear, open-ended civilisation is utterly stupendous; and that doing all of this on a jewel-like planet in an infinitely fascinating universe is the best of all imaginable eventualities – then the whole glorious arrangement is also quite staggeringly convenient.

Suspiciously so.

Some might claim this proves something they think they already know about the literal truth of an ancient fable. I think that would be a mistake. One of the reasons why humanity needs to reach beyond its inbuilt preconceptions, clear its collective head of clutter and see its own context more honestly is that, I suspect, there are quite a lot of very important things about this extraordinary situation which we have failed, thus far, to put our fingers on.

*****

In the sixteenth century the human race experienced a revelation. The established framework of a geocentric cosmology was overturned. Planet Earth was not, it turned out, the centre of the universe. At the time that freaked some people out.

The nineteenth century brought a further revelation, one that redefined our sense of identity. Charles Darwin's candle in the darkness. Evolution by natural selection. All extant life forms are part of a tree which is continuously branching and re-branching. Some people are still freaked out by this.

The twentieth century brought more revelations, this time in physics. We learned that time is relative, that we are surrounded by things we neither see nor sense and that there are orders of creation – in both scale and time – beyond the reach of our minds. Those revelations were more disconcerting than anything Charles Darwin ever said, but because they're so esoteric people aren't as freaked out by them (yet).

That wasn't the end. The scientific endeavour (it is often forgotten) has only recently begun. We're living in a phase of history during which we're going from understanding almost nothing about our own context to understanding it in some detail. As that expansion of knowledge intensifies in the coming decades and centuries there will be further insights, many of which are going to be undermining, defy common sense and, at first, be hard to accept.

Here are three examples of the sort of thing I mean:

1) At the moment, philosophers and neuroanatomists are investigating the nature of consciousness. They are trying to understand what it is, how it relates to the unconscious, how free will works and what, exactly, is happening in these heads of ours when we experience reality. Sooner or later there's going to be a breakthrough. At that point we'll begin to understand what's going on with these 100 billion neurons (that we've all got) to produce this subjective feeling (that we all feel) of being alive. That's going to be interesting.

   What are the possibilities?

   Every system in the universe that's so far been investigated has turned out to be either deterministic (you flick a switch and a light comes on) or random (you roll a die and there's a one in six chance of a six). When we finally deconstruct the principles and processes underlying our own neural circuitry, what might we find? Presumably a process, or set of processes, which are either deterministic or random. What else could it be?

We may be close to finding out – to learning what, exactly, it is that we're talking about when we use terms like 'consciousness', 'free will' and 'think'. If you think Darwinian evolution undermined people's sense of themselves, wait until this baby hits.

2) Questions regarding the possibility of alien intelligence have a widely recognised talismanic significance. At the moment we're only at the stage of organising our ignorance on the subject – ignorance that's loaded with assumptions (regarding extraterrestrial behaviour and technology) which are probably incredibly naive. However, given the age and size of the universe, the fact it's suited to the emergence of life, and the fact this agglomeration of carbon atoms wrapping this planet has started exhibiting such spectacular emergent phenomena, then it would be paradoxical if there were not other such agglomerations wrapping other such planets exhibiting similar such phenomena.

Actually coming across evidence for them may have to wait ten thousand years until robot probes reconnoitre the galaxy; a thousand until we build space-based detectors big enough to pick up intergalactic signals; five hundred until we figure out the decryption algorithms for interstellar communiqués; or one hundred, when we simply point our telescopes in the right direction. But, given the broad trajectory of human affairs, it seems inevitable that, sooner or later, we'll get there.

Seeing that humans can barely relate to dolphins (beings from the same branch of the same tree of life which share most of our genetic code), liaising with something from an entirely different tree of life may be the moment at which it dawns on us just how subjective and arbitrary our way of thinking about the universe has always been.

3) Physicists press on with their quest to grasp the fabric of reality. The more we understand, the weirder it gets. It's already clear that the way we perceive the universe, and the things we regard as real, are a simplified version of a deeper and more complicated picture. But the goal is to achieve an all-embracing theoretical understanding of everything: the fabled Grand Unified Theory.

That may or may not be possible. However, previous experience would suggest that there are conceptual jumps (akin to realising that time is relative) waiting to be made.

Comprehending the underlying geometry of space–time will be no small thing. It will not simply constitute an ingenious piece of mathematics. It's real 'life, the universe and everything' stuff and, if there's a species-wide revelation waiting in the wings, that might be it – the moment at which everything starts to make sense, or the moment it starts to get even stranger.

Maybe it will represent one more step towards a point at which our descendants – or something that springs from them – comprehend what breathes life into the equations that regulate the cosmos in such a way that they grasp more thoroughly what we mean by the word 'God'. Maybe only then will we be in a position to set out a complete, and truly timeless, spiritual architecture and maybe that will be the moment at which history truly begins.

The bottom line is that we live in a complicated and enigmatic universe, we perceive it in an extremely limited way and we're only just learning to model what's happening around us. Given all that, things can still get much weirder than they thus far have. No doubt the most profoundly disorienting developments will come from directions that we do not anticipate.

Taming war, disease, famine and poverty, and sorting out our relationship with the environment, isn't about creating a utopian dream. It's a staging post. It's about dealing with the problems inherent to this phase in the human story, recognising the boxes we think inside for what they are and clearing our heads for the next black-obelisk moment. The future is going to be perplexing and problematic in all sorts of difficult and unforeseen ways.

However, on that note, here is something I believe – an article of faith. We have nothing to fear. Things which are initially bewildering and sinister will, in the end, seem beautiful and right, and the truth will set us free.

*****

Thinking bigger about what's happening on this planet, and what we're part of, can also help us think about mortality. It's something about which humans have a fundamental issue – we are intensely uncomfortable with the idea that the subjective sense of self through which we experience reality will not survive our deaths. Our cultural heritage has bestowed various concepts of an afterlife, the alternatives to which provoke deep apprehension.

C. S. Lewis said that heaven means spending eternity thanking God for not answering our prayers. This is a universe on a mission, not one which messes around throwing infinite garden parties so that carbon-based life forms can drink from flagons. Our individual immortality is enshrined in ways far more complete than those described in our ancestor fables.

Everything that came before us inspires the nature of what we are. Everything we do sets in motion a chain of events which will echo until the end of time – in immediate ways we casually perceive (the work we do, the objects we craft and the children we bring into being), in inconspicuous ways we perceive less fully (the ideas we propagate, the influence we have and the butterflies we affect) and via more subtle routes that we do not, and may never, perceive (such as the interfacing of our personal gravity wells, or whatever). Each one of us is a manifestation of atoms, created at the beginning of time, which have danced across one hundred million centuries to come together at this one unique instant, in this one unique way, to play out the story of our lives.

We are the momentary state of a continuum, stretching back through ages lost to memory, via people of whom we know nothing but to whom we owe everything, through things that were not human, through things that were not even nearly human, and beyond, to something that wasn't even alive. The only meaningful context in which we can, or have ever been able to, exist is as a part of that continuum, and when the entity which is reading these words has sparkled away, that continuum will live on.

There are much more interesting ways of being immortal than simply living forever. Real immortality – immortality which resonates with how the universe truly is – comes from being a part of that greater whole.

And when we deliberate upon the idea of 'living forever', what precisely is it that we're talking about which might 'live forever'?

Those sub-patterns within complex biological decision-making mechanisms that are one element of mortal cell colonies generated by an immortal line of germ cells, which are actually a couple of bacteria that have been replicating together (and throwing up increasingly spectacular by-products) for the two billion years since they became symbiotically joined in the primordial soup and are, themselves, one subdivision of a dispersed agglomeration of carbon atoms which are dancing through the film of liquid and gas wrapping a planet that's spinning around the gravity well of a 4.6-billion-year-old fusion engine?

Those things?

Those things fear death because of a set of boundaries they make inside themselves. The entity which is reading this book, which is seeing these abstract shapes on this page – shapes it's been conditioned to assign meaning to – and which is seeing and assigning meaning to these shapes on this page right now, and letting these thoughts appear inside itself – what is that entity? *Really?*

It's a subroutine in something larger than itself – the same thing as this other entity, which has been sharing this story and these ideas with you by recording them, through the medium of these abstract shapes, from across whichever gulf of time and space lies between us.

And that world I passed through during my journey? That theatre upon which all our designs, navigations and wars have been transacted? That nascent civilisation, just starting to understand itself, which had risen through agriculture to send probes into the solar system? That? That was the beginning.

And this indescribably beautiful planet? This sphere of iron and rock, wrapped in its veil of dancing carbon atoms? This green and blue mote of paradise, hurtling through the blackness of space? This? This is the Garden of Eden.

127: The Redeemer
24 May 2007

I'm on my way home.

Annie, Jamie and I arrived in Rio de Janeiro three days ago. I was physically, mentally and emotionally exhausted.

We found an apartment three blocks from Copacabana beach, then Annie and Jamie set about exploring the city. It was immediately apparent that I was too worn out to join them, so I've spent most of my time in Rio moping around the flat.

The two of them report that 'the marvellous city' is unexpectedly subdued. When I took my only walk to the beach the weather was overcast and the body-beautiful mob were nowhere to be seen. Leonardo, from whom we're renting the apartment, explained that with the onset of winter everyone finds a boyfriend or girlfriend and settles down for long nights in. Then, as spring approaches and blood rises across town, everyone has rows and becomes single again, just in time for the new season. What a great system.

I spent most of yesterday and this morning asleep, but by mid-afternoon I was feeling a little better and realised that if I didn't get out I'd miss the city completely. There was one thing I *had* to see. So, rushing to get there before it closed, I caught a cab across town to the foot of Corvado, the peak on which, between 1922 and 1931, the famous statue of Cristo Redentor ('Christ the Redeemer') was erected.

They say it's best to visit on a clear day. Today it was cold, blustery and wet, so I wore my waterproof and rain hat. Trains take you up the 710-metre peak. I caught the last one. The station at the top had a café (on the far side of the summit from the statue). I got myself a bun and a cup of tea and sat down to warm up.

By the time I was walking around the hilltop, the few others who'd taken the train with me were heading back the other way. When I reached the statue there was nobody else there. It was just me and Jesus – face placid, arms outstretched, palms forward, blessing the city.

Beneath us, Rio was spread out in shades of melancholy overcast – the distant curves of its beaches, the broad expanse of Guanabara Bay, the double hump of Sugarloaf Mountain. With the wind and rain on my face I experienced a surge of elation.

I began running back and forth, going up to the statue's pedestal and touching it, then taking pictures of the statue, the clouds and myself from different angles, then over to the viewing platform and spreading out my arms in imitation of the icon above. All the time I was reciting, then shouting and then singing some lines of a poem I've recently memorised. It's from the Dead Sea Scrolls. As I sang it a sunburst sped across the boiling grey of the heavens, shining beams of white light through the clouds.

> *So I walk on uplands unbounded*
> *and know that there is hope*
> *for that which Thou didst mould out of dust*
> *to have consort with things eternal.*

After sharing my long moment alone with the Redeemer, I retraced my steps around the summit to the station, then caught the last train back down to the city.

Days since leaving London: 727

128: Transcontinental
29 May 2007

After visiting Rio it was time to head for my final destination: the banana republic of Guyana on South America's Caribbean (i.e. northern) coast where two old friends were expecting me. Staying with them and their growing family will draw my pilgrimage, and this story, to their conclusion.

I'd originally planned to do all my travelling in South America overland. However, investigations revealed an almost complete lack of roads in the first half of the 2,500 kilometres of rainforest I had to cross. This was no time for a slow boat up the Amazon.

The morning after visiting the Redeemer I bid farewell to my Atlantic-coast travelling family, who were staying in the city another week. Jamie walked me part of the way to my airport-bound bus. At the far side of the square outside our apartment we hugged and said a last goodbye, he kissed me on the cheek and then off I went.

The first leg of the journey that followed was a 90-minute hop to Brasilia. From my window seat I gazed down at plains spread with multicoloured circles of yellow, brown and green – the imprint of Brazil's giant industrial farms and growing status as an agricultural superpower.

After an hour on the concrete at the capital, the second leg was a three-hour flight to the interior and the jungle city of Manaus. Shortly after we took off the trees started. From above I could see roads running through the ocean of green, with gaps appearing in the canopy on either side in the standard pattern of rainforest clearance. Then a really big river appeared.

At Manaus I went straight onto a 12-hour overnight bus, on which I sat next to a lady called Eyana, who shared her blanket and baffled me with Portuguese as we crossed the Equator together. I disembarked the next morning at Boa Vista, then boarded another bus which took me to Bonfim, the last town in Brazil I would see. From there it was a short walk to the edge of the Takutu River, which forms the border between Brazil and Guyana.

It's a dirt-roads-and-zero-infrastructure part of the world, but I came across a young man by the riverside called Lucas, who had a canoe and an outboard and offered to take me across. On the Guyanese shore I had my passport stamped in a tent by an official named Officer Kennard – the only person in South America to ask me why I write 'Global Muse' on immigration forms.

On that far side of the river I met a buck-toothed 15-year-old called Eddie, whose clapped-out hatchback had a smashed-in windscreen and maxed out at 30 kilometres per hour. I dropped him five bucks to get me to Lethem, the nearest town.

At Lethem, in between negotiations with a minivan company, a surprise rainstorm left me soaked. I towelled myself down while reggae music played and a gentleman called Calvin wearing spectacles told me about how England's cricket team was thrashing the West Indies at Headingley. He clearly assumed that I'd find this news a matter of great excitement.

'Well there's something to be positive about then,' I offered lamely, water still dripping from my nose. At that point Calvin threw wide his arms, grinned serenely (showing three gold teeth) and raised his face to the sky.

'Dea *always* is,' he intoned solemnly.

Welcome to the Caribbean.

The final leg was a ride in an overnight-minivan-sauna-hellbox down mud-and-dust roads through the deep rainforest. I was twisted into a two-person seat with three others and it goes down as comprehensively the worst transport experience of that journey, this pilgrimage and my entire life. At 6 a.m., while we crossed a wide, brown river on a rickety wooden raft, Calvin tried to convert me to Christianity. He didn't ask me any questions but pretty much charged in, telling me that I should study the Bible and look for Jesus. I thanked him politely for the advice.

Our vehicle trundled into Georgetown the day before yesterday, 18 hours after setting out from Lethem, 74 hours after leaving Rio and two years to the day after I cycled away from London. Patrick was waiting for me.

Days since leaving London: 732

	Guyana	Brazil
Population	769,095	190,010,647
GDP per head	US$4,700	US$8,600
Total size of economy	US$3.614 billion	US$1.616 trillion

Global Musings XIV
Ramble On

The twentieth century, and the immense expansion of material and technological wealth it oversaw, ushered in a new phase in humanity's relationship with, and appetite for, long-distance travel. Increasingly, everybody's doing it.

Within that broad phenomenon, a spectrum of activities are taking place: package tourists on sanitised excursions to foreign beaches; adventurous young things travelling around Australia and having a go at bungee jumping; gap-year people immersing themselves in India or South America; and those marvellous souls in Quito who, following years of advanced training in anthropology, spend months learning Quechua then go to live amidst a corner of humanity so very different from their own, deep in the Amazon rainforest.

One way of understanding what all this means for the evolving structure of global society is via the analogy of a web. There are short thin strands representing superficial contact between parts of our world community which are already close (English people going to Spanish beaches to eat fish and chips) and long thick strands representing profound interactions between parts of it that are at a very far remove (Amazonian tribes playing host to American anthropologists).

The overall dynamic of this global humanity web is clear: its intensity is increasing. There are more strands of every length and thickness. More people are going farther and deeper – both culturally and physically – than ever before.

*****

Now that a vast global industry facilitates the hospitality of strangers, and hotels cluster around the world's most beautiful places, it's easy to forget what a nascent phenomenon this is and how rapidly it's evolving. Beaches which were recently pristine are lined with restaurants and internet connections. Obscure villages that were unmapped a generation ago have their own page in several brands of guidebook.

Iconic features of humanity's heritage which were in a raw state well within living memory are now tightly controlled and professionally managed. In the caves of the Vézère Valley, only researchers can now enter places where thousands once tramped. When my children explore this planet for themselves they will not be permitted to clamber over Golubac Grad or Angkor Wat as I did.

There are tantalising indicators of how things will develop. The embryonic fashion for ecotourism promises its perfect fusion of economic and environmental rationalism. In South America, periods of language training and voluntary work are now de rigueur for the serious explorer, and lead to an encounter with the region far more immersive than any traditional tourist experience. Meanwhile, in California's Mojave Desert, there are the first glimmers of what taking a 'trip' might one day involve as a few top-end tourists prepare themselves for short hops to the final frontier.

These are all extremely positive developments. Every strand of the global humanity web, from package tourists to machete-wielding anthropologists, helps bind this world together. Consider the global backpacking phenomenon. It's only decades old, growing out of the pan-Asian hippie trails of the 1960s. Yet it's already become a recognised rite-of-passage for the rich world's young (and not-so-young) adults and, as a cultural institution, it provides exposure to a global peer group and first-hand, de-sanitised knowledge of far-flung, culturally diverse places.

During my journey I observed that institution's twenty-first-century incarnations in cities from Sydney to San José. It had ballooned in the 15 years since my first student trips around Europe and the traditionally well-travelled nationalities – such as the Germans, Japanese and Israelis – had been joined by the Koreans and Czechs. Travellers from India, China, Russia and Brazil are presumably close behind. The youth of planet Earth, thrown together in cheap hotels across the world, are sharing experiences and mixing it up. There will be long-term consequences for the global zeitgeist.

This broadening and deepening of global integration has plenty of dark sides. Some are distasteful: boorish Western men looking for cheap sex or young wives in Bangkok and Quito. Others are embarrassing: culturally oblivious Americans being rude to French priests in the sublime confines of Chartres Cathedral.

It's worth it. Global integration was never going to be all about well-read intelligentsia debating philosophy and showing total respect for each other's cultural preconceptions. A planet of humans is learning to live with itself. We're close to the beginning of a long process of integration that will see notions of national identity broken down and attitudes to global culture transformed. People from different backgrounds are being forced to deal with each other under often imperfect circumstances. It is, by nature, a rough and stressful business. But the only way forward is to start thinking of ourselves as one people, so we may as well get on with it.

As our struggle to make civilisation environmentally sustainable takes shape, one of the cost–benefit decisions to be made is the extent to which air travel should be restricted. We should beware of false economies. In order to solve increasingly globalised issues – such as stabilising our relationship with the environment – people are going to need to become instinctively more internationalist, to really *feel* like they're one world.

In order for that to happen they're going to have to travel more. It isn't possible to understand the majestic pandemonium of Calcutta unless you've actually been to India. No prose, no documentary and no travel book can do it justice. This world is too diverse and resplendent for that diversity and resplendence to simply be imagined. One has to see it for oneself.

*****

As for my own particular brand of full-immersion adventure travel, I'd like to think I did my share of enhancing understanding between peoples and spreading the global love.

As that adventure drew to its conclusion I was asked repeatedly if I was sad about that. People assumed that I'd want to set off again the moment I returned. Not at all. I never wanted to spend my life on the road. I want a life that's rich and multifaceted – one element of which is to see a bit of the world and get into some hare-brained adventures.

Job done.

The dream of spending one's days endlessly drifting from place to place, and playing the wild rover, does have a certain romantic elan. But it strikes me as a bit pointless and self-indulgent.

I'm a big fan of this human adventure of which we're all a part. I think it's a fascinating, magnificent and glorious thing, but keeping it running requires that people maintain its physical, social and cultural infrastructure. There's nothing noble about failing to shoulder one's part of that burden. Maybe there are some who can most productively contribute as eternal hobos, philosophising as they go. But that is not my path.

Following my two-year road trip the people I most admired were not the zany explorers. The people I most admired were the ones who run businesses, go to work every day, maintain households, hold families together and keep this show on the road. Following his grand adventure, this pilgrim intends to do his bit.

129: The Haven
3 June 2007

Patrick and I met at Durham University, where we were geeks together in the early 1990s. When he returned to his home island of Guernsey afterwards, he was chubby, bespectacled and a tad frumpy. The next time I caught sight of him was six years later outside London's Victoria station. He was leaner, harder and about an inch taller. He was moving to the city after scoring a job with a top actuarial consultancy. The next thing I knew he was going out with this Caribbean girl.

Maria and he were married at the turn of the millennium and, since then, their lives have been going from strength to strength. In 2002 they left their hectic UK jobs for Maria's homeland of Guyana. As for Maria, she is half-German and half-Guyanese and has a thick Jamaican-style accent. The overall effect is striking.

They're both bigwigs. Patrick is the proprietor of Caribbean Actuarial and Financial Services, the country's premier risk management consultancy. He works with the Adam Smith Institute, has been CEO of the national stock exchange and writes a weekly column in the business pages. As for Maria, she's the country's Commissioner of Insurance (no less) and even has her own driver.

Patrick and Maria's house is so big that my entire Quito apartment would fit into its living room. The guest room, where I sleep, has a four-poster bed and an en suite bathroom. Ezlin, the wonderful housekeeper, tidies it every day and cooks me bacon for breakfast. The house is also an Aladdin's cave of engaging and mind-expanding reading material. Uncle Peter, the freeloading neo-hippie who's been living there this past week, is spending his days in the back garden, surrounded by Tintin books and copies of *National Geographic*, communing with the dragonflies.

Julia and Mathias – the kids – are a veritable barrel of ongoing high-octane amusement. Mathias (who is two) is at the stage of having lots of worthwhile things to say without actually being able to talk. He deals with the frustration this causes by shouting (quite a bit) and biting his older sister. Mathias is developing a philosophy of property based around the principle that everything belongs to him.

Julia (who is four) is able to speak perfectly well, thank you very much. She is keen to share this ability at every opportunity and to express her joy at the sensation of being alive with everyone around her, especially first thing in the morning. I've taken to barricading my door.

As for Guyana, Patrick and Maria's talk of share prices and company reports is in contrast to the world on the streets. Half the population is of South Asian origin and the other half is Afro-Caribbean. There are two political parties (one for each ethnic group) and everyone votes based upon their race. It's a simple tribal arrangement and it doesn't give rise to an innovative political culture. Although, to be fair, Krishna, who runs the corner shop at the end of Patrick and Maria's road, has got hold of a video of Al Gore's new film *An Inconvenient Truth* and is making everyone watch it. Even here, word gets around.

At the weekend Patrick's family and I travelled up the huge Essequibo River (the mouth of which is 20 kilometres along the coast from Georgetown) on a boat powered by two mean-looking V6s. On the way we passed ruined fortresses built when the Dutch and British used to fight over who was boss around here. Our destination was a villa hideaway in a clearing carved out beside the great river. We spent two days by the water playing board games and taking short walks into the thoroughly impenetrable jungle. I had my first go on a jet ski and, during the hours of darkness, listened to the untamed wilds beyond.

We got back to Georgetown this afternoon. It's raining in Guyana. I go home in three days.

Days since leaving London: 735

Japanese word of the day: 'ichigo-ichie' meaning 'the practice of treasuring each moment and trying to make it perfect'

130: Pilgrim Unplugged
4 June 2007

Because being a delicate and transitory mortal in a harsh and uncaring universe is so difficult, people get all negative. The trials of life and the challenges of the short term are considerable, but overall it's time we started being more optimistic. At the dawn of this twenty-first century, humanity is handling its affairs more adeptly than at any previous period in history. What's more, the human race is in control of its own destiny and, as a species, we're going somewhere. While I have no idea where that is, it's going to be extremely interesting finding out and the adventure taking us there is absolutely gripping.

The cosmologies our ancestors dreamed up while sitting around campfires never really did justice to the great blossoming of which we're all a part, or the complex and enigmatic character of this universe. We get to be part of something far more magnificent than they imagined – something which actually might go on forever.

In addition to being part of this epic, multi-generational, human drama, there's the additional bonus (and it's not an inconsiderable one) that being alive can be great fun. Seeing as fate could snuff any of us out at any moment, I hold that it's appropriate to draw comfort from this.

As our species grows in wealth and self-knowledge, and pursues ever more ambitious games of status and prestige, I hope that some of our descendants bear in mind that happiness comes from within and that even the longest of fame is fleeting, and so take the time to immerse themselves in the now – see the world, embrace it, try to understand.

Homer said that the gods envy us because we're mortal – that everything is more beautiful because we won't be here again. In respect of these past two years walking the Earth, I've done what I can to make the most of the experience and ensure that I share life's rich pageant with those who walk beside me.

Days since leaving London: 738
My visits to different

Countries:	24	Continents:	5
Beaches:	17	Hospitals:	5

Be thou the rainbow in the storms of life. The evening beam that smiles the clouds away and tints tomorrow with prophetic rays. – Lord Byron

131: The End
6 June 2007

It's 1 a.m. local time. I've spent the day cruising around a sun-baked Georgetown with a Rasta taxi driver called Vincent. He played bouncy ska music and said 'no worries, man' while taking me to get my hair cut. It was a good day.

This evening Patrick, Maria and I had dinner with Maria's parents. We got back to the house at 11 p.m. and have just had a three-way heart-to-heart in the living room. During our conversation Maria set out her own vision as to what humanity should do with itself and where it should go from here: plough resources into interstellar travel; embark upon an urgent programme of starship building and then set off to colonise the galaxy. Simple, straightforward and with zero procrastination. Go girl.

Patrick and Maria are now in bed. I'm alone at the computer. There is a rum and coke on the desk.

This is the end.

Tomorrow morning Patrick is driving me to the airport to catch the 10.20 a.m. flight which will deliver me across the Atlantic Ocean via Trinidad and Barbados. At 8 a.m. on Thursday, 7 June 2007 – 740 days after setting out from London – I will return there via Gatwick airport. A landing party has been arranged.

To those who've been with me in spirit during this adventure, your encouragement has been a great strength. Thank you. To those who've shown me hospitality over the past two years, I am in your debt. To the ones who've offered me companionship in the far-off lonely places, I will not forget you.

Merlin the wizard says that it's the doom of men that they forget. I therefore want to note here for you, and for my own record, something about those numerous but soon-forgotten humdrum moments I've spent alone over these past two years: pottering around in my campsites in Europe, standing beside roads in Australia, or working away in my flat in Quito, often singing and almost always daydreaming about some latest imagination.

I want to note how I would catch myself realising how happy I was; how contented and fulfilled I felt; and how my mind was crowded with ideas and a certain amount of awe – a smattering of which has made its way into these words, which have made a record of my journey around the world, and what it meant to me.

Afterword

In my story I've described a pantheistic approach to thinking about the universe: one which sees our sense of individuality as an illusion thrown up by the human psyche's cognitive architecture; and views today's world as a transient phase in a great flowering, as a series of miracles superimpose themselves upon one another.

How might one articulate one's reverence for this grand cosmic opera? What might one substitute for lighting candles beneath the faces of idols or praying to supernatural gods? I'm in favour of whichever form of worship is in harmony with a person's cultural background and life experience. Just because the character of spiritual systems is ephemeral does not rob them of their meaning as frameworks for understanding.

But, perhaps as an alternative, let me tell you what I did – about my personal act of devotion, celebration, adulation and thanksgiving.

I went on a journey. During that journey I attempted to immerse myself in my home world as fully as I was able; to rejoice in its splendour and diversity; and to give expression to the deep and overwhelming sense of wonder I feel at being alive. Then I wrote this book about it.

Appendices

Appendix I: Index of Subchapters

All the book's subchapters are listed below. This index is intended to facilitate re-examinations of particular elements of the thesis and for cross-referencing against the maps. Musings are listed in bold. Global Musings are listed in bold and prefixed with a Roman numeral.

Appendix II: Web Resources

References

Rather than add footnotes to the text, all references are on the website. This section of the site also features extensive additional commentary regarding the ideas and issues discussed in *The Jolly Pilgrim*.

www.thejollypilgrim.org/references

Gallery

An online gallery of images from the adventure (including commentary and notes on each image and where it was taken) can be found on the website.

www.thejollypilgrim.org/pictures

What Happened Next

The website contains extensive notes on the drafting process which began directly after my return to the UK in June 2007. In addition, following my return, I posted six-monthly updates on my progress towards publication. From 2009, this spawned a blog that now sets out in real time the journey of which the events recorded in *The Jolly Pilgrim* were the beginning.

www.thejollypilgrim.org/blog

Appendix III: Technical Notes

Dates

When discussing dates, this book uses the BCE/CE (Before Common Era and Common Era) system. Dates defined using this system correspond directly to the BC/AD system. For example, AD 1000 = 1000 CE, and 500 BC = 500 BCE. The dating convention used in *The Jolly Pilgrim* is to discard the suffix for dates after 1000 CE.

Money

Unless otherwise stated, $ in the text refers to US$. At the time of the journey the GBP to US$ exchange rate was about 1:2. The GBP to AUS$ exchange rate was about 1:2.4.

The total-cost-of-trip figure quoted at the beginning of Part 6 works out at approximately US$40,000, or AUS$48,000.

Bibliography

One of the great things about travelling around the world for two years is that you get to read all the time. Below is a list of the books, documentaries, papers and surveys which: I consumed on the road and that affected my thinking; were crucial to my background knowledge; or were consulted during the editing process.

The Bible. New International Version. London: The International Bible Society, 2002 (I am indebted to Sid McLean for picking out this translation*)*

The Qur'an. Translation by M. A. S. Abdel Haleem. Oxford: Oxford University Press, 2005

Aurelius, M. *Meditations.* London: Penguin Group, 1964

Banks, I. M. *Consider Phlebas.* London: Orbit, 1988

Beddoes, Z. M. 'A Survey of the World Economy 2005' (survey). *The Economist*, 22 September 2005

Carr, G. 'The Proper Study of Mankind, A Survey of Human Evolution' (survey). *The Economist*, 24 December 2005

Carr, G. 'Who do you think you are? A Survey of the Brain' (survey). *The Economist*, 23 December 2006

Carwardine, M. *Whales, Dolphins and Porpoises.* New York: DK, 2002

Clarke, A. C. *Profiles of the Future.* London: Pan, 1964

Collier, P. *The Bottom Billion.* New York: Oxford University Press, 2007

Dawood, N. J. (translator) *Arabian Nights: Tales from the Thousand and One Nights.* Penguin, 1973

Diamond, J. *Guns, Germs and Steel.* London: Vintage, 2005

Duncan, E. 'The Heat is On, A Survey of Climate Change' (survey). *The Economist*, 9 September 2006

Gibran, K. *The Prophet.* London: William Heinemann, 1972

Gibson, W. *Neuromancer.* London: Voyager, 1984

Goklany, I. *The Improving State of the World.* Washington: Cato Institute, 2007

Goodwin, J. *Lords of the Horizon*. London: Vintage, 1999

Graham, B. *In Search of Personal Peace*. Thomas Nelson, 2005

Hemming, J. *The Conquest of the Incas*. Papermac, 1993

Ibn Khaldun. *The Prolegomena* (abridged version, translated by Charles Issawi). Princeton: The Darwin Press, 1987

Kagan, R. *The Return of History and the End of Dreams*. Atlantic Books, 2008

Kaku, M. *Visions: How Science Will Revolutionize the Twenty-First Century*. Oxford Paperbacks, 1999

Keeley. L. H. *War Before Civilisation: The Myth of the Peaceful Savage*. New York: Oxford University Press, 1996

Kluth, A. 'Among the Audience, A Survey of New Media' (survey). *The Economist*, 22 April 2006

Livi-Bacci, M. *A Concise History of World Population*. Oxford: Blackwell, 1997

Lockart, J. and Schwartz S. B. *Early Latin America: A History of Colonial Spanish America and Brazil*. Cambridge: Cambridge University Press, 1993

Lovelock, J. *The Ages of Gaia*. Oxford: Oxford University Press, 2000

Luna, F. *A Short History of the Argentineans*. Buenos Aires: Booket, 2005

Martin, S. (editor) 'Tropical Topics, a Second Companion' (booklet). Cairns: Environmental Protection Agency

Mill, J. S. *On Liberty and Other Essays*. Oxford Paperbacks, 1998

Mulgan, G. *Good and Bad Power: The Ideals and Betrayals of Government*. London: Penguin Group, 2006

Norwich, J. *Byzantium: The Early Centuries*. London: Penguin, 1988

Norwich, J. *Byzantium: The Apogee*. London: Penguin, 1991

Norwich, J. *Byzantium: The Decline and Fall*. London: Penguin, 1995

Palmerlee, D. (coordinating author) *South America on a Shoestring* (Lonely Planet guide). London: Lonely Planet, 2004

Peet, J. 'Fit at 50? A Special Report on the European Union' (survey). *The Economist*, 17 March 2007

Ponting, C. *World History: A New Perspective*. London: Pimlico, 2001

Roberts, J. *The Penguin History of Europe*. Penguin, 1997

Runciman, S. *A History of the Crusades Volume III – The Kingdom of Acre and the Later Crusades*. Cambridge: Cambridge University Press, 1954

Sagan, C. *Cosmos*. London: Abacus, 1983

Sagan, C. *Contact*. London: Arrow Books, 1986

Sagan, C. *The Dragons of Eden*. Random House, 1997

Sagan, C. and Druyan, A. *Shadows of Forgotten Ancestors*. New York: Ballantine, 1992

Seligman, A. *The Voyage of the Cap Pilar*. London: Hodder & Stoughton, 1993

Simon, J. L. *The State of Humanity*. Cambridge, Massachusetts: Blackwell, 1995

Smitz, P. (coordinating author) *Australia* (Lonely Planet guide). London: Lonely Planet, 2005

Sowell, T. *Economic Facts and Fallacies*. New York: Basic Books, 2008

Thomas, M. 'Population Replacement in Anglo-Saxon England' (paper). Centre for the Evolution of Cultural Diversity, 2006

Unger, B. 'Dreaming of Glory. A Special Report on Brazil' (survey). *The Economist*, 14 April 2007

Updike, J. *Brazil*. Ballantine, 1996

Voltaire. *Candide* (translation by John Butt). London: Penguin Books, 1947

Wade, N. *Before the Dawn: Recovering the Lost History of Our Ancestors*. London: Duckworth, 2007

Wilczek, F. *The Lightness of Being*. New York: Perseus, 2008

Williams, N. (coordinating author) *France* (Lonely Planet guide). London: Lonely Planet, 2005

Woodhead, L. *Milosevic: How to be a Dictator* (documentary). BBC, 2002

Other Sources and Influences

The Australian Museum in Sydney was crucial to my understanding of Indigenous Australian affairs. The text for the first of the two narratives regarding the climate change issue in Part 7 was drawn from the websites of Al Gore and Greenpeace. Professor Graham Martin, of the University of Birmingham School of Biosciences, helped polish the element of the thesis dealing with humanity's relationship to the ecosphere.

Even though I did not consciously draw upon his ideas, it has been pointed out that the body of work left by Douglas Adams was of great consequence to the flavour of the intellectual environment in which *The Jolly Pilgrim* was conceived and written.

Finally, the mental energy and curiosity which drove the physical, intellectual and emotional journey which *The Jolly Pilgrim* records could not have been maintained without the influence of the global news media keeping me informed about the wider hum of events, not to mention sane (for the most part), in the far-off lonely places. Those I most often consulted during the journey were the BBC News website, *National Geographic*, *The Hindustan Times*, *The Bangkok Post*, *The Australian*, *The Sydney Morning Herald*, *The International Herald Tribune*, *The Miami Herald*, *The Guardian International Version* and *The Economist*.

Acknowledgements

Seven people were my partners in turning two years of public correspondence (and four battered notebooks' worth of scribblings, numbers, quotes, tables and poetry) into the object you are holding. They are: Tony Bowers, John Devlin, Sid McLean, Simon Peace, Claire Russell, Patrick van Beek and Mark Yzerman-Snare.

In addition, I would like to note the help of the following individuals, who either had direct input during the construction of the manuscript or were pivotal in some way to the overall project: Jack Alexander, Ash, Stephen Brierley, Sol Burt, Simon Cann, Dr Susannah Colbert, Charlotte Eaton, Janet Fulford, Becky Green, Simon Hunt, Jane Isles, Lauren Johnston, Sara Johnston, Heidi Mitchell, Harriet Swatman Manasa, Norge, Sally Rousham, Alan Russell and, of course, my Mum and Dad.

A section of the website provides a more comprehensive list of those involved in producing, editing, packaging and polishing this book, including extensive notes on each individual's contributions.

www.thejollypilgrim.org/the-production-team

Finally, I would like to thank NASA for supplying us with, and approving our use of, the front cover image.

About the Author

Peter Baker grew up in East Anglia and read physics at Durham University. After graduating he moved to Asia, working as a science teacher in India and (briefly) as a club singer in Bangkok. On his return to the UK he became a writer for a global insurance consultancy in the West End, while exploring London's intellectual and cultural scene, pursuing interests in evolutionary psychology, economics and history, and beginning the development of his thesis regarding the shape and character of the human adventure.

In 2005 he embarked upon the journey recorded in this book, during which his ideas concerning the context of contemporary civilisation became fully formed. Following his return home, he spent a year living in a one-room wooden cabin at the bottom of an apple orchard, while writing and caring for his dying mother. He then moved back to London, took a job in the City and spent two years polishing the manuscript.

The Jolly Pilgrim is his first book.